Tribal Television

Tribal Television

VIEWING NATIVE PEOPLE IN SITCOMS

DUSTIN TAHMAHKERA

The University of North Carolina Press CHAPEL HILL

*This book was published with the assistance of
the Anniversary Endowment Fund of the University of North Carolina Press.*

© 2014 The University of North Carolina Press
Manufactured in the United States of America
Set in Utopia by codeMantra

The University of North Carolina Press has been a member
of the Green Press Initiative since 2003.

Cover illustration: Background vector illustration, © 2013 yupiramos; vintage TV from
the 1970s, © 2012 trekandshoot; Indian Head test pattern, 1938.

Library of Congress Cataloging-in-Publication Data
Tahmahkera, Dustin.
Tribal television : viewing native people in sitcoms / Dustin Tahmahkera.
pages cm
Includes bibliographical references and index.
ISBN 978-1-4696-1868-5 (pbk   ) — ISBN 978-1-4696-1869-2 (ebook)
1. Indians on television. 2. Situation comedies (Television programs)—United States.
3. Situation comedies (Television programs)—Canada. I. Title.
PN1992.8.I64T34 2014
791.45'652997—dc23
2014020273

18 17 16 15 14   5 4 3 2 1

Part of this book has been reprinted with permission in
revised form from "Custer's Last Sitcom: Decolonized Viewing of the
Sitcom's 'Indian,'" *American Indian Quarterly* 32.3 (2008): 324–51.

This book has been digitally printed

In memory of
Gran, Uncle Steve,
and
Dr. Campbell

Contents

Illustrations

Sign-on

A SITCOM KID

Nʉ nahnia tsa Dustin Tahmahkera, suku̲ Taiboo tʉpunitʉ yʉ yʉmuhku usʉ nʉ tebuuni kutʉ. My name is Dustin Tahmahkera, and I am a recovering colonized viewer of American television.

I grew up on American sitcoms. I positioned myself from a very young age into half-hour blocks of comedic escapism and entered sitcom worlds seemingly free of real-life violence and chaos and devoid of social and political relevance. I watched reruns of sitcoms like *I Love Lucy, The Beverly Hillbillies, Three's Company, Dennis the Menace, Happy Days*, and *The Brady Bunch*. I tuned in the 1985 premiere of Nick at Nite, whose early promotional ad greeted viewers from a concocted site of televisuality ("Hello, out there, from TV land!"), and saw its airing of sitcom reruns such as *The Donna Reed Show, Mister Ed*, and *My Three Sons*. I remember, too, newer sitcoms like *Alf, Perfect Strangers, The Cosby Show*, and *Full House*, all of which could later be seen on Nick at Nite. I remember once even sketching out a twenty-four-hour lineup of sitcoms for an all-rerun channel, long before the Nick at Nite spin-off network TV Land swiped my idea in the mid-1990s. But I especially remember, above all else, the definitive 1960s sitcom representative of small-town America: *The Andy Griffith Show*.

Each weekday Ted Turner's superstation, TBS, would air back-to-back episodes of *The Andy Griffith Show* at 5:05 and 5:35 P.M., Comanche Country time zone, unless an Atlanta Braves baseball game was on with #3 Dale Murphy or #47 Tom Glavine playing before tomahawk-chopping fans. It was not long before I had seen and reseen all 159 black-and-white episodes. (Do the last 90 post–Don Knotts color episodes really count?) As a cable-subscribing citizen of what Derek Kompare calls the "Rerun Nation," I repeatedly saw Sheriff Andy Taylor and Deputy Barney Fife attempt to maintain law and order in the all-American fictional town of Mayberry, North Carolina, a place of peace and tranquillity where visitors were greeted with the sign "Welcome to Mayberry, the Friendly Town."[1] When criminals occasionally disrupted the serene setting, I knew Taylor and Fife would restore order. In the episode "Crime-Free Mayberry," for example, they caught crooks who posed as FBI agents honoring Mayberry for having the lowest crime rate in the country.[2] I traveled nightly through Mayberry's universe, including Main Street, where Mayberrians gathered to talk, shop, and eat. Barber Floyd Lawson and mechanic Goober Pyle sat in front of the barbershop. Aunt Bee and Clara Edwards window-shopped in front of Weaver's Department Store. Jud and Chester played checkers on the porch of the Mayberry Hotel. Andy and Barney relaxed on a bench outside of the courthouse, or they enjoyed the Businessman's Special served by the wait-ress Juanita at the Bluebird Diner. Or there was Andy and Opie fishing at nearby Myers Lake, "an Edenic place of rest and recreation," Chris Magoc remarks, "where the 'pioneer skills of woodsmen' are practiced and passed on to future generations of Mayberrians."[3] Before long, I could mute the volume during episodes and recite, fairly accurately, chunks of dialogue as scenes reran on television.

As far back as I can remember, *The Andy Griffith Show* and other sit-coms were (long before I heard of a French philosopher named Derrida) *always already* there, significantly impacting my personal pop culture sur-roundings. Like Couer d'Alene and Spokane author Sherman Alexie's self-identification as a "sit-com kid" whose "world outlook is definitely partly shaped by situation comedies," I, too, was a "sit-com kid" whose worldview has been and continues to be influenced by sitcoms.[4] My personal sub-jectivities shaped and were shaped by my reception to televised content. Yes, I was entertained through sitcoms on Nick at Nite and other networks, but, as an Anglo settler and indigenous TV watcher, as a dual citizen of the Comanche Nation and the United States (and as a fan and eventually a scholar), I also began years later to recognize and question sitcoms' repre-sentational influx and diversity of settler characters and, by contrast, rare and repetitive Indian characters intended to represent the indigenous.

Since TV sitcoms began in the late 1940s, their representations of the settler—constitutive herein of white characters portrayed by white actors whose scripted performance reinscribes on- and offscreen historical and contemporary dominance over the indigenous—have made up the vast majority of starring, secondary, and guest roles. Within the critical frame of settler colonial studies, the sitcom's settler, whether sited in Mayberry or elsewhere across TV land, circulates as, frankly, a most unsettling figure attempting to spuriously indigenize and naturalize that from which he or she does not originate. The settler's claims to dominion over indigenous homelands are fed by broadcasted settler-centered narratives of "founding fathers" and pioneers, which, from an indigenous vantage point, are as illogical and unjust as the doctrine of discovery and *terra nullius* (Latin for "lands belonging to no one") that paved the way for constructing the United States and "legalized" dispossession of the indigenous. The formations of settler colonialism and empire have always depended on what Chickasaw scholar Jodi Byrd calls "the foundational paradigmatic Indianness that circulates within the narratives U.S. empire tells itself."[5] Indianness in broadcasted sitcom narratives is too often marked, as it is in innumerable other media sites, by extreme expectations and extremely few options for what it means to be indigenous and by performative expectations built on centuries of such binaries as savagery/civilization and, as exemplified by the historical dictum "Kill the Indian, Save the Man," extermination/assimilation.

In television, the indigenous signifies characters intended to represent Natives, including the dubious indigenous iterations imagined by settler producers. For example, settler characters have often discursively stood in for, or represented, offscreen (that is, absent) Native Peoples. Mr. Furley in *Three's Company* once prepared for a poker game by placing his fingers behind his head to signify feathers as he said, "Poker-hontas." Pinky Tuscadero in *Happy Days*, much to the Fonz's chagrin, questioned Tonto's gender because he wore a feather. Brad Taylor in *Home Improvement* described Aztecs as killers who cut people's hearts out.[6] I also have seen white and, on occasion, African American and Asian American characters symbolically stand in for the indigenous by performing in redface, slipping in and out of a temporary visual Indianness. "Indian play was a temporary fantasy," Philip Deloria observes of American cultural ambivalence with Indianness, "and the player inevitably returned to the everyday world."[7] For example, Dennis played Indian in the Junior Pathfinders Club in *Dennis the Menace*, Lucy played Indian to secure the spotlight in her husband's nightclub act in *I Love Lucy*, and the Brady family became the "Brady Braves" through an Indian naming ceremony in *The Brady Bunch*. In 2002, Michael Kyle, an African American character, played "Chief Bald Eagle" for his daughter's "Indian Princesses" group in *My Wife and Kids*; four months later, a triracial group of fathers and sons in "Indian Scouts" donned plastic feathers and paper headbands in the *Yes Dear* episode "Dances with Couch."[8]

I have viewed, too, visible Indian representations, that is, characters supposedly signifying Native Peoples, even though they almost never performatively resemble such (and are rarely portrayed by Native actors). I saw

Granny shoot at feathered Indians on horseback in *The Beverly Hillbillies*, Mr. Haney hustle what he called his "Indian rain-making machine" Chief Thundercloud to Mr. Douglas in *Green Acres*, Lucy Carter involuntarily marry an "Ug"-talking Indian chief who outlandishly offered her the state of Utah as a wedding present in *Here's Lucy*, and Captain William Parmenter tame (read: civilize) the savage Bald Eagle, identified by the writers as a cousin to Geronimo, and belittlingly tell him he is "a good boy" in *F Troop*.[9]

As for *The Andy Griffith Show*, its overarching dominant narrative aligns with colonial discourse on issues of settlement, pioneer pride and ingenuity, "traditional" gendered performance, and America's determined and destined founding. National and local histories, in particular, constitute several episodes' story lines. In "Andy Discovers America," Sheriff Taylor, the lead settler, explains a vision of America that reinforces a familiar American school version.[10] Andy recounts to his young son, Opie, and Opie's friends a story of the founding of America by the efforts of the boys' "great-great-great-great-great-great-granddaddies," early settler colonials who united to start their own country. The founding of Mayberry is the subject of two plays in the episodes "The Beauty Contest" and "The Pageant." The former presents a wilderness without explicit inclusion of any Indigenous Peoples. The latter shows Barney dressed up in stereotypical Plains Indian costume and speaking what Barbra Meek (Comanche) calls "Hollywood Injun English" in the role of Chief Noogatuck, who leads his unnamed tribe to eventually and conveniently settle for peaceful coexistence with Euro-American settler leader James Merriweather, portrayed by Andy (you were expecting Gomer?), and the rest of the settlers. Neither play offers an account of how early 1960s Mayberry became devoid of Natives. Barney even admits, in another episode, "I ain't never known an Indian," reinforcing the televisual trope that Indians are only of the past, not the present or rerun futures.[11]

The narrative I am sharing so far risks reducing the viewing of sitcoms to being enjoyable or despicable, escapist entertainment or recurring reminders of negative Indian stereotypes, and merely colonizing media texts. But Native audiences, including indigenous sitcom kids, are more complex than the incomplete subject position of *colonized viewers* allows; sitcoms, like other American popular cultural texts, are more complicated than dichotomous generalizations allow; and televisual representations of the indigenous are more intricate than they may appear upon first viewing. The complexities, intricacies, and complications—they are what drive the rest of this book.

To question sitcoms' representations as stereotypes/not stereotypes, positive/negative, or accurate/inaccurate sets up noteworthy but very limited analysis.[12] Years ago, Homi Bhabha called for a "shift from the *identification* of images as positive or negative, to an understanding of the *processes of subjectification* made possible (and plausible) through stereotypical discourse."[13] Such discourse is critical in discussing television representations of the indigenous, but it points to only part of the picture. While Philip Deloria acknowledges that the "stereotype has been an important tool for understanding the relation between representations and the concrete exercise of power," he concludes that "*stereotype* might function better as a descriptive shorthand than as an analytical tool." As "a simplified and generalized expectation" found "in an image, text, or utterance," stereotype has "simplifying tendencies." Calling, then, for a close cultural and historical analysis of the ideology, discourse, and cultural work informing and shaping (un)expected representations, stereotypical or otherwise, Deloria suggests scholars should heed "attention to multiple meanings, contradictions, opportunities, and the shutting down of opportunities" in the formations, messages, and receptions of aural and visual representations of the indigenous.[14] Again, the complexities, intricacies, and complications.

Television, as its scholars and critics have long said, is one of the most pervasive and influential inventions of all time in shaping public perceptions about practically any issue. Far less noted is that the sitcom, one of TV's best-selling genres, and its producers' transmitted representations of relations between the indigenous and nonindigenous have also contributed to public perceptions, more precisely to shaping and being shaped by what the Tsalagi scholar Jeff Corntassel calls the "politics of perception" of indigeneity, that is, of how and what audiences think of Native Peoples, indigenous cultures, and intercultural relations between the indigenous and nonindigenous.[15] If sitcoms have "become a barometer of American culture," then what, I ask, can they tell us about perceptions of historical and contemporary indigenous-settler relations?[16] This significant, overarching question speaks to narratives constructed and broadcasted by television producers and networks in the twentieth and twenty-first centuries that the rest of this book will address but will do so through an indigenous-centered lens that recursively critiques and resituates the situation comedy's politicized and popular understandings of "American culture" and its placements and displacements of the indigenous.

In recent years, scholars have increasingly recognized complexity in sitcoms. As Joanne Morreale writes in *Critiquing the Sitcom*, "Sitcoms address significant ideas and issues within seemingly innocuous narrative frames and analyzing them can help us account for the complexity and complications involved in the production and reception contexts of popular culture." Mary Dalton and Laura Linder argue in *The Sitcom Reader*, "Television sitcoms may be . . . entertaining, but they are never *just* entertainment."[17] Contrary to popular opinion that sitcoms are frivolous entertainment meant only for laughs and not for critical study, they are rich for analysis of their visions of America and its inhabitants, indigenous and settler included. Scholars like Patricia Mellencamp, Robin Means Coleman, Herman Gray, and Victoria Johnson have proven some of the richness in their readings of sitcoms through multiple critical lenses, namely feminist, African American, and queer analyses, to advance the field of sitcom studies and frame important and multifaceted televisual and sociopolitical discussions such as in American studies, communication studies, and critical media studies.[18]

Yet analysis of indigeneity and indigenous-settler encounters in sitcom studies, unlike in cinema studies, has been almost completely nonexistent. Previous scholarship in media and television studies predominantly excludes historical and contemporary televisual representations of American Indians and indigenous-settler politics or, if included, generally writes them off as simply stereotypical and only damaging or irrelevant to Native Peoples and social justice. In comparison, I opt for more nuanced readings to underscore the representations as critical contributors to American Indian studies and television studies and to social and political discourses concerning indigenous identities and relations between Natives and non-Natives. In conversation with approaches to scholarship by Jodi Byrd, Michelle Raheja, James Cox, and others in Native American and indigenous studies who underscore Native Peoples and Native issues in analysis of popular culture figures and texts, I look to contribute as well to the growing field of indigenous cultural studies and its projects that recover and center Native perspectives, representations, and involvement in media and popular culture including literary, cinematic, televisual, musical, and digital production, texts, and reception.[19]

Here's to hoping, then, that *Tribal Television* critically and creatively offers up, to quote a recurring scene-exiting line by indigenous sitcom character John Redcorn, "food for thought"—as a textual testament to the cultural, televisual, and scholarly routes I have long traveled since those early days in Mayberry, to my ambivalent relationship with the sights and sounds of the indigenous in North American sitcoms, and to an indigenous-centered methodology that points toward bridging some of the current gaps, borders, and emerging fissures at the crossroads of television studies, communication studies, American Indian studies, and indigenous cultural studies.

Tribal Television

Decolonized Viewing, Decolonizing Views

Television's first famous Indian never made a sound or moved a muscle. Shown only from the chest up, he always looked to his left and wore a meticulous Plains-styled headdress with eleven feathers, nine of them dark-tipped with fringe, over his long and braidless dark hair and a bone necklace. Similar to wooden Indians commonly found in antique shops, his stoic presence became an international iconic image for representing *the Indian* for multitudes of TV watchers. By the late 1940s and 1950s, this Indian's ongoing appearances during early morning and late night hours on television screens across North America garnered him far more air-time than small-screen stars Milton Berle, Ed Sullivan, Jack Benny, Martha Raye, Lucille Ball, and Jackie Gleason combined, illustrative of why Ojibwe writer and humorist Drew Hayden Taylor once called him "the hardest working Indian in the business" who "has worked on practically every film and television show I have ever seen."[1] TV's first Indian superstar: the Indian Head test pattern (IHTP).

In conjunction with a single kilohertz tone sounding a monotonous *mmm* during the late night and early morning hours, the IHTP featured a fixed and immobile caricature of a generic male Indian amid a scale pattern. Radio Corporation of America (RCA) used the pattern to test early cameras and broadcasting equipment. In the mornings, as programming was about to begin, the test card served "to help people adjust their television sets," that is, to check screens' vertical and horizontal lines and "overall picture" for clarity.[2] As one early TV watcher in Greenville, South Carolina, recalls, his father "got behind [the television set] every morning and fine-tuned the WFBC-TV Indian head test pattern reflected in a mirror placed against a chair."[3]

1

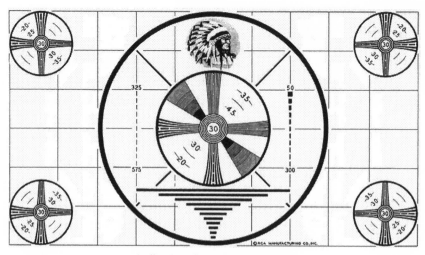

Indian Head Test Pattern, 1938.

Indian Head, as I like to call him, arguably became the most recognizable Indian in the business, signaling to viewers that programming was off the air until the morning and serving as televisual entertainment and an eventual object of audiences' nostalgia alongside episodes of *Father Knows Best*, *I Love Lucy*, and other assimilative, heteronormative, and patriarchal programs of yesteryear. For example, one viewer's early Sunday morning "babysitter would spend most of the hour and a half sitting in front of the set . . . staring at the test pattern" of an "Indian with full-feathered head-dress in the screen center." Another viewer recalls how she and her brothers would "turn on the TV set, and sit in front of it, watching nothing but the Indian on the test pattern. Sometimes we invited our friends over to watch it, too. We all loved it so much that I now remember the test pattern much better than I remember any of the programs we watched."[4]

The original artwork of television's first famous Indian, minus the pattern, simply includes a handwritten "Done by Brooks 8\23\38" in the lower right corner, but whoever "Brooks" is remains a mystery, as is an unequivocal answer for why Brooks drew an Indian.[5] Although the headdress provides some visual intricacy by which viewers could adjust their TV reception, the image contains no *technical* prowess over what could have been test pattern depictions of, say, Christopher Columbus in a detailed Spanish sailor cap, George Washington in a colonial tricorn, or George Armstrong Custer in his Seventh Cavalry Regiment hat (arrows optional). But *culturally* and *politically* speaking, the Indian in the test pattern, among the millions (and millions) of other imagic possibilities, adjoins his representational relatives in Robert Berkhofer's taxonomy of the "white man's Indian."[6] A significant on-screen representative and host of the New World of television programming emerging in the 1930s and 1940s, the test pattern entered into an existing world of settler colonial mass media power and control over representations of Indians, in which the culturally and socially multidimensional and fluid indigenous is practically negated and absent. Given American pop cultural producers' ironic fixations on fixed constructions of stoic, stern, or otherwise savage Indians in nineteenth-century Beadle's Dime Novels and James Fenimore Cooper works, late nineteenth- and early twentieth-century Buffalo Bill Wild West shows, Edward S. Curtis historical photographs, Thomas Edison's kinetoscope film shorts of Indians, and, nearer to Indian Head's prime, *The Lone Ranger* (and Tonto) radio series starting in 1933 and the first cinematic Tonto in the fifteen-part series *The Lone Ranger* in 1938, followed by, among other big-screen westerns, *The Return of the Lone Ranger* and John Ford's *Stagecoach* (starring Hollywood's premiere Indian killer John Wayne) in 1939, the IHTP joined a dominant media tradition of colonizing representations of the Indian.[7]

Representations of anatomically challenged Indian heads include trademarked Indian head logos in sports and business like those commercialized by the Washington Redskins professional football team and the Mutual of Omaha insurance company, suggestive reminders of past bounties that white government and military leaders would pay for Indian heads. Foreshadowing the looks of RCA's test card Indian, American currency's $2.50 Indian Head quarter-eagle and $5.00 Indian Head half-eagle gold coins share a homogeneous head with lengthy wavy hair, headdress, and bone necklace. In 1913, settler artist James Earle Fraser—already known by then for his *End of the Trail* statue in which the topless defeated Indian slumps over on his horse—designed the Buffalo nickel, or Indian Head nickel, by depicting a male Indian head in braids on one side and a buffalo on the other. The nickel's Indian is likely the closest temporal representational relative to the IHTP, for as the Buffalo nickel stopped circulation in April 1938 and exited the monetary scene, television's first famous Indian was drawn just four months later.[8]

My friend Indian Head became another example of a manipulated, intertextual descendant of settler colonial images of Native Peoples in which white producers express ideological dominance over and freeze-frame fascination with idealized and nonthreatening mute Indians who replace the indigenous "real."[9] (In other words, he's messed up!) Scholars Rayna Green, Philip Deloria, Shari Huhndorf, Daniel Francis, and others have accounted for complicated ways the figure of Indians, in its count-less iterations and guises of noble and ignoble savagery, has appeared in North American popular culture and non-Native performance as "Indi-ans." Whether engaging in acts of "playing Indian" (Green and Deloria) or "going native" (Huhndorf), many self-serving settlers have long searched for authentic Americanness and Canadianness through their "imaginary Indian" (Francis) with an unchecked colonizing ambivalence toward real-life Native Peoples. As Vine Deloria Jr. encapsulates it, "Underneath all the conflicting images of the Indian, one fundamental truth emerges: the white man knows that he is alien and knows that North America is Indian—and he will never let go of the Indian image because he thinks by some clever manipulation he can achieve an authenticity which can never be his."[10]

How wickedly fitting, then, that television deployed the Indian to wel-come North American viewers into settler colonial TV land, a symbolic recognition of the indigenous as the only original one who can "authenti-cally" and, given the duplicity and destruction of centuries of colonization, complicitly sign on television programming through airwaves hovering over indigenous homelands expropriated and colonized for the making of the United States and Canada.

Since its inception, television has aired such conflicting images of the Indian, but the televisual narratives I will share in *Tribal Television* are not just those of anxious alien settlers' adjusted and maladjusted representa-tions of the Indian. Native image-makers in television and popular culture also have not "let go of the Indian"; however, Natives' narratives of "clever manipulation" counter, readjust, and recontextualize the Indian through a critical and creative indigenous lens in efforts to deflate and displace the cultural and political power of the Indian and to reinvent pop cultural rep-resentations of the indigenous. In this line of critical and creative work, even Indian Head has received his indigenous makeover.

Nearly seventy years after his debut, Indian Head became the site for readjusting the visuality and perception of the indigenous in the First Na-tions situation comedy *Moose TV*. Created by Ernest Webb (Cree) and Catherine Bainbridge, cofounders of the production company Rezolution Pictures, and recipient of the 2008 Indie Award for best comedy, *Moose TV* premiered on July 19, 2007, on the Canadian television channel Show-case.[11] The sitcom starred indigenous actors Gary Farmer (Cayuga), Adam Beach (Salteaux), Jennifer Podemski (Salteaux), Billy Merasty (Cree), Na-thaniel Arcand (Cree), and Michelle Latimer (Métis), with Drew Hayden Taylor (Curve Lake Ojibwe) as script consultant. In its premiere episode,

Moose TV cast. *Left to right:* Jennifer Podemski, Nathaniel Arcand, Adam Beach, and Michelle Latimer. Used with permission of Rezolution Pictures International Inc.

Adam Beach replaces Indian Head in *Moose TV*.

the charismatic and mischievous George Keeshig (played by Beach) returns from a ten-year hiatus in Toronto to his small hometown of Moose, a predominantly Native community in northern Quebec, where residents sip coffee, engage in small talk, and tread cautiously around George's father, the town's corrupt mayor, sheriff, and sole restaurant owner Gerry Keeshig (Farmer). When George spots a new building in town, his friend Clifford Mathew (Arcand) identifies it as a "television studio . . . a government initiative to bring," he mocks, "'homegrown television to the indigenous peoples,'" but all "they brought [was] the equipment." So, the ever-opportunistic George decides to start "Moose TV," describing it in tribal sovereign terms as "television made by and for the people of this town."[12] During the clever meta-TV series' short eight-episode run, George oversees the station and hires Moose residents to star in extremely low budget, live, and original programming, such as the investigative news series *The Beaver Exposed* (hosted by a busybody beaver hand puppet and his bourgeois conspiracy theorist owner Joan "Littlebear" Whitney), soap opera *Fort Moose* (indigenous characters play French settlers in a dramatic retelling of the town's founding), do-it-yourself series *Ernie Makes a Drum*, and trivia game show *Well, What Do You Know?*[13]

A Native sitcom set at a Native TV station, *Moose TV* showed what happens when on-screen indigenous characters run indigenous television constructed by real-life indigenous producers, allies, and actors.[14] *Moose TV* also did something almost surely unprecedented in television comedy: it replaced beloved Indian Head with the facial image of a real Native. In the third episode, when Clifford oversleeps during his morning time slot for the live workout series *Cliffercize*, the sitcom *Moose TV* and the station Moose TV screen an altered simulation of the IHTP to signal dead air. Superseding Indian Head, the grinning face of Adam Beach-as-George Keeshig is sited front and center on a localized version of the black-and-white test card. In effect, *Moose TV* readjusted pop cultural and televisual indigeneity by covering up the silent and stoic with the fluid and funny and the static past with the vibrant contemporary—not to mention with a Native actor who in real life is practically a household name for many Natives in Canada and the United States after his costarring roles in *Dance Me Outside* (1994), *Smoke Signals* (1998), *Flags of Our Fathers* (2006), *Law & Order: Special Victims Unit* (2007–08), and dozens of other movies and television series.

The juxtaposition of these two test patterns—constructed from early and recent days of television, from settler and indigenous vantage points, and from recognition of the fixed Indian and the flexible Native—illustrates the analytical work at the core of this book: the representational adjustments and readjustments of the indigenous in popular culture. Together the images open up analytical routes into following the vertical/hierarchical and horizontal/nonhierarchical lines sited in the correlating and contentious patterns of televisual representations of the indigenous and indigenous-settler relations from the late 1930s to today. When read intertextually across TV series, the patterns of representations converge and collide in televisual versions of "contact zones"—what Mary Louise Pratt defines as the "social spaces where disparate cultures meet, clash, and grapple with each other, often in highly asymmetrical relations of domination and subordination."[15] Found in TV producers' vertical lines of competing, contentious, and coexisting visions and interpretations of indigeneity, the contact zones of televisual production spaces and fictional narrative spaces are where relations between the indigenous and nonindigenous unfold.

As may already be evident, I am interested in the cultural production of representational genealogies and patterns of televisual indigeneity, or the contextualized production, representation, and reception that constitute contested significations and subjectifications of the indigenous on television. Indian Head exemplifies a representational TV pattern emulated in related iterations in countless texts, but he also is a representational benchmark of sorts for testing the competing patterns and visions of televisual indigeneity. Focusing on the representations produced in fictional North American sitcoms like *I Love Lucy* and *Moose TV*, I foreground critical analysis of indigeneity and interculturality between the indigenous and settler, including representational conflicts and resolutions, to reconceptualize how one approaches and addresses representations of televisual indigeneity. Grounding analysis in what postcolonial theorist Homi Bhabha calls "the processes of subjectification," I outline in the following chapters several approaches to interpreting representations of indigeneity in sitcoms and, for evidentiary support, cite textual examples from the past seven decades to reveal a partial archive of sitcoms' homogeneous-heterogeneous and hierarchical-nonhierarchical visions of indigeneity, representational and discursive boundary disputes, unsettling story line resolutions, and intertextual heritage among sitcom producers and the politics of their representations across and against televisual, sociocultural, and political landscapes.[16]

Setting the stage for thinking through the ideological processes of subjectification of the indigenous in North American television, this chapter formulates a critical approach to analysis of indigenous presence and absence in sitcoms. Situated within indigenous theory and critical media studies, *decolonized viewing* serves as a guiding dualistic framework for coordinating, contextualizing, and critiquing, in subsequent chapters, non-Native and Native producers' visions of indigeneity and indigenous-settler interculturality in sitcoms from the 1950s through the 2010s. Translatable to media-intensive projects within decolonization movements that engage and disrupt colonial productions and discourse, decolonized viewing means to open up indigenous critiques through sitcom reception *and* sitcom production.

As an analytical framework for mapping and navigating through TV producers' visions of the indigenous, decolonized viewing is first introduced in how it functions as a reception-based critique of colonial discourse in sitcoms' recurring productions of the *recognizably Indian*—in broad terms, the one-dimensional, trite, stereotypical, or otherwise problematic discursive and visual constructions of Indians. They represent sitcom Indians, the subject of the case studies in chapters 1, 2, and 3. To complicate matters, as indicative of complex social and political terrains in North America, I also discuss sitcoms' counterintuitive representations of the recognizably Indian, such as in *Barney Miller* in chapter 2 and in *King of the Hill* in chapter 3, which momentarily and ambivalently challenge views of the sitcom Indian as a homogeneous, seemingly fixed constitution.

I then address decolonized viewing as critical production-based work recently practiced by Native sitcom producers who, I argue, adjust—through their indigenous-centered production and reception practices—the familiar patterns of the recognizably Indian and readjust them into *recognizably Native* representations, or those informed by and attuned to, even if conflicting and perplexing, Native individual and tribal recognition of what constitutes indigenous identities and what it means to be indigenous. The recognizably Native in sitcoms denotes formations of indigenous characters flowing from and through indigenous sensibilities and views. Through analysis of their broadcasted visions, the Native producers I highlight in this chapter and chapters 3 and 4 not only apply decolonized viewing but also attempt to *decolonize views* of how Native characters can perform on-screen and are perceived by audiences. The remainder of this chapter is intended to provide introductory context for the following chapters' case studies on the relations, boundaries, conflicts, and resolutions between sitcom producers' characterizations of the recognizably Indian, recognizably Native, and nonindigenous.

Sitcom Kids and Native TV Criticism

Encouraging Native sitcom watchers and other viewers to (continue to) critically approach and analyze television's discursive and imagic inclusion and exclusion of recognizably Indian and recognizably Native representations, decolonized viewing presupposes Native Peoples as long-standing integral TV audiences with reflective, analytical, and creative insights about textual meanings of television's representations of the indigenous and nonindigenous. The following Native perspectives locate a considerable range of responses to television in such forms as narrative, protest, literature, film, textbook, essay, poetry, interview, and television text. Even though none of these critical and creative thinkers and artists have generally been heralded per se as TV critics, they nonetheless shape a growing body of Native TV criticism and eclectic approaches to practices of decolonized viewing.

Sitcoms in particular play significant roles for Spokane and Coeur d'Alene author Sherman Alexie, who says, "I'm a sit-com kid. *All in the Family, Brady Bunch, Three's Company*. So my timing, my sense of humor, my world outlook is definitely partly shaped by situation comedies."[17] The self-proclaimed "first practitioner of the *Brady Bunch* school of Native American literature," Alexie prominently engages television and popular culture in his fiction and nonfiction.[18] The "popular culture invasion," as James Cox calls it, in Alexie's writings provides cracked windows into Native characters' fractured lives. In Alexie's short story "The Lone Ranger and Tonto Fistfight in Heaven," for example, a non-Native 7-Eleven employee initially profiles and fears a Native customer, who then shakes up expectations by asking the clerk if he knows "all the words to the theme from *The Brady Bunch*." When the same Native character returns from Seattle to the Spokane reservation and feels lost, he "watched television. For weeks I flipped through channels, searched for answers in the game shows and soap operas."[19]

Through his characters and his own experiences, Alexie acknowledges indigenous viewership, but he also does more than just state the obvious (that is, the fact that Native Peoples do watch television). As a critic who negotiates and resists settler colonial visions of America and Native Peoples in American popular culture texts, Alexie is well versed in contemporary Native realities and pop cultural surroundings. Growing up as a sitcom kid and an avid fan of *The Brady Bunch*, he surely saw TV episodes featuring Indian characters, such as the Bradys' three-episode Grand Canyon adventure that culminated in the family's adoption into an unnamed Indian tribe by its chief, Eagle Cloud, portrayed by Jay Silverheels, a Mohawk actor originally from the Six Nations Reserve. Silverheels is best known for portraying the Masked Man's sidekick Tonto in the television series *The Lone Ranger*, the same Indian character that Alexie declares he despises. In his essay "Hated Tonto (Still Do)," Alexie claims a previous affinity with John Wayne, whose character kills cinematic Comanches, stand-ins for violent savages, in *The Searchers* (1956). "I loved John Ford's 'The Searchers,'" he says, adding, "I hated those savage Indians just as much as John Wayne did." Alexie also supports the Anglo-Cherokee character Billy Jack, portrayed by Anglo actor Tom Laughlin, in a trio of 1970s *Billy Jack* films:

"We Indians cheered as Billy Jack fought for us, for every single Indian." However, he despises Tonto, an Indian character played by a Native actor. "I was just one little Indian boy who hated Tonto," Alexie explains, "because Tonto was the only cinematic Indian who looked like me." Paul Chaat Smith (Comanche) recognizes the infiltration and pervasiveness of American pop culture and Hollywood across Indian Country and the rest of the world: "The movies" (and, I would add, television shows) "loom so large for Indians because they have defined our self-image as well as told the entire planet how we live, look, scream, and kill."[20]

To self-identify, though, as a sitcom kid or former fan of the Duke does not mean Alexie believes, supports, and perpetuates the colonial discourse in American sitcoms and cinema. Alexie credits sitcoms for shaping his "timing," "humor," and "world outlook," even as he questions television's potentially detrimental impact on Native spectators. Like several of his fictional narrators and other characters, Alexie is a recovering colonized viewer of American film and television. "Does every Indian," he asks in his short story "Imagining the Reservation," "depend on Hollywood for a twentieth-century vision?" "Imagine Crazy Horse invented the atom bomb in 1876," he hypothesizes, "and detonated it over Washington, D.C. Would the urban Indians still be sprawled around the one-room apartment in the cable television reservation?" In this narrative, TV has transformed Native tradition into the basis for a new media tribe located by Alexie on the "cable television reservation." With D.C. still intact, Alexie resorts instead to recognition of blaring TV sets in Native homes ("The TV was always on," he writes at one point) and to pressing "the mute button on the remote control so that everyone can hear the answer" to what it means "to be an Indian man." Through his subversive narratives, Alexie is "muting white noise," Cox argues, "the oppressive noise of white mass-produced culture, the loud demand to abandon all that is Indian and conform to the dictates of the invader's cultural belief system or be destroyed."[21]

"As the source of the white noise," Cox continues, "television is an instrument of late-twentieth-century colonialism."[22] Oren Lyons, an Onondoga and Seneca faithkeeper, similarly recognizes TV as a colonizing instrument that replaces traditional indigenous ways. "If you go into any house that I know these days," he explains, "there are at least two or three televisions in there. There's one in every room; that seems to be standard. That is probably the most invasive and consistent presence in our lives, and it's totally commercial. So you are just bombarded by commerce, and you don't know anything, you don't know any better."[23] Lyons calls for Native Peoples not to mute the television but to turn it off, or at least to reprioritize their lives so that TV becomes far less important and time-consuming.

In her poem "A Postcolonial Tale," Joy Harjo (Mvskoke) critiques television's colonial contribution of shattering indigenous imaginations, but in the spirit of poetic decolonization she also expresses indigenous resistance and hope in "rising up." Television stands in as a contemporary daily presence, a force to be reckoned with, in what Harjo calls "a reenactment of the creation story." She writes, "Once we abandoned ourselves for television, the box that separates the dreamer from the dreaming. It was as if we were stolen, put into a bag carried on the back of a whiteman who pretends to own the earth and the sky. In the sack were all the people of the world. We fought until there was a hole in the bag."[24] Harjo figuratively positions television as a colonizer of indigenous imagination, as an invader that Native Peoples succumbed to but then resisted.

Native Peoples have long engaged in resistance to alter the mainstream television industry. In 1960, indigenous citizens of twenty-one Native nations in Oklahoma, including Comanche, Choctaw, and Osage, recognized TV's potential damage to Native Peoples. In response, they encouraged the Oklahoma state legislature to pass, which it did, a resolution calling for change in the TV industry. Harry Belvin, then principal chief of Choctaws and Oklahoma state representative, commented on the resolution's purpose: "There is no excuse for TV producers to ignore the harm that may be done to the children of America by repetitious distortion of historical facts pertaining to the way of life of any race or creed, including the American Indian."[25] When ABC continued the distortion with its new settler-dominated series *Custer* in 1967, the Tribal Indians Land Rights Association protested. Its director, A. A. Hopkins-Duke (Kiowa), called for a halt to "glamorizing Custer" and announced, "We are lodging a complaint to ABC, petitioning sponsors of the series to boycott it." Under the Federal Communications Commission's Fairness Doctrine, the association also successfully challenged ABC affiliates to allot airtime for Native Peoples to share *their* perspectives about Custer and the Battle of Little Big Horn.[26] In his scathing *New York Times* review of *Custer*, Jack Gould thought such on-air replies to be "misguided" and "superfluous" because both "the white man and the red man are entitled to an equal rebate for wasted electricity in turning on the receiver" to watch it.[27] After just seventeen episodes over the ensuing three months, ABC canceled the series.

Among the few credited indigenous actors in *Custer* was Rodd Redwing, a Chickasaw born in New York who became known for his deft knife throwing and six-gun quick draw and target shooting skills in Hollywood.[28]

From the mid-1930s to 1970, he performed stunts and played Indian roles in scores of movies, including *Flaming Star* with Elvis Presley (1960) and *Shakiest Gun in the West* with Don Knotts (1968), and television series, including the westerns *Bonanza* and *Wagon Train* and the sitcoms *December Bride* and *Mister Ed*. But one of his classic TV moments, I would say, occurred in his 1958 appearance as a contestant on the popular game show *What's My Line?* Redwing's presence on a prime-time series afforded TV viewers a rare on-screen glimpse of a Native person speaking for himself and as himself.[29] The game show brought on relatively unknown people from unique lines of work, to whom celebrity panelists then asked yes-no questions and attempted to guess their occupations. Redwing's line, which panelists failed to determine, was "Teaches Gunplay to Movie 'Cowboys,'" such as actors Henry Fonda, Glenn Ford, and Ronald Reagan. After learning the answer, the talkative panelist and comedian Jonathan Winters (whose Cherokee heritage and work with American Indians will resurface in chapter 2) assertively asked, "How about it? Why don't the Indians win more of the pictures?" Panelist and journalist Dorothy Kilgallen immediately chimed in, "Because he's teaching the cowboys," an ironic reminder that the indigenous manages some control off camera over nonindigenous performance on camera.

With an indigenous wit he had communicated throughout his appearance on the live show in front of the studio audience, production crew, and at-home viewers across the country, Redwing coolly and staunchly replied, "Hollywood doesn't think Indians are the type, so they always have someone else play the Indian." "Isn't that true?" said a sympathetic Winters off camera as Redwing stared sternly at him for nearly three seconds before breaking into a warm smile.[30] Rather than point directly to whom the indigenous (on- and offscreen) are, Redwing addressed who Natives are not: filmic iterations of defeated Indians. He suggested, in effect, that audiences cannot expect non-Native actors in Indian roles to "win" because the nonindigenous generally does not, nor knows how to, perform with the recognizably Native epistemologies and sensibilities that have sustained being indigenous since long before the advent of Hollywood.

These examples urge, explicitly and implicitly, producers and networks to revisit history and to listen to indigenous view(er)s. For artist Teyowisonte Thomas Deer (Tuscarora), whom Taiaiake Alfred (Kahnawake) describes as grounded in the teachings of "the Mohawk Warrior Society in the Kahnawake Mohawk Territory," media becomes opportune space for making innovative cultural connections. The cinematic 1977 classic *Star Wars* is, for Deer, a personal guiding force in a Jedi style that George Lucas likely did not anticipate (and that James "Avatar" Cameron would envy), a force constitutive of Teyowisonte's contemporary Native identity. Addressing his cultural influences, Teyowisonte explains, "I've always seen the Iroquois Confederacy as being just like the movie *Star Wars*! I was weaned on that stuff since it first came out, and since at least 1990, I've seen myself as Luke Skywalker! You know, I'm going to restore freedom to the nation." He adds, "Our traditional Longhouse teachings . . . reinforced what I already knew from *Star Wars*!" Refusing to turn off the movie, to see it as confinement, or to dismiss either Native or non-Native teachings, Teyowisonte knows and interrelates Longhouse teachings *and* George Lucas imaginings, even privileging the latter as primary instructor.[31]

Teyowisonte's and Native sitcom viewers' epistemological assemblage for interpreting televisual texts contain non-Native influences from media and popular culture, all of which influences formations of decolonized viewing. Alexie, for one, is a sitcom kid who admits, "I was obsessed with TV."[32] He identifies as "very much a sitcom American" who is personally "just as influenced by *Three's Company* as I am by powwows."[33] His book *Ten Little Indians* features Spokane characters with transcultural identities, such as William, who "didn't want to choose between [settler author] Ernie Hemingway and the Spokane tribal elders, between [settler soccer star] Mia Hamm and [Lakota leader] Crazy Horse, between [settler Carson Mc-Cullers's 1940 novel] *The Heart Is a Lonely Hunter* and [Coast Salish actor] Chief Dan George. William wanted all of it."[34] These transcultural influences, like pairing Spokane elders and *Star Wars* elder Obi-Wan Kenobi, offer glimpses into Native modes of knowledge production. They contribute to formulating a theoretical framework of indigeneity that accounts for Native Peoples' shared and diverse pop cultures. Rather than entirely separating Native culture from popular culture, or calling for millennia-old Native traditions to be replaced by sitcom reruns, decolonized viewing means not only critiquing American popular culture's contributions to colonialism and invasiveness upon Native traditions but also recognizing Native Peoples as longtime producers, receivers, and traders—"We're Indians, remember. We barter!" laughs Velma in *Smoke Signals*—of a multitude of pop cultural practices and texts spanning generations.[35]

For the Ojibwe and Dakota scholar Scott Richard Lyons, popular TV series play an integral role in perceptions of Indianness and shaping personal identities. Growing up on the Leech Lake reservation in Minnesota, Lyons says he "watched a lot of television" and temporarily thought at a young age that several male TV stars were Native. In framing his deep interest "in impurities, contradictions, and misconceptions," Lyons writes, "This is an age when non-Indian actors can appear Indian to Indian boys, who in turn draw inspiration from those actors." Among them is Ukrainian Jew Leonard Nimoy's *Star Trek* performance as Mr. Spock, whose "demeanor" carried "a dignified Indianish character about him, a stoicism that we all knew masked his hidden passions underneath." Like Teyowisonte's relationship with Skywalker, Alexie's with *Three's Company*, and mine with *The Andy Griffith Show*, Nimoy-as-Spock was, as Lyons notes, "part of his interior landscape."[36]

Decolonized viewing means recognizing, too, the critical role of humor in Native spectatorship, even when TV's representations of Indians are scarce or perceived as racist and stereotypical. "Comedy," Alexie says, "is simply a funny way of being serious."[37] In his screenplay *Smoke Signals*, debuting in theaters two days after his "Hated Tonto" piece in the *Los Angeles Times*, a television airs a black-and-white western in the background. Thomas Builds-the-Fire, an astute and humorous Coeur d'Alene storyteller, observes, "You know, the only thing more pathetic than Indians on TV is Indians watching Indians on TV." An improvised line by the Coast Salish actor Evan Adams, who plays Thomas (as modeled after Adams's indigenous grandmother), it speaks to Joanna Hearne's assertion that *Smoke Signals* invites "*all* viewers to think about Indigenous spectatorship" as it points "to the problematic relationship between the imagined mass audience targeted by television rebroadcasting and Native viewers' apprehension of mediated images of Indians in the context of home viewing."[38] In addition to expressing Thomas's self-deprecating Native humor, the line suggests Hollywood Indian constructs are wretched, doubly so when Natives are entertained by them, as is Thomas, who does not deny seeing *Dances with Wolves*, Kevin Costner's childhood fantasy incarnate, over a hundred times, much to the dismay of his friend Victor Joseph. In Alexie's own words, "Movies have never allowed us to be fully functioning members of the national consciousness and society. This movie [*Smoke Signals*] shows that we are just as influenced by our own particular tribe of cultures as we are pop cultures. That's how we live our lives. That's who we are."[39] Through Alexie's screenplay and Chris Eyre's (Cheyenne Arapaho) direction, *Smoke Signals* functions as a major textual critic of television and film. As Chickasaw scholar Amanda Cobb contends, *Smoke Signals* is "a masterstroke for Eyre and Alexie because they challenge popular culture by creating popular culture, using the very medium that has arguably threatened Native American sovereignty the most—the Hollywood film."[40]

The myriad of cited views across genres herein gel into formations of a body of Native television criticism that talks back to TV producers' perceptions about Native Peoples but also contains within it competing perspectives. Alexie expresses ambivalence toward TV as he deconstructs and reconstructs it. Oren Lyons turns it off, Scott Lyons turns it on, Harjo fights it, Teyowisonte learns from it, Belvin calls for change, Redwing readjusts it, and Alexie's and Adams's Builds-the-Fire calls out both TV producers and Native spectators and reminds viewers of contemporary on- and offscreen Native presence. All, however, engage television through recognition of its varying impacts on Native Peoples. Whether viewing TV as a colonizing and/or decolonizing apparatus, their critiques suggest routes for entering discussions of decolonized viewing as an analytical process of adjusting and readjusting perceptions of non-Native and Native televisual patterns of representational indigeneity.

Tribal Television: Recognizably Indian

The nominal duo of "tribal television" discerns analysis of televisual representations of the indigenous. Television, besides referring to a screened device sold by Sony, Vizio, and other manufacturers, is defined by the *OED* as "the activity, profession, or medium of broadcasting on television."[41] In relation, my use of "television" refers to what gets broadcasted, to producers' activity of creating the medium's transmitted content, including the discursive, imagic, and ideological on-screen constructions of the indigenous and settler in televised episodes. Television entails as well each offscreen vision as communicated through proposed but unaired story lines, interviews with producers, series promos, and other paratexts, or "textual entities" that can shape meanings and views of broadcasted episodes.[42] To pluralize the system and industry known as "television" into "televisions," prefaced by "tribal," is to recognize and provide a frame for the multiplicity of perceptions, imaginings, and, yes, visions of TV producers' representations of the indigenous and interculturality between the indigenous and nonindigenous.

Etymologically, each television of the recognizably Indian is suggestive of the linguistic origins of "television"—*tele* is Greek for "far off"; "vision" derives from the Latin *visio* and *videre*, meaning "to see"—as not only electronically distant in transmission and reception but also socially, culturally, and politically distant and far off from what constitutes the lived experiences and tribal realities of the recognizably Native. Those responsible for producing these distant televisions of Indians—network executives, producers, directors, writers, casts, and others involved in the production process—are televisually and politically related to each other; their representations have attempted to distort and displace the indigenous and shape how the tribal is authored and understood. From one era to another, from one textual moment to another, producers of the recognizably Indian are heirs of previous representations and shared (mis)understandings of the indigenous, as facilitated through an indigenous-centered representational heritage of intertextuality, or "the fundamental and inescapable interdependence of all textual meaning upon the structures of meaning proposed by other texts."[43] In the case of the recognizably Indian, the texts and meanings are marked by an ideologically uneven interdependence that racialized, gendered, and other hierarchical colonial discourses anxiously thrive on in their disavowal of the recognizably Native.

As Diana George and Susan Sanders assert in their poststructuralist analysis of prime-time televisual Indian representations, "Network television, far from being a trivial pastime in the US, is one of this country's primary forms of colonial discourse."[44] Couched in the televisual landscape, North American sitcoms and their longstanding representational lineage have functioned in part as globalized contemporary perpetrators of hundreds of years of misinformation and misunderstandings about Indigenous Peoples, like Belvin's "repetitious distortion" and Alexie's "white noise," which can serve as daily and nightly intertextual reminders of, to quote Bhabha, "the repertoire of positions of power and resistance, domination and dependence," that shape "the boundaries of colonial discourse." For me, "distortion" connotes fallacies and ignorance but also a blurring and bending of representations of the indigenous in repeated attempts to garble and obscure the looks and sounds of the politics of indigeneity, evocative of distortion's havoc to TV screens' resolution-imagic visibility of the broadcasted product in televisual transmissions.

In American sitcoms, the broadcasted distortions began on December 6, 1951, in the original airing of the *I Love Lucy* episode "The Adagio." Set in New York City, the sitcom followed the (mis)adventures of housewife Lucy and her husband and nightclub owner and bandleader, Ricky Ricardo, and their neighbors and landlords, Fred and Ethel Mertz. Each episode typically focused on one of Lucy's madcap ideas, including the recurring theme of Lucy's relentless attempts to break into show business. As soon as Ricky mentions his search in "The Adagio" for an authentic Apache dancer to perform at his club, Lucy responds, "Apache, huh?" Triggering a moment of reflection in response to her own inquiry, she then proceeds to perform a generalized and disrespectful version of a fabricated Apache "Indian" dance at which a presumably non-Native studio audience laughs. For Lucy, "Apache" appears to be synonymous with all Indians as she claps hand to mouth, chants "hey-ya-ya," and shuffles her feet. After Ricky explains that he is looking for a *Parisian* Apache dancer, Lucy concocts a French Indian dance with the same gestures, except she replaces "hey-ya-ya" with "oui-oui-oui." For a few seconds, Lucy, in black slacks and white blouse, transforms into a generic, mocking, pseudo-Native sitcom character that has, like Jacquelyn Kilpatrick says of Hollywood stereotypes about Indigenes, its "origins in over five centuries of perceptions—and misperceptions."[45] To mass audiences at least faintly familiar with visual and sonic Indian representations, Lucy's erratic steps and chants promptly signify whom she impersonates.

From *I Love Lucy* to *The Andy Griffith Show, F Troop, Barney Miller*, and *Three's Company*, to *Diff'rent Strokes, Seinfeld, The Simpsons*, and *South Park*, these and other American sitcoms have aired televisions of American culture in hundreds of episodes with story lines and references involving Indians and settlers. Although recognizably Indian representations have undergone changes, revisions, and updates since the early 1950s and the coinciding emergence of TV as what television historian Erik Barnouw calls "The Image Empire," the production of the Indian still reveals a broadly shared settler colonial logic and sensibility across time, during which white sitcom producers have aimed to claim their televisual territory and have appropriated iterations of Indian characters and references from each other, their cinematic and non-sitcom televisual cousins, and others in the pervasive business of popular culture and the making and remaking of Indianness.[46] If, as Patrick Wolfe argues, "territoriality is settler colonialism's specific, irreducible element" in the settler colonial insistence on the structural "dissolution of native societies," then it might be said that the North American televisual landscape has long been a symbolic space for representing and broadcasting distorted and errant televisions of the indigenous around the world.[47]

Across settler sites of televisual territory, producers' distorted representations of the recognizably Indian (for example, one-episode guest Indian characters, settler characters who temporarily "play Indian," and one-liners referencing Indians) suggest fixity, a multivalent colonial desire to include, contain, disavow, and repeat representations of the indigenous, or what Bhabha theorizes as "a paradoxical mode of representation: it connotes rigidity and an unchanging order as well as disorder, degeneracy and daemonic repetition."[48] Among the intertextual convergences of such contradictory fixity between producers and their recycled story lines, jokes, and representations of Indians, audiences can expect, say, representations of or allusions to sitcom Indians to surface on television every November near Thanksgiving, in which initial tensions or conflicts in a story line between Indian and settler give way to eventual resolutions of intercultural peace or, in metaphorical Thanksgiving conflicts between settler and settler, indigenous erasure.

In the "Turkey Day" episode of *The Beverly Hillbillies*, for example, high-society Mrs. Drysdale, the Clampetts' next-door neighbor, hires two actors from a movie studio in Hollywood to pose as Indians for an "authentic" Thanksgiving picture at her mansion. After a series of misunderstandings, the Indians reveal they are Jewish American as they replace their Indian buckskin costumes with suits and ties for the Clampetts' Thanksgiving dinner, for which the "Indians" bring gefilte fish and matzo ball soup. In the *Brady Bunch* episode "Un-Underground Movie," the settler Bradys reenact the first Thanksgiving in a home movie called "Our Pilgrim Fathers." Peter and Bobby Brady portray, to quote a condescending Mrs. Brady/Pilgrim matriarch, "friendly Indians" before the boys join the rest of the Bradys as Pilgrims by the film's nonindigenous conclusion. In a distorted historical reenactment in the *Happy Days* episode "The First Thanksgiving," the starring white cast also portray Pilgrims, who host, on unacknowledged indigenous land, three male mute Indians (they communicate in sign language with, who else, the Fonz, who then speaks on their behalf) at the Pilgrims' gathering. In the *Everybody Loves Raymond* episode "The Bird," two feuding settler families separate into playing Indians and Pilgrims for an annual tradition of reenacting the first Thanksgiving, replete with starring character Ray Barone as a topless Squanto speaking broken English. In all of these examples, set during a holiday in which America is often reminded of historical indigenous presence, Native Peoples are markedly absent and replaced by the settler stand-ins.[49]

Intertextual iterations of the recognizably Indian in redface play out, too, through faux tribal and communal formations of non-Natives becoming "Indian." These "representations of redface," as I have called them elsewhere, illustrate what Bhabha calls "colonial mimicry" in their "desire for a reformed, recognizably Other," the recognizably Indian.[50] In the *I Love Lucy* episode "The Indian Show," Lucy, Ricky, Ethel, and Fred play Indian with headdresses and tomahawks in a nightclub act. In the *Yes, Dear* episode "Dances with Couch," white American and Asian American fathers and sons don feathers and hokey Indian names in the West Los Angeles tribe of Indian Scouts. Eight months later in the *My Wife and Kids* episode "Michael's Tribe," African American Damon Wayans's lead character declares himself Chief Bald Eagle for his daughter's Indian princesses group. In the "Boston Tea Party" episode of *The Suite Life of Zack and Cody*, nearly two dozen non-Native characters wear headdresses in a flashback to eighteenth-century Boston. In all, redfaced non-Natives abound in "mimicry . . . as the representation of a difference that is itself a process of disavowal," in this case, of the recognizably Native.[51]

In the recognizably Indian deployment of representational self-determination—the subject of chapter 2—producers sometimes envision a temporary "real" indigenous presence, that is, characters intended to be Native yet still constructed as steadfast simulations of sitcom Indians. As representational stand-ins for the actual indigenous, "simulations," White Earth Ojibwe scholar Gerald Vizenor argues, "are the absence of the tribal real." In such episodes as *Barney Miller*'s "The Indian," *Dharma and Greg*'s "Indian Summer," and *Saved by the Bell*'s "Running Zack," guest-starring older male Indians appear briefly and attempt to assert their agency before conveniently dying and leaving a temporary impact on settler characters by the close of each episode, functioning as recurring reinforcements of the vanishing race, last of the tribe, and sage elder tropes. In *Barney Miller*, Charles White Eagle (Lakota) portrays George Ten Fingers, an Indian character who wishes to die in Central Park. Wojo, a Polish American detective, first arrests him for loitering, then takes the stereotypically wise Indian elder back to the park, where Ten Fingers dies. In *Dharma and Greg*, Floyd Red Crow Westerman (Lakota) plays George Littlefox, who first foretells his death on his people's homeland (that is, the roof of settler character Dharma's apartment building) but then, instead of completely vanishing, reappears as Dharma's phantasmic guide in three subsequent episodes over the next four years. In *Saved by the Bell*, Dehl Berti (Chiricahua Apache) plays Chief Henry, who suddenly dies without any expressive warning or previous reference to his health, but not before helping settler star Zack Morris, who has just learned of a personal Nez Perce heritage, to become recognizably Indian.[52] Such episodes attempt to "authenticate" some semblance of a respectable indigenous reality, bolstered more so by casting Native actors, but each eventually succumbs to the colonial power and control over the recognizably Indian in which "tribal realities are superseded by simulations of the unreal," as Vizenor contends, "and tribal wisdom is weakened by those imitations, however sincere."[53]

Recent animated sitcom episodes turn to the "casino Indian" and Indian casino, a dominant representation of and setting for the recognizably Indian. Replacing historical and vanishing Indians with modern-day greedy and cultureless capitalists, the casino Indians and their enormous money-making casinos surface in *South Park*, *The Simpsons*, and elsewhere. In her analysis of televisual representations of Indians in *Family Guy*, *Saturday*

Night Live, Chapelle's Show, The Sopranos, and *Drawn Together,* Celeste Lacroix contends fictional TV has recently ushered in "a new and more virulent form of racism" through "the media stereotype of the casino Indian," or what Katherine Spilde calls "Rich Indian Racism."[54] In their book *Forced Federalism: Contemporary Challenges to Indigenous Nationhood,* Tsalagi scholar Jeff Corntassel and Richard C. Witmer theorize that the "politics of perception" of indigeneity are impacted by the "easily recognizable feature of U.S. popular culture"—"images of rich Indians" such as represented in, he notably cites, the episode "Missionary: Impossible" of *The Simpsons* that depicts "a Native casino [called The Lucky Savage] on a remote island."[55]

In conjunction with the on-screen representations, the paratexts of DVD commentaries also reveal the production of the recognizably Indian in relation to producers' perceptions of Native Peoples. For satirical sitcoms like *South Park* and *Family Guy,* the nonsatirical candor in producers' commentaries is especially enlightening. In the *South Park* episode "Red Man's Greed," series creators Trey Parker and Matt Stone depict the indigenous as colonizers by showcasing Indians as wealthy, self-serving owners of the Three Feathers Indian Casino who plan to take the lands now known as the town of South Park in order to bulldoze the area and build a superhighway to their casino.[56] The episode, Parker admits in the commentary, was inspired by his grandmother's visits to a "most depressing place": an "Indian casino" in Phoenix. From there, Parker and Stone flaunt that the episode and its "obvious" anomalies in flipping the master narrative's script took only around eight hours to write. For example, the "greedy-ass rich Indians," to quote South Park white adolescent Cartman, give SARS-infected blankets to the non-Natives, a play off of white soldiers historically gifting smallpox-infected blankets to Natives. Guest Indian character Chief RunsWith Premise represents a savage capitalist and an inverted Indian killer bent on destroying the livelihood of the non-Native South Park residents in the name of "progress." Overall, Parker and Stone's admission of their production brevity comes as little surprise since they presumably know Indians, that is, Hollywood's televisual and cinematic Indians, as evident from Parker and Stone's dependence on dated colonial logic and the role reversals between the indigenous and settler. "The episode's many reversals," Jessica Cattelino notes, "simultaneously call attention to the colonization of Native America and problematically render this past as something *of* the past by drawing a historically equalizing parallel between it and Indian casino power over small-town white Americans."[57]

The inspiration for the *Family Guy* episode "The Son Also Draws" derives not only from producers' distorted perceptual dependence on the recognizably Indian in indigenous-settler history but also from a distorted deployment of federal Indian politics, a fundamental component of the televisions I address in later chapters.[58] In *Family Guy*, white husband and father Peter Griffin claims to be Indian at the casino Geronimo's Palace in a fraudulent attempt to receive gaming profits and to regain the family car that his gambling addict wife, Lois, has lost to the casino. With names like Deals with his Wrist (blackjack dealer) and Watches You Pee (bathroom attendant), the near-cultureless casino-owning Indians concoct ludicrous vision quest criteria for Peter to fulfill in order to become a member of their unnamed tribe. When Peter succeeds (which includes communing with trees and his spirit guide the Fonz), the Indians feel dejected and culturally lost—the chief whines, "Aw, I want a spiritual vision, too!"—until they soothe themselves with a reminder of their "$6 million a week" fortune. As Renee Ann Cramer observes, Peter "proved that even he was more indigenous than the so-called Indians running the casino."[59] In the DVD commentary, one writer says the episode's Indians are "such a spiritual people, yet they run a casino," as if spirituality and business cannot coexist in Native lives. Another writer explicitly interpellates indeterminate Native Peoples when he adds, "They have these things, too, where they have so much money, like, if you're like 1/64th Native American, you can actually belong to the tribe and collect some of the money, which," he and another writer agree, "was the basis of this episode." In their on- and offscreen (mis)treatment of such indigenous sovereign issues as Native nations' citizenship criteria, economic development, and traditions, *Family Guy* unapologetically showcases its anti-indigenous televisions. Considering that *Family Guy* creator Seth MacFarlane is from Rhode Island, it is not unlikely that he is aware of contemporary mainstream discourse on the Narragansetts or nearby Mashantucket Pequots and Mohegans, including long-standing verbal assaults that question and negate their indigenous identities.

The "Bart to the Future" episode of *The Simpsons*, as one reviewer attests, "actually rips off the *Family Guy*" the following year.[60] Homer pulls into the parking lot of Caesar's Powwow Indian Casino, but Marge refuses to enter due to her self-identified "gambling problem." Rather than go on a vision quest, Bart is shown a vision of his bleak and lethargic future by the casino's "mystic" Indian manager, whose relatives' names include "Crazy Talk" and "Dances with Focus Groups." The same episode also joins a long procession of sitcoms containing recognizably Indian jokes. For example, in *The Andy Griffith Show*'s episode "The Pageant," Barney portrays Chief Noogatuck in Mayberry's annual Founders' Day pageant. Andy says, "I know how you can learn your part real good." Barney asks, "How?," and Andy replies, "See?" In *Friends*, Joey raises a hand to sign an Indian "How" at the start of his catchphrase question "How you doing?" Upon entering the Indian casino in *The Simpsons*, Homer elongates the "How" into an energetic "Hi-how-are-you? Hi-how-are-you? Hi-how-are-you?" spoken to the "sound of Indian" of DUM-dum-dum-dum. (In the *South Park* episode "Red Man's Greed," comedian Johnny ManyMoons' hyper-romanticized and stilted Indian speech includes lame jokes starting with lines like, "Many moons ago, pony and eagle walked up to coyote." The Indian audience's repetitive low-key laughter of "Ha-ha-ha-ha" is also set to the Indian cadence of DUM-dum-dum-dum.)[61] In the "Bart to the Future" DVD commentary, producers offer another variation of indigenous erasure when they erroneously credit non-Native consulting producer Tom Gammill for Homer's joke, not Oneida comic Charlie Hill, who first publicly performed it to open his stand-up routines, such as in his 1977 appearance on *The Richard Pryor Show*. A recognizably Native comedic writer and actor whom I will discuss momentarily, Hill's opening bit—comic legend Steve Allen called it one of the two funniest introductions he had ever heard—speaks back to sonic and rhetorical Hollywood stereotypes in his original line, unlike Homer and *The Simpsons*, who continue the sitcom Indian tradition of non-Native agency, reinforcement of Indian jokes, and lack of indigenous recognition.[62]

The recognizably Indian, however, constitutes more complexity than merely airing repeats and reinforcements illustrative of colonial hegemony. While settler sitcoms share in overlapping televisions, they also include momentary exceptions from supporting what some may deem a homogeneous regime of repetitious and stereotypically false representations of Indians. The productions of sitcom Indians reveal intertextual boundary disputes over heterogeneous representations of the sitcom's Indian and Indian-settler encounters. I locate these discursively and visually negotiated moments toward the margins of sitcom productions, highlighting them as counterintuitive cracks in the settler's always already unsettled representational landscape of colonial discourse. In their analysis of 1990s television drama, George and Sanders acknowledge potential progressive moments in portrayals of Indians in the ABC drama *Twin Peaks* but then leave these momentary exceptions, when positioned within the larger trajectory of the series, to exemplify "throw-away lines."[63] I question if highlighting these moments is more important than noting and subsequently discarding them. Can such lines not help viewers to rethink what constitutes legitimate elements for analysis as well as further precision in cultural criticism? Do they, individually and cumulatively, not open up space to reorient part of how one approaches television texts? In chapters 2, 3, and 4, I attempt to account for some of the complexities of sitcom Indian representations and to resituate analysis of situation comedy within related sociocultural, political, and media contexts. For now, I offer an example of a negotiated moment from a 1960s sitcom that starts to counter previous dismissive critiques of the same series.

As I argue in chapter 2, 1960s sitcoms are not *only* anti-Native texts chock-full of stereotypes and absent critical commentary on Native-settler relations. *The Beverly Hillbillies'* "Jed Cuts the Family Tree," for one, is not simply a throwaway episode. When the Clampetts learn one of their ancestors may have arrived on the Mayflower, cousin Pearl tries to explain to Jed, the Tennessee-raised patriarch of his mountaineers-turned-oil-tycoons family in Beverly Hills, that they will automatically qualify for high society.

> PEARL: The earlier your kinfolk got here, higher up that put ya.
> JED: Well, I reckon the highest society folks is the Injuns.
> PEARL: No, it don't work that way.
> JED: How come?
> PEARL: I don't know how come.
> JED: Well, they was here before anybody else.
> PEARL: Now, now, now, Jed. Let's not try to change the rules. Let's just start enjoying the game![64]

In a moment of common sense, Jed questions Pearl's unchecked social hierarchy and implied white privilege, a colonial class logic dependent on centuries of European immigrations, attempted obliteration of the indigenous, and enslavement of Africans. As Jason Mittell notes, some "critics have read *Hillbillies* as a forum . . . questioning the norms of 1960s modernity." David Marc, for one, contends it "invites the viewer into the epic arena of testing cultural assumptions."[65] Although scholars like Paul Attallah and Janet Staiger have highlighted the *Hillbillies'* recursive commentary on class, Jed's recognition of race and indigeneity in conjunction with class opens up possibilities for expanding scholarly critiques.[66] Jed's acknowledgment, in 1960s rural sitcom parlance, of "Injuns" as first may be the first time in sitcom history not only to recognize pre-settler American history but also to cite the indigenous to illustrate a major fallacy in New England high society logic. Rather than write Indians out of existence, as many sitcoms then and still now have been wont to do, Jed recognizes a *contemporary* Indian presence—he says "*is* the Injuns," not "was"—and offers a counterintuitive moment in early sitcoms' Indian-settler talk, almost anticipating a changing structure and settler anxiety in "the game" that continues to unfold today with hasty, misguided assumptions, like those exhibited in "Indian" casino episodes of *Family Guy* and *South Park*, on tribal sovereignties, identities, and economies. Even though Jed eventually complies with Pearl's request not "to change the rules," Jed leaves a disruptive trace in *The Beverly Hillbillies* universe of settler colonial dominance.

Tribal Television: Recognizably Native

Thus far, my references to the recognizably Native have primarily configured what it is *not*: recognizably Indian. Yet both fundamentally depend on each other for representational recognition. In the dialectical battering of boundaries over representations, the conflicting epistemological formations of the recognizably Indian and recognizably Native stem from competing politics and perceptions of indigeneity. Although the recognizably Indian has occasionally attempted to challenge the boundaries, the recognizably Native works consistently through Native frames of reference, in which recognizably Native representations become the norm, not exceptions, for *changing the rules* in televisual governmentality over representations of the indigenous. Whereas the recognizably Indian has largely marginalized, disavowed, and displaced the Native, the recognizably Native has labored to critically resist and creatively circumvent the Indian. Recognizably Native representations come from an indigenous-centered inclination and contention that they are recognizable to Native Peoples as they synergize the visual, sonic, and affect of indigenous representations into something seen, heard, and felt in a thick resonance by indigenous tribes, nations, communities, and individuals. Without trying to resort to essentialist identity policing to frame indigeneity, I say "recognizably Native" to express what, for many Natives, may feel like second nature regarding how they affectively *just know* Native-ness and its quotidian modes of sensing, carrying, performing, and articulating histories of indigeneity.

Tuned in to experiential formations of indigenous identities and to individual and tribal recognitions of the indigenous, recognizably Native characterizations are performatively grounded in their contemporary familial and tribal ways of expressing indigeneity rather than in cultureless and assimilative performance as, say, televisual and sitcom Indians. As a multifaceted, interlinked recognition of Native presence on-screen and Native viewership offscreen—akin to Joanna Hearne's positioning of

Native recognition as a mode of looking at, remembering, and reclaiming Native-produced mediated images of the indigenous—the cultural work of the recognizably Native counters and upstages the recognizably Indian in its performative proliferation of tribal televisions.[67]

To frame the Native-produced televisions, I turn to Choctaw scholar and writer LeAnne Howe's concept of "tribalography." Encompassing the stories that "author tribes" and connect the indigenous and nonindigenous, tribalography, for Howe, "comes from the native propensity for bringing things together, for making consensus, and for symbiotically connecting one thing to another." Throughout her scholarly and creative oeuvre, Howe engages and expands a traditional-modern-futuristic Choctaw tribalography in a collaborative storying "with the past and present and future."[68] Recognizing that she primarily utilizes "tribalography" in the contexts of indigenous nationalism and tribal storytelling, I borrow the term as a metaphorical encasement of the tribal televisions, the recognizably Native stories, to address the formations of a televisual tribalography that includes the indigenous and their relations with the nonindigenous. I will situate tribalography broadly, in a pan-Native context that includes Oneida, Cree, and other indigenous storytellers, to study Native producers' visions and practices of constructing televisual indigeneity in negotiation with and against TV's generic expectations of representing the indigenous. In all, tribalography is useful for positioning and developing critiques of intertextual connections and representational heritage—an indigenous critical intertextuality—in producers' televisions of tribal peoples and topics.

Intertextuality, to rerun an excerpt from earlier, is indelibly marked by the "inescapable interdependence" of texts, but critical intertextuality discerns contestations of ideological underpinnings and hierarchies of textual power and hegemonic readings. "The territory of *critical intertextuality*," Jonathan Gray explains, includes space for using "paratexts and intertexts . . . to attack a text, to subvert its preferred meanings and to propose unofficial and sanctioned readings."[69] Whereas Gray goes on to use *The Simpsons* to illustrate the animated sitcom's parodic critiques of American TV culture, genres, and representations of familial relations such as in sitcoms like *Leave It to Beaver* and *The Cosby Show*, I have in mind the critical intertextual work between Native producers' interrelated indigenous-centered televisions conceptualized through indigenous frames of reference and sensibilities in image-making. It involves readjusting the televisual and media landscape with recognizably Native (inter)texts that shape and are shaped by perceptions of each other in the ever-expanding genealogy of representing indigeneity.

Indigenous critical intertextuality in television entertainment entails fashioning productive space for engaging Native and non-Native viewerships and perceptions and for countering Hollywood's representations of the indigenous, in which Native and allied producers reconfigure the territory in the colonial apparatus of television to move Native and non-Native audiences toward their own decolonized viewings of representations of the indigenous. By responding to a long history of the recognizably Indian with the recognizably Native, televisionary producers like Drew Hayden Taylor, co-creator and writer for the indigenous sitcom *Mixed Blessings* (which I discuss in chapter 4), and Tracey Deer (Mohawk), executive producer and director of the half-hour dramatic comedy *Mohawk Girls*, attempt in their artistic creations to decolonize audience views of rigid indigeneity.[70] With the tagline "Welcome to Our World," suggesting an inclusive invitation to all viewers, *Mohawk Girls* follows the daily lives of "four young women trying to figure out the answer" to the question, "What does it mean to be a modern day Mohawk woman?," which Hollywood TV series have never really asked nor shown textual evidence of considering, not for Mohawks nor for practically any other indigenous nation or tribe.[71] In comedic TV series, what does it mean to represent the indigenous through a recognizably Native framework in the twentieth and twenty-first centuries?

For this book's focus on sitcoms and the politics of their representations of the indigenous, the critical intertextual tribalography I deploy, particularly in chapter 4, is substantiated with the enactment of what I call *sitcom sovereignty*. Like recent aesthetic and media descendants of tribal sovereignty—a people's inherent right to control their destiny—sitcom sovereignty responds to the Osage scholar Robert Warrior's call for indigenous "intellectual sovereignty" by speaking to Native producers' and audiences' inherent right to construct, critique, and readjust recognizably Native representations of indigeneity. "Native sovereignty," Gerald Vizenor explains, "is sovenance ['a native presence'], the immanence of visions, and transmotion in artistic creations." Beverly Singer (Tewa Pueblo) speaks of "cultural sovereignty" as a movement for "telling our own stories," an assertion shared by Makah television producer and filmmaker Sandra Osawa, who contends that "media has long been an overlooked part of our [indigenous] struggles and true sovereignty cannot exist until we are truly able to tell our own stories." Randolph Lewis's indigenous- and cinematic-centered term "representational sovereignty" concerns "the right, as well as the ability, for a group of people to depict themselves with their own ambitions at heart." Michelle Raheja's cinematic and media concept of "visual sovereignty" is "a creative act of self-representation" that "recognizes the complexities of creating media for multiple audiences, critiquing filmic representations of Native Americans, at the same time that it participates in some of the conventions that have produced these representations."[72] Sitcom sovereignty similarly recognizes the inherent right to produce and disseminate media texts, in this case, for the relatively overlooked genre of the sitcom. Engaging the on- and offscreen politics of creative control in producing Native sitcoms, casting Native actors, developing Native characters, and collaborating with Native-run and Native-supporting networks, sitcom sovereignty works to combat stereotypes, reach diverse audiences, and feature Native perspectives and humor, all through a genre historically distorted in communicating indigeneity through an indigenous lens.

An early experimental forerunner to sitcom sovereignty is the indigenous comedic film *Harold of Orange* (1984), written by Vizenor and starring Charlie Hill in the title role.[73] Prefiguring Native sitcoms, Vizenor's recognizably Native film is reminiscent of sitcom aesthetics and, clocking in at approximately thirty minutes, early sitcom episode duration. For some, however, the film's comparisons to sitcoms become mixed points of contention. In his critique of *Harold of Orange*, Robert Silberman says, "At times . . . the film becomes hokey and moves dangerously close to the shallowness of a TV sitcom." He continues, "*Harold* does occasionally seem rather like an Indian version of *Sgt. Bilko* or *M.A.S.H.* or *Hogan's Heroes* or, perhaps more to the point, *F Troop*, with a group of clever and likeable characters up against the authorities, who are equally likeable if not quite so clever. Yet there are enough significant differences to set *Harold* apart, especially in the political satire and the poetical touches."[74] Silberman, though, does not explicitly recognize, to borrow from Vizenor, the "postindian" sensibility and affect running throughout the production of *Harold*, nor does he note the ideological rescripting of settler colonial dominance over exoticized Others in *F Troop* and his other cited sitcoms. The postindian representations in *Harold*, I contend, deeply distinguish the film, representationally, from non-Native sitcom productions of the recognizably Indian.

As vital conceptual relations to the recognizably Native, postindians are, Vizenor explains in his seminal book *Manifest Manners*, "the storiers of an imagic presence" and "the storiers of actual motion."[75] They include Native storytellers, writers, and activists who recount narratives of lived and imagined experiences that reflect contemporary and presentist indigenous ontologies that are fluently and fluidly familiar to Native Peoples and others whose perceptions of indigeneity are sometimes reactionary to but not wholly dependent on colonial discourse and the almost defeated recognizably Indian representations and televisions in and learned from sitcoms and elsewhere in popular culture, media, and society. Postindians represent those who actively communicate their stories, writings, intellects, and performances to center and reenvision the indigenous and ensure that indigenous views and voices, as intertextually informed by other indigenous views and voices, are breathed into this world. Or as Vizenor says, "The postindian warriors are new indications of a narrative recreation, the simulations that overcome the manifest manners of dominance," or "the modern manners that have carried out the notions of manifest destiny."[76]

Produced in a postindian paradigm to "create a new tribal presence in stories," *Harold of Orange* follows tribal trickster Harold Sinseer and his band of Warriors' travels in Minnesota to a nearby white-run, wealthy foundation, which is interested in funding Harold's proposed (faux) project to use tribal pinch beans to "open coffee houses on reservations around the world."[77] Harold proves to be a multifaceted, comical, and ingenious Native survivor that mediascapes have rarely showcased.[78] Harold the trickster represents the postindian who "stands for an active, ironic resistance to dominance, and the good energy of native survivance." Encompassing and transcending survival and resistance to colonization, Vizenor's critical term "survivance" indicates the modern indigenous state of an "active presence," as illustrated throughout *Harold of Orange*.[79]

"The Warriors of Orange," Harold says, "are trained in the art of socioacupuncture. We imagine the world and cut our words from the centerfolds of histories." He and the Warriors practice their postindian socioacupuncture, described by Vizenor elsewhere as "an active word war with a comic temper," on the Anglo characters through rhetorical encounters about Indians, Columbus, colonization, philosophy, the Bering Strait, anthropologists, Indian mascots, economics, alcoholism, and "mythic revolutions on the reservation." For example, Son Bear, one of the Warriors, responds to the construct of "Indian" when a settler foundation member asks how many Indians were here when Columbus arrived. The Warrior says "none," since Columbus invented the term. When then asked by the same settler how many *tribal peoples* were here, the Warrior quickly and coolly claims, "49,723,196," which silences the settler's arrogant and assumptive inquiries but prompts a reconsideration of "truth" and whose perspectives on history *matter* in the tribal televisions of storying socioacupunctural visions.

After a series of comic situations—an Anglos versus Indians softball game, a hokey parking lot Indian-naming ceremony with Monopoly game cards ("Your new name is 'Baltic,'" says Harold to a settler), and a

Native-led museum protest of anthropologists' collections of indigenous remains—the Warriors, "tribal tricksters determined to reclaim their estate from the white man," eventually secure funding from the foundation by playing to board member Ted Velt's expectations that all Indians are alcoholics.

> TED: My question is, ahh, how did all of you overcome the need and temptation to use alcohol? You are so sober, a credit to your race.
> HAROLD: Pinch beans. Pinch beans, my friend, are the cure.

Harold adds that "the beans block the temptation to take alcohol from evil white men. . . . Our proposal to establish coffee houses will lead to a sober, as well as a mythic, revolution." "Fantastic!" Ted cries out. "You've got my vote for sure."[80]

The socioacupunctural revolution in *Harold* thrives on a Native trickster presence, a band of recognizably Native word warriors, and settler expectations of Indianness within a convoluted conflation of visual and aural ambiguities. In Harold's New School of Socioacupuncture, the serious comedy of socioacupuncture functions as what Vizenor calls a "liberatory tribal striptease."[81] Translated and applied to television, recognizably Native comedy liberates by uncovering and analyzing the recognizably Indian. As a tribal striptease for decolonizing viewers, audiences see postindian producers' televisions of indigeneity.

In Sandra Sunrising Osawa's documentary *On and Off the Res' w/Charlie Hill* (2000), Hill, whose father is Oneida, recalls "sitting in my dad's lap and watching these TV shows, him saying, 'Ah, those aren't Indians, look how dumb they are, look how they're walking, Indians don't walk back and forth, they're not like this.' I realized later he was probably writing my act for me." "The very thing," Hill adds, "that made us survive is what my Dad told me: . . . our humor."[82] Hill carried such teachings not just to stand-up comic routines but also to Hollywood sitcom sets, though he refused sitcoms at first. After performing on *The Richard Pryor Show* and *The Tonight Show Starring Johnny Carson* in the late 1970s, Hill says he "started getting job offers from Hollywood people who didn't understand what I was doing. I got offered sitcoms that was so demeaning." Eventually in the mid-1990s, he was willing to work in two particular sitcoms.

In the *Moesha* episode "Road Trip," Hill appears as Robert, a Hopi owner of a convenience store and diner in Flagstaff, Arizona. According to his wife, Leona, Hill was "able to change how the storyline's going." Hill's critical-creative imprint was soon evident in the episode. When Moesha and her friends enter Robert's store, they see T-shirts for sale sporting the revised faux team names "Cleveland Caucasians" and "Washington Rednecks," reminiscent of Hill's stand-up humor on mascots. For instance, in a 1983 routine, he changed the professional football team the Kansas City Chiefs to the "Kansas City Caucasians" and envisioned a "white guy out there in a leisure suit" who, after the team scores, "[dances] around a mobile home."[83]

Hill also wrote for and guest-starred in the popular 1990s sitcom *Roseanne*. When Hill, possibly the first Native writer of a popular U.S. sitcom, was approached by Roseanne Barr to be in a Thanksgiving-themed episode of *Roseanne*, he expressed concern to her: "You got me two things I've always avoided: sitcoms and Thanksgiving." When Hill received the script, the now comic elder of the recognizably Native sitcom tribalography remarked it was "really kind of demeaning" and told his friend Barr, "I can't do it." According to Hill, Barr replied, "Come on in. Tell us what you want and we'll do it." The result was the Thanksgiving-themed episode "The Last Thursday in November," Hill's readjusted narrative television of early Native-Pilgrim relations.[84]

In the episode, Hill plays a modern-day ninth grade theater teacher named Mr. Hill, who prepares the students for a staged version of the first Thanksgiving. Initially, Hill follows the conventional narrative of Indians welcoming and sharing their food with the Pilgrims, but then he reenvisions the gathering with two male Pilgrims removing their black-and-white Pilgrim attire to reveal dark suits and ties underneath, à la John Travolta's and Samuel L. Jackson's characters in *Pulp Fiction* (1994). The pair of *Pulp Fiction* Pilgrims maniacally shoot and kill all of the Indians. Afterward, one disgruntled parent calls the play "revisionist drivel and tripe" and defends the "brave" Pilgrims who "discovered America." Hill questions how they can "discover America if my people already lived there. You know, that's like me going outside and discovering someone else's porch." After the play, Roseanne, a strong supporter of the performance, references the mid-1960s sitcom featuring the outlandish ragtag tribe of stereotypical Hekawi Indians when she tells Hill, "I will never laugh at *F Troop* again," to which he says, "Don't even get me started on *F Troop*. I mean, I've never seen an Indian person ever go," as he claps hand to mouth, "'woo-woo-woo-woo-woo-woo-woo.' You know, I've seen drunk rednecks do it a lot." From one sitcom to another, *Roseanne* speaks back to and flips the script on representations of sitcom Indians, such as those in *F Troop*, and also opens up new space for the recognizably Native within the sitcom genre.

Like Hill, Ted Jojola (Isleta Pueblo) is highly familiar with representations of televisual Indians. In 1992, Jojola "was contacted by the Division of

Children's Programs at ABC" television to "recreate a cartoon character" for an upcoming Saturday morning cartoon series *Wild West COW-Boys of Moo Mesa*. The main cowboys, who represented the "law" of Moo Mesa, were Cowlorado, Marshall Moo Montana, and the Dakota Dude. Then there was, Jojola explains, "Geronimoo," the violent "Indian sidekick . . . with a Mohawk-style haircut, chiseled out of the likes of the quintessential Indian savage." Originally materialized as an action figure in a line of *Moo Mesa* toys, Geronimoo had "feathers and war paint, animal-tooth necklace, bow and arrow, chopping tomahawk, and G-string and was embossed in red-hued plastic."[85]

ABC rejected Geronimoo and proposed a revised character named Phil Thomas for Jojola's consideration. While Jojola says Thomas "was a dramatic improvement over Geronimoo," he still embodied "the Indian sidekick motif." According to Jojola, ABC "swayed toward a Pueblo Indian image" for Thomas but presented several stereotypes and inconsistencies, such as an early sketch showing "Plains Indian characteristics." "The initial image of Phil Thomas represented a depiction of the Indian from a predominantly non-native perspective and was driven by popular non-native ideals of Native American life and customs. Hence the archetypes of tepees and saguaro cactus [both proposed by ABC] subconsciously crept into what was to be a Pueblo landscape."[86]

In close consultation with ABC producers, Jojola transformed Thomas into J. R. (who would later be voiced by actor Michael Horse [Yaqui, Mescalero Apache, and Zuni descent] during production). "Given the lack of a Pueblo presence in the cartoon world," Jojola explains, "it was necessary to reconstruct the character in its entirety." Through Jojola's work, J. R. became a heroic, philosophical, and Pueblo-informed character modeled after Jojola's "own [Isleta] grandfather." He reconstructed Geronimoo and Thomas into a recognizably Native character from an Isleta frame of reference, not reconstructing, as the producers of Geronimoo and, to a lesser extent, Thomas had done by repeating or reinforcing old stereotypes, such as those from old B-film westerns and *F Troop* reruns. "J. R. was an appropriation," Jojola concludes, "in the revised sense. For me, as a native collaborator on the project, J. R. represented a unique revision from a native's perspective."[87]

Whereas Jojola repeatedly wrote back to ABC and wrote Isleta influences into mainstream children's television, film and television director and producer Chris Eyre and stand-up comic Drew Lacapa (White Mountain Apache) engaged in "talking back" to Hollywood and delivering critically humorous Native perspectives to a sizable audience.[88] Eyre teamed with Lacapa to perform "Talking Couch" at the 2002 Taos Talking Picture Festival. Lacapa said he and Eyre were "big *Beavis and Butthead* fans" and "wondered what if Beavis and Butthead were two Indians making fun of how Indians are portrayed in the movies."[89] So, seated on a couch before a live audience, they watched and satirized, via improvised voice-overs, Hollywood films featuring Indians. Viewing, for instance, Disney's *Pocahontas* (1995) with the volume down, Lacapa says seductively, "Hi. My name's Pocahontas. I never have to brush my hair." To which Eyre, voicing John Smith, responds, "Take my hand. I want to give you syphilis." Lacapa and Eyre reenvision Beavis and Butthead, Mike Judge's pre–John Redcorn and other *King of the Hill* characters, as two seriocomical Natives in a settler-indigenous context informed by confluences between real-life histories, fictional Hollywood texts, and satirical commentary to "provoke," Eyre hopes, "thoughts and conversations" about images of the indigenous in film and television.[90] Used "as a weapon," visual anthropologist Sam Pack says, the two performers' humor "was meant to take the power away from those others who have historically defined them."[91] As producers, performers, and personifiers of the recognizably Native, Eyre and Lacapa appear to recognize Vizenor's argument that "the simulation of the indian is the absence of real natives" in their work to perceptually and representationally confront, deflate, and readjust cinematic and televisual Indians.

Chapter Organization

In the rest of this book, through a chronological series of sitcom case studies spanning representational patterns of positionalities and subjectivities of the indigenous primarily during the 1950s through the 2010s, I look to further unpack the on- and offscreen politics of performance and power, intertextual boundary disputes, and thorny resolutions involving representations of the indigenous and nonindigenous. Chapter 1, "New Frontier Televisions," applies decolonized viewing to analysis of 1960s sitcoms situated within the politics of John Kennedy's New Frontier administration and, as it was called in Indian affairs, New Trail policies and of Lyndon Johnson's subsequent Great Society. As Paul Attallah attests, sitcoms like *The Beverly Hillbillies* have been dismissed as "unworthy discourse" for serious inquiry.[92] Yet their windows into unsettling Indian-settler narratives call for a close viewing that critiques how sitcoms developed a televisual frontier reflective of representational moves in and around the New Frontier political discourse of 1960s Native and U.S. affairs during the Kennedy and Johnson administrations. How, I ask, did *The Andy Griffith Show* and other sitcoms tune in their era's political encounters and ethos in Indian affairs?

Charting the American sitcom's contributions to New Frontier and New Trail discourse of the 1960s, I contend that the first half of the decade represented a shift from the settlers' *physical* violence, reminiscent of 1950s slapstick violence, to the settlers' *discursive* violence of savagery involving stories of conflict often centered on historical Indian-settler relations and a simultaneous contemporary erasure of Indians. By the latter half of the 1960s, sitcoms figuratively tuned in to the political climate in D.C. and represented sitcoms' Indian-settler relations as gestures toward a state of unequal interdependence. In the midst of Johnson's declared "War on Poverty," sitcoms like *F Troop* incorporated business partnerships and transactions between settler supervisors and Indian employees, in effect suggesting troubling hierarchical solutions to indigenous poverty via indigenous assimilation into an American workforce built on profiting from non-Native expectations of "authentic" Indian performance. Indians were viewed as economically unstable colonized subjects in need of paternal supervision. The sitcom's master narrative concerning indigenous-settler histories began to be rewritten for *inclusion, cooperation*, and *development*—all buzzwords in 1960s Indian affairs—but was no less damaging with its on-screen pretenses of pursuing peace and prosperity for all.

A push for representational interdependence, paraded and masqueraded as multicultural inclusion and equality, becomes more explicit in chapter 2, "Settler Self-Determination." Read through the ambivalent Indian policy shifts between assimilation and self-determination in the United States from the 1970s to the 1990s, sitcom Indians and settlers share on-screen space and spoken jabs with each other, yet the Indians remain dependent on settlers for direction and adherence to performative expectations. Textual examples, including episodes of *The Brady Bunch*, *Barney Miller*, *Diff'rent Strokes*, and *Saved by the Bell*, represent liberal multiculturalist televisions of inequitably promoting Indian self-determination without relinquishing settler dominance. The inclusion of sitcom Indians and real-world indigenous issues quickly became overshadowed by partially masked representations of settler self-determination, superiority, and anxiety, in which sitcoms promoted and deflated indigenous self-determination in an anxious rush to imagine a sitcom America free of intercultural violence, unbridgeable difference, and irresolvable conflicts. Sitcom moments of bringing Indian and settler together are, I contend, overshadowed by a contradictory representational self-determination in which settler characters' agency and Indian characters' inferiority in episodic story lines impede sitcoms' attempts for intercultural harmony. The sitcoms encourage instead an unsettling settler self-determination built on a multicultural facade of equality.

A representational pattern of progress ebbs and flows in chapter 3, "The Neo-Indian in *King of the Hill.*" Critiquing recurring character John Redcorn and indigenous-settler relations within the animated universe of *King of the Hill* (1997–2010), I chart evolving on- and offscreen efforts to construct a layered animated indigenous character, who has arguably become the most human Indian character in U.S. sitcom history. Through analysis of broadcasted representations of Redcorn, production materials (for example, rejected story lines and script drafts in the *King of the Hill* Archives), and the offscreen paratextual work of Native actor Jonathan Joss (voice of Redcorn, 1998–2009), I argue that the producers started to challenge, even as they perpetuated, the sitcom's Indian, as if unable to overturn the rerun specter of the recognizably Indian. As the series progressed, Joss attempted to assume a representational sovereign share of his character as he took the Redcorn persona offscreen to start the Red Corn Band in an unorthodox approach to expand his character in *King of the Hill*, which led to new on-screen musical and entrepreneurial developments with mixed results as producers developed at best a new sitcom Indian that moved ambiguously toward and away from the recognizably Indian and recognizably Native. Within the critical genealogy of intertextual and paratextual sites of analysis, I thus situate Redcorn as an unstable representational bridge that traverses the course of the series between shadows of the recognizably Indian and transient semblances of the recognizably Native.

In contrast to the disavowal, marginalization, and ephemeralness of the recognizably Native in previous chapters, chapter 4, "Sitcom Sovereignty in *Mixed Blessings,*" analyzes the centrality of the production, representation, and encoded intent of the recognizably Native in the Aboriginal Peoples Television Network sitcom *Mixed Blessings* (2007–10) in Canada. The story of a widowed Cree woman and Ukrainian Canadian man who marry and merge into a large family of "Ucreenians," *Mixed Blessings* and its co-creators Ron Scott (Métis Nation of Alberta) and Drew Hayden Taylor engage and reconfigure the production and representational parameters of the sitcom genre through a sitcom sovereignty grounded in a creative Native sensibility, self-determination in production, recognizably Native characterization, and representational agency. Sitcom sovereignty is linked to previous chapters' competing conceptualizations of inclusion, self-determination, and other representational politics, but it also transcends their inability to articulate and represent the larger indigenous-centered means for governing the production and representation of the recognizably Native in television. To illustrate the sitcom sovereignty in *Mixed Blessings*, I focus on the sitcom's approach to producing and representing the recognizably Native in the intertwined layers of narrative, casting, characterization, and soundtrack. Together, these aesthetic elements contribute to the cultural work of decolonizing views of fragmented and misguided perceptions of Native Peoples. By engaging in the contact zones of previous sitcoms' scripted representational boundaries, the producers seriocomically contest and reframe the recognizably Indian, represent the recognizably Native, and work toward using the television sitcom to bridge Native and non-Native cultures, all of which is crucial in the politics of shaping views of indigeneity on-screen and off.

After tracing across four chapters a representational evolution of the recognizably Indian into the recognizably Native in North American sitcoms, I conclude with "Sign-off: Digital Test Patterns" to address preliminary work in online indigenous comedy as a new site of analysis for future indigenous sitcoms and for rethinking traditional understandings and uses of "TV." Through their recent original indigenous comedy, such as the anti-Hollywood satirical videos "Wolf Pack Auditions" and "The Avatars," which readjust the patterns of Hollywood indigenous representations in the movies *Twilight* and *Avatar*, members of the Native comedy troupe the 1491s are among the recognizable Natives moving into the future of broadcast comedy through the do-it-yourself ethic on the video-hosting site YouTube. Within a framework of digital sovereignty in cyberspace, the group's *strategies of survivance*—to borrow again from Vizenor—counter, complicate, and transgress the politics of dated perceptions of Native Peoples. Furthermore, in their contributions to the ongoing development of an indigenous entertainment e-network, the 1491s symbolize contemporary creative Natives' anti-sign-off, anti-colonizing, and pro-indigenous ethos.

In all, from the New Frontier and New Trail to representational self-determination and televisual and digital sovereignties, *Tribal Television* argues for enactment of the critical indigenous and media studies approach of decolonized viewing to center and interpret sitcom and other media representations of the indigenous within cultural, social, and political frames. This project also recognizes the decolonized viewing already in practice by Native producers who are applying their indigenous sensibilities and vantage points in their creative work to effect decolonizing views of the recognizably Indian and to produce televisual (and digital) space for recognizably Native characters and story lines. Together, to decolonize viewing (how one watches and interprets) and views (what one interprets) of incessant TV reruns and first-runs in the twenty-first century are critical processes located at the intersections of ongoing decolonization movements and discourses on indigeneity, visuality, and media literacy.

Be it discussing sitcoms through the discourses and representational economies of violence, history, policy, social movements, self-determination, assimilation, interculturality, production, reception, or reconciliation, my analysis of the recognizably Indian and recognizably Native televisions in situation comedies attempts to place indigenous studies, cultural studies, and television studies into a coherent conversation with each other, to account for sitcoms' recognizably Indian and recognizably Native representations from the past seven decades, and to reveal how far producers have traveled (and not traveled) since the mid-twentieth century. Up next, in chapter 1, are the American political visions in the 1960s that would circuitously find their way into sitcoms featuring small-town sheriffs, millionaire mountaineers, and an assorted mix of guest-starring Indians.

CHAPTER ONE

New Frontier Televisions

On June 16, 1960, Senator John Kennedy, on the presidential campaign trail, appeared on NBC's *Tonight Show* with host Jack Paar in New York. In addition to discussing current U.S. relations with the Soviet Union and Cuba and the candidate's Catholicism, Paar and Kennedy also tried, albeit momentarily, for a lighter tone. "Senator," Paar asked, "have there been any amusing things since you have been campaigning that you could tell me in 30 seconds?" To which Kennedy replied, "I was made an honorary Indian and I now cheer for our side on TV. I cheer for our side meaning the Indian side on TV."[1]

Turning to the television western's familiar cowboy-Indian dichotomy and its underlying media violence, Kennedy joked that he had shifted his viewer subjectivity from settler to Indian. But his attempt to amuse the audience, *New York Times* columnist Frank Rich observes, "landed with a thud."[2] At a time when three settler-dominated westerns—*Gunsmoke*, *Wagon Train*, and *Have Gun Will Travel*—topped television ratings, the senator's allegiance to an indigenous "our" may have alarmed Paar's presumably white studio audience, who spent time in their safe viewing confines each week with TV cowboy actors James Arness, Ward Bond, and Richard Boone and cinematic western icon John Wayne. While Kennedy appeared to treat his "honorary Indian" status with more amusement than honor, he did recognize television westerns' recurring settler-versus-Indian story line and the genre's interpellative insistence on whom to identify with: white cowboy heroes overflowing with on-screen bravado.

Kennedy "was made an honorary Indian" in at least two states during campaign stops. In Wisconsin, Paul Boller reports, "Kennedy was made honorary chieftain of an Indian tribe." Wearing a headdress, Kennedy foreshadowed his *Tonight Show* line but this time among an indigenous audience: "Next time I go to the movies to see cowboys and Indians, I'll be us." In South Dakota he wore another headdress, this time for Lakotas.[3] As Robert Burnette, former Rosebud Sioux chairman, would later recall, "When John F. Kennedy flew into Sioux Falls, South Dakota, in 1960, I met him at the airport and had the privilege of introducing him to the entire state. He put a war bonnet on his head, and he left it on for a few minutes. This encounter set the stage for the future."[4]

For a presidential candidate to meet and converse with Native Peoples in Indian Country is, indeed, a rarity and can be perceived as commendable for showing, as Kennedy did, a willingness to listen to Native voters' concerns, though the politician surely desired their votes in return. Kennedy's stops in Indian Country most likely provided him with a stark contrast between the real-life recognizably Native and Hollywood's fictional recognizably Indian. As Kennedy's early primary sources for knowing Indians, film and television offered common ground for discussion between Kennedy and Native Peoples. Early in his presidency, Kennedy would connect Indians and media again in his introduction to *The American Heritage Book of Indians*, which he begins, "For a subject worked and reworked so often in novels, motion pictures, and television, American Indians remain probably the least understood and most misunderstood Americans of us all."[5] Like his campaign trail rhetoric, in which he privileged televisual Indians over real-life Native Peoples, the introduction speaks to Kennedy's recognition of Hollywood's influence on non-Native American (mis)understandings of the indigenous.

Yet "the stage for the future" between Kennedy's administration and Natives would be one not only of occasional meetings, brief tribal addresses, photo opportunities (with headdress or not), and acknowledged misunderstandings but also fraught with controversy in conflicting stances on "issues central to the survival of American Indian communities, including treaty rights, self-determination, tribal sovereignty, and cultural integrity" during what is known as the administration's New Frontier or, as it was called in Indian affairs, the New Trail.[6] As outlined by several scholars, Kennedy's New Trail—supposedly tailored toward strengthening tribal self-determination and diminishing threats of termination—provided a series of accordances and conundrums between his rhetoric and policy directed at Native Peoples. The 1961 "American Indian Task Force Report," released by Secretary of the Interior Stewart Udall, states, "The proper role of the Federal government is to help Indians find their way along a new trail—one which leads to equal citizenship, maximum self-sufficiency and full participation in American life."[7] In historian Thomas Cowger's opinion, "The task force report communicated a mixed message. While encouraging self-determination, it also seemed to endorse goals of termination."[8] George Pierre Castile pinpoints "development" and "inclusion" as the New Trail era's two most prominent themes in early 1960s speeches of Philleo Nash, Kennedy's commissioner of Indian Affairs. "Nowhere," Castile adds, "was heard that discouraging word *termination* despite its status as congressional policy."[9] Nash's stated "insistence on the inclusion of an Indian voice" contrasts with Castile's contention "that JFK and his core staff were not very concerned with the Native Americans." Thomas Clarkin likewise observes increased calls for indigenous involvement in policy but concludes that "the Kennedy administration ignored issues central to the survival of American Indian communities." Naming Kennedy a "hollow icon," M. Annette Jaimes offers the most scathing account. Whereas Castile says the term "New Frontier" could conjure Natives' "bad memories of the old frontier," Jaimes calls "New Trail," its rhetorical replacement, "a phrase smacking of the same assimilationist mentality which had so recently marked the termination and relocation policies of the Truman and Eisenhower administrations."[10] She adds, "The gist of [Kennedy's] federal Indian policy," led by Nash and fellow Bureau of Indian Affairs (BIA) colleagues Stewart Udall and James Officer, "was to get American Indians into the Euroamerican mainstream even at the expense of their cultural preservation of traditional indigenous norms and practices."[11] In the words of an immediate retort to Udall's report, Mel Thom, a Paiute and cofounder and first president of the National Indian Youth Council, asked, "How many Indians want to fully participate in American life? Indians have a life."[12]

Kennedy and the controversial New Trail provide entry into interpreting politicized televisual spaces of the 1960s. In her book *Welcome to the Dreamhouse*, Lynn Spigel deftly interprets 1960s sitcoms and their representations of othered characters through the New Frontier discourse concerning space exploration and Kennedy's mission to land an American on the moon. In conversation with her work, I look at the administration's frontiersman rhetoric and roles in tribal–U.S. government relations in tandem with 1960s sitcom representations of the recognizably Indian and Indian-settler encounters.[13] "Although in distorted and circuitous ways," Spigel argues, "the progressive spirit of the New Frontier and its focus on space-age imagery served as a launching pad for significant revisions in television's fictional forms." Similarly, I turn to the "distorted and circuitous" in the context of extending New Frontier discourse to analysis of Indian and settler formations in sitcoms. Both JFK and sitcoms may have shown only an occasional interest in Indians, but the occasions swirl into a set of fictional and nonfictional cultural discourses on Indian-settler interculturality. Threading together New Trail Indian policy and rhetoric and New Frontier televisual discourse through a case study of the recognizably Indian in episodes of *The Andy Griffith Show*, *The Beverly Hillbillies*, and other series, I suggest that the New Frontier ethos and rhetoric of shifting Indian-settler relations and imagery served as a "launching pad" for shaping, to borrow from Kennedy, the "worked and reworked" televisions of New Frontier sitcom Indians.[14]

When extended to the mid- and late 1960s, Indian affairs in this televisual context concerns more than Kennedy's New Frontier/New Trail relationship with sitcoms. After Kennedy's assassination in 1963, Vice President Lyndon Johnson assumed the presidency until 1969. In addition to continuing and passing Kennedy's proposed legislation on civil rights and other pending laws, Johnson adapted the New Frontier into what he branded the Great Society. Declaring in January 1964 an "all-out war on human poverty and unemployment," Johnson soon signed the Economic Opportunity Act to create social programs across the United States, including, even if by default in the locating of impoverished sites, numerous reservations.[15] Standing two weeks later before the National Congress of American Indians, Johnson "pledged a continued effort to eradicate poverty and to provide new opportunity for the first citizens of America."[16] While historians generally agree that Johnson would go on to show scant interest in Native issues, his Office of Economic Opportunity, a bold initiative in the Great Society's arsenal, notably bypassed the BIA and allocated funds directly to indigenous nations for business start-up and economic growth.[17]

Following Kennedy's and Johnson's economic initiatives, sitcoms increasingly envisioned Indians attempting to earn income, mainly in business partnerships with settlers. Sitcoms gestured toward collaboration as a resolution to Indian poverty. To represent Indians in economic ventures potentially disrupted perceptions of Indians as predominantly poor and shiftless, yet the representations are not without performative and ideological circumstances. The recurring implication in these mid-1960s episodes is that for sitcom Indians to gain on-screen business opportunities, they must perform to settler expectations, in appearance and speech, of the recognizably Indian. Disallowed to be indigenous *and* modern, sitcom Indians in buckskin and broken English also tend to find themselves working in cahoots with crooked settlers or, worse in the context of indigenous self-determination, working under the control of shady settler bosses. Sitcoms, then, configured 1960s mainstream political calls for *development* as further *assimilation* into a dominant American framework that dictated the boundaries of Indian performance and working-class citizenship. As a state of unequal interdependence, in other words, sitcoms' inclusion of cooperative and entrepreneurial Indians considerably translated as representations of submissive and near-cultureless Indians.

Looking to the tribal televisions of the indigenous and indigenous-settler encounters in 1960s sitcoms, I ask how producers representationally tuned in 1960s U.S. policy on Indian affairs. How, in particular, was Kennedy's New Frontier vision of America represented in the televisions of American sitcoms? How did sitcom producers forge a political new trail onto the small screen suggestive of the Kennedy and Johnson administrations' calls for Native-settler cooperation and Native self-determination (over termination) in governance and economic development?[18] How did Johnson's Great Society encourage TV representations of entrepreneurial and employed Indians? Were "notions of the Old Frontier," to extend Horace Newcomb's take on 1950s westerns to sitcoms, "being rechanneled into something new"?[19] Or did producers masquerade and guard old ideological and representational boundaries over how to televise indigenous-settler histories and Indian inclusion?

Within the performative context of a settler colonial continuum between old and new frontiers, in which modern-day white sitcom characters cite dated pioneer perceptions of Indianness, reenact the settlers' skewed historical encounters with the indigenous, or otherwise perpetuate anti-indigenous acts and discourse, I trace sitcoms' shifts in the 1950s and early 1960s from exclusion and erasure to inclusion and re-visioning of the indigenous through the distorted televisions of cross-cultural cooperation and indigenous development. In comparison to readings that stack representations of Indians in *The Andy Griffith Show* and other 1960s sitcoms into a heap of degrading, homogeneous stereotypes, the sitcom frontier that I delineate suggests notable shifts in its televisions. After a predominant discursive and visual absence of the indigenous in 1950s sitcoms, save mostly for a couple of episodes of *I Love Lucy*, that coincided with the 1950s termination and federal relocation era (that is, policy efforts to entice the indigenous to move from reservations to urban cities and assimilate) during the Eisenhower administration, early 1960s sitcoms included recurring Indian-settler representations of *violence*, namely visual Native erasure anxiously punctuated by settler characters' discursive violence—savage speech acts—aimed at non-Native characters posing as Indians.[20] Sitcoms then appeared to tune in and construct variants of the Kennedy administration's New Trail policy buzzwords of "inclusion" and "development."[21] By mid-decade, the settlers' violent speech began to subside for noticeable but still problematic representations of physical *inclusion*, marked by an Indian-settler cooperation that attempted to mask assimilation and racial hierarchies. Amid Johnson's Great Society, economic development for the indigenous also became a prime example of inclusion through sitcoms' Indian-settler cooperative ventures accompanied by inferiority and limited agency for Indian characters whose primary concern, especially in episodes of *F Troop*, *Petticoat Junction*, *Green Acres*, and *The Munsters* airing from 1964 to 1966, is maintaining an employment dependence on the starring settler characters in sitcom Indians' pursuits of prosperity through peddling cultural, and cultural-less items, such as tomahawks and jewelry made locally and abroad, and performing Indian shows and historical re-enactments. Overall, what unfolds is a televisual tapestry of intertextual convergences between New Frontier sitcoms and politics.

Old Frontier Violence in New Frontier Sitcoms

On July 15, 1960, one month after his *Tonight Show* appearance in New York, Kennedy went west, as settlers are wont to do, to introduce his New Frontier. The "honorary Indian" stood before a huge crowd in the Los Angeles Memorial Coliseum to deliver his acceptance speech for the Democratic Party's presidential nomination. Whereas Kennedy had joked about his newfound Indianness with Paar, he now unapologetically sided with the settler in sharing his vision for America. After lauding his Democratic Party and lambasting Republicans over the first fourteen minutes, Kennedy harked back to a nineteenth-century anti-indigenous frontier. "I stand tonight facing west on what was once the last frontier. From the lands that stretch three thousand miles behind me, the pioneers of old gave up their safety, their comfort and sometimes their lives to build a new world here in the West."[22] Echoing the Manifest Destiny doctrine of centuries previous, Kennedy suggested that pioneers had to cross the Atlantic and venture farther west across Indian Country and that their trek had been chosen for them for the betterment of all pioneers. Whereas historian Frederick Jackson Turner had declared the frontier closed in his famous 1893 paper "The Significance of the Frontier in American History," Kennedy imagined its re-opening as the New Frontier of the 1960s, "a frontier of unknown opportunities and perils—a frontier of unfulfilled hopes and threats." In the midst of the Cold War and civil rights struggles, "President Kennedy saw himself, in imagery and substance," Richard Drinnon says, "standing at Frederick Jackson Turner's 'meeting point between savagery and civilization,' fending off the forces of chaos and darkness." Appropriating "'Frontier' . . . a complexly resonant symbol, a vivid and memorable set of hero-tales," Kennedy appealed to, Richard Slotkin contends, "a venerable tradition in American political rhetoric" to spark resonance with "the widest possible audience" across the United States.[23]

In his acceptance speech, Kennedy called for all Americans to align themselves with settlers who "were determined to make that new world strong and free, to overcome its hazards and its hardships, to conquer the enemies that threatened from without and within." While he may have had eighteenth-century British soldiers or twentieth-century German Nazis in mind as two examples of the unnamed "enemies," Indians were a definite possibility as those "from without and within." Kennedy suggestively reinforced the dated dictum that Indians were dehumanized obstacles to the advancements of "the pioneers of old" but explicitly failed to mention the violent actualities that facilitated the ideological dominance of settler colonialism and vanishing Indian tropes. A brief three minutes later, Kennedy unequivocally interpellated and situated his intended multicultural and multiracial audience: "I am asking each of you to be pioneers." Kennedy's rhetoric privileged historical white pioneers as stand-in exemplars of Americanness for all contemporary citizens to emulate. The pioneers represented, for the president, *the* model of Americaneity, which symbolized westward expansion, progress, and survival of "hazards" and "hardships"; at the same time, Kennedy blatantly disavowed any settler colonial responsibility for the attempted genocide of Indigenous Peoples.[24]

On the side of civilization, Kennedy praised pioneers' roles in settler colonialism as he grounded the New Frontier in the old. In front of a predominantly settler audience, Kennedy appealed to pride in pioneer heritage by privileging whiteness and assuming that all listeners could relate and share the same settler ancestors. For all Americans, including the indigenous, Kennedy repeatedly presented his New Frontier (and New Trail) as doctrines of optimism, cooperation, and national development for the greater good of all.

Kennedy told a story of America, centuries in the making, cut from iterations of the master narrative. His New Frontier relied on old frontier perceptions of indigenous savagery and violent attempts at indigenous erasure. Visual and sonic evidence were nearby in Kennedy's aforementioned references to media representations of Indians and Indian-settler dichotomies. Kennedy alluded to movies and TV series supporting the narrative of Manifest Destiny, replete with settler resourcefulness and indigenous savagery and complicity. Like others of his generation, Kennedy grew up with cinematic westerns predicated on violent story lines from the old frontier, such as *Stagecoach*, in which John Wayne's character kills Apaches who attack his settler stagecoach; *They Died with Their Boots On* (1941), starring Errol Flynn as a heroic and courageous George Armstrong Custer; and *Red River* (1948), whose original trailer highlights the words "Comanche Hordes on the Warpath!" in a story of brave white settlement in Texas.[25] The comedic film, an obvious forerunner to sitcoms, showcased violent and nonsensical Indians. In the silent film *Paleface* (1922), writer, director, and star Buster Keaton is tied to a fiery stake by Indians and, upon surviving, worshipped by the tribe. In *The Three Stooges Back to the Woods* film (1937), the slapstick stooges battle Indians near colonial Plymouth. When Larry is captured and tied to a stake by the Indians, Moe and Curly shoot, hit, and burn the captors before escaping. In the satirical western *Ride 'em Cowboy* (1942), comedic duo Abbot and Costello similarly flee violent arrow-toting Indians. TV westerns in the 1950s and 1960s, such as *Gunsmoke* and *Bonanza*, were generally far less hokey in their depictions of heroic settler cowboys. Marshal Matt Dillon and the Cartwrights defend their newfound homes against crooked settlers and savage Indians and occasionally enlist complacent Tonto-like Indians to help settle the west.

By the time Kennedy became a senator (1953) and then president (1961), sitcom producers were well versed in adapting previous cinematic and televisual violence to sitcoms, with intentional slapstick and discursively imagined televisions ushered in by arguably the most popular sitcom, not to mention television program, of the 1950s, *I Love Lucy*. Blatant anti-indigenous televisions in sitcoms date back at least to the episode "The Adagio" in 1951 when Lucy sounds and performs "Indian" by clapping hand to mouth and dancing absurdly in a circle. Two years later, when Ricky develops ideas for his nightclub's performances about American Indians in "The Indian Show," Lucy is determined again to be a star, this time not only by playing Indian but also by physically attacking Indians in an episodic ode to pioneer heroes pitted against encroaching Indians.

Unknown to Lucy, Ricky arranges for two Indians to drop by the Ricardos' apartment to audition, but Ricky has to leave suddenly to handle a situation at the club. Meanwhile, Lucy reads a book titled *Blood-Curdling Indian Tales*, Ricky's impetus for the Indian show and a sensationalized literary descendant of Indian captivity narratives that date back to colonist Mary Rowlandson's *A True History of the Captivity and Restoration of Mrs. Mary Rowlandson* (1682). Pulling her hair in fright at what she reads, presumably an old frontier tale of scalping, Lucy shares a settler's story with Ethel:

Then the silhouettes of the Indians appeared on the horizon. The pioneer men pushed the women and children back into the wagons. [*To Ethel*] Imagine being alone out on the prairie, thousands of miles away from any help. Imagine that. [*Resumes reading*] The Indians crept closer and closer. Fire-tipped arrows pierced the canvas of the first wagon. Women fainted. Children screamed. The Indians were almost upon them. They could see their fiendish faces hideously painted, grotesque in the light of the leaping flames. There was a lull as the last groans of the dying men faded. Suddenly, to the ears of the cowering women and children, out of the stillness of the night, broke the sound of an Indian war cry.

At that moment, the doorbell rings, causing Lucy and Ethel to shriek in terror, a performative precursor to a settler woman's shriek in *The Searchers* when cinematic Comanches descend upon her homestead.

Soon realizing that the sound they heard was not a "war cry," Lucy and Ethel regain composure. When Lucy opens the door to see Ricky's pair of auditioning Indians in costume with toy tomahawks in hand, her fright returns. After slamming the door closed, she screams, "Two wild Indians out there!" Continuing to translate the book's fabrications into the far-fetched present moment, she fears that "they'll scalp us" and frantically runs around. Like the "Indians" who "crept closer and closer" in *Blood-Curdling Indian Tales*, Ricky's stage Indians slowly enter the apartment. Adorned with redface signifiers of paint, buckskin, and weapons, they easily pass as recognizably Indian. Lucy and Ethel then violently knock the Indians unconscious with flower vases in front of a laughing studio audience. As anti-Indianists, Lucy and Ethel reverse the Indian tale's acts of violence. Once Fred enters and explains they are actors for Ricky's show, Lucy simply replies, "We just got carried away," an ironic line considering old frontier rhetoric of settlers being "carried away" by Indians.

When the Indians come to, Lucy attempts to assuage tension by speaking a semblance of "Hollywood Injun English" (HIE).[26]

LUCY: Mr. Indian, me heap sorry me smackum on coco.
INDIAN: Huh?
LUCY: Oh, you speak English?
INDIAN (*in thick New Yorker accent*): Soytanly, I speak English!

Lucy's HIE facilitates an opportunity for her to see the Indians less as one of *them* (Indian savages) and more as one of *us* (white, English-speaking dominant society). To further remedy her savage behavior, Lucy recognizes the two Indians as "real friendly Indians," a stark contrast to those imagined in *Blood-Curdling Indian Tales*. They are "real friendly," that is, as long as they speak the colonizer's language in a familiar (and exaggerated) accent and intend no harm. As for Ethel, later in the actual Indian show, she sings, "Pass that peace pipe, bury that tomahawk" without any hint of irony or self-reflection on her earlier anti-Indian, anti-peace behavior.[27]

Early 1960s sitcoms' representations of Indians predominantly perpetuate the *I Love Lucy* (mis)perceptions, stereotypes, and old frontier violence of the 1950s. In *The Flintstones'* episode "Droop-Along Flintstone," for example, Fred and Wilma Flintstone and their next-door neighbors Barney and Betty Rubble vacation at a ranch in a locale signifying the southwestern United States.[28] When Fred and Barney venture away from the ranch and stumble upon a ghost town, they are unaware that a film crew is there to shoot a violent western with cowboy and Indian actors, the latter of which were found, the film's director says, at an "all-night movie theater." Still thinking the violence is real, Fred and Barney soon find themselves in a cinematic brawl with the cowboys and then run to the ranch with arrow-wielding Indians and the cameraman trailing behind.

Hearing what she says "sounds like some kids playing cowboys and Indians," Betty is curious if "it could be real Indians." "Not a chance," Wilma responds. "There hasn't been a real Indian around here for years." When Wilma *does* see Indians chasing Fred and Barney, she announces, "We have to try and help them. After all, we signed up for better or worse." "And this," Betty adds, "is about as worse as it could get." The two then fear scalping.

> WILMA: Poor Fred. He was starting to worry about his hair falling out. Imagine how he feels now.
> BETTY: Yeah, knowing that those Indians could make him instant bald.

Later, finding Fred and Barney tied to stakes and circled by dancing Indians, Wilma and Betty play Indian and attack. Betty chases one Indian with a tomahawk while shouting and, like Lucy, clapping hand to mouth. Another Indian tells Wilma that "we were only kidding" right before she knocks him down with a rock. The Flintstones and Rubbles never learn that the cowboys and Indians are actors in a movie. All the while, continuing to film the animated clashes from a distance are the director and his cameraman.[29]

The representations of violence enacted by and against Indians in *The Flintstones* are indicative of a much larger milieu of television's and film's violent settler-Indian fare. Just four months earlier, a thirty-five-year-old lawyer named Newton Minow, appointed by Kennedy as chairman of the

Federal Communications Commission, vigorously called for far less violence on television during his first address in 1961 to the National Association of Broadcasters. Yet he showed practically no evidence of specifically considering Native viewers or media representations of Indians, not surprising since his choice of words for communicating his plans drew from a New Frontier discourse that continued to marginalize and erase indigeneity. Speaking on the heels of the infamous quiz show scandals of the 1950s, in which show producers supplied certain contestants with the answers beforehand, Minow began his speech by playfully aligning himself with western heroes and crimefighters.[30] Jesting that the FCC and its seven new commissioners were the "Seven Untouchables," he self-identified as one of "the New Frontiersmen [who] rode into town," in Minow's case, to save television programming by urging broadcasters to serve the "public interest," the phrase Minow wanted remembered from his speech and supported by his repeated settler colonial logic that the "public owns the air." But Minow's single utterance of "vast wasteland" is what stuck when Minow dared the broadcasters to watch their own television sets for an entire day. "I can assure you that what you will observe is a vast wasteland" populated by "a procession of game shows, formula comedies about totally unbelievable families, blood and thunder, mayhem, violence, sadism, murder, western bad men, western good men, private eyes, gangsters, more violence, and cartoons." In accordance with this description, he listed "categories of action-adventure, situation comedy, variety, quiz, and movies" as the primary brands of low televisual entertainment. Countering these, he argued, was a short list of television programming's "hours of greatness," from which he curiously included the made-for-television movie *Peter Pan* and, by extension, its stereotypical, subhuman depictions of Indians.[31]

Whereas others have convincingly accused Minow of categorizing programming into high/low art and countered his assessment of the state of television, critiques generally refrain from any comment on Minow's rhetoric in relation to indigeneity. Heralded by one reporter in old frontier terms as "a bold scout for the New Frontier," Minow unflinchingly appropriated "vast wasteland" from the settler colonial logic that Indians had not utilized the lands properly, that is, to the fullest capitalistic extent for profit by ripping open the Earth and destroying sacred indigenous sites for gold, oil, uranium, and other resources during and since the Industrial Revolution, all in the nominally distorted colonial doctrine of Manifest Destiny and progress.[32] In comparing wastelands, Minow declared, "The squandering of *our* airwaves is no less important than the lavish waste of any precious natural resource" (emphasis on the settler colonial possessive mine). For Minow, as for Kennedy in his 1960 acceptance speech, Indigenous Peoples appear not to consciously register at all, as if televisual violence by and against Indian characters was exempt. Minow bolstered this assessment in 2003 when he clarified his "vast wasteland" characterization as "an endless emptiness, a fallow field waiting to be cultivated and enriched," reminiscent of Henry Nash Smith's take on settler perceptions of early America as "virgin land" and Robert Frost's settler colonial poem "The Gift Outright," which the poet read at age eighty-six at Kennedy's inauguration.[33] In his frontier discourse of not recognizing already-populated vast lands and the subsequent displacement and deaths of Indigenous Peoples at the hands of U.S. settlers and soldiers, Minow never called attention to the televisual representations of violence directed at Indians in two of America's most popular (and rarely deemed as violent) sitcoms, *The Beverly Hillbillies* and *The Andy Griffith Show*.

Debuting the year after Minow's address, *The Beverly Hillbillies* soon became the highest rated television program as viewers tuned in to see Tennessee-mountaineer-turned-oil-millionaire Jed Clampett and his family—Granny, daughter Elly May, and nephew Jethro—navigate through elitist spheres in Beverly Hills. Some critics despised its reliance on hillbilly stereotypes and felt it lowered the value of television. Some lauded it for incisive commentary on the materialism and capitalism of the upper class. Television historian Eric Barnouw claimed *The Beverly Hillbillies* "diverted indignation from the subject of violence."[34] For comedian Bob Hope, the sitcom was a response to the FCC chairman's speech: "Mr. Newton Minow is a man of high ideals, whose needling, prodding and constructive suggestions has led our great [television] industry up the path to the 'Beverly Hillbillies.' That's all we needed: an outhouse in the vast wasteland." Actress Irene Ryan, who portrayed Granny, replied, "All I can say is that . . . millions of folks have moved that outhouse *inside* their homes."[35]

In contrast to the joviality and jesting expressed by Barnouw, Hope, and Ryan, Granny and *The Beverly Hillbillies* led the charge among early 1960s sitcoms for harking back to old frontier violence in the New Frontier era of television while Minow, in this case, sat idly by. Whereas television scholar David Marc lambasts the sitcom as representative of "deep escapism," the sitcom's discursive and physical violence sound anything but escapist when considering Native viewers. Representing an outdated nineteenth-century anti-indigenous mindset that hoped the South and Jefferson Davis will rise again, Granny embodies the old frontier, in part through her unchecked violence aimed at who she perceives to be violent Indians. In *The*

Beverly Hillbillies' episode "Turkey Day," for example, Mrs. Drysdale, the Clampetts' snobbish and class-obsessed next-door neighbor, hires two Indians from an acting agency to pose for an "authentic" photograph recreating the first Thanksgiving. The Drysdales dress as Pilgrims, the Indians as Squanto and Massasoit. Not knowing the Indians are actors, Granny and her niece Elly May, like Lucy and Ethel and Wilma and Betty, fear and attack the Indians, or whom Granny calls "redskin savages." Realizing that Jed and Jethro took the guns with them in their hunt for a Thanksgiving turkey, Granny quotes an old frontier relative: "Just like my Granny always said: 'them redskins wait until the menfolk disappear with the guns and then they attack!'" Granny then leads the charge, ties up the Indians, and hovers over her captives with rolling pin in hand.[36]

Unlike in *The Flintstones*, *The Beverly Hillbillies* includes a settler character who tries to resolve settler-Indian misunderstandings. Representing a voice of reason against Granny's fantastical notions throughout the series, Jed enters the scene and unties the Indians because, as he declares, "how in the world could there be wild Injuns in Beverly Hills?" After acknowledging that "we got a whole heap of misunderstandings to sort," Jed calls for everyone to "sit down and start sorting 'em out." It turns out the hired "Injuns" are Jewish Americans as they discard the Indian costumes and wigs for suits and ties and, upon Jed's invitation, join the Clampetts and Drysdales for a Thanksgiving peaceful dinner, to which one of the pseudo-Indians contributes gefilte fish and matzo ball soup. Yet Jed and his kin, unfamiliar with Jewish cuisine, still think they are Indians. "By dingies!" Granny exclaims in her own moment of reconciliation. "You Indians sure know how to cook."

In "The Family Tree," Jed continues to imagine a social space that includes Indians, but he also shows an ambivalence toward Native Peoples. When Priscilla Ralph Alden Smith Standish—president of the Society for the Preservation of Early American Traditions and a hybrid namesake of colonizers—visits the Clampetts, she is fascinated by Granny's modern use of antique objects, such as an old family churn. At Jed's urging, Granny recounts a story of the time her great-great-grandmother was attacked by, as she labels them, "two big redskins" from the woods. Fearing she would be scalped, Granny's ancestor hit one of them with a churn, and the Indian ran off covered in butter. Then comes Granny's punch line: an "old bear would come around looking for Granny to send him another hot buttered Indian!" All in the room, including Jed, laugh.[37]

Early years of *The Andy Griffith Show* in fictional Mayberry, North Carolina—sitcom exemplar of small-town America—follow a similar televisual pattern to the *Hillbillies'* discursive and physical representations of Indians and Native absence. Set against the turbulent 1960s, Mayberry symbolizes for its settler residents a place of peace and tranquillity, where visitors are greeted with the sign "Welcome to Mayberry, the Friendly Town."[38] *The Andy Griffith Show* follows the generally light-hearted comic adventures of Sheriff Andy Taylor, Opie, Aunt Bee, Deputy Barney Fife, and other friends and locals. Viewers see Andy and Barney, for instance, juggle double dates with Helen and Thelma Lou and the "fun girls" Daphne and Skippy. In another episode, Andy and Barney capture bank robbers who had pretended to be producers researching for a new television show about Mayberry. Aunt Bee enters her disastrous pickles in a local contest, Opie tries to impress a female classmate, and Floyd the barber unknowingly hires a bookie.[39]

Critics tend to read Mayberry as a near-utopian site of innocence where everyone coexists happily. Richard Kelly, for example, says, "[Mayberry] represents a kind of lost paradise founded on the best hopes of people."[40] For Don Rodney Vaughn, Mayberry offers "an avenue of escape from life's vicissitudes by depicting the simple life with small, solvable problems."[41] In the context of nonfiction indigenous-settler histories, Mayberry as "lost paradise" and "escape from life's vicissitudes" are neocolonial fictions. Such critiques of *The Andy Griffith Show* show no evidence of considering who was encroached upon, removed, or erased to enable the founding and daily life of Mayberry.

With no extant indigenous character until season 6, Mayberrians take it upon themselves to distortedly stand in for the recognizably Native through playing Indian. In "Opie's Hobo Friend," guest star Buddy Ebsen plays a hobo who claims an ability to hear fish jumping a mile away because, he says, "I'm part Indian." Yet his crooked and shiftless behavior in the episode suggests a dubious association with Indian heritage. In "The Clubmen," Opie initiates Andy and Barney into his "Tomahawk Club" with toy war bonnets and, yes, tomahawks and recitation of the Tomahawk pledge to "solemnly swear to be fair and square at all times." Opie becomes "blood brothers" with Andy in "Opie's Rival" and with his new settler friend Tres in "Andy and Opie's Pal." In "Aunt Bee's Medicine Man," traveling con artist Colonel Harvey enters Mayberry to peddle his Indian Elixir (later revealed to contain 85 percent alcohol) and, to bolster his product's authenticity, claims to have been kidnapped and then adopted by the Shawnees. He amazes Opie through hokey cigar smoke signals and Indian gibberish. As he profits from an appeal to settlers' perceptions of Indian mystique and feigns a scene of acting out Indian sign language, the colonel also scorns his Indian tribe. In a low solemn tone, he scowls, "Shawnee—I lived among them. They're devils." Whereas Granny would likely concur and add her own savage stories, Andy rolls his eyes, not necessarily to question if Shawnees are devils but likely to express disbelief that the colonel has interacted with Shawnees. When the air conditioning goes out in "Bargain Day," Aunt Bee evokes Harvey's rhetoric as she scolds Opie for not wearing a shirt one morning: "You can't come to breakfast like that, a naked savage!"[42]

The "New Trail" Televisions of Inclusion and Cooperation

By the mid-1960s, the sitcom settlers' savage talk continued (including in *The Andy Griffith Show*), but, at the same time, it began to induce a shift within story lines toward cooperative conflict resolutions between the indigenous and settlers. Sitcoms started to acknowledge historical violence, recognizing, in varying degrees, violence on both sides. Representations of discursive violence in sitcoms, then, became an entrance into establishing a troubling semblance of settlement. As uncomfortable fictions from an indigenous vantage point, sitcoms' representations acknowledged tensions and violent tendencies. The process through which uneasy relations subsided into easy resolutions in story lines suggested a quick-fix approach to resolving not necessarily intercultural disputes but rather settler anxiety and guilt over the lands they now possessed and wished to claim without dispute.

When read through the New Trail, in which Kennedy and the BIA nodded to historical relations and promoted Indian-settler *cooperation*, several sitcoms tuned in and negotiated the aftermath of what Minow labeled the Kennedy administration's "optimistic spirit." As Kennedy said during his inaugural address, "United there is little we cannot do in a host of cooperative ventures." Several floats in Kennedy's inauguration parade displayed such unity over violence to represent historical moments of Indian-settler collaborations for guiding a new trail of future relations. "First New Frontier—1620," a parade float by the National Congress of American Indians (whom Kennedy would welcome to the White House in 1963), "symbolized the hospitality that Indians extended to the first European settlers" in its representation of Indian-Pilgrim relations in 1620. A second float, "Sacajawea and Lewis and Clark Blaze Montana's New Frontier," by the Montana Tribal delegation, showcased similar cultural work of togetherness and cooperation.[43]

Kennedy carried a related message to Indian Country during his campaign. Soon after the election, in a letter dated October 28, 1960, to then president of the Association on American Indian Affairs Oliver La Farge, Kennedy claimed he "would make a sharp break with the politics of the Republican Party," including the "termination program." "Indians have heard fine words and promises long enough," Kennedy said. "They are right in asking for deeds. The program to which my party has pledged itself will be a program of deeds, not merely of words."[44] Foreshadowing his *detrimental* deeds in Indian Country, he spoke honestly here as he would continue the termination policy begun nearly a decade earlier. On August 1, 1953, nearly four months after Lucy attacked and befriended Indians, the U.S. Congress had performed its own attack-and-grin by passing House Concurrent Resolution 108, a call to terminate federal relations and treaty agreements with Native tribes. Kennedy and Johnson, senators at the time, supported the measure that would lead to the termination of treaty agreements and federal recognition of multiple indigenous nations over the next two decades. Under Kennedy's presidential watch, the federal government severed ties with the Klamaths and Menominees in 1961 and the Catawbas in 1962, accompanied by ongoing calls "to terminate some others, notably the Colville."[45]

As the federal government terminated its legal obligations, under treaty law, to the Menominees, Kennedy also violated the 1794 Pickering Treaty. Article II in the treaty reads, "The United States acknowledge the lands reserved to the Oneida, Onondaga and Cayuga Nations, in their respective treaties with the state of New-York, and called their reservations, to be their property; and the United States will never claim the same, nor disturb them or either of the Six Nations, nor their Indian friends residing thereon and united with them, in the free use and enjoyment thereof: but the said reservations shall remain theirs, until they choose to sell the same to the people of the United States, who have the right to purchase." In 1954 Robert Moses, the New York State Power Authority chairman, disregarded the agreement when he proposed building a power plant on nearly 1,400 acres of Tuscaroras' reservation land. Then in 1961 Kennedy violated the treaty when he supported the construction of the Kinzua Dam on Seneca lands, which, upon the intentional flooding, forced approximately six hundred Senecas to relocate. Although alternative plans had been proposed by Dr. Arthur E. Morgan (a former chairman of the Tennessee Valley Authority), the federal government insisted on breaking the treaty. When a reporter asked Kennedy if he had "any inclination at all to halt that [Kinzua Dam] project," the president responded, "I have no plans to interfere with that action," a direct contrast to his earlier rhetoric of enacting "deeds" for the betterment of Native Peoples.[46]

As Native Peoples have demanded that treaties be honored, complicated questions of land ownership, and voiced their perspectives on history, several sitcoms have revisited and reenvisioned history by calling attention to land disputes but shifted to unsettling resolutions of cooperation, almost always tilted heavily in the settlers' favor. Whereas the early message in sitcoms is that the land is only for settlers, settler and Indian then lopsidedly share the land in story lines that leap over land theft and justify the settlers' possession of land through peaceful resolutions. Producers framed New Frontier Indian-settler cooperation in white settlement narratives, suggesting a recognition of starting to deal with unsettled Indian-settler history and competing interpretations of history, but still opting for a blatantly skewed television to rationalize the formations of predominantly white towns through submissive and marginalized Indians.

Exemplifying these shifts in televisions in conjunction with the larger political climate in the 1960s, the multiple narratives on the founding and history of Mayberry aimed directly at the core values of many Americans and *The Andy Griffith Show*, an American public and sitcom that repeatedly celebrates a U.S. history of nation building in which references to Indians are alluded to as an obvious reinforcement of Indians' positionality in the past or, worse, Indians' symbolic annihilation and absence. A critical recurring dispute in *The Andy Griffith Show*, though always quickly resolvable in 1960s sitcom structure, concerns Mayberry's founding in relationship to indigeneity. Representative of early 1960s depictions of Indian exclusion, "The Beauty Contest" briefly reenacts the settlement of Mayberry in a play, one of the scheduled events for Mayberry Founders' Day. Town barber Floyd Lawson plays the part of founder Jacques Mayberry, who leads several ragged Euro-American companions, portrayed by other locals, across the stage. A few months before Minow's pronounced "vast wasteland," Floyd-as-Mayberry proclaims, "Many a mile have we traveled through savage wilderness in search of that promised land." Floyd's naturalist description of "savage wilderness" may be construed as synonymous with *terra nullius*, the "convenient colonial construct that maintained lands were empty of meaning, of language, of presence, and of history before the arrival of the European."[47] Floyd's utterance also is the closest implicit reference to the indigenous, suggesting settlers' historical fears of a wilderness full of Indian savages. He then proclaims to his fellow weary travelers, "This is our land! Here will we settle!" As an unapologetic act of settler colonialism, the broadcasting of "this" represents territory that becomes the explorer's namesake, but it also echoes recognizable speech in settlement after settlement (after settlement) in the United States. With this instantaneous declaration of possession, a discursive ode to the doctrine of discovery and Congress's self-appointed plenary power, the settlement of "Mayberry" begins on land new and strange to the settlers but deep-rooted and familiar to the absent indigenous inhabitants. Upon the instruction of the play's director, Mayberry and his followers then "rejoice." Whether anyone else already occupied or occupies the land is, one can surmise, a trivial detail for the producers in their colonizing televisions. It makes for a comfortable colonial fiction that distances viewers from seeing or hearing about any of the thousands of Cherokees and other Native Peoples in North Carolina who had been forced by the U.S. government to go to Indian Territory, or present-day Oklahoma, many of whom did not survive "the federally enforced death march," in the 1830s.[48]

In *The Andy Griffith Show*'s "The Pageant" episode, the founding of Mayberry is reenvisioned to include an Indian presence of fleeting minor resistance that gives way to strong support of settler colonialism. As Mayberrians prepare for a pageant to celebrate the town's centennial (presumably 1864, though most sitcoms are not generally known for temporal accuracy), a redfaced rejoinder to the colonizing television in "The Beauty Contest" surfaces, albeit in the troubling cooperative spirit of the political times unfolding by the mid-1960s. Debuting November 30, 1964, a year after the 1963 civil rights march in Washington, D.C., and just four months after President Johnson signed the Civil Rights Act, "The Pageant" starts to challenge representational boundaries of black-white segregation through an Indian-settler narrative, but its peaceful resolution points more to assuaging contemporary settler guilt and anxiety over past crimes and land theft than to indigenous justice and racial equality. As Johnson's act, a continuation of the Kennedy administration's ambivalent push for racial equality, focused on lessening tensions between African Americans and white settlers, several sitcoms began including Indians as a possible substitute for black characters. "Native American people," Ojibwe film critic Jesse Wente contends, "became a great allegorical tool to stand in for virtually any oppressed peoples," including "standing in for the Civil Rights movement." Wente cites, for example, *Cheyenne Autumn* (1964), which premiered a month before "The Pageant." After directing such anti-indigenous films as *Stagecoach* and *The Searchers*, John Ford depicts Cheyennes as rightful but inevitably defeated defenders of their homelands in *Cheyenne Autumn*. As one character, a white newspaper editor, says in the film, it is time to shift the headlines from hating "bloodthirsty savages" to grieving "the noble redman." "It's emblematic," Wente adds, "of one of the ways that people in the sixties, Hollywood particularly, were now trying to deal with their own legacy . . . and they were coming to some sort of reconciliation about it."[49]

In "The Pageant," *The Andy Griffith Show* turns to Indian-settler negotiations and settler stardom to reconcile competing land claims. At rehearsal, Andy plays European settler James Merriweather in a coonskin hat. A local, unnamed Mayberrian portrays his wife, Mary, whose only expressed concern in establishing a settlement is Indians.

> MARY: But will the Indians let us live in peace?
> JAMES: Here comes the Great Chief. Let us see.
> MARY: Oh, James, I fear him. He looks so warlike in his paint and feathers.
> JAMES: Now, Mary, we must not show him fear. We must have strength if we are to conquer the wilderness.

Merriweather's determination to "conquer the wilderness" is ambiguous. The line echoes Lyndon Johnson's opening sentiment from his Great Society speech just six months earlier: "For a century we labored to settle and to subdue a continent."[50] Like Jacques Mayberry's self-declared dominion over the "savage wilderness" in 1961 and Johnson's expressed control over an entire continent, Merriweather's hope to "conquer the wilderness," a place for settlers to occupy and dominate, taps into long-standing rugged frontiersman rhetoric. Further, since the "wilderness" is where the indigenous lives, then to conquer the land must also mean to conquer the indigenous inhabitants, or to requote Kennedy from his 1960 Democratic acceptance speech, "to conquer the enemies that threatened from . . . within" U.S. borders.

Merriweather's words, if meant to be spoken in the 1860s, follow real-life conflicts between settlers and Natives and forced removals of Cherokees in the 1830s, but the rest of "The Pageant" rescripts bloody battles and the so-called Trail of Tears into peaceful relations during the violence and protests of the 1960s.[51] Merriweather next addresses the Indian, both of whom sit Indian-style on stage in front of a cardboard teepee: "Greetings to you, Great Chief." Barney Fife, the bumbling and often egotistical but lovable Mayberry deputy, reads for the fearsome, "warlike" (to quote Mary) role of Chief Noogatuck in a long headdress.[52] Initially missing his cue, Barney then nervously stumbles and rushes through his lines.[53] He greets James with a quick "How," the all-Indian "Hello," and, after Merriweather talks of wanting "to live side by side with you, our brothers," a high-pitched nasally Noogatuck responds, "For many moons, Noogatuck has swapped the peace pipe with you, my friend. But now many paleface come and they bring guns. Noogatuck's valley grows smaller." Merriweather then tries to convince Noogatuck of his intentions.

> JAMES: My followers come only in friendship. They bring gifts. They help you plant corn. Our women give calico to your squaws. Is all this not true, Noogatuck?
>
> NOOGATUCK: Everything that Laughing Face says is true, but treaties say that he will not use the land beyond the running stream where the big oak reaches to the sky. Look! Even now you've built your lodges. Paleface is not a man of his word.

Barney asks the pageant's director, John Masters, to change this last line because "it just isn't comfortable. I mean, it's just not Noogatuck." John concurs that the line is "not Indianish enough," so the playwright improvises it to "paleface speaks with a fork-ed tongue." "Oh, marvelous!" exclaims John. Barney tries the new line and smugly flashes the OK sign in approval.

The rehearsal resumes with Merriweather and Noogatuck concluding their dialogue.

> JAMES: Noogatuck, you have my pledge. We will move back across the running water where the big oak reaches to the sky and we will live in peace.
>
> NOOGATUCK: We will live in peace. And this will be called Happy Valley.

Earlier, according to Noogatuck, James had previously lied to the "Great Chief." Here, James promptly convinces Noogatuck that peace will reign through a spoken treaty-like pledge. Noogatuck recognizes the settlers' violence at first, then suddenly joins a narrative of peace and interdependence in distorted historical revisions constituting comfortable colonial fictions and evoking Rayna Green's argument that redface reenactors (like Barney-as-Noogatuck) "reconstruct the Indian presence in an acceptable version" for themselves.[54]

To validate the settler-Indian agreement of peace, Clara Edwards, Aunt Bee's best friend, enters the stage as Lady Mayberry, the leading settler female role who offers the ultimate colonial fiction by situating Indian and settler into a peaceful space. Closing the pageant with a soliloquy, she appears to represent a regal power over both sides in land disputes and naming as she declares a homosocial settler-indigenous union: "I herewith deed these lands jointly to James Merriweather and Chief Noogatuck, knowing that they will rule wisely and that they will share the bounty of this green and happy valley which shall hereinafter be called Mayberry." (Apparently, "Cherokee Princess Happy Valley" did not have the same nominal zip as "[Lady] Mayberry.") Although Jacques Mayberry from "The Beauty Contest" is never mentioned in "The Pageant," the colonizer's name of Mayberry reigns supreme in both episodes and thus serves as an audible reminder of colonization. Noogatuck's English-spoken place name "Happy Valley" lasted for only a few minutes. Unlike Jacques, Lady Mayberry explicitly mentions and recognizes her indigenous neighbors. However, the contemporary Mayberry in "The Pageant" offers no indication of what happened to Noogatuck's people.

After indigenous erasure in previous episodes, the town's one Indian character suddenly (and only) surfaces in the episode "The Battle of Mayberry."[55] The sitcom shifts in representations from no Indians in "The Beauty Contest" to a white character in redface in "The Pageant" to now including a character designated as Cherokee. Yet the continuum of settler majority, superiority, and colonialism remains representationally strong. Airing soon after Martin Luther King's 1963 "I Have a Dream" speech and the 1965 Watts Riots, *The Andy Griffith Show* rewrote history, again, to fit contemporary calls for peace, to suggest calm and understanding over violence and protest, and to reassure white viewers that their settlement on others' homelands was nothing to be ashamed of. By the time the episode debuted, the series had switched from black-and-white to color (not good, by the way, for Indian Head of test pattern fame) and hired new writers, and costar Don Knotts had abandoned his Barney Fife role—save for a few subsequent guest appearances—for a full-time movie career in Hollywood, including the violent anti-Comanche film *The Shakiest Gun in the West*. The mood in and outside of *The Andy Griffith Show* was changing, including increasing attention, albeit in circuitous ways, to racial politics that appeared unavoidable even for Mayberry. The first five seasons had credited presumably only white characters, and a few African Americans on camera had appeared fleetingly in the background and in crowd scenes. Whereas no characters of color had speaking parts in the black-and-white episodes, two Chinese American characters, a father and son, co-owned Mayberry's new Chinese restaurant with Aunt Bee in February 1967.[56] The next month, an episode featured for the first and only time in the series a credited African American character, a former professional football star from Mayberry who returns home to coach Opie's football team. But before those characters of Charlie and Jack Lee and Flip Conroy, there was Tom Strongbow, Mayberry's lone Cherokee in "The Battle of Mayberry," the final installment in the trilogy on the unsettling settlement narratives of Mayberry.[57]

When the newspaper editor of the *Mayberry Gazette* announces to Opie's class an essay contest on "that historic [1762] battle between the early settlers and the Indians that established Mayberry's place [in] our state history," *The Andy Griffith Show* once again reenvisions the origins of Mayberry.[58] "As Mayberrites," teacher Miss Crump chimes in, "you already know something about that battle and about the heroism of the founders of our town, but I want you to do some real work on your essays." With all of the children interpellated as settlers, the editor adds that the winning essay will be published on the front page of the newspaper's upcoming fiftieth anniversary edition. Settler narratives and positionalities in "The Battle of Mayberry" continue to dominate through almost all of the episode. Like several earlier references to Indians in *The Andy Griffith Show*, the episode then promotes settlers' discursive violence through competing tales of whose white relative was the most heroic. After Floyd, for example, tells Opie that the battle started when Indians ran settlers' cattle off a ledge, he claims that his ancestor "Colonel Lawson came upon the Cherokees. And they were in their war paint; they were dancing and 'hooping it up." Chased by Cherokees "with arrows buzzing all around him," the colonel warned everyone at the settlement of pending violence. Floyd adds that his relative "personally accounted for fourteen of them savages during the battle." Mayberry mechanic Goober Pyle interjects with reference to his ancestral namesake: "Colonel Goober Pyle of the North Carolina Seventh Cavalry" was the real hero who "held them bloodthirsty savages off." Wanting to ensure Opie learned "all the true facts," Clara Edwards later says her ancestor Colonel Edwards "was the commanding officer" who "led them [the settlers] in a sterling charge that broke the spirit of the Indians and brought the final victory."

Unsatisfied with the competing (anti-indigenous) settler accounts of whose ancestor was the most heroic in defeating the Cherokees, Opie deduces, "The only thing that people agree on is that those Indians were pretty mean." He follows with an unexpected line, at least in the context of sitcoms leading up to the mid-1960s: "Sure would like to know what the Indians said." Realizing he knows *one*, Opie says, "Hey, Pa! Tom Strongbow is an Indian! . . . Maybe I oughta go to talk to him." The next day, Andy and Opie visit Mayberry's lone Cherokee, whose account of the battle starkly contrasts with the settlers' competing perspectives. That *The Andy Griffith Show* acknowledged an Indian side may figuratively attest to a growing awareness of 1960s civil rights issues, at the heart of which entailed providing space for sharing and listening to stories of injustice and strength of peoples of color. Although previous sitcoms had not expressed such interest in including an Indian perspective, Strongbow turns out to be a representational descendant of Noogatuck, both of whom prove to be very limited in their supposedly inclusive roles. Through white actors, the characters speak up at first to voice their views and their displeasure with settlers; then both submit to an uneven resolution of peace that glosses over undeniable indigenous history in North Carolina to make for some of the more daunting comfortable fictions in sitcom history.

Packed into approximately seventy seconds of footage within the episode, the scene at Strongbow's residence opens with familiar menacing music (imagine a sonic "Indians on the warpath" trope) overlaid by symbolic cues that Strongbow (and, by extension in his burden of representation, other Indians) has become modern, partially coded as assimilated. The first shot features a close-up of Strongbow's mailbox, emblazoned with his name and address ("Box 222 R.R. #3") and a newspaper slot for the *Mayberry Gazette*, against which Strongbow places his pitchfork, blatantly signaling he may be a farmer, as he begins his side of the story. "It was my revered ancestor Chief Strongbow," Tom recalls to Opie, "that led the Cherokee in the defense of their original hunting ground," contrasting Floyd's account that Cherokees initiated the conflict. When he adds that "it was fifty braves against five hundred settlers" and "bows and arrows against muskets," Andy disbelieves the disparate numbers. When Strongbow calls the conflict "the Battle of Tuckahoosie Creek" (an unintentional play off of "Nooga*tuck*"?), Andy further challenges him.

> ANDY: Tuckahoosie Creek? [*smiles*] We're talking about the Battle of Mayberry, Tom.
> TOM: Well, that's what the settlers called it. But to us Indians, it's still the victory of Tuckahoosie Creek!
> ANDY: Victory?!
> TOM: Yeah, that's right. Us Indians forced them settlers and their cattle off our huntin' grounds.

In disbelief, Andy asserts that "the settlers won that battle" before Strongbow assimilates into the parade of perspectives competing for heroism: "Opie, I hope you'll mention Chief Strongbow in your paper. After all, he was the real hero of the battle." Strongbow speaks up to voice an Indian perspective, yet his claim to the supposed Cherokee naming (Tuckahoosie Creek) is very temporary within the episode's dominant narrative. Like Jacques Mayberry's "savage wilderness" and Chief Noogatuck's English-spoken "Happy Valley," Tuckahoosie Creek becomes and remains "Mayberry."

At a crossroads as to what to write (and apparently uncomfortable with narrative contradictions), Opie then travels to the settler-run Raleigh Public Library (not, say, the complex of the Eastern Band of Cherokees in Cherokee, North Carolina) to search for newspaper accounts of the battle.[59] He locates one article, dated May 18, 1762, which is unquestionably and, hence, disturbingly held up in the rest of the episode as *the* truth. According to the reporter, who had traveled from Raleigh to Mayberry sometime after the settler-Cherokee encounter to talk to both sides, there was no battle. After a Cherokee accidentally shot a settler's cow, "fifty settlers found themselves," the story reads, "facing fifty Cherokee braves who had about as much desire to fight as they did. Taunts and insults filled the air but no bullets or arrows." Then a Mayberrian approached the Cherokees with "a fearsome weapon in his hand: a jug of Mayberry's finest corn liquor." Once both sides became "happy and friendly," the Cherokees tried to compensate for the cow by entering the woods and shooting three deer, one of which turned out to be a mule. "Both sides realized that the true story of the battle would be a sorry tale to tell their womenfolk," so they concocted a violent narrative, with differing heroes, to impress their spouses and to satisfy hypermasculine expectations of frontier violence.

After Opie's essay, presumably a rehashing of the newspaper report, wins the contest, shocked Mayberrians, settler and Indian alike, shun Opie. The violent account each had inherited and recounted was shattered by the front-page reprinting of Opie's paper in the *Mayberry Gazette*. However, when Opie, Andy, other settlers, and the lone Cherokee are summoned to the courthouse for a special announcement, all strife will soon dissipate in the Mayberry universe. It turns out North Carolina's governor has read Opie's essay in the paper and wants to recognize it in his weekly radio address. Like a deus ex machina, the governor replaces Lady Mayberry from "The Pageant" to save the day and keep intact the comfortable fictions for the Mayberrians crowded around the radio. Intervening as a mediator to reconcile the Indian-settler and settler-settler conflicts over competing heroics and historical truths, he says, "The frankness of the article and the honesty of its publication can serve as an inspiration to all the people of the state. Too often we're hindered by old myths and legends that have no real meaning today. There's a lesson to be learned from the true story of the Battle of Mayberry, and that is that things can very often be settled peacefully. You all have every right to be proud of your town and its wise founders."

In the courthouse, tension immediately subsides into unifying pride and smiles as Clara leads a round of three cheers for Opie. Abandoning his earlier talk of "savages," Floyd responds, "Mayberry has always been an honest and peaceful town, and we all have a right to be proud." With no lines since his initial encounter with Andy and Opie, Tom complies with the merry mood in the room as he smiles at Goober. No one questions why Tom would be proud of settlers' invasion of indigenous homelands. No one asks where his relatives are. No one shows remorse for the relatively recent forced removals and deaths. Instead, the sitcom's television of reconciliation, quelling accounts of settler-Indian violence (and possibly subconscious settler guilt over indigenous erasure), opts for the third time for historical and contemporary myths of peace. From indigenous absence in the first settlement story line (1961) to the stereotypical Chief Noogatuck and his sudden shift to concessions (1964) to Strongbow's eventual submission to published settler "truth" and state governmental authority, *The Andy Griffith Show* works through highly selective old frontier representations toward its settlement of New Frontier fictions of peace and nonviolence as ideal aspirations for audiences in 1960s America.

The Televisual Office of Economic Opportunity

The Andy Griffith Show was not alone in its attention to resolving land ownership conflicts, erasing historical violence, and lessening white guilt through nonviolent means. The New Trail ethos of indigenous inclusion and settler-indigenous cooperation also tracked its way into the Great Society's economic and business sectors as a wave of entrepreneurial Indian characters entered the televisual landscape in the mid-1960s. The Kennedy administration had previously called for attention to poverty in Indian Country, such as in March 1963 when BIA commissioner Philleo Nash said, "The New Trail along which we are moving with the Indian people is the sound path of economic development."[60] In accordance with New Trail goals, development plans were "to study the Indians' potential for achieving" what the BIA called "economic self-sufficiency" and "participation of citizenship."[61] With "considerable effort devoted to attracting various industries to locate on reservations," Kennedy's New Trail was "a sort of entrepreneurial governmental agency."[62] By the mid-1960s, the federal government increasingly encouraged contemporary Natives to rise up out of poverty and to be players in the American economy.

In his inaugural State of the Union address on January 8, 1964, President Johnson called for sustained attention from Congress on civil rights, transportation, health care, foreign aid, housing, and education. Emerging, too, in his ambitious address was talk of what became one of the cornerstones of his Great Society administration. Johnson "declared all-out war on human poverty and unemployment in these United States." "Unfortunately," he added a few moments later, "many Americans live on the outskirts of hope—some because of their poverty, and some because of their color, and all too many because of both. Our task is to help replace their despair with opportunity." As noted earlier, Johnson also spotlighted poverty "on Indian reservations." In a speech two weeks later to the National Congress of American Indians, Johnson stated, "I have directed that in our attack on poverty program we put our Indian people in the forefront," after identifying the "fact that America's first citizens, our Indian people, suffer more from poverty today than any other group in America."[63]

By the next day, newspapers across the United States began publishing an article by reporter Raymond Crowley. "The phrase 'vanishing American,'" Crowley began, "is out of date. For American Indians are experiencing a population explosion. But if you say 'lo, the poor Indian' you will be right. Most Americans [sic] Indians are beset by numbing, spirit-sapping poverty. But leaders of the National Congress of American Indians cheered at the White House this week when President Johnson promised to pay special attention to Indians in his 'war on pockets of poverty.'"[64] Soon thereafter at the American Indian Capitol Conference on Poverty, Nash affirmed, "President Johnson's declaration of unconditional war on poverty was welcomed as enthusiastically by the Bureau of Indian Affairs as it was by the Indian people." In the spirit of the New Trail calls for cooperation, Nash added, "we will fight this war side by side."[65]

Amid this backdrop in Washington, D.C., where a few politicians, the BIA, and Indian task forces continued to call for increased cooperation between indigenous nations and the federal government and sought, to quote Johnson, "to see what we can all do together to make life better for all of us," several sitcoms ushered in a conspicuous business-oriented path for Indians, including joint ventures with settler characters, to resolve Indian-settler aggressions and, in effect, to promote televisions of cooperation and anti-poverty through employment and income. Over an approximate three-year period, 1964–66, producers of F Troop and other sitcoms constructed tribal televisions of economic opportunities in conversation with Johnson's recurring message on Capitol Hill to end poverty on reservations and elsewhere, but dominant underlying messages generally showcased Indian workers as occupationally dependent on and inferior to settlers, often subservient to shady settlers, desperate for work, adherent to settler expectations of "real" Indian performativity, and, in all, devoid of the recognizably Native.

In the *Green Acres* episode "The Rains Came," for example, the Indian tries to profit through deception by a failed attempt to deliver on expectations. A fish-out-of-water sitcom by Paul Henning, *Green Acres* featured married New York City couple Oliver and Lisa Douglas in their recent move from New York to Hooterville, Tennessee, to settle down on a farm. In "The Rains Came," Oliver's crops are in danger due to a drought. Enter Chief Thundercloud, a sitcom Indian working for local conniving and traveling sideshow huckster Mr. Haney. Thundercloud speaks the typical HIE, greeting Mr. Douglas with "How" and claiming, "Me make big heap water anytime I want." Peddling the Indian's advertised rainmaking services to Oliver, puppet master Haney directs the compliant Indian to dance, sing, and drum. Ten seconds into the nonsensical performance, Thundercloud keels over in exhaustion. When no rain comes and Haney fires him, Thundercloud soon returns to the Douglas house, where Lisa hires him to wash their car, and sure enough it rains, prompting Haney to sue Douglas for failing to pay for the "rendered services" by Thundercloud. Throughout the episode, the "chief" is a dubious marginalized pawn who beckons to multiple settlers' direction.[66]

Petticoat Junction, Henning's other sitcom, includes a couple of one-time Indian pawns similarly in cahoots with a conniving settler, this time a corporate executive. Set in Tennessee and starring Bea Benaderet as Kate Bradley (the actress previously played Pearl, Jethro's mother, in *The Beverly Hillbillies*), *Petticoat Junction* centers on Bradley's operations of the Shady Rest Hotel and a small train called the Hooterville Cannonball. In "The Umquaw Strip," initial Indian-settler tension over a treaty dispute gives way to a resolution of peacefully renewing the treaty and securing steady work for the Indians.[67] Kate's recurring adversary Homer Bedloe, a railroad executive who wants to monopolize the train business, tries but fails again to shut down the Cannonball. When Bedloe learns the Umquaws had never signed a treaty that would have given the local settlers permission to run the Cannonball over a strip of Umquaw land, he pressures Chief Fleet Eagle and his son Black Salmon of the Umquaw tribe into assisting him by staging a teepee barricade on the railroad track in protest. In exchange, Bedloe, whom the Indians call "Snake in the Grass," promises the Umquaws an exclusive franchise to sell their surplus stock of what they call "Indian souvenirs." Otherwise, Black Salmon frets, they will be "back on the reservation doing beadwork." Eventually, Bradley saves the day when she turns to the plot of a (made-up) film called *Revenge of the Redskins* starring, she says, real-life silent film star Monte Blue.[68] She recalls "this big corporation using the Indians to put Monte Blue out of business," similar to

Bedloe's plan in "Umquaw Strip." When Kate borrows the movie's sketchy resolution to inform Bedloe that he, like those in the film's "corporation," could go to prison for trying to "coerce Indians into doing his dirty work," Bedloe finally relents. The Umquaws, he assures Kate, will "get their franchises to sell the souvenirs," and the Cannonball will continue running, all thanks to Kate's compassion and Homer's agency. Although left unsaid, the Umquaws presumably signed the treaty once Kate's stipulations were agreed upon.

Sitcom Indians also have a dismal economic outlook in the episode of *The Munsters* called "Big Heap Herman" when they seek to profit from historical reenactments of their ancestors' daily life.[69] Along with such television series as *The Adamms Family* and *My Favorite Martian*, *The Munsters* was part of a wave of the "fantastic family sitcom" in the 1960s about friendly and quirky families of monsters, aliens, and others. During a family vacation to Buffalo Valley (think Death Valley), Herman Munster reads from a travel guide about local tourist stops formerly inhabited by Olwahgee Indians and settlers attracted to the "vast expansive wasteland": "Legend has it there may be one or two lost tribes still living in the desert." He later conveniently wanders alone into an Indian village of teepees where Indians perform shows for tourists. One of the performers admits, "The whole tribe's going broke with this kooky Indian village gig." (They had discontinued selling tomahawks and blankets because, another performer says, "the Japanese wholesaler raised the price.") However, when the village's chief mistakes Herman to be the "ancient spirit Manitoba" whose return is believed to bring "prosperity" to the tribe, Herman, a jovial settler modeled after Frankenstein, is billed as the new tourist attraction and, in a recurring theme in 1960s episodes with working sitcom Indians, the non-Native financial rescuer of the Indians during their challenging times. Before the first show begins, though, Herman's family shows up to take him back to settler life, and the Indians are left without their new star and are back to "going broke."

In *Get Smart*'s episode "Washington 4, Indians 3," the idea of a sitcom Indian playing to settlers' expectations of authentic violent Indianness is eventually abandoned in order to secure an economic opportunity by becoming a part of the federal government. *Get Smart*'s lead character, secret agent Maxwell Smart, travels to a reservation in Arizona to stop what he calls an "Indian uprising in the twentieth century," but he fails to persuade an Indian leader in headdress and buckskin named Red Cloud not to blow up the White House.[70] When Maxwell's negative reminders of the historic arrival of "our settlers and then our soldiers" and the current policy of "nice tiny little reservations" do not convince Red Cloud (and himself), Max shifts to "talk about the future. Now, if we take the promises of the past and join them with the policies of the present, then there's only one thing left to say." Unsure how to continue, Maxwell concedes: "Let it rip, Red Cloud." After Red Cloud uncovers an absurdly giant arrow in the teepee and launches it into the West Wing of the White House, *Get Smart* suddenly concludes the narrative on a note of potential support for the federal government to oversee Natives and to hire civilized (read: "good") Indians into the system, namely the BIA.[71] The threat of further violence is crushed, fears are alleviated, and settler order is restored through a co-operative agreement in which Red Cloud becomes "the newly appointed Undersecretary of the Interior for Indian Affairs." Now sporting a suit, hat, walking stick, and gloves, Red Cloud surprises Maxwell at the secret agent headquarters in D.C.: "I travel over high mountains, across wide rivers to bring you medal from my people." Thus, Red Cloud leaves behind his Indian community and rebellious behavior to assimilate into the American mainstream and work for the very government he had fought against.

Running the preceding spectrum of working sitcom Indians who comply with deceptive settlers, perform historical reenactments to match tourists' static Indian expectations, and sell Indian souvenirs in cooperative economic ventures for mutual but often uneven gain, *F Troop* extends the partnership beyond an individual episode to the entire series across two seasons, sixty-five episodes in all. In a recurring story line of joint business development, Indian and settler discreetly work together as co-managers of the settler-overseen souvenir business O'Rourke Enterprises. Set at the fictional Fort Courage in Kansas just after the Civil War, *F Troop* features the troop's leaders Captain Wilton Parmenter, Sergeant Morgan Sylvester O'Rourke, and Corporal Randolph Agarn, among other comical misfits. O'Rourke and Agarn, who use the fort as a front to store and sell Indian-made products and purchase supplies with government monies, regularly travel to the nearby village of the Hekawi Indians to visit with their business partners Chief Wild Eagle and his assistant Crazy Cat.[72] As O'Rourke explains in the first episode, the Hekawis make "arrows, quivers, bows, shields, tomahawks, . . . souvenir war bonnets, . . . barrels of perfume war paint," and other items.[73] They also make whiskey for O'Rourke to sell at his Fort Courage saloon.

In the series premiere, O'Rourke says the Hekawis need to feign an attack on Fort Courage in order to convince a "snoop lieutenant coming out here from [the inspector general's office in] Washington . . . that we're having Injun troubles." O'Rourke fears his "enterprises" will be over after "sending in those phony reports about knocking off two tribes in two weeks, drawing rations for thirty men when we only got seventeen." He believes "if that snoop finds out how peaceful it really is, there'll be no more Fort Courage." Wild Eagle initially refuses: "Attack you? You honorary Hekawi!" before adding, "You got wrong tribe, brother. Hekawis not fighters—invent face pie!" Wild Eagle even fictitiously announces that the complicit and pro-cavalry Hekawis are the "only tribe that ever live up to paleface treaty." As the theme song goes, "Where Indian fights are colorful sights, and nobody takes a lickin' / Where paleface and redskin both turn chicken," conjuring the lack of fighting and concocted violent narrative between Cherokees and settlers in "The Battle of Mayberry." For Indian and settler to work together, *F Troop* implies, both parties must agree to nonviolence. Evoking the Umquaws' fear of returning to beadwork on the reservation if they do not cooperate with Bedloe, Wild Eagle readily submits to staging an attack when O'Rourke and Agarn, who like other sitcom settlers apparently control the purse strings, threaten to send the Hekawis "back to hunting and fishing" and "weaving your own blankets." As in the other cited examples, settlers are clearly in charge on-screen as the troop and producers are able to dictate the future survival of the tribe.[74]

Conclusion: Running for the Old Frontier

In the 1960s, the New Trail of sitcom Indians wound through significations of violence, conflict, physical and cultural erasure, partnerships, economic ventures, and, at least for settler characters, resolutions of peace. Following the trajectory from the 1950s to the latter half of the 1960s, one might suspect friendlier, slightly more progressive relations, even if still unequal, to characterize the decade's closing New Frontier and Great Society televisions between Indian and settler. The later sitcom episodes, however, show distorted counters to the politics of Kennedy's and Johnson's proposals for new relations and a return to sitcom Indians of the 1950s and early 1960s. The era's conclusion circled back to its start, led by two familiar and unsurprising characters: Granny in *The Beverly Hillbillies* and Lucy in *Here's Lucy* (formerly of *I Love Lucy*).

After the Hekawis in *F Troop*, Chief Red Cloud in *Get Smart*, Chief Thundercloud in *Green Acres*, and the Umquaws in *Petticoat Junction*, a new pair of sitcom Indians in 1967 proved to be the most economically successful of them all, not to be rivaled until casino Indians surfaced three decades later in *The Family Guy*. In *The Beverly Hillbillies* episode "The Indians Are Coming," Chief Running Wolf, owner of several oil derricks and banks, and his son Little Fox represent the fictional Crowfeet tribe from the Clampetts' home state of Tennessee. Dressed in full suits, the chief and his son graduated from Oxford and Harvard, respectively, and speak several non-Native languages. They arrive in Beverly Hills to settle an oil boundary dispute back home with Jed. Although they privately and peacefully settle it offscreen—Jed later tells the chief it was a "real good deal, fair to both of us"—Granny fears the Crowfeet will attack her family, and banker Drysdale fears the Crowfeet want the Clampetts' fortune, especially after his redface routine as Chief True Tongue fails to keep them away from Jed. Replacing her rolling pin from the "Turkey Day" episode with her shotgun, Granny prepares for the worst, even shrouding Elly and herself in wigs in case of scalping. To keep Granny and her money safe in Beverly Hills and to satisfy one of his largest depositor's desire to kill Indians, Drysdale arranges for Indian stuntmen (from Jed's own movie studio) to stage an attack on the Clampett mansion on horseback with bows and arrows. Unknown to Granny, Drysdale replaces her bullets with blanks before she commences firing repeatedly at them. He also arranges for John Wayne, exemplar cinematic Indian killer, to show up, but he arrives late, after the attack. In a suit and tie not designed for on-screen battles, the Duke approaches her: "I understand you were looking for me. I'm John Wayne." A somber Granny just stares up at him and asks, "Where was you when I needed you, John?"[75] That Wayne shows up late to the Clampetts and not in his famous cowboy duds foreshadows, unintentionally I suspect, the coming years when iterations of Granny's question would be posed and rejected in response to a changing televisual landscape that would become less welcoming for the blatant violence and settler swagger of the anti-indigenous Grannys and John Waynes.[76]

Finally, Lucille Ball, whose Lucy Ricardo character began the sitcom genre's blatant anti-indigenous televisions in 1951, closed the 1960s similarly with her sitcom *Here's Lucy*, costarring her son, Desi Arnaz Jr., and daughter, Lucie Arnaz. In the 1969 "Lucy and the Indian Chief," Ball shows that not much has changed comedically in her televisual logic of sitcom Indians since the early 1950s.[77] During a four-episode adventure that touts tourism across the United States to viewers, Lucy's RV breaks down in Navajo Country in Utah. When she finds a nearby stream for water, Lucy begins to reprise her "Hiawatha" soliloquy from the 1953 "Indian Show" episode of *I Love Lucy*. She is soon interrupted by an aggressive Navajo chief in a Hollywood costume of buckskin and headdress. Two of his tribesmen lead Lucy back to his hogan, where she inadvertently marries the chief in a ceremony performed by the medicine man. For a wedding present, the chief gives her what his family still claims as their own: the state of Utah. Boisterous slapstick echoes of *I Love Lucy* ensue all the way to her eventual divorce and escape from the Navajos.

In the 2009 DVD introduction to the episode, Ball's daughter proudly heralds *Here's Lucy* as "the first and only situation comedy to be shot on location with a real Indian tribe." She then speaks of the Navajos on the set: "Mom was always very impressed with the Navajo people not just for their acting abilities but also for their overall stoic appearance, which served to enrich the humor in this story." The introduction is rather unsettling and bizarre, not to mention ambiguously inaccurate, when Arnaz concludes, "So now, *without reservation*, enjoy 'Lucy and the Indian Chief.'"[78] The episode's reservation setting and the Diné/Navajo extras—they basically stand around, watch the episode's narrative unfold, and speak no lines—serve primarily to authenticate the backdrop for the non-Native cast and crew. Curiously, the Native extras do dress in jeans, skirts, and concho belts, presumably their own clothing in real life and not Hollywood wardrobe left over from the set of a John Ford western. In contrast, the two speaking Indian roles are filled by German American actor Paul Fix as the "Indian Chief" and Sicilian American actor Iron Eyes Cody as "Medicine Man," both in Hollywood Indian garb. The visual on-screen clash between recognizably Indian and recognizably Native clothing is furthered when Lucy and her children, upon being welcomed into the tribe, change into what appear to be Indian costumes, presumably gifted to them by the chief. At the end, when Lucy and the others run away from the village to their RV, they conveniently take the clothing with them. Overall, the episode reeks of representational throwbacks to older sitcom Indians, but with a partial visual change in décor. Yet even the scenery and its ties to U.S. invasion and colonialism become implicated. In the closing credits, whether haphazardly or not, *Here's Lucy*, after offering kudos to the U.S. Department of the Interior and its overseen Bureau of Reclamation, Glen Canyon Dam, and National Park Service, then thanks "The Navajo Tribe" *last*, at the bottom of the screen, in an unsurprising hierarchical visual display.

In 1974 CBS canceled *Here's Lucy*, the last sitcom to go in the "rural purge."[79] In 1970 the network canceled the rural sitcom *Petticoat Junction*, to be followed the next year by *The Beverly Hillbillies*, *Green Acres*, *Mayberry R.F.D.*, and others, to clear space in the televisual landscape for *All in the Family*, *Maude*, and additional so-called relevant sitcoms.[80] But the Indian types of the 1950s and 1960s were only partly canceled as shades of them would continue to appear in the forthcoming decades. Soon, new twists on Indian-settler representations and "worked and reworked" visions of sitcom Indians would emerge in the televisual landscape, including through the adjoining stories "of a man named Brady" and "a lovely lady" who would load up the station wagon—the settlers' preferred Conestoga of the 1970s—with six kids and the housekeeper for a family vacation to the Grand Canyon where they would transform into the first sitcom settler family of Indian adoption: the Brady Braves.

CHAPTER TWO

Settler Self-Determination

On July 8, 1970, almost ten years to the day since John Kennedy's appearance on the *Tonight Show*, President Richard Nixon delivered his "Special Message to the Congress on Indian Affairs." He began:

> The first Americans—the Indians—are the most deprived and most isolated minority group in our nation. On virtually every scale of measurement—employment, income, education, health—the condition of the Indian people ranks at the bottom. This condition is the heritage of centuries of injustice. From the time of their first contact with European settlers, the American Indians have been oppressed and brutalized, deprived of their ancestral lands and denied the opportunity to control their own destiny. Even the Federal programs which are intended to meet their needs have frequently proven to be ineffective and demeaning.

Acknowledging "centuries of injustice," Nixon's message thus far painted a portrait for pitying Natives and viewing them as hapless and homogeneous victims with bygone glory days. "Nixon," according to the president's consultant Leonard Garment, "felt an empathy for Indians, America's home grown victims, losers, and survivors." Garment's executive assistant Brad Patterson agreed, "[Nixon] had a warm spot in his heart for Indians."[1] Although the president's message to Congress avoided pinpointing the perpetrators of injustice and oppression, save for quickly citing "frequently" failing "Federal programs," Nixon's rhetoric followed Kennedy's and Lyndon Johnson's sporadic steps toward shaping public opinion about "the condition of the Indian people."

In the next part of the message, Nixon shifted to recognition of indigenous strength and accentuation of advancing the era of indigenous self-determination.

But the story of the Indian in America is something more than the record of the white man's frequent aggression, broken agreements, intermittent remorse and prolonged failure. It is a record also of endurance, of survival, of adaptation and creativity in the face of overwhelming obstacles. It is a record of enormous contributions to this country—to its art and culture, to its strength and spirit, to its sense of history and its sense of purpose. It is long past time that the Indian policies of the Federal government began to recognize and build upon the capacities and insights of the Indian people. Both as a matter of justice and as a matter of enlightened social policy, we must begin to act on the basis of what the Indians themselves have long been telling us. The time has come to break decisively with the past and to create the conditions for a new era in which the Indian future is determined by Indian acts and Indian decisions.

Although he perpetuated the familiar "us/them" dichotomy and subsumed all Natives within the monolithic category of "Indian in America" (hence, not explicitly arguing for validation of indigenous nationhood nor for abandonment of paternalistic federal authority trumping indigenous sovereignty), Nixon's political and temporal juxtaposition of acknowledging historical and contemporary injustice *alongside* calling for indigenous-settler futures of interdependence and indigenous agency reflected changing perceptions in the United States about Native Peoples during the relatively young era in indigenous policy known as self-determination. To some extent, Nixon's message echoed those of Kennedy and other politicians in the 1960s, which occasionally highlighted U.S. wrongdoings in general against Indigenous Peoples and called for cooperation between Indian and settler for the democratic betterment of America. But the late 1960s and the 1970s saw increasing numbers of people, especially Natives, in politics and media pressure the federal government to go further, to not only talk about justice but also enact and sustain it.[2]

"Congress responded" to Nixon's address, David Wilkins (Lumbee) and Heidi Kiiwetinepinesiik Stark (Turtle Mountain Ojibwe) explain, "by enacting a series of laws designed to improve the lot of tribal nations and Indians generally in virtually every sphere," such as the Indian Education Act of 1972, the American Indian Religious Freedom Act of 1978, and the Indian Child Welfare Act of 1978. Intertwined with all of these was the landmark Indian Self-Determination and Education Assistance Act of 1975, passed near the end of Gerald Ford's presidency, which "recognizes the obligation of the United States to respond to the strong expression of the Indian people for self-determination by assuring maximum Indian participation in the direction of educational as well as other Federal services to Indian communities so as to render such services more responsive to the needs and desires of those communities." "Maximum Indian participation" did not necessarily connote indigenous self-determination and indigenous control as much as it denoted Natives as participants and players in mainstream U.S. politics. But the phrasing did jibe with Nixon's plea to Congress "to create the conditions" for self-determination. Congress, in turn, called upon the federal government to *help* Native Peoples determine their future and to insist that more Natives assume leadership roles in (limited) decision making, echoing Lyndon Johnson's 1968 "Forgotten American" message to Congress: "I propose a new goal for our Indian programs: A goal that ends the old debate about 'termination' of Indian programs and stresses self-determination; a goal that erases old attitudes of paternalism and promotes partnership self-help." All of it, including the idea that the federal government would *help* Natives *help* themselves, is curiously worded, considering that *self-determination* sounds *self-explanatory*.[3]

It is this kind of ambiguous and perplexing political language that leads me not only to question the apparent inconsistencies of federal policy up against truly indigenous self-determination but also to inquire how sitcoms during this era represent ambiguous televisions of self-determination. Primarily through episodes of *The Brady Bunch, Barney Miller, Diff'rent Strokes,* and *Saved by the Bell,* I analyze Indian-settler interactions as the two parties worked together (or so it may seem) in decision making and conflict resolution, accentuated and avoided settler colonial history and modern Indian affairs, educated and miseducated audiences, and promoted and deflated sitcom Indian self-determination to envision a future America free of neocolonialism, intercultural violence, unbridgeable difference, irresolvable conflicts, and, sometimes, even Native Peoples. In conjunction with a changing political climate and news media's increased attention to Native activism, sitcoms airing during the era of self-determination signaled the next shift in representations of the recognizably Indian. Sitcoms of the 1950s and 1960s unapologetically showcased Indians as wild savages, modern remnants of an imagined past, uncredited Hollywood extras, settler characters in redface, culturally inferior, speakers of broken English, mutes, assimilated supporters of settler colonial narratives, and anti-indigenous, all of which is suggestive of 1950s termination discourse and its lingering aftermath. The 1970s answered with representations of seemingly different characters that are, for the most part, physically and discursively nonviolent and visually and audibly modern. From *The Brady Bunch* to *Dharma and*

Greg, sitcoms became considerably more *sympathetic* to the proverbial Indian "plight" and began to seriocomedically address issues of Native identity, land rights, and repatriation.[4] Like Nixon, sitcom producers showed a warm spot in their hearts for Indians through on-screen representations, commencing with the Bradys' romanticized Indianness and capped off by New Age characters Dharma and her parents' instantaneous liberal love for anything Indian, not to mention Floyd Red Crow Westerman's phantasmic character George Littlefox in four episodes.

These sitcoms' televisions feature, albeit intermittently, settlers who sympathize with Indians and listen to them voice dilemmas, who recommend and determine nonviolent solutions to the dilemmas, and who attempt to educate the general viewing public about Indians, all of which subsume the indigenous and talk of self-determination within a rubric of settler-driven determination. Against previous representations of the indigenous in sitcoms, the recognizably Indian characters in this chapter *appear* as progressive portrayals as they try to promote a pro-Native agenda cognizant of the importance to readjust the old patterns of the recognizably Indian, such as by developing multidimensional characters over stock caricatures. Yet attempts for indigenous inclusion, voice, and issues are overshadowed by partially masked representations of settler self-determination, superiority, and anxiety. Furthermore, in their liberal schema of televisions of the tribal, producers attempted to masquerade, in my opinion, recognizably Indian characters as recognizably Native.

Ultimately, the status quo in television, like its political counterpart in D.C., was left practically unscathed, and the indigenous representations became additions to the genealogy of the recognizably Indian, ushered in as the next wave of inferior iterations of Indianness, who recursively bow down and literally smile in response to settlers' quick-fix solutions and superior logic for tackling immediate symptoms, not underlying long-term systemic causes, of the conflicts. In the context of representational self-determination, Indians occasionally quip humorous comebacks in response to settler characters' misperceptions about Natives, but they rarely initiate and control the comedic direction. They lack settler lead characters' expressions of agency, or what television studies scholar Jason Mittell defines televisually as "the ability to undertake actions and make choices with narrative consequences." In response, I argue that sitcoms' televisions of self-determination, unlike the sitcom sovereignty that I will address in chapter 4, are largely built on a facade of indigenous-settler togetherness, equality, and overly "happy multiculturalism," which continues to represent Indians as compliant, inferior, and another tacked-on racialized strand of fabric in the uneven quilting of multicultural America, and of America's talk of celebrating difference as it incessantly and anxiously searches for a harmonizing and nonthreatening sameness.[5]

In her book *Represent and Destroy*, Jodi Melamed critiques the "production of liberal multiculturalism" through the 1980s and 1990s canon wars in literary studies, which she contends were "restricting discussions of race, culture, and antiracism to either assimilationist cultural pluralism . . . or positive cultural pluralism" over critical paradigms attuned to racialized histories and systemic inequities that prompted the formations of progressive social movements. At the same time, the sitcoms I analyze reveal, too, the coexistence of those "competing visions" of "assimilative pluralism" and "positive pluralism" as illustrative of "liberal multiculturalism's stress on representation and cultural recognition [that] screened off differential power [and] dematerialized conceptions of race."[6] As real-life calls for and enactments of indigenous self-determination increased and as Natives made headlines in mainstream America, sitcoms imagined and performed interrelated televisions of indigenous politics and protest. Perhaps more precisely, sitcoms distortedly and selectively tuned in and tuned out real-life indigenous identity politics and social movements by constructing ambivalent but eventually, for the nonindigenous, comforting televisions of liberal multiculturalism's safe inclusion of the recognizably Indian. As Chickasaw scholar Jodi Byrd writes, "The familiarity of 'Indianness' is salve for the liberal multicultural democracy," and "it is through the elisions, erasures, enjambments, and repetitions of Indianness that one might see the stakes in decolonial, restorative justice."[7] Through the recurring liberal multicultural discourse around Indianness, the sitcoms I analyze start to recognize contemporary indigenous identity and issues but largely keep at bay the essential discourse of tribal sovereignty and indigenous-centered activism necessary for actualizing indigenous self-determination, the innate right of Native Peoples to socially and politically determine, form, and manage the conditions necessary for indigenous livelihood and nationhood.

Rather than conceptualize space for indigenous self-determination, the sitcoms figuratively tune in televisions of settler self-determination founded on a political paternalism that the United States has long exercised over Indigenous Peoples, which includes the submissive recognizably Indian but excludes the recognizably Native and the indigenous-determined future that Nixon referenced. Contrary to presumed progressive intentions by producers, sitcoms continue to circulate on-screen settler superiority and promote tribal televisions in symbolic support of federal government dominance over indigenous self-determination policy. Within liberal multicultural fantasy, the indigenous-settler relations in sitcoms resemble the product of what Homi Bhabha calls "colonial mimicry," or "the desire for a reformed, recognizable Other, as a subject of difference that is almost the same, but not quite." As the ambivalent set of indigenous characters in this chapter mimics the settler's desire for peaceful and smiling resolutions, the indigenous remains recognizably Indian, the "recognizable Other" whose "mimicry must continually produce its slippage, its excess, its difference."[8]

The self-determination I have in mind with sitcoms is not about identifying the obvious creative control and determination over broadcasted content held by white TV executives and producers. That non-Native producers in U.S. sitcoms have almost always determined how sitcom Indians and Indian issues are represented on screen *is* important and explicitly goes against indigenous nationalists' calls for indigenous control in all areas of life, including media. Within the confines of this chapter, however, self-determination speaks more to the broadcasted product, that is, the sitcoms' fictional televisions of on-screen characterizations and story lines concerning the recognizably Indian. How, I ask, do the on-screen relations between the indigenous and settler play out when considered against an offscreen backdrop of self-determination in Indian affairs, Native activism, and a changing tide of thought about Native Peoples?

Representational relations involving Indian masculinity also play an integral role in the televisions of self-determination. In a representational variance of self-determination, Native actors finally began to be routinely cast, albeit in recognizably Indian roles. Whereas few Native actors found work in sitcoms before the 1970s (for example, Eddie Little Sky [Lakota] in *Mister Ed* and Ned Romero [Chitimacha] in *The Munsters*), now Jay Silverheels (Mohawk) guest-starred in *The Brady Bunch*, Charles White Eagle (Lakota) and Mark Banks (Anishinaabe) in *Barney Miller*, Romero in *Diff'rent Strokes*, Dehl Berti (Chiricahua Apache) in *Saved by the Bell*, Charlie Hill (Oneida) in *Roseanne*, and Westerman (Lakota) and Romero in *Dharma and Greg*.[9] Reinforcing mainstream male-dominated portrayals of the American Indian Movement (AIM) and the Red Power Movement in the 1970s even as Native women like Mary Jane Wilson (Leech Lake Ojibwe) and Madonna Thunder Hawk (Cheyenne River Sioux) were also at the forefront of AIM, female Indian characters with speaking parts were practically nonexistent in the sitcoms. The glaring omission and silencing of Native women not only reproduced the federal government's historical insistence on discussing policy and treaties with Native men but also subsumed Native women within a representational patriarchy that relegated them to roles of subservient homemakers and objectified backdrop.

By considering sitcom representations of Native masculinity as a frame for analysis, I argue that sitcoms in the 1970s through the 1990s present curiously tame and noble Indians through an anti-savage liberal multicultural paradigm. In moves favorable to federal Indian policy, sitcoms construct televisions of Native masculinity that suggest representational submission by the sitcom Indians over cultural equity. Airing televisions that largely counter mainstream news portrayals of AIM participants as militant and angry Natives, the recognizably Indian is visually marked on-screen as nonviolent and nonmilitant while representational hints of militancy and protest are performed offscreen.

Repressing much of the cultural work of indigenous social movements, the liberal multicultural slant in the episodes drives the sitcoms to locate common ground, literally, for constructing a renewed harmony between diverse characters for reforming the recognizably Indian into "almost the same, but not quite" as the settler. The general setup goes something like this: the episodes introduce a conflict between the settler and indigenous, then show them "determining" resolutions together but, as I contend, inequitably. In accordance to their conventional structure for plot lines, the sitcoms insist on offering resolutions. My concern here is that they repeatedly situate the resolutions in the guise of fictional variants of self-determination in which the indigenous performatively complies with the settler's conflict resolution. Although he occasionally speaks up for himself, the recognizably Indian yields in the end to the settler's agentive sway over the final say in resolving conflicts. The recognizably Indian corroborates white fantasies of temporarily becoming Indian, teaches settlers how to play Indian, vanishes to leave only the settler as *the* symbolic Indian stand-in, and adheres to the settler's upper hand in decision making and control in determining the fate of the indigenous, all of which subsume the momentary glimpses of screened gestures toward the recognizably Native indigenous strength and sensibility.

In this chapter, I unpack such juxtapositions of appearances and masquerades, encoded intentions and decoded implications, in the form of recognizably Indian televisions within the political and ambiguous interpretive framework of representational self-determination. To look at the intercultural encounters and story lines through the interpretive lens of self-determination opens up space to consider how sitcom producers translate the nonfictional politics of Indian-U.S. affairs into fictional TV representations, which can provide insight into how "self-determination" is understood televisually within contemporary notions of Indianness, multiracial harmony, and quick-fix resolutions to indigenous-settler conflicts. In short, whether speaking of the producers' creative control or the control and decision-making power they bestow upon their predominantly white male starring characters, self-determination in sitcoms is primarily settler self-determination.

Self-Determination Televised

The sitcom and other TV genres began to increasingly tune in modern Native issues and reenvision historical narratives amid the release of an influential mix of print sources authored by Natives and non-Natives that shared in privileging Native perspectives, or at least telling a version of history that most Americans likely had not heard. For example, in its special December 1967 issue, "Return of the Red Man," *Life* magazine featured contemporary portraits of young Natives at the Institute of Indian Arts in Santa Fe. "Never had the tired, shopworn platitude . . . about walking and living in two worlds," Paul Chaat Smith observes, "looked so vibrant, so exciting, so sexy, so alive. We could have Rothko and beadwork, Motown and the British Invasion and the tradition of our Crow and Navajo and Apache ways."[10] New books vastly different in tone and content from previous texts also influenced how American history would be told and understood. In 1969 Scott Momaday (Kiowa) received the Pulitzer Prize for Fiction for *House Made of Dawn*, and Vine Deloria Jr. released *Custer Died for Your Sins: An Indian Manifesto*. Dee Brown's best-seller *Bury my Heart at Wounded Knee*, released in 1970, soon became the more popular account of telling the American public who "Indians," or "the victims," to quote Brown, *were*.[11] Focusing on nineteenth-century atrocities, not on contemporary acts, committed by white Americans against Native Peoples, Brown's work appeared to strongly stir sympathy in settlers for Natives. As Deloria observed, "It seemed as if every book on modern Indians," including *Custer Died for Your Sins*, "was promptly buried by a book on the 'real' Indians of yesteryear" in feeding and shaping the public discourse on indigeneity.[12] Furthermore, Deloria added, the main topic "was not American Indians, but the American conception of what Indians should be."[13] A case in point occurred when Native Peoples protested ABC's new TV series *Custer* in 1967 for its glorification of the general. Unable to accept the kinds of intercultural confluences highlighted in *Life* magazine, the *Pittsburgh Gazette* mocked, "We can't conceive of Cochise slapping an injunction on a television network. Neither can we imagine Geronimo consulting his mouthpiece. We hate to say it, but we think red man talks with forked tongue."[14]

As more of mainstream America heard that modern indigenes were still *here* and actively adding their perspectives on and to mainstream media, such discursive boundaries among an imagined past and realistic present would literally play out on television screens. During "a period marked by the highest rates of Indian protest activism in the twentieth century," televised media attention to real-life contemporary Natives and their struggles for indigenous culturalhood grew exponentially in mass audience exposure in the 1970s.[15] For the first time on television, Native-led events received recurring mainstream news coverage, such as the 1960s fish-in protests for treaty-protected fishing rights in the Pacific Northwest, which, Philip S. Deloria notes, "had an enormous impact on the public consciousness and on tribal and individual self-awareness."[16] The Alcatraz occupation beginning in November 1969 (two months after the debut of *The Brady Bunch*) "captured more press attention than all the Indian struggles of the entire century" up to that point.[17] The group Indians of All Tribes sought to reclaim the island under an 1868 treaty and proposed plans for a Native cultural center and university. Further media exposure of Alcatraz filtered through John Trudell's (Santee Sioux) radio program *Radio Free Alcatraz*, carried by stations in Berkeley, Los Angeles, and New York.[18]

The American Indian Movement soon set a new standard for garnering the most extensive network coverage. Founded in Minneapolis on July 28, 1968, AIM started just three months after the ratification of the Indian Civil Rights Act, the first major law of the self-determination era.[19] Compared to the National Congress of American Indians and other "social movement organizations," AIM "dominated the headlines" from the late 1960s through the 1970s, though with mixed results. In his study on how NBC nightly news covered indigenous protest from 1968 to 1979, Tim Baylor finds that the network framed AIM as "militant" in 90 percent of more than fifty news segments. He adds that CBS's first coverage of AIM, a "six minute segment" on June 28, 1970, called AIM "militant" an average of once per minute. "Yet AIM," Baylor counters, "had not yet engaged in any of the major confrontations for which it would achieve notoriety."[20] The author alludes to events like the Trail of Broken Treaties, which saw AIM members travel across the United States to address treaty rights and living conditions. The Trail's most salient stop in the media was AIM's takeover and subsequent trashing of the Bureau of Indian Affairs building, or what members renamed the "Native American Embassy," in Washington, D.C., in response to "the BIA's failure to work with and for Indian tribes."[21]

Most critics agree that AIM's seventy-one-day occupation of Wounded Knee, South Dakota, in 1973 was the main media event as all three TV networks—NBC, CBS, and ABC—set up camp nearby. Numerous Natives exhibited media savvy, yet as Greg Sayer observes, mainstream media commonly called AIM leaders not only "militants" but also "insurgents," "tall, graceful, bronzed," and, in fusing past and present, "modern day Sitting Bulls."[22] Catching more than his fair share of the spotlight, AIM leader Russell Means (Lakota) "seemed particularly skilled at exploiting the media to gain political support, but also financial aid from volunteers and churches."[23] Among the financial backers visiting Wounded Knee was actor Marlon Brando. During the AIM stand-off against the federal government, Brando famously sent Sacheen Littlefeather (White Mountain Apache and Yaqui) to reject his Best Actor Oscar for his role in *The Godfather* because "the motion picture community has been as responsible as any for degrading the Indian and making a mockery of his character, describing his as savage, hostile and evil."[24] Elsewhere on the big screen, American audiences saw white males play Indian roles in the 1970 films *Little Big Man* and *A Man Called Horse* and 1971's *Billy Jack*. In addition to watching white actors Dustin Hoffman, Richard "Horse" Harris, and Tom Laughlin play Indians, audiences also saw movie actor Iron Eyes Cody, or Espera Oscar de Corti, "redfacing" in *A Man Called Horse*. A Sicilian American who claimed to be Cherokee and Creek, Cody's work in a commercial on the small screen became his most recognizable role. On Earth Day in 1971, he debuted as the ghostly "crying Indian" in a Hollywood Plains Indian costume and canoe in the public service announcement "Keep America Beautiful." As the announcer says, "People start pollution. People can stop it," the camera zooms in on Cody's tear to symbolize failed earthly stewardship and an ecological Indianness longing for romanticized pristine pastures of yesteryear.[25]

"That's the Way We Became the Brady [Braves]"

Amid the increasing nonfictional and fictional attention on-screen and in print, modern indigenes' numbers were also increasing rapidly. The federal census reported a considerable upsurge of Americans self-identifying as "American Indian"—from 523,591 Natives in 1960 to 792,730 in 1970 to 1,418,195 in 1980. Joane Nagel attributes this major upswing to an indigenous cultural revitalization motivated by "federal Indian policies, ethnic politics, and American Indian activism."[26] Policy, protest, cultural pride, and media coverage, not to mention growing numbers of non-Native allies and settlers self-identifying as Indian, contributed to the renewed understandings and invigorating support of (and, for others, vehement disdain against) indigeneity. "Public opinion," Vine Deloria remarked, "was significantly tilted in favor of Indians at the beginning of the seventies. Alcatraz and succeeding activist events may have galvanized the Indian image and made it seem romantic, perhaps even mysteriously exciting, to claim to be an Indian."[27] For *The Brady Bunch*, romanticized and mysterious excitement would become an understatement.

In the episode "The Brady Braves," the settler Bradys, including Carol and Mike and their six children (Greg, Marcia, Peter, Jan, Bobby, and Cindy) and housekeeper, Alice, take a family vacation to the Grand Canyon and become the first sitcom family to be adopted on-screen into an Indian tribe following their encounters with a "chief" and his grandson.[28] Their transformation from the Bradys, the quintessential groovy sitcom family of peace and love, into the "Brady Braves," as Bobby announces at the conclusion of the episode, is a centuries-old form of playing Indian that found a relatively new performative outlet in American sitcoms. Whereas previous series portrayed settler characters briefly feigning the recognizably Indian in Indian shows (for example, *I Love Lucy*), childhood games (*Dennis the Menace*), fraudulent schemes (*The Beverly Hillbillies*), bogus interracial marriage (*Here's Lucy*), and pageantry and historical reenactments (*The Andy Griffith Show*), the Bradys are elated and eager to become members of the tribe.[29]

The Bradys' pre-adoption representational history of signifying Indianness points toward this elation but also contains trite and aggressive moments of redface and violent expressions of Indian-settler masculinities. *The Brady Bunch* first references Indians in its sixth episode, "A Clubhouse Is Not a Home." Seeing his sister Cindy in his toy headdress, Bobby announces, "I'm gonna scalp her." Alice intervenes, "Oh, I think she makes a heap pretty squaw." Similar play off of invisible indigenes and violence continues in the 1970 episode "Slumber Caper." Overseeing a slumber party at the Brady house, Alice refers to herself as "General Custer" when she tries to keep the Brady boys, or, as she says, a "tribe on the warpath," from playing pranks on the Brady girls and their friends, who by default symbolize historical notions of innocent and helpless female settlers.[30]

In the following week's episode, "Un-Underground Movie," Greg, the oldest Brady kid, makes a film starring his family in a reenactment of the Pilgrims' first Thanksgiving with Natives for a history class project. Dually titled "Our Pilgrim Fathers" and "Through Hardship to Freedom," Greg's collective "our" already indicates his bias, in line with his membership in the Frontier Scouts, an iteration of the Boy Scouts. During casting for Greg's film, Bobby foreshadows his 1971 self-identification as a "Brady Brave" by exclaiming, "I wanna be an Indian!" Although Greg initially casts his brothers as Pilgrims, Bobby and Peter later play Indians. "Me Samoset!" shouts Peter. "Me Squanto!" adds Bobby. Dressed as a male Pilgrim, Alice, upon Greg's direction, fears them initially, in line with settler expectations of indigenous violence; but then, in a benevolent moment of recognizing the other representation extreme of noble savagery, she says, "They're friendly Indians." The other women temporarily join the Indian play as they greet "Samoset" and "Squanto" with "How." Carol, playing a female Pilgrim, even speaks to them in a tone typically reserved for patting babies and petting puppies: "Oh, friendly Indians. Aren't they *nice* Indians?"[31]

When *The Brady Bunch* opens its third season (1971–72) with a three-episode adventure to the Grand Canyon ("Ghost Town, U.S.A.," "Grand Canyon or Bust," and "The Brady Braves"), a television of liberal multiculturalism reigns throughout the Bradys' encounters with numerous "nice" Indians.[32] "The Bradys' Grand Canyon adventure is a saccharine story," Mark Neumann observes, with "regular comic mishaps, one-liners, and the constant din of a studio laughtrack."[33] They begin their trek in September 1971, three months after the federal government forced Indians of All Tribes to end their occupation of Alcatraz on June 11 and two months after the Raiders scored the #1 Billboard song "Indian Reservation."[34] Emblematic of the next wave of sitcoms with occasional guest-starring Indians and possibly in response to previous TV Indians, *The Brady Bunch* first attempts to educate a settler and multicultural audience about Indigenous Peoples with factual snippets attuned to colonial pleasantries.

As the Bradys prepare for their trip, the producers prepare their audience for the ensuing on-screen Indian encounters. From the start, before the family ever loads up in the station wagon, Mr. Brady is held up as the leading representational authority on Indians. He tells the children they will learn about the Havasupai, Hopi, Hualapai, and Navajo.[35] When Peter asks the origins of "such strange names," Mr. Brady replies, "Each name means something," such as "Havasupai" translating to "Great people of blue-green running water." In contrast to this tone of romanticized rhetoric, Mr. Brady neglects to mention, and frankly cannot in this liberal multicultural vein, that "Navajo" may be a name given by the Tewa Pueblo to mean "thieves" or "takers from the fields."[36] Later at the campsite, Mr. Brady flattens nation-specific terminology into pan-Indian rhetoric. He translates *Ya'at'eeh* not as a Diné, or Navajo, word but as an "Indian word [that] means 'hello' or 'welcome.'" Mrs. Brady similarly excludes indigenous specificity when she says, "The Indian word for Grand Canyon means . . . 'mountains lying down.'" Numerous sources indicate the Southern Paiutes' word *kaibab* means "mountains lying down" in reference to the Grand Canyon, but *The Brady Bunch* fails to mention this as well as the fact that "the federal government created the Kaibab Indian Reservation" in 1907 to confine the Southern Paiutes. The government also prohibited them from hunting for deer, as the Southern Paiutes had done for centuries, on what became known as the Grand Canyon National Game Preserve in 1906.[37]

The settlers' feel-good "education" continues when Bobby and Cindy wander from their campsite and encounter Jimmy Pakaya, a young Indian standing silently (read: mysteriously) on a rock before suddenly fleeing the Brady siblings (read: vanishing). "Gee! An Indian boy!" Cindy exclaims. They chase after him and soon become lost. Later, when they see Jimmy again, Cindy asks him, "Are you a real Indian?" Bobby figuratively turns to his dated Hollywood influences to test Jimmy's racial authenticity by greeting him with a raised hand and stern "How." To which Jimmy asks, "How what?" "Uh," Bobby fumbles, "how are you?" Curious about why Jimmy ran away from them, Bobby later asks, "Don't you like us paleface?" Jimmy snaps back, "Aw, cut out the paleface stuff." The retort is aimed at Bobby, yet could it not also be a corrective to previous television programming guilty of Hollywood Injun English?[38] Then in a gesture rarely emulated by settler to Indian in sitcoms, Bobby says, "Sorry." The apology opens up a small window of space for now including a modern Indian in a modern story line. In a nod to Jimmy's familiarity with his homeland, the Indian next leads them back to their camp even as the act also evokes the Indian guide trope, popularized by historical indigenous-settler trio Sacajawea and Lewis and Clark as well as by many of Jimmy's Hollywood Indian relatives.

Jimmy soon explains that he has run away from home and fears someone will see him and tell his grandfather where he is. When Mr. Brady finds the kids, Jimmy suddenly and almost inexplicably opens up to tell the figuratively great white sitcom father (move over, Ward Cleaver!), practically a stranger, why he ran away and what he wants to do, all of which he curiously had never told his Indian grandfather, who, according to Jimmy, "thinks only about the old Indian ways."

> JIMMY: He always talks about great things that happened a long time ago.
> MR. BRADY: Well, I can understand that. He's proud of those things, son.

JIMMY: Mr. Brady, I'm tired of being an Indian. I want to be an astronaut!

MR. BRADY (*chuckles*): Well, look, Jimmy, you can be both of those things. Look, you can be proud of your heritage just like your grandfather, and you can still do what you want to do or be what you want to be.

Revealing an internalized anti-Indian attitude, Jimmy appears in the shadow of the termination era to represent a prime candidate for assimilation into mainstream America. But Mr. Brady advocates a both/and approach in line with the multicultural era's stance on embracing certain aspects of cultural diversity. During a time in which increasing numbers of Native Peoples renewed their indigenous pride, demanded cultural freedom and justice, and increasingly attended college to attain their career goals, Mr. Brady speaks to Indian "heritage" and multicultural idealism, not to assimilation and separatism.

What is disconcerting, however, considering the long, sordid history of white male politicians, boarding school administrators, and missionaries claiming to know what is best for Native Peoples, is that producers situate Mr. Brady into the elder position of adviser (the Indian grandfather's role) to a young, impressionable Indian on the Indian's homelands. Just two years removed from the recommendation of the "Kennedy Report" for "increased Indian participation in and control over their own education programs and schools," a settler is the one to encourage Jimmy to pursue a career generally requiring higher education.[39] Mr. Brady's role as adviser seems to go against the report's envisioned means to such career goals. As if taking up the challenge of the "Kennedy Report" to ensure Natives have the freedom "to grow to their full potential," *The Brady Bunch* subjects Jimmy, a symbolic televisual stand-in for all Native youth, to similar settler-determined advice "to be what you want to be."[40] The writers' motive for the advice also sounds suspect when it later functions primarily as the rationale not only to unite Jimmy with his grandfather but also, as viewers soon learn, to secure an invitation for tribal adoption. Thus, the writers position Jimmy's reluctance to *be* Indian as the cultural avenue through which the Bradys come to *play* Indian.

The episode's discursive entanglement with self-determination policy is most symbolic after Jimmy leaves the Brady camp for home and returns with his grandfather, Chief Eagle Cloud, who is portrayed by the Mohawk actor Jay Silverheels, most recognized for his proverbial sidekick role of Tonto in the 1950s TV series *The Lone Ranger*. Appearing seemingly out of nowhere, standing silently on rocks like his grandson had in a gesture of intergenerational Indian oneness with nature, Eagle Cloud mistakes Alice, the housekeeper, for Mrs. Brady. Alice greets him with "Ya'at'eeh," which she had learned from Mr. Brady and intertextually said at the time, tongue-in-cheek, that the word would "come in handy if I happen to bump into Tonto." After speaking a few Diné words in response, the chief wastes no time in indulging in romanticized claptrap in his first English-spoken line: "My heart soars, Mrs. Brady!" Later, when he meets the Brady parents, he explains his excitement. (For those who have not seen this scene, imagine the actors' faces with near-constant feel-good smiles.)

> CHIEF: Mr. Brady, because you brought my grandson back to me, I offer you thanks, many thanks.
> MR. BRADY: Well, I really didn't do very much, Chief Eagle Cloud. I just talked to Jimmy. He made the decision.
> CHIEF: But you helped him to decide. I offer you thanks.
> MR. BRADY: Well, you're very welcome. [*To Jimmy*] Uh, Jim, did you speak to your grandfather?
> JIMMY (*bashfully*): Yeah, I did.
> CHIEF: The foolishness of this child. He thinks because I speak of buffalo, I do not understand "blast-off."
> MRS. BRADY: We have the same problem, Chief Eagle Cloud. We call it the generation gap.
> CHIEF: That's what we call it, too. [*The Bradys laugh and, yes, smile.*]

Speaking with tonal traces of Tonto, Eagle Cloud quickly sounds defeated and nearing submission to settler expectations for authentic Indianness and for finding common multicultural ground in "the generation gap."[41] Amid increasingly tense encounters and debates between the federal government and indigenous nations during this time, Mr. Brady and Eagle Cloud symbolize the ideal federal-tribal relationship of the 1970s, in which the two work together for mutual success and congratulate each other on a job well done. Like a BIA how-to video demonstration of discursive self-determination, the settler humbly claims he "didn't do very much" and that the young Indian "made the decision." But the thankful chief insists the settler "helped him to decide" to return home and now feels indebted to him.

Having known the Bradys for all of about two minutes, Eagle Cloud says to the children, "I speak in honor of your father. I ask you to journey to our village tonight. In a ceremony, I will ask you to become members of my family and tribe." He assures them that they will have a "groovy time," in effect becoming quite possibly the first sitcom Indian to utter "groovy" in a prime-time comedy. The Brady kids plead with their sitcom patriarch to accept the invitation, which he does. (For those keeping score, Jimmy received hot dogs and beans served in a flashlight's battery slot for guiding Bobby and Cindy back to their family, while the Bradys get adopted after disjointedly helping the chief's grandson, symbolizing yet again, with no disrespect to Van Camp's or Oscar Mayer, an imbalanced trade between the indigenous and settler.)

To set the Hollywood stage, literally and ideologically, that evening at some sort of Indian camp, Indian flute music plays. A few Indian characters sit in the distance for recognizable backdrop. Temporarily replacing Mr. Brady as the cultural authority figure, Chief Eagle Cloud stands stoically and declares, "All these people [the Bradys] sitting around this fire shall belong to my tribe from now until forever."[42] He then walks past each of the Indian-style-seated Bradys and gives them stereotypical Indian names. The males receive animalistic monikers, such as Mr. Brady's "Big Eagle of Large Nest" and Greg's "Stalking Wolf." Peter rejects "Leaping Lizard" and "Middle Buffalo" before the chief says, "I'll get back to you." The females mainly receive flowery, more effeminate names, including Mrs. Brady's "Yellow Flower with Many Petals" and Cindy's "Wandering Blossom." Next, Eagle Cloud instructs the Bradys to dance around the fire, which they do recklessly with flailing movements of erratic hops, skips, and spins. The nine newly found Indians take center stage while Eagle Cloud and the other Indians watch. The scene then abruptly cuts to a culminating three-second shot of the Bradys and their Indian relatives holding hands in a round dance, symbolizing a temporary multicultural mosaic of recognizably Indian adoptees and Indians before the latter vanish from view.

As the Bradys exit the park the next day, Cindy asks the park attendant, "Remember us? We're the Brady family." Bobby interjects, "You mean we were. Now, we're the Brady Braves!" In the nearly seventy-five remaining episodes of *The Brady Bunch*, the Bradys never refer again to their tribe or Indian names, typical of the sitcom's storytelling enclosure within a single episode (or, in this case, three-episode Grand Canyon adventure). The brief interlude into Indianness carries considerable precedent outside of television. "Indian play was a temporary fantasy," Philip Deloria explains, "and the player inevitably returned to the everyday world. But the world to which one returned was not that of Indian people, and, in that sense, play allowed one to evade the very reality that it suggested one was experiencing."[43] The Brady family entered a part of Indian Country in the Grand Canyon area, saw and heard what they wanted (dancing and singing by real Indians), were guided by a "real Indian" boy, served unnecessarily as white guardians before reuniting the formerly self-hating Indian boy and his traditional grandfather on the Indians' own lands, were adopted into an unnamed tribe and received Indian names, and, finally, left their romanticized Indian relatives for home in sunny Southern California. To remix the theme song, "That's the way," in sum, "they became the Brady [Braves]" of self-determination.

Televisions of Recognizably Indian Protest:
Barney Miller and *Diff'rent Strokes*

Elsewhere on television, some producers devoted on-screen nonfictional attention to modern Native Peoples. In June 1975, NBC aired a ten-part special simply titled *The Native American*, described by one reporter as "an in-depth look at the American Indian's life and culture—both past and present. Native American Indians from many tribes perform and interpret their heritage on the shows." In December, the Cree musician and actress Buffy Sainte-Marie joined the cast of *Sesame Street* and appeared frequently through 1981. Additionally, during the 1970s, the Federal Communications Commission mandated local stations to provide airtime to underserved populations, which opened space for new public access shows by Natives. For example, starting in 1973, Harriet Skye (Standing Rock Sioux) directed, produced, and hosted *Indian Country Today* on the NBC affiliate in Bismarck, North Dakota. In 1974, Sandra Osawa (Makah) produced, directed, and wrote *The Native American Series* for NBC in Los Angeles. Both programs, along with others like it across Indian Country, featured contemporary Native guests and addressed contemporary Native social and political issues. By 1975, Osawa's series screened right before *The Today Show* in major cities across the United States.[44]

As for sitcoms' representations of the indigenous, the "groovy time" that Chief Eagle Cloud spoke of at the start of the 1970s was arguably the decade's pinnacle for the recognizably Indian. In 1972, *The New Dick Van Dyke Show* aired "Running Bear and Moskowitz" in which two costarring settler characters "open a boutique in a delicatessen with an old Indian." In the 1973 *All in the Family* episode "Archie Learns His Lesson," bigot settler Archie Bunker and his liberal settler son-in-law, Mike, briefly exchange vastly different and predictable views about Native Peoples. Archie believes Indians "sell all their horses for booze and then they can't ride into town"; Mike counters that "we [the United States] lied to them, we cheated them, and then we drove them off their land without paying for it." *Happy Days*, set in 1950s Milwaukee, turned repeatedly to Indian references during its 1974–84 run, such as Ralph Malph's demonstrated faux ability to "count to five in American Indian," as if such a generic language exists. When Richie asks for tribal clarification, a question of irrelevance in 1950s and 1960s sitcoms, Malph responds, "I don't know. My mother always makes things up," suggesting to viewers that the Indian rhetoric is bogus. The Fonz (with his catchphrase "Aaaay!" sounding like a bad rendition of the Native jokester's "Aye!") showed a recurring love for Indians, though almost always to those in the past, especially the fictional Tonto. "Hey, I don't like the cavalry, man," he exclaims in one episode, "I like the Indians!" Another time, when his girlfriend Pinky Tuscadero mocks the Lone Ranger's sidekick, Fonzie responds, "Hey, don't you joke about Tonto!" Visual but mute Indians crop up in at least two 1978 episodes: first, in "Westward Ho!," Soft Doe, a mute female Indian in buckskin and on horseback, serves briefly as Fonzie's affectionate guide to a modern-day dude ranch in Colorado where settlers talk of an "Indian legend" about an "Indian princess" whose tears formed a nearby lake after her "brave" did not return from a buffalo hunt; then in "The First Thanksgiving," three male Indians are frozen in history while overseen by their protector and Indian sign language expert Fonzie in a reenactment of the first Thanksgiving. In 1977, *Blansky's Beauties*, a short-lived *Happy Days* spin-off, included the character Gladys "Cochise" Littlefeather as one of the showgirls at a Las Vegas hotel. Then finally, in 1979, *Barney Miller* took its first turn with an Indian story line.[45]

Set at a police station in Greenwich Village in New York City, *Barney Miller* follows the lives of a group of detectives and a vast array of guest-starring complainants and suspects. Known for its multiethnic cast, the sitcom has been heralded as televisually groundbreaking in its portrayals of ethnic and race relations. In his article "Unmelting Images," on ethnic representations in TV, James Craig Holte says, "*Barney Miller* represents a major change in television's depiction of ethnic characters" in which "the actors portray people, not caricatures."[46] Jack Soo, "the first Asian American to be cast in the lead role in a regular television series," the early 1960s show *Valentine's Day*, portrayed the Japanese American sergeant Nick Yemana. Ron Glass played the African American detective Ron Harris with what the *Saturday Review* then called "the slyest wit on commercial television." According to film and TV historian Donald Bogle, "Glass created an ambitious, bright character that was the antithesis of what viewers had been conditioned to expect from Black males."[47] Gregory Sierra was the Puerto Rican sergeant Miguel "Chano" Amenguale, Max Gail was the Polish American detective Stan "Wojo" Wojciehowicz, and Abe Vigoda portrayed the Jewish American sergeant Philip Fish, the subsequent star in the sitcom spin-off *Fish*.

However, the inclusion of the indigenous in the episode "The Indian" raises questions to Holte's reading of peopled characters. Guest star Charles White Eagle portrays George Ten Fingers, or as settler Detective Dietrich dryly says, "old Indian."[48] When Dietrich and Wojo bring him to the station for "trespassing" (on possibly his traditional homeland) and "disturbing the peace" in a restricted area at Central Park, Ten Fingers calmly offers the defense, "It's a good place to die."[49] With a distinguishing gentleness, passivity, submissive fatigue, and faint smile, Ten Fingers soon talks of a wolf he rescued years earlier from "the white man's trap" and who recently appeared to him again. Having been without food for four days in order "to communicate with the spirit of the wolf" and "to help prepare me for death," Ten Fingers quietly adds, "It is time to go, says the wolf."

When the Parks Department drops the charges, a concerned and intrigued Wojo refuses to let him leave. Wojo asks the Indian, for instance, where he resides. "Where you do," Ten Fingers replies, "at the center of the universe." Concluding that Ten Fingers is homeless and broke, Wojo decides to contact the BIA for assistance. "I called Washington," he tells Barney. "I told them there might be some sort of a treaty involved," a blatant but effective lie to lure in the federal government bureau. In a consistently unflattering portrait of a major segment of the federal government, the BIA arrives in the form of an impatient and egotistical white male in a suit named Philip Owens who, upon realizing he was called in "under false pretenses," angrily shouts that he works "with entire Indian nations, not people." When Ten Fingers slyly smiles at him, Owens exclaims, in a moment of settler recognition of anxiety, "No, you don't pull that 200 years of guilt stuff on me!" Telling the detectives that there is nothing he can do for an urban Indian like Ten Fingers in New York City ("Out here, he's just like everyone else"), the two-faced BIA employee exits with an empty apology: "I'm sincerely sorry there isn't more I could have done."

The BIA representative fits the mood of other fictional television portrayals of the BIA at the time. In his 1978 appearance on *The Tonight Show Starring Johnny Carson*, Oneida stand-up comic Charlie Hill joked, "I attended the Bureau of Indian Affairs School for Comedians." As Hill would later say, his father had advised him early on to "attack the Bureau of Indian Affairs" and its "nearsightedness." In a comedic skit on the short-lived 1980 NBC variety and musical series *The Big Show*, Hill converses with a settler who delivers several insulting remarks, such as "You people should be glad Columbus discovered you!" After unsuccessfully attempting to school the stranger ("Hey, we knew where we were!"), Hill finally asks what he does for a living. The settler simply says, "I work for the Bureau of Indian Affairs." Acting not the least surprised, Hill pans to the camera and smiles as if to say, "That figures." The BIA portrayal in *Barney Miller* also prefigures an Indian character's more serious reaction to the BIA in the 1980 episode "Indians" in the TV drama *Lou Grant*. When a settler newspaper reporter helps a young Tohono O'odham boarding school runaway search for his uncle, the reporter announces he will check with the BIA. Suddenly, the boy disappears from the scene. "I shouldn't have mentioned the BIA out loud," the reporter admits. "That must have scared him."[50]

With no help, nor determination to assist, from the BIA, *Barney Miller* complicates typical sitcom narrative convention by suggesting, for the time being, no clear answer for what to do with Ten Fingers. "The manual," Captain Miller says, "doesn't cover something like this." Wojo reluctantly opts for Bellevue, a psychiatric hospital, which appears to deeply disappoint and silence Ten Fingers as he slowly exits the station and his on-screen performance. Wojo later returns alone to tell Barney that he went against police procedure and took Ten Fingers back to the park instead: "He wanted to go, so I took him." Wojo then announces, "He's dead, Barn. I stayed with him a while and we talked and then we just sat and he died." In line with centuries of the vanishing Indian trope in popular culture, Ten Fingers's death does not sound too unexpected for mainstream film and television, unless perhaps one had recently seen *Little Big Man* (1970), in which Chief Dan George's elder Indian character erroneously and humorously thinks it is time to die. Nor is it unexpected that a settler character remains to recount the Indian's story. "It made me feel good, Barn," Wojo says. "It's what he wanted. I mean, I don't mean like he wanted to die. He wanted to be in the park." In a way, the sitcom affirms Ten Fingers's understanding that "it is time to go." Yet within the larger history of settler storytelling, one may inevitably feel that *Barney Miller* opts for a *cop-out* resolution (bad *Brady Bunch*–like pun intended) of death. In this case, the cops were anything but out as they stayed central to the plot, determined when and where the Indian could go, and, by the end, remained the only ones left to be in charge of the narrative, including the Indian's story.

Barney Miller would attempt three years later in the episode "Bones" to counter its contribution to the vanishing Indian trope.[51] If not, however, for Max Gail, the actor who portrayed Wojo and the character at the epicenter of representational self-determination in "The Indian," the episode may have never been produced and aired. During production of "The Indian," Gail recognized the "convenient" and clichéd resolution to have another underdeveloped "old Indian" die in the end. As Gail told me, "This guy's a traditional elder" and "probably has a lot of family, but," the actor also recognized, "it could happen" if an Indian is separated from his people, ages, then eventually dies. Regardless of believability in the fictional world of *Barney Miller*, "The Indian" struck such a chord with viewers that it became, Gail says, the "*only* episode to be rerun" that season due to an outpouring of viewer support, suggestive of not only the entertainment value but also the comfortable fictions and colonial anxiety reduction the episode's plot and resolution may have provided.

Gail had long been interested in indigenous politics and philosophy. He has repeatedly commented on the deep impact that Native Peoples have had on him and on his way of seeing the world. During the 1970s, he visited diverse urban indigenes in Los Angeles, Chicago, and Denver at the Intertribal Friendship Houses. "Usually functioning on garage sales resources," Gail recalls, "they always seemed to have a rich intercultural and intergenerational life. I believe this had to do with regard for future generations, the respect for different ways, the connection to place, and the recognition of the relationship of all life that 'in-forms' Native American cultures as immensely varied as they are otherwise." In addition, Gail joined the Longest Walk participants in solidarity during the first stretch of the five-month trek in 1978 from San Francisco to Washington, D.C., to protest eleven proposed bills in Congress threatening tribal sovereignty. To increase awareness of "the Walk" along the way, Gail used his TV celebrity status to go on talk shows. Gail also visited the walkers' camp in D.C. as Congress passed the American Indian and Religious Freedom Act. In 1980, Gail filmed the "documusical" *For All My Relations* about "video storytellers" and musicians "on the Mohawk reservation" and "in the Black Hills," and then produced the documentary *Wrong Side of the Fence* about "Hopi/Navajo land issues."[52] In 1983, Gail, along with Jonathan Winters and other Hollywood actors, was invited by actor Will Sampson (Mvskoke), costar of the 1975 film *One Flew over the Cuckoo's Nest*, to serve on the advisory committee for the newly established American Indian Registry for the Performing Arts.[53] In 1989, Gail and his Oneida friend Charlie Hill performed together in the First Nations television comedy *Indian Time*. In one skit, Gail plays an insensitive TV producer of a deodorant commercial. He wants Hill to wear a faux headdress and speak broken English while holding the product. Due to his principles and recognition that other Natives will see the commercial, Hill refuses . . . until he learns the gig will pay $10,000.[54]

After "The Indian," Gail focused more attention on future possibilities for a second episode featuring the indigenous. Seasons 6 and 7, though, passed by without it happening. So, in negotiating his contract for the eighth and final season, Gail required and, indeed, was granted one episode to include a story line with at least one Native character. The stipulation likely surprised the writers, who acted like *Barney Miller*, Gail infers, had already "done that," as in done the Indian story. When producers suggested he provide an Indian story line, Gail assumed they would reject it but prepared one anyway. For inspiration, he looked to the Lakota AIM leader Russell Means and his Vietnam veteran brother Bill Means. The first outline featured a young Native man who wants to bring attention to repatriation. Gail has the character remove indigenous remains, possibly from a museum, and carry them to a construction site in New York where, Gail continues, he "freezes" in fear atop a building. A male Mohawk character, suggestive of the famous iron steel Mohawk workers who helped to build New York City, soon arrives to talk him down. A third Native character, an "apple" cop from Minnesota who is racially red on the outside and behaviorally and attitudinally white on the inside, has followed the first character to arrest him. A fourth Native character proposed by Gail to enter into the representational bricolage is a Six Nations female cop and spiritual follower of the Longhouse teachings. Within the history of sitcoms, to represent four Native characters with lines must have sounded like a representational revolution! It appears to have been no surprise to Gail, then, when the writers rejected it, possibly due in part to someone else attempting to do their job. "We [in the cast] always respected," Gail recalls, "that the writers were the writers." Still, Gail expresses some disappointment that after his seven years on *Barney Miller*, there seemed to be an insufficient trust in his ideas. What the writers *were* "infatuated" with, much to Gail's chagrin, was their own idea of constructing cultural tensions via a generational gap between an old Indian attached to the past and his son who embraces change and, to some extent, assimilation. The intergenerational angle had long been narratively played out in Hollywood, including in the aforementioned *Petticoat Junction* episode, "The Umquaw Strip" (chapter 1), and *The Brady Bunch* episode, "The Brady Braves." Eventually, *Barney Miller* co-creator Danny Arnold rejected the father-son story in favor of "Bones."[55]

As the sitcom neared the series finale, Gail reminded producers of their contractual obligation to him. Finally, in the 165th episode, the last episode before the three-part series finale, *Barney Miller* aired "Bones."[56] Gail now turned to directing the series' only other episode featuring an Indian.[57] Directed by arguably the most politically invested and informed sitcom producer, "Bones" is also the most politically engaging episode representing the indigenous by the early 1980s. Gail's Wojo mostly stays out of the

Indian-themed story line this time, which appears to allow the Indian to speak fervently for himself.

After producers considered Charlie Hill to play the Indian, Mark Banks (Anishinaabe) landed the role of James Long, an outspoken Mohawk character who breaks into a white male archaeologist's office and, as in Gail's previously proposed story, takes indigenous remains.[58] Banks, older brother to AIM cofounder and eventual part-time actor Dennis Banks (Anishinaabe), was AIM's press secretary. During Wounded Knee in 1973, Mark Banks "spent much of the siege in Los Angeles raising money and generating publicity through connections in the local media, whom he had cultivated during several years as a Los Angeles radio and television personality known as 'Johnny West.'"[59] Banks's breakthrough into television came when comedic actor Jonathan Winters, reportedly of Cherokee heritage and a longtime indigenous ally who once served as honorary chair of the National Congress of American Indians, called Banks one day at the radio station, invited him to emcee a benefit for the American Indian scholarship fund, and then asked him to be a guest on *The Jonathan Winters Show* on CBS. He would eventually be in six episodes, performing comedic skits with Winters, and eventually filled guest spots on *The Carol Burnett Show* and *The Mary Tyler Moore Show*.[60]

Banks's offscreen politics with AIM found an on-screen communicative outlet when Banks-as-Long in *Barney Miller* enters the police station, handcuffed, in a discursively assertive bang, suggestive that a sitcom and, by extension, television network (ABC) had finally afforded a fictional space for AIM: "Hey, look, I'm talking respect here. I don't go messing with your grave. Don't go messing with mine!" Wojo, one of the arresting officers, is dumbfounded. Facing pending charges of "burglary and disturbing the peace," Long offers the defense that he "was trying to preserve the cultural and traditional integrity of the Mohawk Nation," a far more active stance on cultural continuity than Ten Fingers's initial reply connoting readiness for death. Suspecting the Greenwich Museum of Natural History (nominally and geographically close to the American Museum of Natural History in Manhattan) had excavated indigenous bones from upstate New York, Long took the museum's remains and, instead of leaving, held a sit-in at the museum's entrance of a Native exhibit. "What would you do," Long asks the detectives, "if someone stole the remains of your ancestors, then shoved them into some garbage bag, then threw them into a closet somewhere?"

"Bones" aired during a tumultuous time of related real-life struggles in the American Indian repatriation movement. In her book *Grave Injustice*,

Kathleen Fine-Dare says, "The 1970s saw a growing discussion regarding the general role of museums in possessing, displaying, and representing Native American cultural objects and human remains."[61] She copiously cites instances of theft and desecration of indigenous remains and artifacts, such as in New York, the setting of *Barney Miller*, where the Onondagas fought for the return of their historic wampum belts.[62] Since 1909, state law had dictated New York to be the sole possessor of Iroquois wampum; but in the early 1970s, Onondagas "demanded that their belts be returned," which they were, finally, in 1989. The former Museum of the American Indian in New York City held eleven other wampum belts from 1910 until their repatriation to the Six Nations Council of Chiefs in 1988.[63] Elsewhere, Natives had recently responded to the desecration of remains by an anthropologist and archaeologist. "In 1971 the Narragansetts of Rhode Island conducted a ceremony to rebury remains that had been removed from a tribal cemetery by an anthropologist. . . . In 1976 the Canadian Union of Ontario Indians performed a citizen's arrest of an archaeologist for failing to comply with the Canadian Cemeteries Act of 1976."[64] By the early 1980s, theft continued, but certain organizations also raised concerns. In 1980, a Chicago art dealer sold three Hopi masks he had initially stolen. The dealer later pleaded guilty but received just a $1,000 fine. The collectors of the masks then received tax deductions after donating them to the Art Institute of Chicago. Theft continued in 1983 when "ritual objects [were] stolen from the Museum of the American Indian." The following year, "the Smithsonian return[ed] five Modoc remains to their living descendants." In 1981, the American Association of Museums released "a statement regarding ethical standards for the treatment of Native American collections." In 1982, the National Park Service implied Natives "should be consulted" concerning indigenous remains. Louisiana repatriated over two tons of remains and artifacts to the Tunica-Biloxi Nation in 1985, and the University of Minnesota finally followed through in 1989 on repatriating indigenous remains according to a 1981 law.[65]

Barney Miller entered into such tumultuous political and legal discourses that previous sitcoms generally ignored, circuitously skirted around, or heavily distorted. As a televisual rejoinder to the ongoing movement, "Bones" presents an indigenous character whose rhetoric, tone, and actions were all relatively new in the then thirty-five year history of American sitcoms. James Long, in effect, shakes up the boundaries of what constitutes Indianness on American television. He is not a "chief," a settler actor in redface, or a passive performer. He appears culturally competent, angry, and fed up with injustice against Indigenous Peoples. Long literally shouts a television of "truth" that sitcoms had never dared to broadcast. That he primarily does so from behind bars in the station's holding cell, symbolic of long-standing colonizing restriction and captivity of expressive indigeneity, presents what can (and does) happen on one's own homeland when one breaks settler colonial laws for indigenous freedom. "You people," he says to Wojo, a stand-in for immigrant-settler America, "have ruined this land. You've wasted our animals, our forests, fouled up the air, polluted the rivers. Keep that up and Manhattan is gonna be worth even less than you paid for it."[66]

In these heated moments, *Barney Miller* also looks to educate viewers, bordering the *Brady Bunch*'s slightly instructive forays into Indianness but offering something more substantial than the Bradys' "Indian"-to-English translations for rivers and mountains. "The law," Long bellows at one point. "Who do you think inspired the Articles of Confederation and the Constitution? Washington? Jefferson? Forget it. It was the Iroquois, man!" The erudite Sergeant Dietrich, well versed in an array of subjects, confirms it for nearby astonished characters. Long turns as well to indigenous foods: "Where do you think you got tomatoes, potatoes, and squash and popcorn?" As for "jails," from one of which he stands and stares at Barney, "that was *your* contribution!"

Despite Long's uninvited history lessons and blunt charges, the detectives and Long are mutually supportive in holding the latter due to standard procedure. Miller, in particular, expresses an understanding of Long's actions and cause for justice. Almost apologizing when he places Long in the cell, Miller says, "Well, we sympathize [with your situation], Mr. Long, but I'm afraid we're gonna have to hold you anyway. Nothing personal." "Hey," Long kindly interjects, "it's okay." Miller later tries to gently dissuade the archaeologist, without insulting him, from pressing charges: "Now, obviously, you have the power to put Mr. Long in jail," but "considering the circumstances, you got your bones back."

From the moment that the archaeologist, an older and gentle but seemingly bumbling and absentminded man named Otto Traven, arrives at the station, he is unsure of how to proceed. Even after Long quickly launches from behind bars into name-calling—"Desecrator! Violator of sacred soil! You people got no respect for nothing!"—Traven is hesitant to press charges. Finally, Long attempts to plead calmly with Traven through an analogy.

LONG: Doctor, water in liquid form exists only on this planet, and man is 60 percent water. Without water, there's no life, don't you understand? We're destroying our water supply.

TRAVEN: You want to go to jail?

LONG: Of course. People have to be reminded.

TRAVEN: I understand. I will press charges against you.

LONG (*smiles*): Thank you.

TRAVEN (*smiles*): You're very welcome! [*Smugly to Miller*] Put him away, Captain.

As Traven exits the station and says he looks forward to the trial, Long smiles proudly as he says in his closing line, "What a nice guy."

Curiously, the only one insistent on jail time is Long. He utilizes jail, it appears, more as a platform for publicity and his rhetoric than out of necessity. Rather than attempting earlier to flee the museum with the remains, Long made certain he was seen and caught. "If you want to draw attention to the issues," he explains to the detectives, "you got to get publicity." Asked who noticed at the museum, Long notes just a "Japanese tourist group" but reasons "it's still early." When a detective says someone from the museum may press charges, Long eagerly replies, "That's fine with me. I've been arrested before. Three Mile Island, Washington, D.C. . . . I go where I'm needed."[67]

Added together, Long's motives for breaking the law, demanding justice by jail, and thirsting for media attention sound self-serving *and* community-driven. He breaks federal and state laws and welcomes imprisonment even when he technically does not have to. Suggestive perhaps of the actor Banks's real-life role as AIM's press secretary, Long insists on doing what he believes is necessary for publicity. (According to Gail, Banks even went off-script in "Bones" at one point to reference AIM during taping, but the line was cut because it rang more of "flag waving" than something emanating from the writers' vision of the character.)[68] Within the ongoing push in Indian Country for self-determination, Long wants indigenous remains in museums to be repatriated to Native Peoples so that Natives can *determine* and enact proper cultural protocol. Still, by deciding to take the remains and intentionally situating himself within, to some extent, a foreign judicial process, Long rests his fate in the hands of the non-Native detectives, archaeologist, and, upon being charged, a judge and jury at the pending trial.

Just three months before "Bones" and set a few miles north of *Barney Miller*, the *Diff'rent Strokes* episode "Burial Ground" premiered. Guest star Ned Romero portrayed, in comparison to Banks's role, a more reserved on-screen Indian with his own discursive markings of offscreen militancy.[69] Reportedly of Chitimacha, Spanish, and French ancestry from Louisiana, Romero performed as an opera singer for approximately twenty years before compiling a lengthy list of acting credits in movies, television dramas, and westerns from 1963 to 2006, when he played a humorous indigenous storyteller in the morbid cinematic comedy *Expiration Date*. Romero also knows sitcoms, evident from his guest roles as Indian and non-Indian characters in *The Many Loves of Dobie Gillis*, *McHale's Navy*, *Get Smart*, *The Munsters*, *Spin City*, and *Dharma and Greg*.

In "Burial Ground," his character Chief John Longwalker of the fictional Oswego tribe enters the upscale Park Avenue residence of the Drummonds, including white patriarch and wealthy government contractor Phillip, his white teenage daughter, Kimberly, and two younger adopted African American sons, Willis and Arnold. Along with the 1980s sitcoms *Webster* and *Gimme a Break!*, *Diff'rent Strokes* reads as feel-good integrationist comedy. Communicating from the opening credits a message of interracial harmony, its theme song begins,

> Now, the world don't move to the beat of just one drum,
> What might be right for you, may not be right for some.
> A man is born, he's a man of means.
> Then along come two, they got nothing but their jeans.
> But they got Diff'rent Strokes.
> It takes Diff'rent Strokes.
> It takes Diff'rent Strokes to move the world.

Or as teenagers Kimberly, Willis, and Charlene (played by a pre-superstar Janet Jackson) sing in an episode a few months after "Burial Ground,"

> Ebony and ivory
> Live together in perfect harmony
> Side by side on my piano keyboard
> Oh, Lord, why can't we?[70]

This lyrical message of black-and-white solidarity originally performed by Paul McCartney and Stevie Wonder is not to be missed, but conspicuously absent is a line of racialized piano symbolism indicating which keys are foundational (white), larger (white), and numerically higher (white).

The sitcom's backstory is that before Willis and Arnold's mother, the Drummonds' former maid, died, she made her boss promise he would take care of her sons. Instead of including an on-screen black maid for a white family, as early 1950s sitcom *Beulah* and *Gimme a Break!* and numerous movies had done, *Diff'rent Strokes* kills her off before the series begins.[71] In her place, Donald Bogle observes, "are no Black relatives or a Black community to care for the children. For the late 1970s/early 1980s audience, the millionaire Drummond becomes a *great white father figure*, able to provide the material comforts (as well as the subliminal emotional ones) and the cultural milieu that the Black community supposedly could never hope to match" (emphasis in original).[72] In "Burial Ground," Drummond again "becomes a great white father figure," or who Robin Means Coleman labels the "White savior" type in his representational power to save the day by determining a conflict resolution that appeases all parties, including the accommodating and, yes, smiling indigenous representative Longwalker.[73]

During its run, *Diff'rent Strokes* attempted to address a number of important social issues, such as bulimia, drug use, bullying, pedophilia, and racism. In "Burial Ground," the issue concerns whether to build a new structure over what may be an Indian burial ground. When Longwalker hears that Arnold found a bear rock carving on Drummond's building site (aka Oswego homeland), the chief shows up at the Drummonds' door and exchanges banal pleasantries.

> LONGWALKER: Forgive me for dropping in like this, but it's important that I speak to Mr. Drummond. My name is John Longwalker, and I'm chief of the Oswego Indian tribe.
> DRUMMOND: I'm Philip Drummond. I'm chief of the Drummond tribe.
> LONGWALKER (*smiles*): White man speak with funny tongue.[74]
> DRUMMOND: It's very nice to meet you. Come into my teepee.

Screening Longwalker as polite, jocular, and respectful, *Diff'rent Strokes* seems careful not to offend a modern multicultural sensibility and to refrain, for now, from signifying anything remotely savage even as "Chief" Drummond plays loosely with Indian signifiers.

Once inside, Arnold and Longwalker address the thorny topic of indigenous authenticity. Evocative of the *Brady Bunch*'s attempt to clear space of 1950s–1960s recognizably Indian representations by engaging them, an excited Arnold first echoes Cindy Brady's inquisitiveness with Indians:

> ARNOLD: Are you a real Indian chief?
> LONGWALKER: Well, that's the way it says on my credit cards.
> ARNOLD: Well, where are your feathers?
> LONGWALKER: Oh, I don't wear my feathers when driving my taxi. In some neighborhoods, I'm liable to get plucked.

Longwalker tritely challenges stereotypes but also inspires others, such as when he exits his first scene. After giving Arnold a tribal fur hat, adorned

with a single feather and colorful headband, and deeming him "an honorary member of the tribe" for finding and loaning the bear carving, Longwalker says, "Hang in there, Little Big Cheeks," and raises his hand in a
"How" gesture that Arnold eagerly replicates. In a subsequent scene, Longwalker and Arnold replay the "How"s as the chief affectionately calls him
his "little brave." As Bogle explains, "*Diff'rent Strokes* enjoyed poking fun at
racial attitudes rather than at racism," the latter of which is portrayed not
"as a national sickness" but "as so much nonsense."[75] In support of Bogle's
assessment, the Indian play, for Longwalker, appears to be in jest even as
he reinforces recognizably Indian signifiers for a young Arnold to emulate. Indeed, the nonsensical acts and rhetoric of playing Indian in "Burial
Ground" offer more approval and allowance than critique and disruption
of the redface behavior. Producers do not appear to consider the representations as even remotely *racist* when, for example, Arnold dances wildly
and yells "hey-yay-yay-yay" in an attempt to summon, he says, "the spirits"
to help Longwalker. His sister, Kimberly, demands Arnold stop "before it
starts raining in here." At the end of the episode, Arnold leads Longwalker
in a Hollywood Indian dance. Playing Indian, then, with an Indian chief's
(and, by extension, a Native actor's) smiling support appears permissible
in *Diff'rent Strokes*.

In between the one-liners and strained education, a serious conflict
arises between Drummond and Longwalker. Upon seeing the bear carving that Arnold found, Longwalker is "sure" Drummond's construction
site is "our ancient burial ground." For further evidence, he stares off into
the distance and, in the vein of Longfellow's 1855 epic poem "The Song of
Hiawatha," cites "the legend handed down by the elders [that] it is located
'by the river of the wide waters where the trees touch the sky.'" Not surpris-
ingly, Longwalker's performance prompts Kimberly to gush, "Ah, that's so
beautiful. Just like a poem." The chief says the legend's "description fits the
site," and Drummond believes the news for the Oswegos is "wonderful"—
that is, until Longwalker requests he "stop construction." When Drummond refuses ("I can't stop a multimillion-dollar government project just
because of a legend and a rock"), the chief says he will "go to court to get
an injunction."

Soon a third party, representing the federal government and a strong
opposition to the Oswegos, arrives at the Drummonds'. Cliff Hammer of
the General Services Administration ("the vice president in charge of red
tape," says Drummond) reports that "the judge denied the Indians their
injunction." He adds that Longwalker "was perfectly calm. He thanked the
judge and said he was going on a hunger strike [Hammer mimics him by

standing upright and feigning a stoic tone] 'until his people regained their lands,' as he put it." Hammer later tells Drummond that the Oswegos "have set up a blockade" to the site. "Some of the Indians," he scoffs, "are lying down on the ground in front of your bulldozers."

Hammer says Drummond can sign a complaint to forcibly remove them (that is, "get beaten up and tear-gassed" according to Willis).[76] When Kimberly asks, "Dad, does there really have to be any violence?" her father replies, "Not if I can help it." Drummond's concern here and elsewhere in the episode is suspect. His portrayed compassion appears to serve as justification for the great white father figure's recursively ascribed paternalism and power in the episode. When Arnold and Willis defend the Indians, for example, Drummond says, "Listen, boys, I appreciate your *sympathy* for the Indians, but the court has made a decision, and now I have to live up to my contract. There's nothing I can do about it." When they decide to join the chief in the hunger strike, their father similarly says, "I *sympathize* with your feelings, fellas, but my hands are tied" (emphases added). Just a few hours into the hunger strike, Arnold whines, "Why doesn't Dad give the Indians back their burial ground?" as if the government contractor can determine to do so.

Producers continue to bestow upon him, despite his expressed powerlessness, the authority to decide the fate of the Oswegos and his contract. Eventually, Drummond calls for a meeting with Longwalker to "try to avoid a confrontation." Once the chief arrives, Hammer berates him: "Don't think for a minute that we approve your kind of resistance. It is illegal, and we are prepared to do everything in our power to clear you and your people out." Longwalker pleads for the government to excavate the site to "see what you turn up," but Hammer says, "The government doesn't care what turns up." As Hammer presents his government employer as an insensitive and self-serving force bent on bullying, Drummond's benevolence shines even brighter.

"I do happen to care," Drummond explains, "what might be on that site." Staunchly believing "there must be a solution to this, something that will satisfy" everyone, Drummond then has an epiphany. Seated between the two opposing forces, the mediator describes what he calls a "compromise":

DRUMMOND (*draws*): Let me try and sketch this for you. The building will be on stilts. That way, it will be standing over the burial site, that way we can preserve the sacred ground. And we can open up the inside to the sky with an atrium or with a courtyard for an Indian museum. What do you think of that, Chief?

LONGWALKER: There's only one thing I don't like about that idea.
DRUMMOND: What's that?
LONGWALKER (*smiles*): That I didn't think of it.

His envy that he "didn't think of" Mr. Drummond's solution undercuts the work of prominent Native leaders who think for themselves and are obviously capable of making important decisions concerning the interests of their peoples and nations. Longwalker's disturbing playful shame and submission to a settler character's agency counter his previous offscreen determination to stop construction and the real struggles for indigenous self-determination. Meanwhile, the heroic settler's children congratulate him. "Hey, Dad," the honorary Oswego declares, "you must be the one who put the 'pow' in 'pow wow'!" Hammer is not so quickly convinced about the museum; so, in an extended paternalistic move, Drummond says his "company will pick up the tab for that. It's deductible." He humbly adds that "settling a potentially explosive situation without violence" may even garner Hammer "a commendation," which appeases Hammer and further distances Drummond from taking credit for his resolution and establishing his place as a self-determining settler do-gooder.

After all the smiles and agreements, handshakes and pats on the back, not one character comments that the "stilts" will still touch the ground and that the building and museum housing Oswego relics will hover over what still may be a sacred burial ground! That Longwalker approves, and without further pleas, as earlier in the episode, to "dig deeper" and "see what you turn up," suggestively goes against a lyric from the sitcom's theme: "What might be right for you, may not be right for some." In this case, the line eventually translates into something like "What is right for me, is also right for you," especially when sung from Drummond's perspective of settler self-determination.[77]

After "Burial Ground," the Drummonds did not interact again with the Oswegos or, for that matter, any other Indians. A ghosting effect, though, would follow them west in 1996. Gary Coleman and Conrad Bain, who portrayed Arnold and Phillip Drummond, respectively, reprised their characters' roles very briefly in the series finale of *The Fresh Prince of Bel-Air*. The father and son show interest in purchasing the starring family's mansion. When character Will Smith, the sitcom's starring "prince" who does not want to move, concocts a story that it was built over a "haunted Indian burial ground" that features a nightly "wailing of the dead," the Drummonds remain undeterred, echoing their fearless days in the early 1980s.[78] If only Mr. Drummond had even remotely believed Will's tale, then perhaps the millionaire mediator of self-determination could have slightly reconfigured his previous solution with the Oswegos: "The mansion will be on stilts!"

Conclusion: November 16–24, 1990

The contentious battles over indigenous remains and burial sites in *Barney Miller* and *Diff'rent Strokes* circuitously found a nonfictional legislative tangibility in the Native American Graves Protection and Repatriation Act (NAGPRA). After decades of critical work by indigenous activists and allies, President George H. W. Bush signed NAGPRA into law on November 16, 1990. Designed "to protect burials, sacred objects, and funerary objects on federal and tribal lands," NAGPRA also "disallows trafficking of Indian skeletal remains, allows American Indian remains and sacred objects held by museums and federal agencies to be repatriated to tribes, and requires federally funded institutions to release inventories of their human skeletons to tribes."[79] For James Long in *Barney Miller*, he might consider NAGPRA to be the result of his readiness for protest and jail to stir up publicity and awareness of issues that are at the core of NAGPRA. For John Longwalker in *Diff'rent Strokes*, NAGPRA might be chalked up to the fast-thinking work of non-Native negotiators like Drummond who showcase their cerebral and financial clout for saving the day. Yet as numerous scholars continue to address, NAGPRA also is a contentious and limiting piece of legislation, influenced in part by media portrayals, fictional and nonfictional, of Native Peoples and self-determination.[80]

NAGPRA became a major highlight amid an unkind year of major news stories in Indian Country. Within a week of NAGPRA's passing, the *New York Times* published Robert H. White's article "Indians' New Harvest." Before discussing a series of modern economic coups for indigenous nations and communities, he summarized "the negative accounts [that] still outweighed the positive depictions" in mainstream media coverage of Native Peoples.[81] "The only news," White began, "to travel from Indian country to the major media in 1990 has been news of disaster: a violent standoff between Mohawks and Government officials in Quebec; fatal gun battles over casino gambling at the St. Regis reservation in New York State; the ignoble fall of Peter MacDonald from the helm of the Navajo Nation. America has been saturated with images of incompetent Indian leadership and harebrained business schemes."[82]

NAGPRA also entered the political landscape on the eve of an action-packed week of pop culture Indianness that suggested more affinity with imagined, romanticized, and exoticized Indians of the distant past than with an awareness of the political, social, and cultural realities of today. First, after a slow decade for cinematic Indians in the 1980s, Hollywood found a renewed interest and fascination with Indians that may have resonated with fans of "The Brady Braves." On November 21, the day after the Dallas Cowboys defeated the Washington Redskins 27–17 on Thanksgiving, director Kevin Costner's eventual seven-time Oscar winner *Dances with Wolves* premiered across the United States. The film set the new standard of settler-going-Indian, this time of Lieutenant John Dunbar, portrayed by Costner, who leaves his Civil War outfit and joins Lakotas during the 1860s. Dunbar metamorphoses into Dances with Wolves, falls in love with the Lakotas' lone white female captive, and, at the film's conclusion, goes away with his new love and leaves behind the tribe, his newfound people, to a pending cultural destruction. The closing on-screen message leaves viewers to imagine the subsequent offscreen doom: "Thirteen years later, their homes destroyed, their buffalo gone, the last band of free Sioux submitted to white authority at Fort Robinson, Nebraska. The great horse culture of the plains was gone and the American frontier was soon to pass into history."[83]

Costner's movie grossed over $184 million in U.S. theaters. In comparison, *Last of the Mohicans* (1992), another historical film with the vanishing race trope, garnered approximately $75.5 million. U.S. sales of the less-romanticized historical Canadian film *Black Robe* (1992) were slightly more than $8 million. *Powwow Highway* (1989), starring Cayuga actor Gary Farmer in a story about contemporary Native Peoples with brief nods to AIM, grossed less than $250,000. *Thunderheart* (1992), another contemporary-based Indian film but starring another settler actor, Val Kilmer, as a mixed Anglo-Lakota in a Hollywood version of an AIM-like setting, grossed over $22 million. The immensely popular reception of *Dances with Wolves*, which ultimately grossed $424 million worldwide in theaters, greatly overshadows other films of the time with Native representations. To some extent, Costner's work became the 1990s cinematic response to the 1970s book *Bury My Heart at Wounded Knee*. Devon Mihesuah notes that "countless Americans and Europeans adore the movie *Dances with Wolves* because it depicts Plains tribes exactly the way fans prefer to think of them—handsome, buffalo-hunting, and tipi-living (and didn't address the messier reservation period that makes them feel guilty)."[84]

Three days later, on November 24, NBC showcased its own cultural blinders by airing a sitcom episode that reads like a summary of the recognizably Indian from the previous four decades. Nearly twenty years after the Bradys' adoption, settler star Zack Morris makes his first and last red-face performance in *Saved by the Bell* when an Indian named Chief Henry, portrayed by Chiricahua Apache actor Dehl Berti, surfaces in Southern California to transform Bayside High School's great white hope into the Indian "Running Zack." As the most popular teenager at Bayside, Zack is known for his chic (dyed) blond hair, good looks, clever schemes, quick comebacks, low grades, and numerous girlfriends. In "Running Zack," he is set to compete in the hundred-yard dash in a track meet against archrival Valley High—if he passes his family tree school project.[85] Over the course of the episode, Zack undergoes a racial makeover from perpetuating ignorance and degradation of Native Peoples to becoming "educated" on and temporarily proud of his newly found Nez Perce heritage. As a representative of the early 1990s multicultural relationship between settlers and Natives, "Running Zack" joins a long list of Hollywood productions demonstrating non-Native America's renewed fascination with its original inhabitants. At the same time, the (mis)education of Zack appears to be an attempt by *Saved by the Bell*, akin to efforts by *The Brady Bunch*, to educate and to bolster pro-Indian support from television audiences.

The episode almost runs the gamut of tropes and stereotypes, particularly during Zack's first non-researched presentation in which non-Natives play Indian, use markers for war paint, speak monotone lines like "Need meat . . . me hungry," self-identify as Cherokee, conjecture Cherokees originate from California, and position Indians as primarily in the past, all mostly performed tongue-in-cheek to set up a subsequent supposedly informed presentation. To educate Zack, *Saved by the Bell* introduces the mysterious and quirky loner Indian, Chief Henry, who readily accepts and accommodates a stranger's (Zack's) story about finding a family photo of a person whom Zack claims "must be" a distant Indian relative. Henry also presumably provides Zack, for his second school presentation, with the Indian costume of Hollywood headdress and buckskin and instruction to fold arms and talk stoically. Starting his new presentation with a solemn "My name is Running Zack," a name given to him by Henry, the newly found Indian adds a heavy dose of romanticized rhetoric as he quotes Hin-mah-too-yah-lat-kekt/Chief Joseph's immortalized 1877 "I will fight no more forever" speech. An earlier close-up of Zack's family picture, however, shows the person to be Allalimya Takanin/Looking Glass, not, as Chief Henry claims, "Whispering Wind." Looking Glass reportedly refused to surrender, as Chief Joseph had finally done, and continued to fight but was killed the same day Chief Joseph delivered his speech, historical details that, you might say, could seriously alter Zack's presentation.[86]

To further its television of a settler-centered occupation of Indianness, *Saved by the Bell* concludes with an invocation of the vanishing Indian trope. After Zack learns that Chief Henry, who had shown no desire to die or signs of illness, has suddenly died, Chief Henry returns in Zack's dream (yes, perhaps symbolizing a "vision") to encourage "Running Zack" to do his best in the track meet. When Zack asks, "Why'd you have to die?" Chief Henry, dressed in a heavenly white suit, does not explain that settler writers have been erasing indigenes from stories for hundreds of years, especially after their work to help settlers is complete. He does not say that sitcoms like *Saved by the Bell* continue the long-standing televisual work of rescripting indigenous-settler histories and modern-day relations to keep the settler superior at the contemporary forefront and the indigenous inferior in the distant past. Looking upward, Chief Henry just says, "They don't give you much choice up there." Then, extending the tone of cultural doom in the sitcom's invocation of Chief Joseph's speech, the elder Indian vanishes. Having completed his purpose of substantiating Zack's transformation into Running Zack, Chief Henry leaves the newly found Nez Perce descendant who has now become the only on-screen Indian in *Saved by the Bell*.[87]

Sitcoms' failure to be progressive beyond a few moments of footage supported their subsequent failure to represent *Native* self-determination. Sitcoms' facade of representing the recognizably Indian as recognizably Native overshadowed the moments of potential for a genuinely and consistently new trail of representations. The sitcoms also attempted to screen, as in air, televisions of Indian-settler equality and reciprocal relations even as they tried to screen, as in hide, the compliancy and very limited agency of the Indians. Evoking the era's political atmosphere of self-determination in Indian affairs, settler self-determination over the course and direction of story lines and resolutions pervaded producers' televisions of the recognizably Indian. Mike Brady, not the grandfather Chief Eagle Cloud, advises runaway Jimmy Pakaya to embrace his Indianness and aspirations to be an astronaut. In return for helping Jimmy to "decide" to return home, the chief adopts the whole Brady bunch into the tribe. In *Barney Miller's* "The Indian," Wojo ultimately gives the OK (against police protocol) to Mr. Ten Fingers to die in Central Park. In "Bones," a settler archaeologist finally decides to press charges against the Indian for stealing back stolen indigenous remains. In *Diff'rent Strokes*, the most explicit episode featuring anti-indigenous self-determination, Mr. Drummond determines the conflict's resolution, leaving Chief Longwalker to regret, but with a smile, "that I [the Indian leader] didn't think of it." In *Saved by the Bell*, Zack Morris, like Costner's character among Lakota characters in *Dances with Wolves*, becomes *the* Indian in the wake of Chief Henry's vanishing act.

Unlike the one-episode Indians in this and the previous chapter who came and went, up next is a recurring indigenous character who arguably became U.S. television's most complex indigenous sitcom character, both on- and offscreen: the loving father, New Age healer, former rock 'n' roll roadie, and emerging children's entertainer John Redcorn in the animated sitcom *King of the Hill*.

CHAPTER THREE

The Neo-Indian in
King of the Hill

During a 2010 visit with students at his alma mater Our Lady of the Lake University in San Antonio, actor Jonathan Joss said, "*King of the Hill* . . . has been one of my favorite things I have done for the reason that it's known, it's a piece of history, it's changed the way people look at Native Americans a little bit." He paused, then added with a sly grin, "good *and* bad."¹ As the voice of recurring *King of the Hill* character John Redcorn III from 1998 to 2009, Joss spoke fervently, coolly, and ambiguously on the animated sitcom's popularity, televisual heritage, and intersecting politics of representations and audience reception of the indigenous. Considering Redcorn's marginal status in approximately three dozen episodes and visual absence in over two hundred others, Joss's descriptor "a little bit" sounds apt.² Collectively, though, Redcorn's appearances paint a portrait of arguably the most developed and complex indigenous character in U.S. sitcom history, thanks in critical part, as I will discuss, to the on- and offscreen work of Joss. At the same time, to think of Redcorn, a cartoon character whom audiences mostly do *not* see on screen, as the most human and multidimensional Indian in the genre is a disheartening and stark reminder of the history of indigenous representations in network television. Yet there is far more to Redcorn than the broadcasted version. What follows is a project in centering this marginal character, namely an on- and offscreen representational genealogy of John Redcorn as developed and shaped by *King of the Hill* producers, including Joss, in the context of tribal televisions of a contemporary neo-Indian identity.

By "neo-Indian," I mean a new and contemporary Indian character who simultaneously moves about in the shadows of Indianness as he or she searches for, but never fully grasps, something representationally "new," especially something recognizably Native, within twenty-first-century media. As a liminal figure, the neo-Indian complicates indigenous representations by searching and struggling for a breakthrough recognizably Native status in the sitcom genre against production forces and a generic tradition that mandate representational settler superiority over recognizably Indian inferiority. For Redcorn (and Joss), he searched throughout the series for an elusive love, happiness, and satisfaction by way of his relations (namely his son, Joseph) and his shifting entrepreneurial work. In the intertwined politics of race, representation, and American network television, he made progress over the years, but the specter of the Hollywood Indian, coupled with a settler-determining community in the production and story lines of *King of the Hill*, kept an unsettling presence. Still, Redcorn (and Joss) pressed on and attempted to break through a largely unkind and unflattering history of representations of the indigenous, including those analyzed earlier from the 1950s to early 1990s. As a new Indian marked with an underlying televisual version of what Homi Bhabha calls "sly civility," Redcorn is an ambiguous character whose representations of slyness and civility—sited in Joss-Redcorn's ambivalent responses to the settler-dominated universe of *King of the Hill*—repeat and reinforce televisions of the recognizably Indian but also break representational ground in later seasons for what constitutes American televisual indigeneity.[3] How these dueling processes of submission and resistance play out and overlap each other on- and offscreen are my main focus.

I locate my critique at several sites, including *King of the Hill* broadcasts and archives and Joss-Redcorn's offscreen travels. Analyzed intertextually and paratextually, the broadcasts, archives, and Joss's multimedia work open up possibilities to alter critiques and understandings of the recognizably Indian, at least "a little bit." In the case of *King of the Hill*, the production of Redcorn signals the emergence of a new Indian in sitcoms, one whose *recurring* on-screen presence (a rarity for indigenous characters in the history of American television) and absence (the norm) build up a genealogical case study to map and analyze but also whose representational variances in utterance and depiction show Redcorn as an ambivalent new Indian.

The term "new Indian" has been stated elsewhere, usually to describe a new or next generation of Native Peoples who are recognized new leaders, activists, and warriors of the twentieth and twenty-first centuries. In his 1968 book *The New Indians*, Stan Steiner turns to Native activists, thinkers, and leaders like Vine Deloria Jr. (Standing Rock Sioux) and Mel Thom (Paiute) to illustrate that the new Indians were (and are) Red Power members who "had become visible" and unashamed to be Native as they fought (and fight) socially and politically for the right to live indigenously. In the words of "fancy dance revolutionary" Clyde Warrior (Ponca), "new Indianness" is "a fresh air of new honesty, and integrity, a fresh air of new Indian idealism, a fresh air of a new Greater Indian America." In Elizabeth Cook-Lynn's 2007 *New Indians, Old Wars*, new Indians are twenty-first-century Indigenous Peoples, such as American Indians and Palestinians, who "resist the colonial effort to seize their lands and resources; make them beggars; convert them to an unknown religion, Christianity; and destroy them economically."[4]

King of the Hill producers attempted to construct Redcorn as a character who knows, supports, and embodies this new Indianness of what Kevin Bruyneel characterizes as "postcolonial resistance."[5] Within the scope of the burden of representation (Redcorn was one of the extremely few recurring indigenous characters in U.S. network television, all genres included, at the time), Redcorn was more than just a cartoon character as *King of the Hill* deployed him to tune in and around current indigenous politics and topics.[6] He entered the televisual landscape as President Bill Clinton signed Executive Order No. 13084, "Consultation and Coordination with Indian Tribal Governments," and exited *King of the Hill* as President Barack Obama vowed to renew and improve upon Clinton's collaborative initiatives.[7] During the series, in between the presidential pledges, Redcorn endured struggles—sometimes alone, sometimes in partnership with nonindigenous characters—that resonate, though in very uneven ways, with current issues in Indian Country like land reclamation, economic sovereignty, gaming, education, religious freedom, and, as a running thread through all of these, cultural identity, all of which typically go unrecognized and uncommented on by most of the American public.[8] At the risk of sounding overly dramatic, never before had so much been asked of an Indian character in American sitcoms, to stand in as a sort of *everyIndian*.[9] In hindsight, the sitcom Indians in *I Love Lucy*, *The Beverly Hillbillies*, *The Brady Bunch*, *Diff'rent Strokes*, and *Saved by the Bell* had it relatively easy in their one-off roles of recognizably Indian inferiority, nonsensical dancing, submissiveness, feigned indigeneity, and vanishing.

Although Redcorn shows signs of occupying the new Indianness of cultural resistance and restoration, *King of the Hill* does not, nor appears to want or even know how to, shed the spectral shadows and expectations of the recognizably Indian in a settler-dominated, U.S.- and Texas-centric Arlen community that vastly suppresses indigeneity. It would take the series nearly five years before it significantly, albeit slowly, started to tune in relevant issues in Indian Country and began to recognize that an Indian in Arlen, Texas, could contribute more to story lines, or in Joss's estimation, do more than "grunt" and "jump out of windows."[10] But like a microcosmic televisual illustration of federal Indian policy within U.S. politics, of indigenous populations within the vast majority of predominantly non-indigenous towns and cities across the United States, and of competing perceptions and expectations of constituted indigenous performance, Joss and Redcorn were vastly outnumbered by non-Natives in their real-life and televisual settings and repeatedly found themselves problematically limited in a genre, network, industry, and nation-state that very rarely recognize and represent something resembling the recognizably Native of informed indigenous resistance and survivance. For decades, the sitcom genre in the United States and its decision makers, conventions, and settler colonial politics have disavowed admission to representations of Cook-Lynn's "new Indian" and Bruyneel's "postcolonial Indianness." What contemporary producers construct in their place is, at best, their own brand of neo-Indianness, such as illustrated by Redcorn, whose actions and rhetoric position him in an unstable representational space buttressed against the boundaries of the recognizably Indian and recognizably Native in U.S. television.

Through critical analysis of the tribal televisions in the sitcom's aired episodes, I address how representations of Redcorn reproduce *and* challenge the colonial discourses informing the recognizably Indian and indigenous-settler relations. How, I ask, do the producers start to recontextualize yet also reproduce on-screen sitcom traditions of the recognizably Indian, to the extent that Redcorn eventually becomes a version of the sitcom's new Indian and, in effect, bridges some of the recognizably Indian–recognizably Native representational gap? Like the descriptor "neo-Indian," the sitcom's televisions of the tribal depend on subtly and explicitly reinforcing the recognizably Indian so that Redcorn is positioned contingently upon mainstream settler audience expectations even as he starts to disrupt, or perhaps so that he *can* disrupt, what non-Native and Native audiences likely would have expected at the time from mainstream TV representations of Indians.

To situate Redcorn as a reconstructed subject of neo-Indianness, I also turn to the *King of the Hill* Archives at Texas State University in San Marcos, located approximately halfway between Joss's home in San Antonio and *King of the Hill* creator Mike Judge's residence in Austin. As a critical site for comparative offscreen/on-screen analysis, the archives house paratextual "research notes, story pitches, outlines, and drafts of scripts" for

King of the Hill episodes, each of which is also arguably a paratext within the "text," or the "entire storyworld as we know it," in this case, *King of the Hill.*[11] By including archival and aired paratexts, "textual entities" that "create . . . manage . . . [and] fill texts with meanings," I concur with Jonathan Gray that scholars can tune in a larger picture of a television series via its on- and offscreen representations and discourses.[12] For my purposes here, the *King of the Hill* Archives reveal alternative and eventually rejected directions for Redcorn that, if accepted, would have expanded his character in interesting though troubling ways. The rejected and accepted ideas and internal creative differences evoke a set of creative representational boundaries over how to represent sitcom Indianness in the form of competing readjusted televisions and, when considering producers' revised drafts, tele-*re*-visions of Redcorn.

Producers of *King of the Hill* include co-creators Judge and Greg Daniels and executive producer Jim Dauterive (who donated the archival materials and loaned his family name to character Hank Hill's friend Bill Dauterive). An additional but uncredited producer I have in mind for critical analysis of Redcorn is Jonathan Joss. Of White Mountain Apache heritage, Joss shaped Redcorn's on-screen representations in efforts to move toward the "good" and away from the "bad," which I translate as televisually *progressive* and *regressive*, respectively.[13] In the context of Redcorn's portrayals, progressive and regressive are slippery and highly subjective concepts as Redcorn's "new" representations, shaping the bulk of his neo-Indian status, are not exclusive to either ideological camp.

As stated on the actor's personal website, *King of the Hill* used Redcorn "in an attempt to educate the public regarding Native American views." Although Joss is credited in episodes only for voice-overs, he is partly responsible for the televisual indigenous education as he repeatedly challenged offscreen a narrative of "John Redcorn," to quote from the official *King of the Hill* "bible," as just "a Native American healer." Penned by Dauterive, the description briefly continues, "He and Nancy are lovers. Everyone in town knows about Nancy and John Redcorn, except Dale."[14] Joss went on to influence *King of the Hill* producers in later episodes to move Redcorn beyond a healing occupation and the extramarital affair with Nancy Gribble. His multifaceted media work *as* Redcorn in music recordings (Joss's lead vocals and lyrical visions of Redcorn in his offscreen Red Corn Band), interviews (for example, Joss's hour-long interview in Redcorn character for the call-in radio program *Native America Calling*), and a personal website (jonathanjoss.com, almost an e-stand-in for what could be called johnredcorn.com) suggests several new interpretive routes for thinking through representations of Redcorn and his cultural work. In tandem, this work further blurs the boundaries between televisual animation and real-life realities and personas when recognizing that Redcorn also shaped (and still shapes) Joss, prompting one reporter to observe, "Actor Jonathan Joss credits a cartoon character for letting him discover who he is."[15] Redcorn's occupational struggles in the series may reflect Joss's own challenges and frustrations as a modern-day Native actor in the beast known as Hollywood. In turn, Joss's work in shaping and performing "new" representations of Redcorn for Judge and other producers warrants credit for expanding Redcorn's presence and assisting in providing viewers with a mixed education of "good and bad" on and around Native issues. In some ways, particularly in the actor's negotiated efforts for obtaining a share of "representational sovereignty" with the character, this chapter is as much about Joss as it is about Redcorn.[16] The conclusion further supports this observation by looking at contemporary moves by Joss to keep Redcorn alive beyond contemporary syndicated reruns of King of the Hill.

In what follows, I look to synthesize these sites of analysis—broadcasts, archives, and production—and politicized tensions into a discussion that complicates perceptions of contemporary indigenous portrayals in sitcoms as primarily one-dimensional and cultureless caricatures. I also challenge readings of John Redcorn as predominantly a sexualized adulterer and insignificant character who, at most, might receive a quick reference in a publication as "the Indian New Age healer sleeping with Nancy." To fill in part of the picture of the "good and bad" swirling around Redcorn, I follow certain representational paths in Redcorn's travels from 1997 to 2012: his televised early years during roughly the first four seasons of very limited screen time, early rejected story lines, Redcorn's eventual expanded story arc in land reclamation and business ventures, and Joss's unorthodox and entrepreneurial on- and offscreen performative roles in his character's comparable unorthodox on- and offscreen expansion in entrepreneurial endeavors. In all, this case study charts a fragmented history of one character and the forces behind his production in an attempt to consider the challenges, frustrations, and breakthroughs embodied in the colliding performative moves by Redcorn, Joss, and King of the Hill.

Fox, Animated Sitcoms, and Racialized Discourse

In their essay "The Flintstones to Futurama: Networks and Prime Time Animation," Wendy Hilton-Morrow and David McMahan identify several conditions for the reemergence of animated sitcoms in the 1990s, also known as the "second prime time animation boom," after the prime-time original runs of animated sitcoms *The Flintstones* and *The Jetsons* in the early 1960s. First, "animated programs," along with former programs in other TV genres, "were . . . syndicated and aired during the late afternoons and early evenings" on cable. Second, "the new generation of network executives" and "adult members of the viewing audience" had grown up as "fans of animation." *Simpsons* co-creator Matt Groening says, "One of the reasons *The Simpsons* got on the air in the first place was that there were finally some executives who remembered watching *The Flintstones* and *The Jetsons* and *Johnny Quest* at night as children." Additional factors, Hilton-Morrow and McMahan contend, include improved animation quality and the production of non–Saturday morning animation. But "perhaps the most important factor," they say, "was the introduction of a new network," Fox, which would eventually become home to numerous prime-time animated series.[17]

In efforts to reach a young audience and to join the Big 3—networks NBC, CBS, and ABC—Fox garnered initial success in the late 1980s with the live-action sitcoms *Married with Children* and *It's Garry Shandling's Show* and sketch comedies *In Living Color* and *The Tracey Ullman Show*, the latter of which first screened a yellow-hued family named the Simpsons in 1987 in one-minute snippets around commercial breaks. In December 1989, Fox debuted its half-hour series *The Simpsons*. By the early 1990s, with *The Simpsons* leading the way, Fox solidified its position as the fourth major network. The other networks tried but failed to capitalize on the success of *The Simpsons* with new prime-time animated programs. Meanwhile, the cable network MTV, upon seeing Mike Judge's submitted 1992 animation short "Frog Baseball" starring male teens Beavis and Butthead, quickly hired Judge to develop it into a series that first ran until 1997, when he left MTV and signed with Fox to create, along with *Simpsons* writer Greg Daniels, Fox's next animated sitcom hit, *King of the Hill*.[18]

Following the adventures of series star Hank Hill—intertextually labeled the "anti–Andy Griffith" by Judge, who voiced Hank—and his family and friends (including Redcorn) in fictional small-town Arlen, Texas, as based on a Dallas–Fort Worth suburb where Judge once resided, *King of the Hill* premiered on January 12, 1997, in between episodes of already-popular series *The Simpsons* and *The X-Files*.[19] An original member of Fox's "animation domination" lineup (along with *The Simpsons*, *Family Guy*, and *American Dad*) starting in 2005 and a five-time nominee and one-time recipient of the Emmy for Outstanding Animated Program, *King of the Hill* was eventually canceled in 2009, possibly to clear room for *Family Guy* spin-off *The Cleveland Show,* and Fox aired the final new episodes in 2010.

During its thirteen-season run, *King of the Hill* routinely conversed with racialized discourse. In addition to representations of whiteness, especially in the context of white Texan masculinities,[20] varying characters of color appear in every single episode, yet always marginally in secondary or guest-starring roles. The Souphanousinphones—married couple Minh and Khan and daughter Khan/Connie—are the Hills' Laotian American neighbors. Khan, an anagram of Hank, often calls Hank and his friends "hillbillies" and "rednecks," but he also occasionally joins forces with Hank to resolve conflicts. Ted Wassonasong, appearing in a few episodes, is an elitist Laotian American whom Khan attempts to impress. Latino character Enrique is Hank's propane coworker who asks Hank, more an acquaintance than a dear friend, to speak at his daughter's quinceañera. Octavio, a Latino with a giant Rob Zombie tattoo on his chest, is initially Dale's burly hired-but-failed hitman and subsequent go-to guy for an assortment of outrageous actions. Roger "Booda" Sack, first voiced by Chris Rock, was an African American stand-up comedian and later one of Hank's coworkers at Strickland Propane. In one episode, Bernie Mac voiced an African American water heater repairman who was attacked by Hank's dog, Ladybird. After most of Arlen deemed Hank racist, Ladybird—generally as lethargic as Jed's hound, Duke, in *The Beverly Hillbillies*—attacked a white repairman, causing the Hills to realize that Ladybird detested, as did Hank, anyone attempting to fix what the anal-retentive Hank could not and providing a rather convenient resolution to black-white tensions that downplays real instances of racism.[21]

Fox has long expressed interest, like other networks, in expanding diversity, including racially and ethnically, in the televisual landscape. Since 2001, Fox has held its Writers Initiative program to provide opportunities for "experienced writers with unique voices, backgrounds, life and professional experiences that reflect the diverse perspectives of the audiences we [Fox] create for."[22] Notably, among the nominating organizations for program applicants is the Sundance Native American and Indigenous Program. On-screen indigenous representation in Fox series, however, has been sporadic and slow. Floyd Red Crow Westerman (Lakota) and Dakota House (Cree) appeared in a few episodes of *The X-Files*.[23] Representations of indigenes in *Malcolm in the Middle* include recurring Alaska Native character Piama Tananahaakna (though portrayed by Filipina American actress Emy Coligado) and two different Indian roles played by Michael Horse (Yaqui, Mescalero Apache, and Zuni descent). After a couple of aired episodes of *Malcolm in the Middle* featuring Indian casinos, the Oneida Nation honored the sitcom in 2002. "They got the portrayal of Indian country just right," Oneida Nation representative Ray Halbritter explains, "so we thought we'd try to reward shows that have a positive portrayal and focus on that and not just the negative." For Indian casinos on a mainstream network to be the setting for "positive" and "just right" portrayals sounds unsettling, more so when celebrating a series on the same network that aired the anti-indigenous *Family Guy* episode "The Son Also Draws" in 1999, in which the starring settler character out-Indians the sitcom's indigenously ignorant and capitalistic casino-running Indians.[24] Like *Family Guy*, other Fox animated sitcoms *The Simpsons*, *Futurama*, and *American Dad* have included recognizably Indian characters but did not employ Native actors for the roles. The most recurring and long-lasting indigenous characters, then, on Fox (and in North American sitcom history) have been John Redcorn and his biological son, Joseph John Gribble.[25]

John Redcorn: The Early Years of a Sitcom Indian

In season 1, Redcorn was voiced by and possibly modeled in appearance after Yaqui actor Victor Aaron, whose lean physique and lengthy hair could be seen in such productions as the 1993 film *Geronimo: An American Legend*, television miniseries *Dead Man's Walk*, and television drama *Dr. Quinn, Medicine Woman*.[26] For the 1998 male Indian calendar "Native Visions," Aaron is featured on the cover and inside as Mr. September, reporter Marley Shebala of the *Navajo Times* says, with "long dark hair" and a "black leather vest with silver clasps, a four-tiered bone choker, a silver bracelet on his right wrist and a smaller inlaid stone bracelet and watch on his left wrist."[27] After his character's very brief and nonspeaking debut in the pilot episode (Redcorn waits for Nancy outside of her house in his Jeep Wrangler), Aaron first voices Redcorn in the second scene of episode three, "The Order of the Straight Arrow." Stepping out of his tan Jeep, Redcorn sports what would be common attire signifiers (and reminiscent of Aaron's looks) throughout the series: bone choker, faux arrowhead earrings, light green T-shirt, dark suede vest, and white Sergio Valente jeans. The Redcorn look of a tall athletic build is draped partly by long and flowing dark hair that is prone to suddenly blow in the wind when he speaks, like an animated version of the *Dances with Wolves* Lakota character Wind in His Hair.[28] Redcorn evokes the quintessential Plains warrior gracing the covers of romance novels, particularly when *King of the Hill* depicted a topless Redcorn abounding with rippling muscles in several episodes and, in his last episode, as a topless self-embodied logo for his children's entertainment video production company.

In "The Order of the Straight Arrow," John Redcorn's appearance lasts for only sixty-seven seconds, but his visible and discursive presence marks something different and "new," yet familiar and dated, within the on-screen genealogy of sitcom Indians. Hank and his three best friends, Bill Dauterive, Dale Gribble, and Boomhauer, stand outside, drink beer (as they do in most episodes), and discuss an upcoming camping trip involving Hank's son and other boys for a Straight Arrow retreat, where "Indian Guides" mesh with "Boy Scouts," according to the episode's director Klay Hall.[29] Looking for, as Hank says, "new material" for the retreat, they spot Redcorn driving up and exiting his Jeep in front of the Gribbles' residence.

HANK: Hey, Dale. Uh, there's your wife's, uh . . .
BILL: Healer.
HANK: Yeah. John Redcorn. Let's get some funny Indian stuff to do.
BILL: Hey, John Redcorn.
REDCORN: Hank, Dale, Bill, Boomhauer.
DALE: We've got this Order of the Straight Arrow retreat tomorrow and I was wondering—
REDCORN: I'd be honored to look after your wife.
DALE: Oh. Gee, thanks. But what I was really wondering is if you had some good Indian stuff for the ceremony around the campfire.
REDCORN: Mmm. Our rituals are considered sacred and are passed down only in the nation.
HANK: Oh, well, that don't bother us.
DALE: Hell no. We'll take a sacred one.
REDCORN (*camera zooms in, hair blows in the breeze amid Indian flute music*): There is a very ancient ceremony that I learned from my grandfather. We call upon the sacred We-mawt-uhn-aw and we ask him to breathe life into our spirit bag.[30]
HANK (*jots notes*): Let's see. Spirit bags. Wematanya. [*Glances at Redcorn, then continues writing*] Funny looking headband. Ah, the boys are gonna eat this stuff up.
REDCORN (*extreme close-up on raging eyes*): The spirit bag is very sacred. You should not make light.
DALE: I like how you say everything's sacred. That's funny, too. Let's do that, Hank.

Rather than engage the settler characters further, "Redcorn, fed up, walks off, unnoticed," as written in the script. He exits not only the scene but

John Redcorn in
King of the Hill.

the rest of the episode. In addition to more allusions of John and Nancy's affair in this brief exchange, a consistently somber Redcorn sounds culturally grounded, recognizes an elder relative (presumably the first John Redcorn), and shares knowledge of "a very ancient ceremony." Rather than resist Hank's flippant disregard for the "sacred," he curiously accommodates Hank with ceremonial material to appropriate in their Indian play at the retreat and, in the process, sounds defeated.

Earlier drafts and notes of the episode, however, reveal Redcorn not as a willful discloser but a trickster accommodationist, whereby he is willing to compromise with Hank by satisfying white expectations of Indianness through trickery while not disclosing anything sacred or exiting angrily, as he does in the broadcasted episode. Early on in production, Cheryl Holliday, the credited head writer of "The Order of the Straight Arrow," shows Hank and Redcorn as increasingly cognizant of performance and appropriation. She portrays Redcorn as outsmarting white audiences and depicts Hank as partly in the indigenous know with both supporting and continuing the trickery at the retreat. In the pre-draft "storynotes" document, Holliday says Hank wants "anything Redcorn has that can make it [the retreat] *authentic*" (emphasis in original).[31] Then in the first draft, she simply notes, "Tallequah Powow [*sic*]" after Hank asks Redcorn for "anything that's not so sacred" and adds, "We're not going to really do 'em, you know—just for the kids."[32] In the second draft, Holliday begins to clarify the powwow reference when Redcorn says, "I'll give you the ones we do for the white man at the Tallequah Powwow every year." To which Hank concurs, "That'd be fine." Whereas Redcorn never actually travels to or references Oklahoma at any point in the series, Holliday initially locates Redcorn off-camera in Tahlequah, capital of the Cherokee Nation of Oklahoma.[33] She pens Redcorn outmaneuvering ignorant white audiences and suggests he may be Cherokee, the largest Native nation and arguably the most oft-cited nation of choice for non-enrollees who claim Indian heritage. However, why would a powwow in Tahlequah, where culturally grounded Cherokees may attend, entail a mere show of antics or even a performance of conforming to white expectations of Indian authenticity? In the second draft, a large handwritten *X* is marked through all references to Tahlequah. Based on the aired episode, I doubt my previous question was a factor (or even a thought) in rejecting the Tahlequah references. In the broadcasted episode, Redcorn is shown as almost unambiguously providing ceremonial content to a disrespectful Hank, in which more of the comedy shifts from earlier drafts to coming from series star Hank, not Redcorn. The final cut opts for a reinforcement of Hank and the others playing Indian and mocking Redcorn's shared information.[34]

The story notes also show Redcorn as more invested in the life of his biological son, Joseph, who appears to never realize he is indigenous. Holliday notes that audiences would first see Redcorn playing baseball with Joseph and then the two holding hands, two actions that never occurred in broadcasted episodes. She also has Redcorn show interest in attending the Straight Arrow retreat, years before a season 6 episode in which Redcorn does follow Joseph on a camping trip to assist in guiding his son on a vision quest and before his first on-screen interaction with Joseph in season 3 (all of thirty-three seconds), in which he gifts his son an old family knife for Joseph's first hunting trip with Dale.[35] In Holliday's second draft of "The Order of the Straight Arrow," Redcorn says, "I'd be honored to attend," instead of the eventually aired line, "I'd be honored to look after your wife."[36] In that critical moment, priority is given to bonding with Joseph, not to the affair with Nancy. Hank, however, says that would be "inappropriate," and Holliday adds, "Dale says it's for fathers and sons only." Then as Dale drives away to the retreat, he throws a cup out of the vehicle "and John Redcorn has a tear in his eye from watching Dale litter," a clear reference to the famous anti-littering commercial of the early 1970s in which Sicilian American actor Iron Eyes Cody sheds a tear in response to the trash on the ground around him. Yet the trash and tear, both dependent on settler notions of ecological Indianness and an actor's Indian performativity, never air in *King of the Hill*. Nor does Redcorn's expressed interest in attending the retreat. By revising the line to "I'd be honored to look after your wife" in the broadcasted "The Order of the Straight Arrow" and thus rejecting unaired ideas of indigenous wit and fatherhood, *King of the Hill* sets into motion, through Redcorn's on-screen debut, the dominant tone and association for many of the character's three dozen appearances over the next thirteen seasons.

Redcorn appears only once more in season 1. At Ugly's Saloon in the fifth episode, Redcorn walks up to the Gribbles and, in Aaron's last line in the series, says, "Dale, I bought you a beer. Mind if I dance with your wife?" As if he owns Nancy, Dale replies, "Take her." A quick drink later, thinking he has outsmarted Redcorn, Dale sneers, "Sucker."[37] The representations of Redcorn over the next four seasons continue to revolve around his adulterous affair with Nancy, their sexual relations coded as migraine treatment sessions conducted through Redcorn's New Age healing practices. Representative of what I have called elsewhere a "limited logic of the sitcom's Indian," Redcorn's limited variability in roles are evident not only in what the writers put forth for Redcorn but also in audience reception. The on-screen Redcorn is reduced primarily to representations of adultery and absent fatherhood with occasional quips and jabs at other characters. Critics in the press and academia as well as fans on Internet message boards tend to glean from such representations a similar overarching message about Redcorn as, in short, the licensed New Age Indian healer sleeping with the neighbor's wife with whom he has a son.[38]

Redcorn's other appearances in the early years shed some new light on the character but are still explicitly tied to his affair with Nancy. In season 3's "Peggy's Headache," a stressed Peggy Hill, unaware of the affair and Redcorn's renowned "healing" techniques with female clients, turns to Redcorn for help. While the episode centers on Peggy, her realization of the affair, and a personal quest to become a writer for the local paper, viewers do see, briefly, an Indian running his own business out of his trailer adorned with a hanging dream catcher, plug-in water fountain, Brookstone massage chair, and burning incense. As he massages Peggy and softly plays a New Age recording of whales, Redcorn cites a popular country music singer for his settler client: "The whales sing of joy and sorrow, of gain and loss, like LeAnn Rimes" (who, incidentally, is purported to have Native heritage). The references to Brookstone and Rimes can be heard as discursive challenges to conventional portrayals of the indigenous in sitcoms, yet they also prompt laughter, what Philip Deloria calls an "ideological chuckle" facilitated "through a thickness of consciousness" dependent on settler-driven descriptive ideologies of the indigenous that produce and reproduce limited perceptions of recognized constitutions of indigeneity. Encouraging a laughter contingent on settler colonial discourse that refuses to associate "real" Indians with modern cultural references and practices, Redcorn's references to chamomile tea and lattes in later seasons suggest producers never fully refrain from making such lines, in the context of a limited settler vantage point, unexpected for the indigenous to utter.[39]

Redcorn may have functioned in *King of the Hill*, especially early on, by playing to and momentarily disrupting settler expectations of performative indigeneity, but his modern-day pop cultural citations were encoded to solicit ideological chuckles, altogether configuring Redcorn as somewhat of a trickster accommodationist with more accommodation than trick. Or to riff on Bhabha's "sly civility" in the context of indigenous-settler relations, as someone with more civilized conformity than resistant slyness.

Representations of Redcorn also suffer from abrupt conspicuous exits and subsequent visual absences, such as in season 1's "The Order of the Straight Arrow." In the season 2 episode "The Arrowhead," in which Joss makes his voice-over debut, Hank goes next door to the Gribbles' home to ask Redcorn, who is in a healing session with Nancy, about an Indian object he has found in the front yard.[40] Initially showcasing Redcorn's insight, the exchange soon returns, in accordance with Redcorn's dominant representation, to his affair with Nancy.

> HANK: Listen, I found this Indian, uh, Native Indian thing in my yard, and I was wondering if you knew what it was.
> REDCORN: It's a tool used for straightening the shaft of an arrow.
> HANK: Uh-huh. In a pinch, though, you could jam it into someone's brainstem, right?
> REDCORN: Yes, but that's true of almost any tool.
> HANK: Well, yeah, sure, I guess.
> REDCORN: A treasure such as this is priceless to my people.
> HANK: Really? What do you suppose it's worth to my people?
> REDCORN: A museum or university might give you $50.
> HANK: $50, huh? Well, that'd get me a new rototiller blade.
> REDCORN: Hank, think about what you're doing. It is wrong to take what belongs to another person and—[41]
> NANCY (*offscreen*): John Redcorn!
> REDCORN (*embarrassed*): Well, food for thought.

In comparison to his first appearance in season 1, Redcorn once again starts to challenge Hank, but this time with an intended irony and humor lacking before in his earnest We-mawt-uhn-aw talk. In "The Arrowhead," Redcorn matter-of-factly counters Hank's savage notion of "brainstem" violence ("that's true of almost any tool") and encourages Hank to reflect on his intentions as cultural usurper before Nancy beckons Redcorn. Redcorn's initial counters to Hank become entangled in a conflation of cultural appropriation and adultery. Echoing his brief appearance in "The Order of the Straight Arrow," Redcorn then disappears from the rest of the episode, save for a few seconds to pick up Nancy in his Jeep for a rendezvous, coded as a migraine workshop trip, to Corpus Christi. The rest of the episode focuses on tensions between a jealous Hank and a self-serving university archaeologist who intellectually sweet-talks Peggy and secures her permission and assistance to dig for more Indian artifacts in the Hills' yard, which Hank, as viewers know, dearly loves and reserves for his John Deere riding lawnmower. In the end, Hank admits he wishes Peggy would spend more time with him before he repeatedly pushes the archaeologist, who says he "could have scored with [Peggy]," into the newly dug large hole.[42]

The Indian object merely helps to propel the triad of narrative conflicts between Hank, Peggy, and the archaeologist. Redcorn shows momentary interest in educating Hank on cultural appropriation, then retreats to his dominant representation and leaves town. While Redcorn also plants the idea for Hank to go to "a museum or university," archival paratexts for "The Arrowhead"—originally titled "Indian Artifact Story" and then "The Indian Giver"—posit several substantial possibilities for Redcorn, which, if not rejected, would have resulted in his first major episode. In the writers Jonathan Aibel and Glenn Berger's pre-draft "Indian Artifact Story Pitch," the episode's earliest printed outline in the *King of the Hill* Archives, Redcorn features prominently but problematically in his still early years as a sitcom Indian. Situated in a limited cooperative role with Hank, the representations of Redcorn gesture toward familiar uneven sitcom iterations of indigenous-settler coexistence.

In the "Story Pitch," Hank finds himself up against, Aibel and Berger note, "academia and government bureaucracy," and his "yard is roped off as a sacred Indian burial ground" after Hank digs up a "pottery shard" or "arrowhead." (In the aired episode, a burial ground is never mentioned.) Hank still turns to Redcorn for assistance but in a more sustained manner. First, in lieu of merely hearing Redcorn calmly caution Hank about his new find, the writers have "John Redcorn getting upset about the artifacts" as the two engage in a tense conversation spurred by Hank's attempt "to sell [an object] to John Redcorn."

REDCORN: You do not understand. You cannot sell me what is already mine. . . . You insult me and my ancestors.

HANK: 30 bucks. Take it or leave it.

REDCORN: This is not a negotiation. A piece like this belongs in a museum.[43]

Redcorn boldly claims the object belongs to him, yet his solution is to house it "in a museum," a stark contrast to his initial outrage and to Natives' historical and ongoing repatriation efforts and calls for museums and universities to return, not possess and preserve, their people's cultural items. Then on the following page, Redcorn all but admits he has previously sold tribal objects to the archaeologist when he advises Hank to proceed with caution: "Do not take his first offer." More damning for Redcorn's cultural integrity is a producer's handwritten note next to Redcorn's line concerning "what is already mine": "looks valuable I sold stuff to univ[ersity] 300 bucks."[44]

In act 3 of the beat sheet for "The Arrowhead," "Hank hears from Redcorn that Native Americans' land was taken—just as Hank's land is being taken. This is interesting [to] Hank. They go off to talk more about it." Once they arrive "at Redcorn's, Hank is interested to learn about history."[45] Hank and Redcorn share narratives of land loss, but to equate the two land thefts drastically downplays the indigenous-settler specificities of broken treaties, violence, assimilation efforts, and racism, not to mention absolves Hank of any personal guilt or responsibility (evocative of the outcome in the aforementioned episode with Bernie Mac) as a contemporary settler living on a piece of land that, according to Aibel and Berger's pitch, was formerly inhabited by Redcorn's grandfather.

When Hank digs in his yard and finds "an old retail sign which reads 'Souvenirs,'" Hank pursues its origins at "the downtown Hall of Records and finds out that his parcel of land was zoned as a souvenir store in the 1920s. . . . John Redcorn's grandfather ran it."[46] Meanwhile, the archaeologists resume digging up Hank's yard and suspect they have found "mysterious and wondrous glyphs" on "an old metal sign of some kind." After Aibel and Berger make a migratory turn toward the highly contested Bering Strait theory—"It bears a striking resemblance," they note, "to Asian text characters and Indio-European writings"—"Hank proves them all wrong by whipping out his garden hose and s[p]raying the dirt off the sign—an old retail sign which reads 'Souvenirs.'"[47] What began as the development of a resolution involving Hank and Redcorn working together soon becomes Hank's show in representing his version of settler self-determination.

Redcorn, however, was not the only indigenous character to intervene in Hank's land dilemma in the pitch. Aibel and Berger posed an additional story line that, if aired, would have introduced several other opportunistic Indian characters. The writers' submission of other Indians is highly unusual, considering that Redcorn's only blood relation ever depicted in any of the 259 episodes of *King of the Hill* is his son, Joseph, and, in one late episode, his previously unknown daughter, Kate. Other relations very briefly reference Redcorn's father (John Redcorn II), grandfather (John Redcorn I), and a sister. For Aibel and Berger to pitch multiple Indian characters could be deemed a feat in itself, yet their Indians quickly slip into a regressive camp of representations.

In the pitch's opening paragraph, Aibel and Berger write, "Maybe Thanksgiving episode: Indians want their land back."[48] Following this thread through Redcorn and several other local Indians who intervene upon Hank's find, the writers emphasize distorted representations in which the Indians cannot escape "jokes" and settler colonial discourse over tradition and modernity. In the pitch's tritely titled section "Native American Givers," they note, "Once the land is declared ancient Indian burial ground—or something like that, the representative of the local Arlen Native American Council shows up, laying claim to the land as sacred Indian territory." The representative declares, "This lands belongs to the people of the Commanche [sic] Tribe . . . Incorporated. (Or Souix [sic] Indian Corporation, Lacota [sic] Corp., Sioux Preservation and Gaming Commission.)" In addition to the emphasis on Indian enterprise over indigenous nationhood to feed into popular perceptions of contemporary Natives, the tribal misspellings and Lakota/Sioux misplacements, reminiscent of the Sioux in Tennessee in the *Green Acres* episode "The Rains Came," suggest ignorance and carelessness by Aibel and Berger. One wonders, though, what to expect from the writers of such non-Native animated films as *Kung Fu Panda* (2008) and *Alvin and the Chipmunks: The Squeakquel* (2009) and the Fox television series *MADtv*.[49] In the aired *King of the Hill* episode, no reference is made to Comanches or Lakotas. In their place, Caddo and Tonkawa are referenced and mispronounced, apparently in all seriousness without correction, by the archaeologist and Peggy, respectively.[50] In the pitch, the writers soon abandon references to the gaming story line, though facets of it will air, as I will explain, in season 9's "Redcorn Gambles with His Future."

Aibel and Berger propose that those on the Arlen Native American Council were not the only Indians depicted as opportunistic. For Redcorn, Aibel and Berger demonstrate near their pitch's conclusion that they were thinking early in the series of how to slightly expand his character. Instead, though, of questioning how his grandfather's land became Hank's land—like Santee Sioux John Trudell's question once on CNN, "How did my land become someone else's country?"—Redcorn focuses on his grandfather's line of work. Standing before Hank, the archaeologists, onlookers, and his grandfather's sign, Redcorn declares, "Since the sun has risen in the east, my people have sold crap to your people." Aibel and Berger tack on, "Maybe Redcorn opens up a new souvenir stand to take advantage of the gawkers." Although *King of the Hill* never broadcasts such, it does go on to feature Redcorn, as I will now explain, in a number of business ventures, some of which are partly attributable to the creative thinking and negotiated performance by the actor Joss.

Redcorn and Joss: Entrepreneurial Endeavors and Indian Ingenuity

During the first four seasons, Redcorn's representational inclusion is recursively dependent on the affair with Nancy. In addition to the episodes cited earlier, six other episodes in seasons 3 and 4 represent or reference his adulterous affair.[51] Most notable is the late season 4 episode "Nancy Boys," which marks a narrative halt to the affair, though references to the tryst persist well into the last season.[52] Although most of "Nancy Boys" revolves around the dissipation of the fifteen-year affair between Nancy and Redcorn as she and Dale suddenly rekindle their marriage, a new political story line over a land claim begins for Redcorn in the closing minutes, which also commences Redcorn's more visible on-screen search for a happiness and fulfillment that are historically very rarely evident or seen as worthy of any attention for Indian characters in American television.

Realizing he and Nancy are through and that he still has "no wife, no land," Redcorn reflects how "over half of Arlen used to belong to my people." When he mentions to Dale a lawsuit he had filed ten years earlier against the Bureau of Indian Affairs, which, he says, "refuse[s] to return the land that is rightfully ours," Dale suggests he go through the Freedom of Information Act (FOIA) to access federal documents. After Dale discusses how he previously (ab)used FOIA "when I took on the IRS for disallowing my status as a tax-exempt church," Redcorn, handing a pad of paper to Dale, asks, "Would you mind?" Rather than reject another land-based collaboration, like between Hank and Redcorn in the production of season 2's "The Arrowhead," Dale and Redcorn now join forces to "[bring] down," Dale salivates, "the federal government." After an indigenous-settler trade—Dale, the antigovernment conspiracy theorist, fills out the

FOIA paperwork while Redcorn, the New Age healer, massages him—the two move toward a strained personal and intercultural reconciliation.

REDCORN: Dale, you are a good man. All of this effort on behalf of my struggle, and you are not even a Native American.

DALE: Isn't it time we put aside our differences? On behalf of the white man, I would like to formally apologize for everything my people have done to your people.

REDCORN: And I would like to apologize for everything I've done to you, [*they shake hands*] uh, and your people.

Evoking the earlier uneven exchange over appropriation between Hank and Redcorn in "The Arrowhead," Dale and Redcorn's exchange of apologies unapologetically equates colonization with an extramarital affair, possibly to assuage the characters' respective guilt over differing, if not incommensurable, circumstances. "It was brought to my attention," Joss would later recall, "that one of the few apologies to the Native American . . . where the white person said I apologize [for] everything I've done to you was on *King of the Hill*." This televisually rare reconciliation is narratively significant. For Redcorn, it seems he needed to agree to stop the affair and reconcile with the cuckolded Dale to open up new, albeit curious, collaborative space for land claims and entrepreneurial endeavors in subsequent episodes. Amid a climate of gradually increasing recognition of historical atrocities committed by the United States against Native Peoples, the exchange also originally aired five months before Kevin Gover, a Pawnee and then assistant secretary of the BIA, offered an apology to all Native nations on behalf of the agency.[53]

In the epilogue of "Nancy Boys," after submitting the FOIA paperwork, Redcorn receives a truckload of boxes containing documents from, who else, the BIA. He dons reading glasses as he sits alone perusing the documents in his trailer while listening to Judas Priest's song "Living after Midnight," from which the audience can hear the line, "I took the city 'bout one A.M.," a metaphorical wish perhaps for Redcorn's plans to take back "the land." "This is good," Redcorn says while reading. "This is dynamite!"

"Nancy Boys" launched a series of sporadic but interconnected entrepreneurial ventures for Redcorn during the rest of the series. The story line resumes the following season on November 19, 2000, right before Thanksgiving, in the season 5 episode "Spin the Choice." Redcorn and his now self-identified "legal advisor" Dale (whose real profession is bug exterminator) file a claim for 130,000 acres of land. Citing for Dale the January 2000 decision for the federal government to return 84,000 acres of land to Northern Utes, Redcorn identifies the case as "a good precedent for our tribe's lawsuit."[54] To which Dale responds, "Well, with me acting as your legal advisor, I am confident that you have an airtight case, although I am not sure what you mean by 'precedent.'" That Dale is Redcorn's legal representation is narratively plausible, as illogical and humorous as it is encoded to be, but what stands out further and progressively in this exchange is Redcorn's reference to the real-life story about the Northern Utes. Unlike countless previous episodes in other sitcoms, "Nancy Boys" actually involved research into the indigenous issue of land claims. In the recent genealogy of the recognizably Indian, it also becomes a rare on-screen citation of a real (non-gaming) headline that may have helped to inspire the continuation of Redcorn's lawsuit story line.

By the end of the episode, in possibly the fastest land claim settlement of all time, Redcorn receives only twelve acres, eleven of which are connected; one is next to the highway. Furious at first, he conflates the government's meager offer with the fact that Dale is raising his biological son—"They take our land *and* our sons!" Eventually, out of his love for Joseph and commitment to a semblance of indigenous cultural continuity, Redcorn tells Dale he will accept the dozen acres with certain stipulations.

REDCORN: I think I will take those twelve acres after all, and then upon my death, I would like to pass the land on to you, Dale, for all the help you've given me.

DALE: Score!

REDCORN: Then Joseph will live on my forefathers' land after you die.

DALE: Thanks, Captain Bringdown.

In a temporal gesture of past and future interconnections, the land acquisition in "Spin the Choice" spawns not just a circuitous possibility for a Redcorn familial futurity with Joseph but also future episodes featuring Redcorn's healing line of work as well as other entrepreneurial endeavors on what he calls his forefathers' lands. The land literally becomes ground for Redcorn's subsequent inclusion as a business owner, albeit thirty-seven episodes later, and a rather opportunistic entrepreneur. Near the end of season 6, in "Returning Japanese, Part I," viewers see his massage business move from his trailer to a new building. The oxymoronic "John Redcorn's New Age Healing Center & Tax Free Cigarettes" offers, according to signs out front, "Color Therapy," "Massage," and "Mineral Baths." Inside, Redcorn sells such items as candles, dream catchers, medicine bags, and necklaces.[55]

In the same episode, Redcorn's land also becomes the site of a dubious exchange, which may further his neo-Indian status. When Hank and his friends show up to use what Hank calls the center's "steam room," Redcorn counters, "It's not a steam room. It's a sweat lodge. It's one of the most intense, spiritual experiences known to my people." After Hank asks if he is "talking about that thing by the Porta-John that looks like a compost heap with garbage bags on it," Redcorn retaliates by charging them "$20 [pause] each." Likely intended to be a humorous exchange, Redcorn's indignation resembles his reaction to Hank's flippancy in his season 1 debut ("The spirit bag is very sacred. You should not make light"). This time, though, Redcorn refuses to walk away and seeks to profit from Hank's critique of the lodge. Demanding $20 from each person pales monetarily in comparison to, say, James Arthur Ray's bill of nearly $10,000 per person for a 2009 retreat that included his version of a vision quest and sweat and led to three deaths.[56] The ethical implication of Redcorn requiring payment risks placing him in company with such New Age frauds who charge individuals for supposed Indian spirituality. Profiting in this context is likely disconcerting, to say the least, to those who adamantly say spirituality is not for sale. Furthermore, inside the lodge, after Redcorn warns Hank and the others that "things can get a little trippy," the customers have varying hallucinations, from the absurd and comical to acutely serious, which could evoke negative associations between Native spirituality and LSD or peyote.[57] Bill, for example, sees himself driving a motorcycle into a gigantic pie. Dale is in bed with a praying mantis that then decapitates him; Hank sees his father, Cotton, finally admitting his love for him. Cotton, in his "vision," sees Japanese soldiers he claims to have killed in World War II. In all, the two scenes in the healing center and the lodge appear to reproduce questionable (mis)perceptions of Native spirituality.

Skewed visions aside, though, Redcorn's line of "$20 . . . each" could be read more resistively. During production, Joss voiced his concern with Redcorn's decision—that is, the writers' decision—to make Redcorn charge Hank for the sweat. "I had a problem with that," Joss explains, and "didn't want to do" it, but the executive creative powers did not budge. Actually, for Redcorn to charge something is in accordance with his identity as a New Age healer, a profession that tends to lead him more into sexual relations with female clients than into establishing him as an upstanding healer. At the same time, one can question if Redcorn charged for the sweat for reasons other than mere self-profit. What if, as Joss observes, Redcorn decided to charge Hank only because of Hank's dismissive and disrespectful attitude? "In my mind," the actor says, "John Redcorn wasn't going to charge him" until Hank disrespected Redcorn's lodge. In this light, Redcorn exhibited a show of one-upping Hank in the exchange.[58]

In conjunction with an episode to air nine months later during season 7, this reading becomes further plausible when Redcorn (humorously) reveals that settlers playing Indian, including playing with and disrespecting Native traditions, is of utmost concern to him. In the episode "Vision Quest," Redcorn collaborates with Hank to inconspicuously lead Joseph on a vision quest in the woods. But Dale, having not eaten for a couple of hours and feeling overly fatigued from a brief walk, intercepts when he hallucinates. "I see the buffalo!" he exclaims. "I see the Indian! I *am* the Indian!" In response, Redcorn fumes one of his most memorable lines: "500 years of oppression and somehow I find *this* the most irritating."[59]

Joss-Redcorn's Off- and On-Screen Gambles

Redcorn's awareness of "oppression" and cultural appropriation as well as his expressed love for his son, Joseph, appear to fuel Joss's motivation for how Redcorn moves about in the *King of the Hill* universe. For Joss, Redcorn stayed in Arlen, even after the breakup with Nancy in season 4, to stay near his son. "Redcorn put up with a lot," Joss recalls, "to be close to Joseph." That includes not just negotiating daily expectations of Indian performativity, settler characters' disrespect and misunderstandings of Redcorn, and the personally expressed pain that Dale was raising his biological son without Native traditions, but also the absence of expansive story lines and character development for Redcorn and, by extension, for Joss to voice, all of which genuinely matters to the actor.[60]

"After a few episodes," *News from Indian Country* reported in 2005, "[Joss] suggested to the show's writers that there was more that John Redcorn could do."[61] As Joss says, "I got tired of *King of the Hill* [having] John Redcorn jumping in and out of the [Gribbles' bedroom] window." Joss knew, however, that "you just couldn't go to Fox and say, 'I want to do something differently.' [I] had to show them a little bit of who I thought Redcorn was." He proposed several possibilities, including Redcorn as a "professional wrestler" who wears a mask to hide his identity and facilitate a closer relationship with Joseph, but they were all rejected.[62] To reduce Redcorn's recognizably Indian status and expand his character into something "more," Joss then took Redcorn *offscreen* to inspire more on-screen lines and work for Joss and more on-screen story lines and airtime for Redcorn. Joss takes the figure of Redcorn as a "Hollywood Indian" and attempts to manage, or at least expand and reconfigure, the character's narrative through musical performance. Rather than fully abandon the network system and *King of the Hill,* Joss works both to his and, eventually,

Redcorn's representational and slight economic advantage. Remaining, though, in a mainstream settler-dominated system and its sitcom product also meant an inevitable negotiated catering to Hollywood executives' notions of acceptable Indian performance and Indian-settler relations.

Searching for a creative release from his frustrations with the powers that be on *King of the Hill*, Joss-as-Redcorn stepped onto a new stage, literally and occupationally, to perform lead vocals for his assembled band John Redcorn Big Mountain Fudgecake.[63] "To be an actor, to be an artist," Joss explains, "you got to be creative, whatever outlet you can do. And since I can't sing, I thought what better thing to do than pretend."[64] He worked with musician Kristen Kiser on Joss's thirty-foot boat in Marina del Rey, California, where they set up microphones for Joss's vocals and Kiser's acoustic, and recorded rugged blues and "hardcore rock and roll" songs on a Digital Audio Tape player. "We did it all in one track, recorded it in two hours," Joss explains. Characterizing the recorded product of eight songs as a "frustration CD," Joss named it "Golden Driblets."[65] The opening song was, for both Joss and Redcorn, aptly titled "I Gotta Do Something to Help Me Out."[66] Heeding his song's thesis along with the track's clamorous question in the second verse ("Hey, you! Can you help me out?"), Joss and his bandmate personally delivered CD copies to approximately fifteen writers in an uninvited visit during the middle of a production meeting. Standing before a roomful of stunned writers, Joss says he paraphrased a line from *Pulp Fiction* to acknowledge he was, as Natives almost always are in Hollywood, outnumbered: "Should've brought shotguns!" About "five hours later," Joss received a "call from executive producers" that *King of the Hill* was interested in pursuing Redcorn's musical angle.[67]

Near the end of season 7 in "The Witches of East Arlen," Big Mountain Fudgecake receives its first plug.[68] With flyers in hand at the 9th Dimension Bookstore, Redcorn approaches a customer: "Have you checked out John Redcorn's New Age Healing Center? You really should. On Friday nights, John Redcorn and his band Big Mountain Fudgecake will be playing. I'm John Redcorn." He then spots Hank and Peggy's son. "Hey, Bobby. You like to rock?" It would be, however, almost two years (and, for Redcorn, six appearances later) before viewers saw Redcorn and his band start to rock on-screen.

Meanwhile, Joss went offscreen again with the music and revamped the hardcore Big Mountain Fudgecake into the "Native American alternative blues" act the Red Corn Band.[69] As lead vocalist and lyricist, Joss teamed with producer and manager Adrian Brown (Viejas) and musicians Tim Sampson (Mvskoke and son of actor Will Sampson) on rhythm guitar,

George Multine III (Navajo) on lead guitar, and Charles Button on bass. Sung from the perspective of blurred Hollywood Indian personas of Redcorn and Joss, with all music arranged by seasoned guitarist Sampson, the Red Corn Band recorded five songs for its first album, *The Red Corn Sessions*, in 2004 at Button's Sacred Mountain Studios in Flagstaff, Arizona. Garnering some buzz in Native music circles, the album was nominated for the 2004/05 Best Jazz/Blues Nammy at the Native American Music Awards.

Although the Red Corn Band was "originally conceived as a back-up band to front Joss' stand up lyrics about contemporary Hollywood Indian life," *The Red Corn Sessions* serves as further sonic and lyrical response to Redcorn's challenging and limiting placement in *King of the Hill*.[70] In the opening track, "The Mouse," Joss-as-Redcorn sings as a loner mouse looking for a house to entice him with cheese. The lyrics sound rather metaphorical for desiring, partly in line with Redcorn's on-screen TV character, a one-night stand. The next song, "Reservation Crime," an earlier version of which appeared on the "Golden Driblets" CD, also incorporates metaphor but as possible commentary on the larger climate of Hollywood politics for Native actors as well as on Redcorn's outlook within *King of the Hill*. The song seems to insinuate that to reduce one's historically expansive homelands, as the federal government has done, onto a reservation and impose major statutory restrictions on indigenous enactments of tribal sovereignty is criminal. Joss-as-Redcorn sings, "Restricted freedom is my Hell / I'm at home, not a white man's cell," and later declares, "I want freedom, freedom, on my land, on my land," suggestive of Redcorn's frustrations and struggles over his life and land claim in several episodes of the sitcom. Although Redcorn does not live on a reservation (Arlen is a fictional town in Texas), the song's reservation sounds symbolic for tapping into the "imagined space" that informs Michelle Raheja's term "virtual reservation." In line with her concept's definition, Joss and the Red Corn Band carve out "a space where Indigenous artists collectively and individually employ technologies and knowledges to rethink the relationship between media and Indigenous communities."[71] In this case, Native actors provide a musical soundtrack for a sitcom neo-Indian in an effort to alter how he is represented on mainstream television.

After the reflective song "Come On," about yearning for someone (or something) to fill a void left unsatisfied by "alcohol," "cigarettes," and "weed," and the traveling song "Blades of Grass," about seeing grass stained with "ancestors' blood" on the "Trail of Tears," the album starts to close with "I Can't Remember," an open-ended last track about a relationship gone wrong. Around the six-minute mark, however, a hidden track begins in which Joss-as-Redcorn sings the refrain, "I am a surfing man," followed later by the assertions, "I surf the sands with no white man's waves" and "my teachings are the old ways" that leave reverberating "footprints of an Indian." Altogether, the hidden track rings of a supratribal nationalism and aspirations of cultural preservation, continuity, and perseverance in cultural renewal. For Redcorn, the album's closing note of continuance through the ebb and flow of life's waves, always with the risk of colliding against and merging with others' waves, in and around Hollywood, metaphorically suggests a determination and personal confidence that leads to and finds an on-screen performative outlet in the April 9, 2005, premiere of the *King of the Hill* episode "Redcorn Gambles with His Future."

As the only episode with Redcorn's name in the title, "Redcorn Gambles with His Future" illustrates, I contend, a visible and sonic manifestation of Joss's longtime efforts to develop Redcorn into, as a lyric in the Red Corn Band song "Still No Good" goes, being "king of the hill." But Joss's work met mixed results once credited producers and network executives had the final say in how the broadcasted narrative would unfold, even to the point of determining which settler characters would receive credit (Hank) and take credit (Dale) for Joss-Redcorn's work in the story line. A new variant of the settler self-determination in the previous chapter, the self-determination in this episode reflects distorted efforts to recognize Joss-Redcorn's representational work in the sitcom's settler-dominated setting.

The episode opens at an Italian restaurant, where Hank's boss, Bud Strickland, gives a calmly ecstatic Hank the crucial job of organizing the Strickland Propane Family Fun Day, including hiring the entertainment.[72] Their conversation is soon interrupted by Maria's Pasta and Pizza's evening entertainment, John Redcorn and Big Mountain Fudgecake (BMF) in their broadcast debut. Joss's offscreen Native bandmates Sampson and Multine have been replaced on-screen by settler characters and guitarists Lucky Kleinschmidt, Luanne's boyfriend/future husband, and Elvin Mackleston, one of Lucky's "redneck" buddies. Lucky is voiced by rock star Tom Petty and Elvin by country star Trace Adkins, but neither sings in the sitcom. Interestingly, amid the pair of established real-life music stars and singers, Joss, with just two side music projects to his name, sings lead on *King of the Hill* as he does in the Red Corn Band. The BMF sound, as described by the band's future manager Dale Gribble, is a mesh of Bachman-Turner Overdrive, Deep Purple, and Electric Light Orchestra. After just one hardcore rock song featuring Redcorn's blaring vocals ("There's a hole in my pocket where the money should go!") and Lucky's and Elvin's thrashing electric guitars, the restaurant kicks the band out of its free gig.

John Redcorn and his band, Big Mountain Fudgecake.

Looking for another opportunity to rock, Redcorn focuses on persuading Hank to hire BMF for the Fun Day picnic, but the propane salesman is certain the band is not right for the family-oriented event. Redcorn remains persistent. Evoking the story of Joss's "Golden Driblets" CD delivery to *King of the Hill* writers, Redcorn shows up unannounced at Hank's work with demo tape and cassette player. Standing on the Strickland Propane sales floor, Redcorn presses "play" as employees and customers, including a mother and daughter, gasp in response to the song's lyrics:

I am the reaper
The collector of souls!
I am the taker
And the smasher of bowls
Mothers cry
Children die
Alone!

Hank stops the tape and says, "I'm sorry, John Redcorn. I'm not hiring you. No way!" Redcorn then starts to break down before Hank figuratively picks him up.

REDCORN: You know, you start doing massage to pay the bills and you tell yourself, "Just a few more years of this, Johnny." And one day you look up and you're 40. [*Shouting*] You're 40, Hank![73]

They step outside and continue what joins the racialized ranks of, as I discussed in chapter 2, Mr. Brady's advice to Jimmy Pakaya in *The Brady Bunch* and Mr. Drummond's determined resolution with Chief Longwalker in *Diff'rent Strokes*:

> HANK: Look, maybe you should stop waiting for other people to make things happen for you.
> REDCORN: What does that mean?
> HANK: Uh, well, maybe what you need to do is to, uh, bet on yourself. A lot of really successful people did that.
> REDCORN: Bet on myself?
> HANK: Sure. It's your dream, you make it happen. Bet on yourself.
> REDCORN: Wow, Hank. You are very wise. Thank you! Thank you!

Redcorn takes the advice rather literally as he begins construction on his land to build a casino to "have," he says, "a permanent venue for Fudgecake to play. Like Wayne Newton and the Stardust."

With "Redcorn Gambles with His Future," *King of the Hill* joins the new wave of anxious casino-filled representations of the indigenous in animated sitcoms, in which nonindigenous characters, overseen by nonindigenous producers, recurringly position themselves to (still) be representationally superior to the indigenous. Whereas legal, political, and cultural studies scholars have addressed the distorted anti-indigenous discourse of the "casino Indian" in *Family Guy*, *The Simpsons*, and *South Park* to illustrate unfavorable perceptions of contemporary Native populations through the filter of "rich Indian racism"—following the Indian Gaming Regulatory Act in 1988 (which paternalistically *permitted* tribes to conduct gaming on their *own* lands)—*King of the Hill* complicates even as it reinforces previous representations.[74]

On opening night at Redcorn's new Speaking Wind Casino and Entertainment Center, an obvious play off of the Tigua Pueblos' former Speaking Rock Casino in El Paso, Indian signifiers run rampant with door greeters in headdresses and buckskin, dealers sporting feathered headbands, and the walls adorned with Indian masks, shields, buffalo paintings, and tomahawks. Redcorn spots Hank, hugs him, and says, "Thank you. None of this would have been possible without your advice." Yet Joss's touches on the episode remain in play as the band then prepares to play songs "inspired" by, Joss says, his "Golden Driblets" recording, including the aforementioned song "I Gotta Do Something to Help Me Out," which contains the lyric "I need your money to help me out." Redcorn says to Elvin and Lucky,

"Let's open with 'I Need Money.' We can transition to 'Gotta Get Money,' and do a whole money medley."[75]

Just as they start to perform, authorities step in to shut down the casino, as the state of Texas had done to the Tiguas' Speaking Rock Casino in February 2002.[76] As one of the officers states, "Texas tribes traded their federal gaming rights for state recognition of their tribes," a line left unchecked in the episode not only for its discursive infringement upon tribal sovereignty but also for its erroneous distortion of tribal and state relations.[77] In 1999, six years after Speaking Rock had opened, Texas attorney general John Cornyn sued the Tiguas for running what he and then governor George W. Bush deemed a violation of state law on gambling. Cornyn reportedly even swayed a judge to reduce the sovereign status of the federally recognized Tiguas, as well as that of the Alabama-Coushattas also located in Texas, to "an association" like a "sorority or fraternity," a blatant and inexcusable refusal to recognize tribal sovereignty.[78] Under the 1987 federal Indian Restoration Act, just a year before the Indian Gaming Regulatory Act, the Tiguas and Alabama-Coushattas had "allegedly agreed not to sponsor any gaming that was otherwise illegal in Texas," though the tribes counter that their gaming establishments were "structured to meet the requirements of the [1991] state Lottery Act" and, therefore, were "legal as long as the state lottery is legal." In response to Cornyn telling "a U.S. District judge that Texas is not a gambling State," Alabama-Coushatta chairman Kevin Battise told the U.S. Committee on Indian Affairs in June 2002, a month before Texas authorities shut down his tribe's casino, "I must live in another State," before referencing the state lottery, horse races, and other gambling activities.[79]

After Redcorn's casino closure, another settler character, Dale, steps in to help Redcorn. As the manager of Big Mountain Fudgecake, Dale says, "I'll focus on a way to fix this," which comforts no one in the band. When Dale finally secures for BMF a gig at the Strickland Propane company picnic, Redcorn's bandmates refuse. "The Cake," Elvin states, "don't play picnics." When Redcorn shows up to tell Hank the band broke up, Dale once again intervenes to lift him up and, suggestive of Mike Brady's advice to the young indigenous character Jimmy Pakaya, persists in telling Redcorn what he can and should do.

DALE: John Redcorn, you're the heart and soul of The Cake, man! You can play this gig yourself!
REDCORN: Alone? Me? Besides, kids aren't going to want to listen to me.

DALE: The BMF sound is universal. You can adapt.

REDCORN: Hmm. I guess there is that song about killing myself. I could rewrite it so it's about personal hygiene.

DALE: Love it. Now, go!

Accompanied only by his acoustic guitar, Redcorn steps onto the stage.

REDCORN: Hello and welcome to the Strickland Family Fun Day. I am John Redcorn. Here's a song I wrote after government agents shut down my gambling establishment and I wanted to die. [*Starts singing*] "Wake up, just want to [*pauses to improvise*] wash myself, clean my wrists, scrub my brains out. Heya, heya, heya-hey, heya-hey, heya-hey. They'll miss me when I do."

The crowd applauds enthusiastically, Redcorn and Hank exchange approving nods, and the scene cuts to an exterior shot of the revamped enterprise "Redcorn's Land," a family fun center that invokes the Tiguas' casino becoming the Speaking Rock Entertainment Center.

Now seated on his own stage before a room of small children, Redcorn sings:

There's a hole in the jar where the cookies should go
There's a hole in the tank where the fishies should go
There's a hole, and a hole, and a hole.

Standing nearby, Dale takes credit for the newfound success as he smugly tells parents, "Yeah, when I first found Redcorn, he was in some go-nowhere, Whitesnake-meets-White-Lion-meets-Great-White rip-off group, but I recreated him as the Native American Raffi."

Joss's struggles and frustrations in Hollywood are nothing new for Native actors working in mainstream television. Nor is the story development of settlers saving the day. But what is striking, albeit unsurprising, in "Redcorn Gambles with His Future" is the transference of on-screen credit to Hank and Dale for the offscreen work of Joss-Redcorn. After Joss persuaded *King of the Hill* producers, via his offscreen music, to expand Redcorn's character, settlers stepped in to heavily and unnecessarily assist. *King of the Hill* and Redcorn repeatedly thank Hank for his advice, and even misguided and unpredictable Dale arranges the picnic music gig and tells Redcorn to go solo onstage. Although Dale's managerial skills are questionable and his claim to making "the Native American Raffi" is laughable, Dale nonetheless spurs a series of events into motion. Still, Joss and Redcorn deserve credit for their performances in the episode. Redcorn is

John Redcorn,
the children's
entertainer.

the one, after all, who improvises under pressure and finally finds his audience in a profession as children's entertainer that would be revisited in
future episodes. At best, producers show Redcorn, Hank, and Dale sharing
in taking center stage in decision making in an episode partially resulting
from the performative ingenuity of Joss.

Two years later, Redcorn is an established children's entertainer in season 11's "Hair Today, Gone Tomorrow," in which Redcorn and Nancy almost get back together.[80] After learning he has a daughter and after running a fireworks stand in season 12, Joss-as-Redcorn makes his concluding
on-screen appearance in "Manger Baby Einstein."[81] Redcorn moves from
being a children's entertainer to a children's entertainment producer. Representing an on-screen determination and skill for personal agency as a talent agent and the owner of "John Redcorn Presents," Redcorn approaches
Luanne, Hank's niece, who has just completed a puppet show at a kid's
birthday party. "I want to produce a line of children's educational videos,"
he tells Luanne, "to turn you and [her puppets] the Manger Babies into the
next *Baby Einstein*," a nod to a real-life line of educational videos for infants.
He adds that he has "a camera, editing equipment, and," in a lingering discursive trace to BMF, "a bass guitar left over from a previous enterprise."

In "Manger Baby Einstein," Joss's favorite episode due to his character's
self-sufficiency, Redcorn starts and conducts his own business but not on
his own land this time. Instead, in a strip mall, a makeshift banner with
the agency's title flaps over a former company's affixed sign reading "De-
pendable Mortgages: The Subprime Specialist." This time, Dale does not
attempt to manage Redcorn's business affairs, and Hank does not advise

him to bet on himself. Redcorn started a new business without their assistance. Right after he recorded his final *King of the Hill* voice-overs, Joss told a reporter, "[Redcorn's] been a fun character to play, and it's been a fun show. I like how he's grown from the early episodes, where he was just this character who climbed in and out of the window, to where he has his own band, his own casino and he even becomes an agent, working with kids to make them stars. He matured and became a self-sufficient character."[82]

Conclusion: Joss and Redcorn, Post–*King of the Hill*

As *King of the Hill* wrapped up production in 2010, Joss lamented, "It's kind of sad the show's come to an end. With the cancellation of 'King of the Hill,' it's like there's another dead Indian whose spirit is out there wandering."[83] In line with a number of his aired appearances, the obituary might read that John Redcorn was a biological father to Joseph and Kate; massage therapist; founding member and lead singer of hard rock band Big Mountain Fudgecake; self-employed healer; entrepreneur and five-time business owner (John Redcorn's New Age Healing Center & Tax Free Cigarettes, Speaking Wind Casino, Redcorn's Land fun center, a fireworks stand, and John Redcorn Presents children's entertainment); solo children's singer and songwriter (with guitar and xylophone) once dubbed "the Native American Raffi"; talent agent and DVD producer of children's entertainment; former roadie for Winger; music fan of Foreigner, Meatloaf, Pat Benatar, Bad Company, Billy Idol, and Ratt; invited guest speaker at Tom Landry Middle School on Thanksgiving and colonization; avid reader of *This Land Is Our Land*; traditional vision interpreter; athletically superior in softball; and athletically challenged in kickball.

Metaphorical morbidity reconsidered, Redcorn *is* "wandering" but, for Joss, refuses to be "another dead Indian." Redcorn presses on offscreen in efforts to be, re-quoting Joss, "self-sufficient," thanks not to Mike Judge or Hank Hill but to Joss, whose work with Redcorn looks to be mutually beneficial. "I like keeping this animated character alive in the real world," Joss recursively explains. His message of extant determination, carved out of and around *King of the Hill* productions and televisions, Joss's musical visions and acting roles, and the give-and-take between the sitcom and Joss, has been in the making for years and continues to play out today.

After recording the album *The Red Corn Sessions*, Joss said in 2005, "We [the Red Corn Band] have the torch and we're moving forward. If the show gets canceled tomorrow, John Redcorn will have a life after TV. Sure I'm a frustrated actor, but I want to leave a mark. Like Redcorn, I'm trying to do better, I care about my family and want to leave the world a better place. And maybe give people something to smile at and think about at the same time. The music is making us all better."[84] To ensure a post-TV life for Redcorn, Joss continues to pursue a musical route. As noted earlier, the Red Corn Band released a second CD in 2006. More recently, in 2012, Joss began performing under the stage name The Redcorn Experience with the Gray Wolf Blues band, who won a Nammy for Best Blues recording in 2009. Joss also performed in Redcorn voice as a judge for the 2008 Austin Rock Band Championships at the Alamo Ritz theater, where bands play and perform to the Rock Band videogame onstage.[85] In a press release, the theater noted Joss is "the voice of John Redcorn" but clearly emphasized the character to potential contestants: "Your fate rests in Redcorn. Who happens, by the way, to be the real deal," a claim presumably based on his on-screen days as lead vocalist of Big Mountain Fudgecake, not necessarily Joss's lesser-known offscreen musical travels.

The news release raises another key point concerning discursive and performative slippage between Joss and/as Redcorn: the wording risks not distinguishing between the actor and the character, something the former appears not to discourage. As Joss says, "It's a lot of fun being John Redcorn. I really like the character. It allows me to do things that I, Jonathan Joss, couldn't do."[86] As the voice of a well-known animated, not live-action, television character, Joss could choose *not* to let folks know he was the voice of Redcorn. Instead, he works to play with and fashion the on- and offscreen identities of the fictional and nonfictional into a multifaceted and dynamic (read: ambiguously animated) performance, which may be a factor in interviewers' occasional confusion and nominal slips. In a 2012 interview, for example, on *One Voice Radio* hosted by Kenneth Hieber and Felipe Rose (the "Indian" in the Village People), Joss was asked how much of himself is Redcorn. "The good-looking parts," he quipped. Main host Hieber may have thought there was more to him than just appearance, though, when he advertised the call-in show with Joss as an opportunity for listeners to talk to "Jonathan Redcorn." Moreover, when Hieber blanked on the actor's last name during the interview, Rose had to step in to say "Joss." The actor's name was never mentioned in a 2011 interview on 1200 WOAI News Radio, in which a San Antonio radio host visited with Joss in the station but kept referring to the actor, apparently in all seriousness, as "John Redcorn," even saying that Redcorn, not Joss, attended nearby McCollum High School years earlier and recently guest-starred on *Parks and Recreation*.[87]

Today, the actor maintains the website jonathanjoss.com to post descriptions of his former and current projects and pictures with fans, but johnredcorn.com could be almost as apt. The self-branded "first real voice of a Native cartoon character," as the opening page states, also utilizes the site to advertise a rather unique crossover mix of Redcorn products, such as "Redcorn's King of the Dill Spice" and "Redcorn's King of the Grill Massage Rub."[88] As the site's "King of the Grill" page reads, "Jon was raised in his parents' San Antonio restaurant and spent quality time perfecting the family recipes!" Joss sells the products online and at numerous venues, such as anime conventions that he has begun to frequent not only to sell the rubs and spices but for interviews, autographs, and networking with other voice actors and producers.

In all, Joss and Redcorn are working together to ensure each other's post–*King of the Hill* futures by embracing their ups and downs on the series, seeking out new ways to profit, and bringing further crossover attention to the actor's talent and the character's persona in hopes, at least for Joss, to see where the roads may lead and to assume a partial representational control of Redcorn, all the while keeping the comical in play. As reruns of *King of the Hill* continue on Adult Swim and Netflix, it sounds plausible that Joss will continue to manage Redcorn elsewhere in reproducing and reconstructing representations of the persona. In the process, the performer blurs identities, with Jonathan Joss as John Redcorn, and vice versa, which is ambiguously apt (and aptly ambiguous) for functioning as a performative bridge between the recognizably Indian and recognizably Native; for becoming, in all its animated slippage, a sitcom neo-Indian; and for moving, under Joss's savvy management, further toward other possibilities for indigenous performance. Through his longtime and ongoing work with and as Redcorn, not to mention his dozens of indigenous roles in cinema (for example, 2001's *Christmas in the Clouds*), miniseries (*Dead Man's Walk* and *Comanche Moon*), television drama (*Walker, Texas Ranger* and *Charmed*), animation (*Justice League*), and sitcoms (*Parks and Recreation*), Jonathan Joss has endured Hollywood to assume an earned and significant negotiated share of representational sovereignty over the Redcorn character.

The conversation now moves from a single character's quest for indigenous futurity and self-sufficiency and an actor's efforts for a share of creative sovereignty over that character into the next chapter's discussion on the indigenous sitcom sovereignty over an entire series co-created and coproduced by and costarring Native Peoples. As I will explain, the indigenous sitcom tribalography has opened up in the twenty-first century far north of Arlen, Texas, in Fort McMurray, Alberta, where producers of the "Aboriginal *Brady Bunch*" readjust the recognizably Indian and represent televisions of the recognizably Native.[89]

CHAPTER FOUR

Sitcom Sovereignty in
Mixed Blessings

On June 21, 2012, Natives and non-Natives across Canada kicked off summer and the longest day of the year by celebrating First Nations, Inuit, and Métis cultures during National Aboriginal Day. In Vancouver, British Columbia, on Coast Salish homelands, people gathered for breakfast and a Friendship Walk. In Ontario, Thunder Bay residents held a sunrise ceremony and powwow, and Ottawa organized the Summer Solstice Aboriginal Arts Festival. In Alberta, the Edmonton National Aboriginal Day Committee organized an arts and music festival featuring the electric powwow musical trio A Tribe Called Red.[1] Across the country, the coordinated and collaborative efforts of Natives and non-Natives resulted in an eclectic amalgam of free events featuring historical and modern forms of indigenous expression to entertain, educate, and promote iterations of the recognizably Native and intercultural dialogue and healing.[2]

On a day of publicly celebrating and performing indigeneity, writer Drew Hayden Taylor contributed to conversations in all three areas—entertainment, education, and healing—through his article "What . . . You Think You're Funny?!" The article was posted "in honour of National Aboriginal Day" by Canada Writes, a Canadian Broadcasting Corporation (CBC) site for publishing creative writing, and in support of the CBC documentary series *8th Fire: Aboriginal Peoples, Canada, and the Way Forward*, "an original series by some of the country's leading and emerging Aboriginal writers," including Taylor, who discuss contemporary relations between Natives and non-Natives in Canada. The series title, as the documentary's official site states, "draws from an Anishinaabe prophecy that declares now is the time for Aboriginal peoples and the settler community to come together and build the '8th Fire' of justice and harmony," directly supportive of aspirations of National Aboriginal Day.[3]

For Taylor, as reflected in his article and the corpus of his recognizably Native work, a major key to cross-cultural unity and to paving a healing way forward is humor.[4] Taylor's National Aboriginal Day article offers a celebratory yet stark reminder of two of his favorite writing topics: the existence of Native humor and its usage for intercultural healing. It begins with a simple and profound reflection: "Being a humourist is serious business." An Ojibwe playwright, novelist, filmmaker, columnist, guest lecturer, screenwriter, and, yes, humorist born and raised on the Curve Lake First Nation reserve, Taylor continues, "Academically and critically, it's not a particularly well respected profession. If you've noticed, so much of our [Native] literature (plays, novels, television, etc.) deals with the darker aspect of our culture, the trials and tribulations of Aboriginal life. . . . All Native people have to be either oppressed, depressed or suppressed. Those are the three major tribes in Canada. So I've spent a career trying to tell people that we, the Native people of Canada, are a very boisterous and fun people, who love to tell funny stories and have a great time."[5]

As Gerald Vizenor says, "Natives are storiers, and humor is a touchstone of native presence."[6] An exemplary indigenous storier of Native presence, Taylor has spoken around the globe reporting what may still be surprising, if not shocking and rather unfunny, news for some, including producers in charge of the recognizably Indian: Native Peoples not only exist but are also comical. Or as Taylor calls his edited collection of essays on indigenous humor, *Me Funny*, which incidentally was inspired by another venture into studying indigenous humor, his 2000 documentary *Redskins, Tricksters, and Puppy Stew: Native Humour and Its Healing Powers*. In short, Taylor writes, films, studies, and speaks Native humor, such as in his recurring playful threat—in response to tiresome questions on his being Native with non-brown skin and blue eyes—"to start my own separate nation. Because I'm half Ojibway, and half Caucasian, we will be called the Occasions. And of course, since I'm founding the new nation, I will be a Special Occasion."[7] In addition to his scores of lectures and newspaper columns on and illustrative of pan-Native and Ojibwe humor, intercultural relations, and multiracial identity, Taylor has over seventy produced plays, over twenty books, and numerous television writing credits, almost all of which include considerable doses of comedy.

Taylor also has on his résumé the title of co-creator and head writer in a genre of strong interest to him since childhood and clearly in conversation with his comedic columns and creative works in theater and television: the sitcom. In 2006, he penned the pilot for what soon became the indigenous and intercultural family sitcom *Mixed Blessings* (2007–10), or what he dubs "an Aboriginal *Brady Bunch*."[8] With *Mixed Blessings*, Taylor expanded the indigenous sitcom tribalography through a genre historically and contemporarily unaccustomed to recognizably Native humor, let alone the existence of recognizably Native characters. Within the contexts of social and televisual politics of cross-cultural perceptions through indigenous frames, the tribal televisions of the recognizably Native in production, representation, and encoded intent in *Mixed Blessings* guide the ensuing discussion.

Producing an Indigenous Sitcom

Airing for three cycles, twenty-six episodes in all, on the Aboriginal Peoples Television Network (APTN), *Mixed Blessings* costars Tina Lameman (Beaver Lake Cree) as Cree waitress Josie Fraser and Gary Basaraba as Ukrainian Canadian plumber Hank Kowalchuk. Both characters are widowed and friends before the series starts, then soon fall in love, elope, and, at the end of season 2, welcome into the sitcom world a little bundle of "Ucreenian" joy.[9] As the sitcom's official site states, *Mixed Blessings* "explores the realities, the complexities, and the humour of blending two families and two very different cultures."[10] On the Cree side are Josie's mother, Kookum; sister, Kate; grown son, Mick; teen daughter, Bobbie; and ten-year-old son, Donnie. On the settler side are Hank's sister, Doreen; teens Walt and Vicki; and best friend, Tazz.

Ron E. Scott (Métis Nation of Alberta) co-created *Mixed Blessings* through his independent production company Prairie Dog Film + Television.[11] As Scott explains, "I came up with this idea, along with Ric Bearisto from Vancouver, about mixed relationships. My own background is Métis [First Nations and European heritage], and I realized I was pretty typical, being raised in a family with multiple heritages." Looking to the sitcom's setting in Fort McMurray, Alberta, near the Fort McMurray First Nation of Cree and Dene peoples, Scott says, "Ukrainian represents a large percentage of the population of the prairies so it seemed like a natural blending."[12] From there, *Mixed Blessings* began to craft situations and conflicts on "Native culture versus Ukrainian culture" within a framework of twenty-first-century personal, familial, and tribal-community identities that would be interpretively accessible to Native *and* non-Native viewers.[13] Rather than separate cultures and families (and viewership), the producers brought diversity together to search for common ground through comedic and dramatic intercultural situations. Conflicts ensue from the "clash of cultures,"

Mixed Blessings logo. *Left to right:* Griffin Powell Arcand, Wilma Pelly, Emma Ashbaugh, Allen Belcourt, Michelle Thrush, Tina Lameman, Gary Basaraba, Timothy "Big Daddy Tazz" Norris, Jesse Frechette, Kirklin Maclise, and Emma Duncan. Used with permission of Prairie Dog Film + Television. Photograph by Dan Power.

Mixed Blessings director Frances Damberger explains, but the inevitable interculturality also leads to "breaking down barriers."[14]

Continuing the thread of common humanity and struggles in the series, Scott insisted on bridging cultures through story and comedy. "The message," he states, "is simply that people are people. But especially in the Native culture, there's a great sense of humour which help[s] us deal with the conflicts, which are typical to what we all go through in our relationships."[15] Rather than promote an approach of mere colorblind sameness, as "people are people" may initially suggest, *Mixed Blessings* interjects humor to locate common intercultural ground *and* to foreground difference. Crees and settlers coexist and share with each other, but their identities are marked visually and discursively in explicit epistemological discussions of distinct cultural ways. For instance, when Kookum gifts Hank's son, Walt, with a ribbon shirt for an upcoming powwow, he asks, "Are white people allowed to wear them?" Josie translates Kookum's teasing Cree response into English: "She says she'll 'write you a note.'"[16] *Mixed Blessings* privileges, as in this cited example, indigenous humor to expand perceptions of on- and offscreen indigeneity while also utilizing it, in the form of indigenous teasing, to build intercultural bridges through a gesture of acceptance.

To adapt Native humor into the sitcom, facilitate content accessibility for multiple audiences, and increase public awareness of interculturality and the integral component of humor in Native cultures, *Mixed Blessings* brought in veteran author Drew Hayden Taylor to be head writer. Among the earliest known Native scriptwriters of Canadian television, Taylor first worked as a script consultant in the mid-1980s on *Spirit Bay*, for which producers would "give me the scripts to read and ask me if they were accurate or not, and I'd say, yeah, Native people do eat toast." Then, in 1987, he wrote the article "Adapting Native Scripts" to address "how to develop Native-oriented stories into a television and film format." During the course of his research, Taylor contacted producers "to see if they'd ever had a Native scriptwriter, and there hadn't been one." After the story producer for *The Beachcombers* (1972–90), a multicultural Canadian drama-comedy series with non-Native and Native characters, welcomed Taylor to submit story ideas, he did, and at the age of twenty-four, Taylor received his first TV writing credit for the 1988 episode "A House Divided."[17] Since then, he has amassed writing credits for such television series as the Toronto-based lawyer drama *Street Legal* (1987–94), sub-Arctic aboriginal drama *North of 60* (1992–97), and the children's puppet series *The Longhouse Tales* (2000), not to mention the made-for-television movie *In a World Created by a Drunken God* (2007), the half-hour "Aboriginal *X Files*" TV drama *The Strange Case of Bunny Weequod* (1999), and over a dozen documentaries. Elaborating on *The Strange Case*, Taylor says it was, as far as he knows, "the first film, to be broadcast on CBC, written, directed, produced, and staring [*sic*] Native people, and completely in an Aboriginal language—Ojibway to be exact. The only words of English left in the script were 'Hank Williams Jr.'—evidently there is no suitable translation."[18] He also pitched, unsuccessfully, "Seeing Red," an indigenous sketch comedy modeled after the African American series *In Living Color*, to CBC.[19]

Taylor's previous written work on screen and stage and in print exudes the accessible pan-Native and tribal storytelling and intercultural comedic clashes that Scott sought for *Mixed Blessings*. Except for developing an unaired sitcom pilot in 1990 based on his play *The Bootlegger Blues* for the CBC, Taylor had little writing experience in the sitcom genre, though several of his plays have drawn comparison to critically smart sitcoms. Dale Young, for example, notes that "*The Bootlegger Blues* resembles the sitcom sensibilities prevalent in popular television," which the CBC likely detected as well; but Young contends, as does Taylor, that the Native oral storytelling tradition has been more influential in Taylor's writing than the TV sitcom.[20]

As for many writers, Taylor's early formations of humorous storytelling began at home, in his case, the everyday-ness of his reserve reality of sovereign storying by and about his people.

> I grew up in an environment of sitting around and telling stories out in front of my grandparents' house. There was a big old willow tree and a couple of chairs and a firepit and we'd sit there. I'm not talking oral tradition in terms of Nanabush legends or "Legends-of-my-people" or that type of thing, but more stories about funny things that had happened in the community, just talking late into the night—I think that's where I got my concept of oral narrative and also the structure of humour, and the structure of how to write.

Influenced by regularly listening to and learning from relatives' funny stories, Taylor intrinsically uses humor to communicate that Natives are still *here*, Natives like to laugh and tell funny stories, and Native humor bridges cultural gaps. As a self-identified "old-fashioned storyteller" who desires nothing more than "to tell a good story," Taylor typically aims to communicate a good *humorous* story.[21] Taylor's upbringing, then, amid Ojibway humor on the Curve Lake reserve and his career in comedic creative writing, including on-screen work, provide a strong cultural and adaptable backdrop for his entry into *Mixed Blessings*.

Of course, it does not hurt that Taylor knows sitcoms, as well as sitcom representations of Indians, through his repeated viewings of various series, such as *Friends* and *The Simpsons*.[22] He also cites and critiques several U.S. sitcoms, such as *Seinfeld* and *Barney Miller*, that have "donated at least a token episode or two to Aboriginal causes . . . however accurate they may or may not have been."[23] Taylor is, in many ways, like Sherman Alexie, "a sit-com kid" whose "sense of humor" and "world outlook" appear to be "partly shaped by situation comedies."[24] This designation is further supported in Taylor's article "Aboriginal TV," in which Taylor dabbles in re-writing premises of U.S. sitcoms into recognizably Native texts that adapt Native social conditions and sensibilities into the sitcom format.

In one of his faux proposals for a new TV series on his made-up Aboriginal Broadcasting Network (ABN), similar to APTN, he reconstructs *Three's Company* into "Cree's Company," with a synopsis embroiled in colonial policy and First Nations citizenship politics. "The fun continues as we join the wacky and comic adventures of a small, overcrowded reserve. Jack is introduced to two beautiful women who have just recently been reinstated. Due to the lack of adequate housing, they are forced to all live together in his small cramped house." Another proposed show by Taylor is a readjusted *Married with Children* into "Shacked Up with Kids": "And for the Native community's most dysfunctional family—Al, Peg, Kelly and Bud Benojee—don't miss 'Shacked Up With Kids.' This is actually closer to life than you'd think." Taylor reconfigures *Facts of Life* into "The Micmacs of Life" featuring "the misadventures of five wildly different teenage girls . . . living together at the Maritime Residential School." He also reconstructs *All in the Family* into "All in the Clan": "The comic everyday lives of a family embroiled in the fast-changing world of its reserve as different generations often bump heads over important social issues." But then Taylor reconsiders. "Nah, too silly, viewers would be expecting White people in sheets or something."[25] Even though he writes of flipping the channel after each sitcom's synopsis (nobody said one had to be a *fan* of all-Native TV series), Taylor's work is invested in proposing something new and indigenous for television. In the critical-creative proposals for "Cree's Company," "Shacked Up with Kids," "The Micmacs of Life," and "All in the Clan," Taylor imagines possible indigenous sitcoms, akin to his questioning in 2003 what an indigenous *Gilligan's Island* would look like as "Wapole Island, Lennox Island, Georgina Island, [or] Christian Island," all home to First Nation reserves.[26]

These examples speak back to sitcoms that excluded physical representations of Indians. *Three's Company*, *Married with Children*, and *All in the Family*, the latter of which critics heralded as groundbreaking for promoting public dialogue on race relations, never included an indigenous character and rarely referenced Indianness. For instance, in one episode of *Three's Company*, lead character Jack Tripper calls a conniving New Age guru, in all seriousness, an "Indian giver" over a monetary scam. In another episode, Jack's landlord Mr. Furley plays cards as he holds two fingers behind his head to signify feathers and says, "Poker-hontas!" In *All in the Family*, Archie Bunker, one of television's most popular bigots, and his liberal son-in-law, Mike "Meathead" Stivic, disagree about how the United States claimed control over indigenous homelands. Whereas Mike adamantly argues that "we [the United States] lied to them [Natives], we cheated them, and then we drove them off their land without paying for it," Archie claims Indians "never had no land. They couldn't read or write. How could Sitting Bull sign a lease?" Curiously garnering laughs from the studio audience, Archie adds, "All the Indians ever do is ride around and scalp the wagon trains." Mike literally screams and runs upstairs to get away from what he calls Archie's "lunacy," thus ending the debate. In his indigenized versions of U.S. sitcoms, Taylor borrows from and reimagines each series by including and centering those they never did: indigenous characters.[27]

Taylor's imagined sitcoms also challenge indigenous segments of the television industry and programming. Referencing early on in his "Aboriginal TV" article an ongoing "war of the airwaves," Taylor substitutes ABN for the familiar APTN, which began broadcasting in 1999, the self-declared "first national Aboriginal television network in the world with programming by, for and about Aboriginal Peoples, to share with all Canadians and viewers around the world." Taylor, among the network's more vocal critics, wondered during the network's infancy if it could provide "an Indigenous light at the end of the cultural tunnel," particularly for fictional Native series.[28] He was unconvinced later in 2003 when he lamented that "there's little chance of us [Natives] doing our own shows, though that would be fun." Taylor sardonically says, "We can watch APTN and learn how to gut a seal, caribou, deer, arctic char or elk (each day of the week gets its own animal-gutting lesson)."[29] In his article "57 Channels and No Indians On," a play off of Bruce Springsteen's 1992 song "57 Channels (And Nothin' On)," Taylor adds, "My mother swore after watching the first few months of [APTN] that she never wanted to see another Inuit/Dene hunting or seal/caribou gutting again." While he applauds APTN's talk shows and cooking shows, Taylor also questions the "endless parade of documentaries or current affairs shows" and the recursive airings of the "pseudo-Indian movie," saying open-endedly, "if I see either *Thunderheart* or *Billy Jack* aired one more time . . ."[30]

Similarly critiquing the CBC's tribal populations of "oppressed, depressed [and] suppressed," Taylor states, "We can watch CBC news and be filled in on the dysfunctional Aboriginal story of the day." Or viewers could turn to *North of 60* (1992–97), a drama set in a First Nations community (the Dene of the Northwest Territories) that Taylor characterizes as "a tour-de-force for dysfunctionalism."[31] Featuring several indigenous characters but starring the proverbial "pesky White central character," he says the series focused so much on tragedy that it failed "to show the other side of Native life—the humour and good times." Taylor's critiques supposedly influenced the producers, as he heard from one of the show's writers that the following handwritten quote, which Taylor has no recollection of saying, appeared in a *North of 60* production room: "*North of Sixty* is one of the most depressing shows on Canadian television and it does not accurately reflect Native life—Drew Hayden Taylor."[32]

Sovereign Television

Overall, underlying Taylor's pre–*Mixed Blessings* imaginings and critiques of indigenous television are a determination and drive for something I call "sitcom sovereignty." What would sitcoms like *Three's Company* and *Gilligan's Island* look, sound, and feel like, Taylor hypothetically inquires, if *Natives* held creative control in production, characterization, and broadcast? And what if the Native-run APTN were to include them in their lineup? Rooted in a sitcom sovereignty of creative Native sensibility, self-determination in production, recognizably Native characterization, and representational agency, Taylor's vision of an indigenous sitcom transferred from creative what-ifs and critiques of TV programming in brief news articles to an on-screen reality with *Mixed Blessings*.

This sovereign vision for indigenous TV contributes to what drove the eventual creation of APTN in the first place. As several scholars have outlined in their written histories of indigenous television in Canada, the route leading to the creation of APTN, a space where an original series like *Mixed Blessings* can even *exist*, is fraught with entanglements between Native Peoples and the Canadian government. Indigenous media scholar Lorna Roth points to June 1969, when Minister of Indian Affairs Jean Chrétien unequivocally called for a repeal of the Indian Act (and, hence, termination of Canadian recognition of the indigenous and indigenous nationhood) in favor of Native assimilation into Canadian settler colonialism. Chrétien's "White Paper" of assimilationist policy, Roth argues, "catalyzed First Peoples' recognition that, while living within a circuit of mediated stereotypes, political manipulations and misrepresentations, they would have to seize control of the means of media production and distribution so that they could circulate information to the Canadian public from *their* multiple perspectives."[33] That same month, the Canadian House of Commons approved the Telesat Act to provide live TV programming to the indigenous and nonindigenous in the North through a domestic satellite system that launched in 1972.

During this time, the Inuit organizations Inuit Tapirisat of Canada and the Northern Quebec Inuit Association "worked persistently to bring federal government communications priorities in the North into line with those of the Inuit themselves."[34] After the Canadian Radio-television and Telecommunications Commission (CRTC) in 1980 called for broadcasting of indigenous programs spoken in Native languages for language preservation, the national governing body created, with indigenous support, the Inuit Broadcasting Corporation in 1981. The next year, the federal Applebaum-Hébert *Report on Federal Cultural Policy* acknowledged its Canadian government "has by treaty, law and custom a special responsibility for the well-being of these peoples" as a preface for declaring "that federal policy should give special priority to promoting both traditional and contemporary creative work by artists of Indian and Inuit ancestry." In response, Roth calls the report "the first formal pronouncement of any significance to demonstrate federal appointees' support for a separate status that could be used to argue for a distinct Northern Broadcasting policy." In 1983, "after years of aboriginal lobbying," the establishment of the Northern Broadcasting Policy spawned the Northern Native Broadcast Access Program.[35] In 1991, an updated Broadcasting Act "supported the establishment of a First Peoples infrastructure." The CRTC approved Television Northern Canada (TVNC) for a broadcasting license for "cultural, social, political and educational programming for the primary benefit of aboriginal people in the North."[36]

In the late 1990s, indigenous broadcasters and media proponents strongly advocated for a national pan-indigenous TV network to extend access of its northern programming and to include more southern programming for all audiences throughout Canada. On February 22, 1999, the CRTC approved the TVNC's application to become a national network, and TVNC then became APTN. Finally, on September 1, 1999, APTN began broadcasting "to over 9 million homes throughout Canada via cable television, direct-to-home and wireless service viewers."[37] As its first chairman, Abraham Tagalik, said in March 1999, APTN "will be a major step in building bridges of understanding between aboriginal and non-aboriginal people in Canada."[38] Although APTN, as Taylor suggested in his critique of the network, was slow to air an original indigenous comedic series, its inclusion of *Mixed Blessings* starting in 2007 served as a creative actualization of recent decades of work among Native media proponents and Canadian government officials to facilitate indigenous programming that would educate audiences about Indigenous Peoples and, in line with Tagalik's expressed vision, promote intercultural understanding and community building.

As I will explain, *Mixed Blessings* adeptly and comically contests and reframes sitcom and televisual Indianness and represents variegated postindianness with the intent to alter, or at least expand, non-Native and Native perceptions of Native Peoples on television and to promote intercultural understanding and healing through humor. Like Herman Gray's argument that the late-1980s sitcom *Frank's Place* was "an attempt to rewrite and reposition African American culture and black subjectivities" from African American vantage points, I contend that *Mixed Blessings* rescripts and resituates indigeneity from indigenous sensibilities.[39] If, then, Scott and Taylor are indigenous sitcom televisionaries cognizant of colonial inscriptions on TV representations of Native Peoples, then what are their rescripted televisions of the indigenous and relations between the indigenous and nonindigenous? By turning in this chapter to the sitcom's politics of recognizing and negotiating the representational boundaries between the indigenous and indigenous and between settler and indigenous, I analyze how producers humorously reconfigure the televisual discourses and performances of the recognizably Indian, recognizably Native, and mixed indigenous-settler families.

Acting on sitcom sovereignty to contest the colonial inscriptions marked upon sitcom Indians and unfunny perceptions of Native Peoples, *Mixed Blessings* decolonizes views of how Native characters are cast, portrayed, and developed in the sitcom genre. The indigenous producers rescript representations of indigeneity in the sitcom and, in effect, encourage many viewers to rescript their perceptions. As aesthetic activists attuned to Native identity politics and intercultural relationships, *Mixed Blessings* producers encourage solidarity and cross-cultural understanding across its intended diverse viewership.

To illustrate how *Mixed Blessings* represents the indigenous, I will focus on its approach to producing the recognizably Native in the intertwined layers of narrative, casting, characterization, and soundtrack. These layers, among others, contribute to the producers' important work in decolonization. With their own decolonial views in tow, Scott, Taylor, and others work toward engaging the politics of racial casting, expanding views of Natives beyond the categories of dysfunctional and unfunny, decolonizing views of popular misconceptions of Native Peoples, decolonizing views of what constitutes Native music, and, all the while, decolonizing the representational parameters of the sitcom genre through recognizably Native inclusion. And perhaps most significantly for Taylor, sitcom sovereignty must include the funny, a humor chiefly (yes, adverbial Tayloresque pun intended) written and enacted by Natives and broadcast for cross-cultural audiences in Taylor's ongoing efforts to remind "people that we, the Native people of Canada, are a very boisterous and fun people, who love to tell funny stories and have a great time."[40]

Television: Readjusting the Recognizably Indian

"Humour requires intelligence," Taylor theorizes. "It calls for the ability to take in information, deconstruct it and reconstruct it in a new, improved, refined format. The humorist then reintroduces that information to the world to achieve a completely different reaction."[41] In his efforts to reconfigure televisual Indianness in *Mixed Blessings*, Taylor takes simulations of the Indian construct, pervasive across practically all media genres in their sordid histories, and readjusts them through a Native sensibility steeped in indigenous approaches to storytelling, humor, and popular culture. By flipping the mainstream script, so to speak, on the recognizably Indian, Taylor and *Mixed Blessings* begin to readjust the recognizably Indian early in the series and suggest the Indian should be acknowledged, confronted, and displaced by the recognizably Native to open up further spatial possibilities for representing the indigenous and to help pave paths for future indigenous TV series. In the first season, for example, *Mixed Blessings* evokes, resituates, and then marginalizes, in favor of Native tradition, one of the largest cultural icons of the twentieth century and, though lesser known, a contemporary part-time symbol of indigeneity: Elvis Presley. In the second episode, aforementioned lead characters Josie Fraser, the widowed Cree waitress and mother of three, and Hank Kowalchuk, the widowed Ukrainian Canadian plumber and father of two, prepare to sneak away for their first date. Like numerous sitcom characters before him, Hank turns to Elvis, his admitted "personal hero," for direction, in this case to sweet-talk and impress Josie with his knowledge of the King. Proudly professing he has seen all of the "Elvis Presley movies," like a genre unto themselves, Hank asks her, "What movie's the only one he didn't sing in? *Flaming Star.*" Hank pauses before adding approvingly, as if in the indigenous-know with his Cree date, "He played an Indian." Rolling her eyes, Josie replies dismissively, "What a guy."[42]

The exchange, including Josie's terse response, may sound uninspiring, yet it invites further exploration about Elvis in relation to the televisual indigeneity in *Mixed Blessings*. In contrast to almost all other sitcoms, *Mixed Blessings* repeatedly reframes the politics of indigenous identity from a recognizably Native perspective. Moreover, with pop culture Indians buff Drew Hayden Taylor as the episode's credited writer, Elvis is unlikely a haphazard selection here.[43] Although Hank is wrong—Elvis's *Flaming Star* character Pacer Burton *does* sing the cowboy bachelor and womanizer song "A Cane and a High Starched Collar" on camera—more intriguing is that *Mixed Blessings*, a show about intercultural relations between Crees and Ukrainian Canadians, references early on an intercultural movie about two peoples practically at war with each other.[44] In *Flaming Star*, everyone is deemed either Kiowa/Indian or settler/white, except for Elvis's character, who has a Kiowa mother and settler father. Not feeling he ever fully belongs to either culture ("I don't know who's my people," he says at one point), Pacer eventually rides with the Kiowas to avenge his mother's death at the hands of a settler but then turns against his tribe when they attack his white half-brother. Elvis, with no Vegas impersonators for backup, versus an entire band of Hollywood Kiowas! Just before he rides into the movie's concluding sunset to die alone, Pacer says to his brother, "Maybe someday, somewhere, people will understand folks like us."

The "us" rings of mixed families, like those featured in *Mixed Blessings*, who challenge either/or subject positionalities and negotiate personal, family, and tribal identities. It also hints at Elvis's offscreen identification as Cherokee, not just white. Elvis cited, from his mother's side, a Cherokee great-great-great-grandmother named Morning White Dove (and as far as I know, he did *not* call her an Indian princess). Inspired perhaps by his declared Cherokee heritage, Elvis agreed to play another Hollywood Indian named Joe Lightcloud, "a modern-day Navajo" and "a Trickster who survives by his wits," in the cinematic farce *Stay Away, Joe* (1968). Together, the on- and offscreen indigenous identities contribute to Peter Nazareth's contention that Elvis "was conscious of his Cherokee ancestry, which means he was conscious of having colonizer and colonized in him."[45]

Mixed Blessings further incorporates the indigenous-settler Elvis as a decision-making guide for Hank before the King fails to become an intercultural communicative bridge into their Cree-Ukrainian family conflicts. During their first date, Hank suddenly has an idea that, he announces, "the King would love": he and Josie fly to Las Vegas and marry at Graceland Wedding Chapel at six in the morning. Elvis then resurfaces in episode 4 when the newlyweds contemplate how to break the news to their unsuspecting families.

> JOSIE: Do you have any idea how much grief we have ahead of us?
> HANK: What would Elvis do?

Up to this point, Elvis has guided Hank, but it appears Hank's invocations have now run their course. Hank could turn again to *Flaming Star*, but even Presley's Pacer was unable to reconcile the film's Kiowa-settler conflicts without further anguish and his character's eventual death. Hank could try the Vegas Elvis, yet the Graceland Wedding Chapel is known far more for kitschy rash marriages, not for solving post-ceremony drama. After a momentary silence following Hank's WWED ("What would Elvis do?"), Josie's Cree wisdom supersedes Hank's faith in Elvis and inability to cull another answer from the King's filmography.

> JOSIE: We'll have a talking circle with a talking stick.
> HANK: What is that?
> JOSIE: Well, it's Native tradition. Everyone sits in a circle and no one can speak unless they're holding the talking stick.

HANK (*quizzically*): And if they do, you hit 'em with the stick?
JOSIE (*slaps him playfully*): No.
HANK: Well, it sounds very, uh, civilized.
JOSIE: Amazing what us heathens can come up with, huh? [*Hank cracks a half-smile*] There's no shouting, there's no interrupting. It'll work.[46]

Trumping Hank's WWED approach, Josie turns to a nonconfrontational indigenous practice for resolving the anticipated familial grief and resistance. Josie's agency in determining a potential interfamilial solution serves not only to remind viewers of Native tradition and its feasibility today but also to recognize settler colonial semantics and an indigenous-driven attempt to wrest some discursive control over the term "heathen."

The exchange here adds another example of speaking back to a type of Hollywood Indianness that films like *Flaming Star* perpetuated. Although *Flaming Star* shows a lead actor who identifies as Kiowa and temporarily and restrictively pledges allegiance to his tribe, Pacer also presumably dies due to Indian-inflicted wounds that contribute to the dominant portrait of Kiowas as instinctively violent savages. The civilized-savage dichotomy is often used flippantly regarding the indigenous in media, but *Mixed Blessings* reframes it. Coming from Taylor-to-Josie's shared recognizably Native script, "civilized" is a loaded discursive reminder of settler-constructed histories of Indian savagism, including in the audibly absent presence of "savage" that arguably elicits one of the meanings of Hank's audible "civilized." Josie's "us heathens" counters Indian savagery by engaging, destabilizing, and diminishing its ability to legitimate for settlers the ideology of Natives as uncivilized, particularly since Josie was the one who proposed the nonhierarchical Native tradition for breaking the marriage news to relatives.

At the end of season 1, when Elvis makes his last discursive appearance in *Mixed Blessings*, Hank drops the King, even when Josie attempts to persuade Hank by referencing his guide. When Hank initially refuses to attend a local powwow with Josie, she asks him, "What would Elvis have done?" The rhetorical question suggests the Indian-settler Elvis would have attended in support of his family, but Hank's blunt reply—"Elvis was dead at 42"—dismisses Josie's inquiry. Failing to convince him through his supposed love for Elvis, Josie succeeds when she turns to another Native tactic of explaining the personal significance and inclusivity of the powwow. Perhaps Hank finally learned, as Taylor notes in his own philosophy of reserve life, that "family will be there when strangers won't."[47]

Hank, too, takes his turns at speaking back to and resisting settler perceptions of Indianness. Perhaps attributable to his new relationship with Josie, Hank seems to recognize instances of when settler perceptions are *not* recognizably Native, as evident in settler-settler exchanges over the marriage. Upon learning of his father's new Cree wife, Walt, around sixteen, first asks with a reserved curiosity, "So, does this mean we're like part Indian now?" To which Hank counters absurdly to dispel Walt's immediate response of cultural curiosity: "Yes, Walt, you are now half-Indian. You must go on a vision quest and only in your underwear and strangle a hoofed animal with your bare hands."[48] The outlandish "vision" evokes a scene in the 1995 Canadian movie *Dance Me Outside*, in which a topless and drunken white character (married to a Native) chases in his own quest what he believes to be a gopher or beaver after shouting his spirit animal identity, "I am the wolverine!" No such nonsense plays out in *Mixed Blessings* as Hank's deadpan jest to Walt refutes such misguided cultural appropriation and the idea of a settler's sudden claim to indigeneity.

Walt has his romanticized, unaggressive, and naive notions of fictional Indians learned likely from fictional media, such as when he mentions in one episode seeing Indians perform smoke signals on TV. Hank's friend and coworker Tazz, however, initially reacts in disbelief to Hank's marriage news. "Can you do that?" Tazz asks. "She's an Indian [pause] waitress." Realizing his faux pas, Tazz quickly struggles to articulate his uneasiness with the marriage. Before storming off, Hank shouts back, "I'm not going there with you!" Tazz's utterance of "She's an Indian" interpellates volumes of racist and sexist rhetorics directed toward indigenous women and that possibly occupy some of Hank's "there." Tazz is generally friendly with Josie in person, but in this rare moment for his character, he expresses a potentially ingrained settler prejudice toward indigenous-settler unions. Feeling ashamed, he attempts to right his wrong as he turns from anti-Indian to pro-Indian by referencing cinematic noble savages. Strongly suggestive of Taylor's style of humorous writing (including numerous articles devoted to satirizing Hollywood Indians and the often white males who portray them),[49] Tazz declares, "I love the Indians! I got *Dances with Wolves* on DVD. I got the *Indian in the Cupboard*. I got all kinds of stuff. You know what, I love 'em. I've seen the *Last of the Mohican* [*sic*], the 'Second to Last of the Mohicans.' I like Indians. I just wasn't ready for this [marriage announcement]!"[50] Tazz names popular films (minus the made-up "Second to Last"), in which Cherokee actor Litefoot portrays a miniature toy in a settler boy's cupboard and settler actors Kevin Costner and Daniel Day-Lewis temporarily play Indian before their Hollywood Lakota and Mohican relatives vanish, reruns notwithstanding.

Set to the sitcom's intercultural tenor of collaboration, Native and non-Native also work together to performatively and discursively combat Indianness when a guest settler character in *Mixed Blessings* goes beyond just loving Indians to claiming to be the most Indian of all in the sitcom. A tense triad of the recognizably Indian, recognizably Native, and settler offers competing perceptions of the indigenous throughout the episode "Dances with Wolfy," an obvious play off of Costner's movie. Other sitcoms have performed similar word plays, such as *Yes, Dear*'s "Dances with Couch," in which non-Native fathers and sons don feathers in an Indian Scouts group, and the *Ten Items or Less* episode "Dances with Groceries," in which an otherwise bumbling adult settler suddenly learns he is "1/16th Shawnee" and proceeds to simulate an absurd vision quest that he researched online.[51] Unlike in *Mixed Blessings*, they show practically no semblance of knowing anything more than recognizably Indian performance. "Dances with Wolfy" calls into question Costner's *Dances with Wolves*, the white-male-gone-Native trope, and accompanying politics of cultural appropriation through the episode's performance of an Indian hobbyist from Germany named Wolfgang who moves onto the land next door to Josie and Hank and sets up a teepee and inuksuk amid a decorative buffalo skull, reindeer hide, and other signifiers that support Wolfy's attempt for "authentic" Indianness. "It looks like," Josie says upon first glance, "the United Nations of First Nations."[52]

As the episode's credited writer, Taylor likely culled the fictional character of Wolfgang from the his personal encounters with Germans and their "romanticized, exoticized, and adorized" perceptions of Natives, or what the German scholar Hartmut Lutz calls "Indianthusiasm."[53] As Taylor explains in the 2012 article "Experiencing Fine German 'Injuneering,'" he has visited "Germany, that far away land of schnitzel, white asparagus, and Indian enthusiasts," at least fourteen times, including for invited lectures, book tours, and conferences, such as the 2012 conference "Fake Identities: Imposters, Conmen, Wannabees in North American Culture."[54] He attributes German "fascination with Indians to probably a combination of everything from Karl May to the fact that Germans used to be very tribal themselves," nodding to "the Germanic tribes of the Rhine."[55] Like May, the late nineteenth-century German writer who popularized fantastical notions of cowboys and Indians in his home country, Wolfy in *Mixed Blessings* presumably had never visited North America and Native Peoples—that is, until he moved next door to Josie and Hank.

In a thick and exaggerated German accent, Wolfy greets his new neighbors: "Welcome to my reservation."[56] He raises a hand in the proverbial

Indian "How" gesture, to which Hank comically holds up Josie's hand to awkwardly reciprocate. Unlike Chief Longwalker's performative "How" play in *Diff'rent Strokes*, Josie refuses to corroborate and playfully slaps Hank.[57] Wolfy then serves Hank and Josie moose meat and bannock in his teepee, an interpellated indigenous gesture of welcome steeped in his limited perception of what he deems genuine Indianness. Then, like the casual adage "Let's do lunch," Wolfy tells Josie, "We must get together sometime and build a canoe, yeah?" As unenthusiastically as her "What a guy" reply to Hank's Elvis-as-Indian remark, Josie answers with a forced smile, "Yes, let's do that."

Wolfy overcompensates, to say the least, in his quest to become Indian. Foreshadowing the aforementioned conference theme, Josie tags him back at home as "just a wannabee" followed by a temporary acceptance of what she senses is a challenge: "He wants to play Indian? I can play Indian. I'll show him who's really Native and who isn't." Angered and perhaps intimidated by Wolfy's brazen appropriation of Indian and Native signifiers and performance, Josie attempts to one-up Wolfy by inviting him to dinner for a personally prepared "*real* traditional Native meal" (emphasis in original). Soliciting Walt's computer prowess, she and Walt commence researching online for a Cree meal that will scream Native and impress Wolfy. When Walt locates a recipe for "roast prairie chicken with an elk sage stuffing," Josie says it "will be great soon as I figure out how to stuff an elk up a prairie chicken." Unable to find elk, though, she opts for caribou.

At the dinner, Wolfy deems his host's efforts to be far short of his expectations of authentic edible Indianness.

WOLFY: What kind of caribou is it?
JOSIE: Cooked.
WOLFY: No. Is it a woodland or lichen-fed?
JOSIE: Woodland or lichen—I don't know. I didn't know there was a difference.
WOLFY: Of course. How can you not know this?

Wolfy is appalled at what he perceives to be the Cree family's assimilation into settler culture. "I do not understand you all. You should be ashamed of yourselves!" Angered, Josie snaps back, "Ashamed? Did you just say 'ashamed'?" But Wolfy continues, "You have no teepee at this house. Or even a sweat lodge." He disapproves that Josie is "married to a Russian" before bluntly telling everyone, "You do not know anything about the very animals that give you people sustenance. This is unforgivable. The only thing that is totally and 100 percent Native in this house is our beloved elder [Kookum]," to which she cordially responds, "Actually, I have a plastic hip."

Shocked at Kookum's discursive puncture to his unchecked colonizing mindset of quantifying indigeneity, Wolfy's anger escalates as he finally declares, "In Germany, we have names for people like you. We call you 'Coca-Cola Indians.' You have all been corrupted by the twentieth and twenty-first century. I think, no, I actually know, I am more Indians [*sic*] than all of you," and he exits abruptly.

Earlier in the episode, when Hank presumed Wolfy was "not Native," the German said he was personally "trying to be" and that he was "very devoted." The irony, suggests *Mixed Blessings*, is that Wolfy *is* more Indian than the Native Josie and other Cree characters in the context of the colonial invention of Indian. Although Wolfy has learned, from unnamed sources, how to set up a teepee and how to prepare caribou, he personifies arrogant appropriation of Native culture with a polemical mindset on who and what counts as Native.

How, then, might a recognizably Native character like Josie respond to such a blatant discursive act of disrespect by someone personally claiming to be the most Indian of all? Josie's previous performative gestures in *Mixed Blessings* could be considered. For example, there are Josie's earlier smiles of feigned politeness to Wolfy in response to the prospect of a canoe building date, or her recognizably Native glare at Wolfy for his disrespectful "ashamed" talk. Yet the smiles and glares as well as engaging in competition over Indianness with Wolfy all come up short of resolving her own frustrations with "Indians" like Wolfgang. There also is Josie's recurring Native gesture of slapping Hank when he supports Indianness, as if she literally slaps away absurd and appropriated Indian talk and performance, such as his "hit 'em with the stick" crack and his raising Josie's hand for "How." But Josie reserves the slaps only for Hank and performs them far more endearingly than spitefully. Hank, too, appears playful in those moments and reserves his Indian performativity for his wife, whom he knows he can tease.

In response to Wolfy's concluding diatribe of claiming more Indianness, no one immediately speaks back. Josie, Hank, Kookum, and Josie's sister, Kate, sit silently and stare in quizzical disbelief at each other for approximately ten seconds. They appear to allow Wolfy to sink himself and exit with his static ignorance of indigeneity before they partake in one of the oldest Native traditions in existence today: laughter.[58] The three Crees and one Ukrainian-Canadian erupt into a powerful performance of resounding laughter for nearly all of the episode's closing twenty seconds, performing quite possibly the longest on-screen recognizably Native laugh in North American sitcom history. In comparison to the earlier short-lived responses by Josie, the laughter delivers a fitting and humorous indigenous comeuppance directed at Wolfy and, by extension, other non-Natives like the American wolfy Costner who culturally and unapologetically usurp Indianness and fashion their own recognizably Indian identity. As Taylor said in a 2002 interview, he looks at non-Native appropriation of indigeneity "with more humor than annoyance."[59] Rather than angrily lash back at Wolfy and stoop to his level, Josie and her family laugh back at and laugh off his preposterous notions that "real" indigeneity is quantifiable and frozen in history and that an outsider can somehow become super-Indian with a hodgepodge of tribal signifiers and tidbits of indigenous knowledge.

Television: Being Recognizably Native

As a recognizably Native sitcom attesting to the ongoing presence of "the aesthetic ruins of Indian simulations," *Mixed Blessings* is highly cognizant of the Indian construct.[60] The producers' televisions, however, are not only explicitly reactionary to Indianness; they also proactively envision recognizably Native representations through a tribalography of televisions grounded in "the new stories of survivance over dominance."[61] "Survivance," Vizenor claims, "is more than survival, more than endurance or mere response; the stories of survivance are an active presence."[62] As Jill Doerfler (White Earth Anishinaabe) comments, survivance "highlights Native people's ability not merely to exist, but to flourish."[63] In *Mixed Blessings*, indigenous survivance flourishes through a fusion of aesthetic elements, including but not limited to recognizably Native storying, casting, characterization, and music. The sitcom's interrelationships of narrative, indigenous actors, character development, and soundtrack provide audiences, in turn, with a rich collective of indigenous affective, visual, and sonic representations. As I turn to the sitcom's politics of Native subjectivities in the cast, roles, and songs, I will reference story lines from *Mixed Blessings* to provide further context and narrative support for the creative choices informing the making of layered indigenous representations.

Mixed Blessings underscores conversations about contemporary indigenous identities and presents a sustaining visuality of the Cree characters' daily lives, in which viewers get to know the characters, unlike the former skewed glimpses into the highly marginalized and irregular on-screen presence of the recognizably Indian in scores of previous productions. For *Mixed Blessings* to present similar and different Cree characters, notably in the plural, who move, speak, and laugh illustrates contemporary Native populations' transmotion over fixity. In comparison to sitcoms with just the occasional one guest Indian character, a recurring Redcorn (in *King of the Hill*), or rarer still, multiple sitcom Indians in an episode, *Mixed Blessings* reclaims a share of the on-screen indigenous visuality by representing culturally and socially shared and diverse ways of being Cree and indigenous in the twenty-first century through the active presence of numerous recognizably Native characters.

From the start, the production of *Mixed Blessings* was built on perceptions of indigenous and intercultural realities. As Scott says, "We just wanted to present a situation that we thought (portrayed) real people and real situations."[64] In the video *The Making of Mixed Blessings*, Scott adds specificity by alluding to Josie's sister, Kate, and son Mick and Hank's daughter, Vickie: "With family, you can introduce characters, you can introduce situations that are real, that people can really relate to . . . we all have the kooky aunt or we all know some son that's gone sideways or we know a daughter who talks back to the father. These are all real things."[65] Although *Mixed Blessings*, commonly known like other sitcoms as a work of fiction, screens the standard disclaimer in each episode's closing credits ("The events depicted in this program are fictitious. Any similarity to any person living or dead is merely coincidental"), the sitcom nonetheless taps into realistic moods and situations and relatable characters to stake out an important and rare indigenous and intercultural space in the televisual landscape.

Scott suggests here efforts to produce a universal appeal, albeit through a fictive reality, in his television projects. On his recent Gemini- and Leo-award winning First Nations drama *Blackstone*, Scott says, "As a content creator, as someone who wants to tell stories, it's important the series is accessible to everyone." The sentiment is clearly applicable as well to *Mixed Blessings*. "For my comedies to work," Taylor similarly insists from a comic writer's standpoint, "the humor has to be universal."[66] At the same time, however, Scott and Taylor do not exclude indigenous specificity. Rather, they unabashedly privilege the production of recognizably Native characters and humor, a draw to non-Native Francis Damberger, who directed all of the episodes in seasons 2 and 3. "What is really attractive to me," Damberger says, "is that the aboriginal characters are played with such humour. It's important to see that other side of them."[67]

In *every* episode, Native characters and Native actors occupy representational spaces of survivance in an on- and offscreen "presence and continuation of Natives."[68] Unlike televisual texts that have cast practically any non-Native in indigenous roles, *Mixed Blessings* shows cultural consideration in casting, to the degree that the sitcom, in constructing and delivering its narratives, blurs performative boundaries between cast and characters. All of the Cree characters, recurring and guest, are portrayed by indigenous actors, several of whom are Cree in real life. Tina Lameman, for example, is Beaver Lake Cree in Alberta and the daughter of a Beaver Lake Cree Nation chief. Lameman's real-life nephew Griffin Powell-Arcand, who plays her on-screen son Donnie, is Plains Cree from the Alexander First Nation Reserve and the son of well-known actor Nathaniel Arcand.[69] Veteran actress Michelle Thrush (Kate) is Cree, as is her mentor the late Gordon Tootoosis.[70] Wilma Pelly (Kookum) is Salteaux Ojibwe, and Emma Ashbaugh (Josie's daughter, Bobbie) is K'ómoks. Allen Belcourt (Josie's older son, Mick), a Métis actor and filmmaker from Edmonton, affirms the sitcom sovereignty in *Mixed Blessings*. "For us [Native Peoples] to really go ahead with our future in the television industry, we have to tell our own stories."[71]

With Josie, Kate, Kookum, and Bobbie, *Mixed Blessings* notably represents four similar yet diverse female Cree characters, a first in the sitcom genre. Despite the considerable pool of indigenous acting talent, sitcoms (and fictional TV in general) have scarcely ever depicted a female Native character, let alone multiple characters with speaking lines from the same indigenous nation. In 1993, Kimberly Norris Guerrero (Colville/Salish Kootenai/Cherokee) guest-starred and verbally sparred with Jerry Seinfeld in the U.S. sitcom *Seinfeld* ("The Cigar Store Indian" episode). In the next decade on the show *Malcolm in the Middle*, Filipina American actress Emy Coligado portrayed recurring Alaska Native character Piama Tananahaakna. *The Rez*, a late 1990s dramatic Canadian comedy adapted from the popular 1995 film *Dance Me Outside*, cast Salteaux sisters and actresses Jennifer and Tamara Podemski as Sadie Maracle and Lucy Pegamegaaba, respectively. In season 2 of *The Rez*, Elaine Miles (Nez Perce/Cayuse), perhaps best known for her quiet but strong role as Marilyn Whirlwind in the early 1990s in *Northern Exposure*, played Mad Etta. In the 2007 show *Moose TV*, an eight-episode First Nations sitcom co-created by Ernest Webb (Cree) and Catherine Bainbridge of Rezolution Pictures International with Taylor as a script consultant, Jennifer Podemski and Michelle Latimer (Métis) costarred as sisters Alice and Robin Cheechoo.[72]

In comparison, *Mixed Blessings* heightens the standard for sitcoms in its recognizably Native realism in casting. Of all the indigenous actresses in film and television, such as Irene Bedard (Inuit and Métis), Tantoo Cardinal (Cree), and Misty Upham (Blackfeet), Scott says, "Tina Lameman is one of only a few actresses who could have filled the character we envisioned for Josie." His observation, I would hope, does not necessarily slight other Native actresses; it suggests respect to Lameman as a Cree actress who knows her Cree relatives and knows how to portray and embody a recognizably Cree woman on-screen.[73] In return, Lameman, who received the 2008 Best Actress honor at the Alberta Film and Television Awards for her role, connects deeply with her character. Remarried in real life to a non-Native in Alberta, where Crees and Ukrainians are known to intermarry, Lameman claims Scott and Taylor "wrote my life." In further affective connections, Lameman turns to female Cree relatives for inspiration for her role. Like the comedy duo "Susie and Sarah," featured in Taylor's *Redskins* documentary on Native humor and who perform as their indigenous elders to entertain real-life audiences of elders, or like actor Evan Adams who admits his character Thomas Builds-the-Fire's storytelling techniques in *Smoke Signals* were inspired by his grandmother, Lameman's Josie also is influenced by her relatives.[74] "Josie is my Grandma, my Kookums, and a lot of my aunts." Lameman laughs before adding, "She's a bossy Cree woman, very independent, very strong, and knows what she wants basically and isn't afraid to live her life and raise her kids, and she's a lot like the Cree women that I know: she's a matriarch."[75]

For example, when her on-screen daughter, Bobbie, is interested in becoming a vegetarian, Josie sternly says, "If you think it's wise to abandon 10,000 years of tradition, there's a few things I would like to tell you about that." When her younger son, Donnie, asks if hot dogs are "part of our Cree culture," she seriocomically replies, "Only for the last two generations." Or when Hank asks why Kookum is dancing toward him at a local powwow, Josie shares her cultural knowledge and a directive on protocol.

> HANK: Why is she coming over here?
> JOSIE: Oh, she wants you to go in and intertribal.
> HANK: She wants to adopt me?
> JOSIE: No. Intertribal is a dance. Anybody can go, from any tribe, including you.
> HANK: Dance?
> JOSIE: You have to go. She's an elder. It's tradition. She calls you. You go. Go![76]

Wilma Pelly, the Salteaux Ojibwe actress who plays Kookum (Cree for "grandma"), had previously acted on Taylor's favorite series, *North of 60*. She played the recurring role of Elsie Tsa' Che', "the town medicine woman and no non-sense elder."[77] On *Mixed Blessings*, Pelly says Kookum is also "the elder. An elder in my community or other Native communities [is] very well respected. That's what I like—the respect." When her nephew Charlie, for instance, delivers a moose carcass to the family house, he tells her, "Don't worry, Kookum. I saved you the nose!" prompting a big grin from her in a comical moment of shared Cree recognition that elders are known to enjoy the nose.[78] Throughout the series, Pelly portrays Kookum as culturally and familially responsible, gentle and giving, and mischievous and wisecracking. In her debut appearance in season 1, Kookum arrives at Josie's house to pick up Bobbie and Donnie while Josie goes on her first date with Hank. Recognizing Hank as her plumber, Kookum makes rather ambiguous and funny remarks in Cree (with English subtitles):

KOOKUM: I remember you! You brought your snake to my house.
HANK (*to Josie*): What did she say?
JOSIE: She said nothing. It doesn't translate.
KOOKUM (*to Bobbie and Donnie*): C'mon kids. Your mother has some snaking of her own to do![79]

Kookum's humorous wit also translates into a comical impatience with her other daughter, Kate. At the bingo hall in one episode, Kookum asks her overly dramatic and culturally proud but misguided daughter, "What kind of Cree woman are you, you can't even play a decent game of bingo?" When Kate's chicken stuffed "with sweetgrass as opposed to sage" repulses her family at dinner, Kookum humorously advises her, "You should try frying it in lard." Or when Kookum has a doctor's appointment and leaves the inexperienced Kate in charge of the Ucreenian baby, Kookum assures her she will be back in an hour, then smiles and says in an aside, "Indian time," thus affording herself no fixed time for her return. In the series finale, when Kate panics over not knowing the whereabouts of Josie and Hank (it turns out they were on a weekend getaway and had no cell phone reception), Kookum says, "Somebody smudge her!"

In extended support of representing the recognizably Native, *Mixed Blessings* consistently hires indigenous actors to portray guest-starring indigenous characters. Richard Monias, a former tribal administrator from the Heart Lake First Nation in Alberta, plays Uncle Charlie, Josie's ex-brother-in-law, in three episodes. Sokaymoh Frederick (Métis/Cree), cofounder of the performance company Alberta Aboriginal Arts in Edmonton, portrays the hospital's nurse attending to Josie and the baby at the end of season 2. Actress and mentor to Native youth from Saddle Lake First Nations Teneil Whiskeyjack (Cree) plays Josie's niece in a couple of episodes. Thrush's *Blackstone* costar Roseanne Supernault (Métis)

Michelle Thrush and Wilma Pelly in *Mixed Blessings*. Used with permission of Prairie Dog Film + Television. Photograph by Dan Power.

guest-stars as Hank's plumbing apprentice and a single mother in a season 3 episode.

In accordance with the sitcom's intentionality of bridging cultures, elder Helmer Twoyoungmen from the Stoney First Nation in Morley, Alberta, is another apt casting choice for a guest character in the episode "Traditional Wedding."[80] Two weeks after the Elvis-themed wedding in Las Vegas, Josie announces that she wants a "traditional style" ceremony. "We're gonna have it like Native, Native all the way," she explains, "sweetgrass, pipe ceremony, the blanket." She also mentions needing a priest and an elder, the latter of whom Twoyoungmen portrays on-screen as one of the individuals who solidifies the union between Josie and Hank, suggestive of further bridging between indigenous and settler. He has only two lines in the episode but presents a strong recognizably Native presence as he conducts an on-screen cleansing ceremony near a teepee and assists the groom. Twoyoungmen's presence also carries a history of his former and current creative and critical work in Hollywood and indigenous communities. An extra in *Little Big Man* (1970), set designer in *Legends of the Fall* (1994), the character "Elder #1" in the 2005 HBO miniseries *Into the West*, guest star in the comedic documentary series *Fish Out of Water* (2008), and musician in the powwow rock band Koskanuba, Twoyoungmen is now a community addictions counselor and teacher of First Nations medicine to Native youth.[81] "Everywhere I go," he says, "I try to promote better understanding between my culture and the culture of the dominant society," a sentiment directly shared by Scott and Taylor in the production of their creative works. Twoyoungmen's philosophy on Native and non-Native relations also resonates with the encoded intent of *Mixed Blessings*. "We are each other's best medicine," he says, "no matter what culture we come from."[82]

Within the historical context of televisual indigenous talent, representation, and viewership, *Mixed Blessings* shows that casting and characterization matter immensely. As noted earlier, the actors and characters denote the active presence of survivance and elements of the relatively new indigenous sitcom sovereignty. Lameman, Pelly, and the other indigenous actors prove that Natives can sufficiently fill all indigenous roles in a sitcom and counter the symbolic annihilation, the absence, of Native representations.[83] By creating multiple recognizably Native characters and casting recognizably Native actors for the roles, *Mixed Blessings* simultaneously refrains from indigenous erasure and from support of the recognizably Indian. *Mixed Blessings* also contributes to the growing genealogy of recognizably Native characters for future indigenous generations to see and connect with on-screen. For Indigenous Peoples to see themselves and to know that some producers work hard to ensure an on-to-offscreen indigenous relationality between fictively realistic characters and real-world viewers can provide for deeply affective connections through what Faye Ginsburg calls "screen memories."[84]

The music in *Mixed Blessings* also provides a layer of indigenous fictive reality, affective resonance, and aesthetic boundary expansion in the making of the sitcom through its soundtrack of survivance, as especially heard in seasons 2 and 3, for current and future listeners-viewers. Season 1 includes familiar sonic signifiers of Native music, moves that could also be essentially critiqued for catering to non-Native musical expectations of indigeneity. A Native flute surfaces occasionally in episodes as a sonic bridge, a transitional cue to slide viewers from one scene to the next.[85] For example, as Hank and Josie move a conversation about Hank's love for Elvis from outside of her house into her dining room, a Native flute plays softly over the scene change. The flute returns in several other episodes, such as during a two-line exchange spoken in Cree between Kookum and the elder in "Traditional Wedding." The other most recognizably Native instrument appears in the same season 1 episode along with the season finale, in which drum groups perform at Josie and Hank's traditional wedding and at the powwow.

In every episode of season 1, the sitcom's upbeat instrumental theme song plays in the introduction and over the closing credits. Symbolically suggestive of sliding the settler and indigenous into safe musical genre corners, an electric guitar and presumably Native flute respectively trade licks over quick shots of each cast member and images of Fort McMurray. Starting in season 2, however, *Mixed Blessings* replaces its recurring use of the theme music during the closing credits with a developing sitcom soundtrack that spotlights contemporary indigenous artists. Like the indigenous actors who fill the major and minor indigenous roles, Native musicians fill the soundtrack with their musical contributions to the Native sitcom tribalography. As I contend, the sitcom's selected songs play noteworthy roles in the narrative development of the series.

The songs also decolonize what, for many, constitutes indigenous music by crossing socially constructed perceptions of sonic boundaries. That sense of decolonizing reverberation is foundational in a song performed at the end of season 2 by Inuvialuit and Dene musician Leanne Goose from Inuvik. Right after the Ucreenian baby is born, Goose's hard-hitting electric guitar–driven alternative rock track "Burns" plays over the closing credits with the repeating lyric, "Music, it burns inside my head." The line metaphorically suggests the fluid sonic imprint and impact that the lyrically undefined and uncategorized "music" has on the artist. As the song leaves open, unbounded possibilities for listeners, all Goose appears to request in return, as she emphatically states on her MySpace site, is that listeners "Be REAL BE YOU" (capitals in original).[86]

Goose's directive is echoed in the "Dances with Wolfy" episode. After Josie finally lets go of the needless competition with Wolfy over "who's really Native and who isn't," the episode concludes with Mohawk descendant Kinnie Starr's upbeat hip-hop and club song "Rock the Boat." Sounding forth ambiguously open-ended lyrics aimed at Natives to resist imposed cultural fixity (like that espoused by Wolfy) and to be true to themselves, and hence recognizably Native, Starr sings,

> Heed the heart of everything near you
> Be who you are
> Shine like you do
> Aboriginal, I'm speaking directly to you.[87]

Songs continue to help sonically and lyrically frame the sitcom's narrative in additional episodes. As Mick boards a bus for South Dakota to find his Lakota biological father, Stó:lo Nation (Coast Salish) hip-hop artist Ostwelve raps "Feather in My Rearview Mirror," a traveling track of reflecting back while also moving forward in one's journey in life. When Mark, Mick's father and Josie's and Kate's ex-boyfriend, shows up in Fort McMurray in a subsequent episode, the closing song symbolizes a dangerous warning heard in Six Nations musician Derek Miller's blues rock song "Devil Came Down Sunday." When Kate tells the devilish and unreliable Mark she is pregnant in the following episode, he leaves her standing alone at a party while Inuit musician and environmental activist Lucie Idlout, who has previously opened for Buffy Sainte-Marie (Cree) and the White Stripes, sings, "Would you turn me away if I let you know? / If I asked you to stay, would you go?"[88] Each song selection, in other words, adds a sonic layer to the story while also affording airtime for contemporary indigenous artists to showcase their music.

In addition to the relevant and applicable lyrics and the unbounded sounds of indigenous musics, the sitcom's soundtrack provides a lasting resonance in support of the sitcom's narrative approach to intercultural bridging. Drawing from diverse musical influences, the included artists significantly support the overall tenor of *Mixed Blessings* and its intercultural work in bridging societal gaps. Although the music of "Uke-Cree Fiddler" Arnie Strynadka, whose mother is Cree and father is a first-generation Ukrainian Canadian, would have been an intriguing choice, other indigenous artists contribute to the soundtrack.[89] One episode features Leela Gilday's indigenous pop song "Indian Girl" about being a mixed Native-white girl. (Gilday's father is white; her mother is Dene.) The track refutes the either/or racial identification from the opening verse,

I am an Indian girl
I hold my head up high for the world
I am a white girl
I hold my head up high, this is my world.

Another episode closes with a song by M'Girl, an indigenous group with Métis/Cree, Mohawk, and Ojibwe female artists. Situating their music in such genres as a cappella, R&B, and reggae, M'Girl blurs the temporal binary of traditional-contemporary as they merge older and newer musics into one. Their 2006 album, *Fusion of Two Worlds*, is described as "eclectic with aboriginal sensibilities at the core of the overall sound that keeps it honest and true to their voice & hand drum roots."[90]

Conclusion: Televising Indigeneity

In all, *Mixed Blessings* fuses numerous indigenous sensibilities in its narratives, casting, characterization, and soundtrack to provide for the makings of an indigenous sitcom that readjusts the recognizably Indian and represents the recognizably Native. Whereas previous sitcoms failed time and again to represent the recognizably Native and counter the recognizably Indian in their representational productions of a new frontier and new trail (as discussed in chapter 1), *Mixed Blessings* does both. Whereas sitcoms have failed to produce an indigenous-centered self-determination (chapter 2) that represented Native agency and survivance in characterization, *Mixed Blessings* enacts indigenous self-determination in production and representational agency. Whereas John Redcorn (chapter 3) started to challenge the recognizably Indian, he also was severely outnumbered and seemingly compelled to reinforce the sitcom Indian, albeit in old and new contexts, and to negotiate and play to surrounding expectations of Indianness. Unlike *King of the Hill*'s lone Redcorn, *Mixed Blessings* features five regular indigenous characters along with additional guest Native characters whose active presence provide an array of recognizably Native sensibilities and possibilities.

Unlike the marginalized Tom Strongbows, Chief Eagle Clouds, John Longwalkers, and Chief Henrys in today's reruns of *The Andy Griffith Show*, *The Brady Bunch*, *Diff'rent Strokes*, and *Saved by the Bell*, respectively, *Mixed Blessings* maps out a space where Natives take precedence over Indians, Natives collaborate more equitably with non-Natives, and Natives remain plural in number and diversity of character. Representational tensions and conflicts ensue between the indigenous and nonindigenous, but they unfold through the lens of a recognizably Native and intercultural fictive reality, not a misguided settler dominance over the recognizably Indian. Although the intercultural collaborations and celebratory undertones in *Mixed Blessings* may not cater to everyone's televisual tastes or politics, Ron Scott, Drew Hayden Taylor, and others involved in the making of the sitcom imprint a brand of comedic televisions of indigeneity upon the televisual landscape as they move audiences toward a *decolonized viewing* of the recognizably Indian and toward intercultural dialogue on future relations among the indigenous and nonindigenous.

CONCLUSION

Sign-off
DIGITAL TEST PATTERNS

In the late 1930s and early 1940s, the Indian Head Test Pattern began to sign viewers on to the New World of television programming. Once the situation comedy, led by its grand marshal *I Love Lucy*, became a programming staple in the 1950s, the tribal televisions in the genre's representations of the indigenous ensued. From the politics of the recognizably Indian and settler-Indian relations in subsequent eras of New Frontier, New Trail, Great Society, and self-determination policies to the new Indian challenges and interventions in *King of the Hill* to sitcom sovereignty and the recognizably Native in *Mixed Blessings*, my intertextual and paratextual ventures in this project have covered a wide range of televisual terrain in efforts to center textual sites of analysis where representations of the indigenous and nonindigenous collide and converge in contact zones creatively adjusted and readjusted by generations of sitcom producers.

As a sitcom kid, I have had an ambivalent relationship with the sights and sounds of the indigenous in sitcoms over the years. Yet the "sitcom kid" designation may sound dated for today's younger generations and their vastly expanded media options. Whereas I do not recall using the Internet until I was in my late teens in the mid-1990s, my children practically entered the world (and the World Wide Web) with their own Gmail and Facebook accounts. Whereas I was born within months of Marie Winn's controversial anti-TV book *The Plug-in Drug* (1977), today's youth, particularly teenagers and twenty-somethings, are labeled as highly amplified and wireless inheritors of the plugged-in descriptor.[1] My so-called Generation X was deemed overly saturated with TV, but today's Millennials are whom the Pew Research Center recently called "history's first 'always connected' generation" due to their connectivity to and usage of "digital technology and social media."[2] With that said, "I'm a YouTube kid" is, I presume, more likely to be heard from Natives and non-Natives now and in the near future than Sherman Alexie's, Drew Hayden Taylor's, and my sitcom kid narratives.

Sure, sitcoms are still around and available on more TV channels than ever before, but the media sites for viewing them have expanded exponentially since my childhood, even since I began writing this book. Besides the now old school options of VHS tapes (boxes of which sit in my attic), DVDs (which may soon join their VHS relations), and cable (canceled it in 2008), new media streaming sites like Hulu and Netflix (subscriber since 2009), video hosts like YouTube and Vimeo, and social networks like Facebook and Twitter with posted links to online videos are reconceptualizing "television" with computers doubling as TV sets as the sites lead Internet users to almost instantaneous access to complete episodes of most sitcoms cited in this book, not to mention videos from all other TV genres.[3]

Of all the video-sharing sites, however, YouTube arguably leads the way in affording to its billions of users access to more programs and more programming control. During the course of my research for primary sources of television series, YouTube became essential in accessibility. In numerous instances, YouTube seemed to be the *only* site for access. For example, when I tried to track down the *Barney Miller* episode "Bones," all searches fell short. At one point, a media center in Los Angeles purportedly had a copy. Then finally, in 2012, someone uploaded it to YouTube.[4]

From searching for uploaded videos of users' personal home movies and Smartphone footage to classic sports moments, obscure music videos, lawnmower repair, Internet TV series, dancing cats, dancing babies, and banter between Elmo and Ricky Gervais, YouTube provides access to countless media and popular culture texts.[5] With its users creating, starring in, and uploading video blogs, skits, musical performances, and other "original" videos, YouTube is, as Henry Jenkins says, the tentative "epicenter of today's participatory culture" in which "fans and other consumers are invited to actively participate in the creation and circulation of new content."[6] Founded by three former employees of PayPal in June 2005, just thirteen months before my oldest was born, and purchased by Google in November 2006, YouTube has dramatically altered and expanded the televisual and media landscapes with its user-generated content, or what *New Yorker* writer John Seabrook calls "user-generated anarchy," of original and previously aired videos. In early 2012, YouTube had "eight hundred million unique users a month" and received over "three billion views a day," making it the third most visited Internet site after Google and Facebook, both of which constantly lead viewers, via searches and posts, back to YouTube, where nearly fifty hours of extremely diverse content from around the world are added every single minute. "It is," Seabrook deduces, "the first truly global media platform on Earth."[7]

YouTube also functions, as it does of most other peoples and cultures around the globe, as one of the primary visual-sonic hubs for screening the indigenous. As a transnational tool, YouTube provides access to indigenous programs from other countries, such as the indigenous sitcom *Moose TV* from Canada that I have viewed only on YouTube in the United States. In a book, then, that has followed representations of the recognizably Indian and recognizably Native in TV sitcoms into the twenty-first century, I turn now to some of the original online anarchy on the ever-expanding "television" e-network YouTube for a precursory peek at what's next in comedic tribal televisions of indigeneity.

Digital Test Patterns

As Faye Ginsburg, Laurel Dyson, and other scholars have discussed, online representations of Indigenous Peoples have long circulated and contributed to what Kyra Landzelius calls the "virtual face of indigeneity."[8] I am interested here in critically *entertaining* (as a verb *and* adjective) strategies of survivance that inform how Native producers are shaping that face. To illustrate, I turn to the critical-creative viral videos of the 1491s, a Native comedic troupe whose members envision, write, produce, perform, and upload videos to share with the world on their 1491s site and YouTube channel and to effect laughter, smiles, critical reflection, cultural recognition, debate, and steps toward indigenous justice. Since gathering for the first time on the set of "Wolf Pack Auditions," the group's premiere broadcasted video in Bemidji, Minnesota, in late 2009, the 1491s have been testing the relatively untested digital waves of online indigenous comedy with a myriad of satirical digital patterns.[9] Although not all viewers are always fans of these patterns, indigenous producers like the 1491s showcase a rich network of texts whose visual, sonic, and affective representations are encoded with the intent to empower Native Peoples, to represent love and humor over hate and anger, to challenge and spur reflection on indigenous understandings of indigenous identities, to foster and support the activist work of decolonizing views of Native Peoples and cultures, to move audiences toward decolonized viewing as a visual and intellectual given, and to inspire current and future generations to create and broadcast their own recognizably Native tribal televisions for the world to see, hear, and feel.

As the group states on its site,

The 1491s is a sketch comedy group, based in the wooded ghettos of Minnesota and buffalo grass of Oklahoma. They are a gaggle of Indians chock full of cynicism and splashed with a good dose of indigenous satire. They coined the term All My Relations, and are still waiting for the royalties. They were at the Custer's Last Stand. They mooned Chris Columbus when he landed. They invented bubble gum. The 1491s teach young women how to be strong. And . . . teach young men how to seduce these strong women.[10]

The group's name connotes a playful tone with a sophisticated indigenous sensibility. Although the main players—cofounders Dallas Goldtooth (Santee Dakota/Diné), Ryan Red Corn (Osage), Bobby Wilson (Sisseton Dakota), Migizi Pensoneau (Ponca/Ojibwe), and Sterlin Harjo (Mvskoke)—were born well into the twentieth century, the name 1491s suggests they were always already here, including before Columbus's wrong turn in 1492. Reminiscent of Tom Joad's "wherever you can look" cinematic speech in *The Grapes of Wrath* (1940), the 1491s imply they are wherever Indigenous Peoples were, are, and will be continuing a thriving indigenous presence, livelihood, and laughter anchored in ancestral logics moving across generations, space, and time.[11]

In comparison to mainstream sitcoms, which I suspect will continue the predominant absence and, when rarely present, highly restrictive portrayals of the indigenous, do-it-yourself indigenous videomakers like the 1491s are breaking creative, broadcasting, and representational ground online. In comparison to indigenous sitcoms, which are very rare and costly to produce on cable television, some indigenous YouTube users are taking digital routes to produce, represent, and broadcast their recognizably Native creations. Rather than deal with the disruptive abundance of mainstream TV restraints, uninformed TV executives, and corporate sponsors (which may inform Ryan Red Corn's personally designed "Kill Your TV" T-shirt featuring an exploding TV screen for a head detached from a body in suit and tie), the 1491s pursue and hold creative digital sovereignty over their product in cyberspace. Sure, ratings and viewers' opinions can and do vary and commercial sponsorship is optional, but the videos continue without fear of cancellation.[12]

By going digital to create and distribute their original videos on their site and YouTube channel, the 1491s are "trying," cofounder Red Corn explains, "to combat the control of media" by acquiring more of the representational "bandwidth."[13] To illustrate, Red Corn says one should Google

"Native American" to see "what images recur and what images rank highest." Narrowed to Google's "Images" search feature, hundreds of millions of results ensue. Similarly, a video search for "Native American" on YouTube produces hundreds of thousands of hits. Both searches bring up vast amounts of images or clips featuring historical Natives frozen in the past, New Age portraits of Native spirituality, and songs with Native flutes amid graphics of animals, nature, and nineteenth-century stock Indians. Native-created videos featuring contemporary multidimensional Native Peoples are also present but far less in comparison to the dominant imagery of "Native American." For the 1491s, then, making videos of modern-day Native survivance increases indigenous media and indigenous control over it. As Red Corn contends, "Create more and better art and you'll take up more bandwidth and tip the scales."[14]

For example, in 2011, Red Corn and filmmaker Sterlin Harjo made the short video "Smiling Indians." It opens with the stark message, "This Film is Dedicated to Edward S. Curtis." Curtis's famous late nineteenth- and twentieth-century photographs of Native Peoples continue to influence perceptions and newer images of the unsmiling and stoic Native. "We need to add more of our own images," Red Corn says, "to compete against Curtis's," whose photographs "permeate every history book . . . [in] grade school to even the documentaries that are shown on TV now."[15] So, the two filmmakers held digital cameras in front of dozens of Natives, who literally smile back, and often appear to uncontrollably laugh back, at the dominant photographic image of dour Natives. Set to Laura Ortman's melodic and dreamy song "Can't Stop This Feeling"—in the case of "Smiling Indians," the feeling of *happiness*—the musical message and slow tempo mesh well with the slow-motion shots of Natives' facial expressions. The 1491s literally reconfigure a part of the "virtual *face* of indigeneity" (emphasis mine) into an indigenous collective of smiles that are, to quote Mishauna Goeman (Tonawanda Seneca), "upsetting the terrains of settler colonialism" and heeding Himani Bannerji's call for "returning the gaze."[16]

In their videos "Wolf Pack Auditions" and "Hunting," the 1491s attempt to seize more of the bandwidth by setting their sights on Hollywood Indians, like non-Native Taylor Lautner's character Jacob in the *Twilight* series and non-Native Daniel Day-Lewis's Hawkeye in *Last of the Mohicans*. In the former, Goldtooth, Red Corn, Wilson, and Pensoneau portray four outlandish Hollywood Indians who audition for the "Indian" roles of the wolf pack in *Twilight*. Positioning the video at the "intersections of cynicism and humor," Julia Goodfox (Pawnee) contends the bogus auditions are "as much about the burden of authenticity (with non-Natives being chosen as best representing Indians) as it is about the Hollywood infrastructure that refuses to employ Tribal actors." In the end, the only one presumably hired is a last-minute arrival, an African American with, he says, "a little bit" of Indian. In "Hunting," a *Last of the Mohicans* parody filmed on the Menominee Reservation in Wisconsin, Red Corn is Hawkeye and Goldtooth is Chingachgook. Like the movie version, the two run seemingly forever through a forest amid upbeat inspirational music; but unlike in the film, the 1491s find their destination not at the end of a bleak cultural outlook for Mohicans but at the fast food restaurant Hardee's, where the two hungry "Mohicans" order, as they say, a combo #4 with cheese, in effect running the characters out of the romanticized ghostly past and into the lively contemporary.[17]

Although their comedy resembles, as Goodfox notes, the sketch comedy of *Kids in the Hall*, several of the group's videos suggest possibilities for becoming conceptualized into indigenous Internet sitcoms.[18] "The Avatars" (2012) especially suggests a sharply satirical sitcom sensibility. In response to James Cameron's going-native blockbuster *Avatar* (2009), the indigenous family in "The Avatars" is diverse in characterization and rich with episodic possibilities. In Cameron's film, lead settler character Jake Sully is sent by his colonizing military to the moon of Pandora to obtain (read: steal) a precious mineral resource from the homelands of the twelve-foot-tall and blue Na'vi indigenous humanoids. In the guise of a Na'vi, Sully learns their ways (from the chief's daughter), eventually sides with them, and serves as *the* Na'vi to lead them into battle against the ruthless military that is determined to destroy the land and anyone in its path for the minerals. The film has its unabashed commentary on environmental planetary destruction and mechanized warfare, but its narrative route is nothing new. CNN reviewer Tom Charity calls it "'Dances with Wolves' in outer space," and Randy Szuch illustrates how closely it resembles a certain Disney film in his ingenious "Avatar/Pocahontas Mashup" video.[19]

Then came the September 2012 response by the 1491s in which they mock back with blue middle fingers pointed toward Hollywood and satirize *Avatar* from within an indigenous world communicated through indigenous sensibilities and collaborative filmmaking. Conceptualized by Pawnee and Yakama artist Bunky Echo Hawk and filmed by Navajo director Black Horse Lowe, "The Avatars" stars several members of the fictional blue Makto family. The members, Wilson explains off camera, "went to a costume shop and bought fake ears and all this [blue] makeup." As the cranky and foul-mouthed elder and intergalactic veteran Grandpa Turok Makto III, Wilson's character opens the film in a satirical slur spoken to the camera in mockumentary style and possibly aimed at inquisitive and indigenous-intrusive filmmakers like Cameron: "You want to know about indigenous? Indigenous is my big blue Na'ai foot in your little Sky People a—hole if you don't get the hell off of my planet . . . f——ker."[20] His relative K'luk K'luk Makto (Rose Simpson, who also worked as makeup artist) speaks more pointedly to the male settler–dominated control, from Cameron to Sully, in *Avatar*: "That movie's bulls—. You know why that movie's bulls—? 'Cause Na'vi women wouldn't fall for that kind of Skywalker bulls—. Piece of s—t, [Sully] thinking he's Na'vi. Motherf—er. Hell, no. He doesn't even talk right, he doesn't ride right, doesn't do nothing right. Can't even plug in right. F—him!" K'luk K'luk's passionate review of *Avatar* strongly argues that self-respecting, culturally-informed Natives would not have been so compliant in the face of Hollywood's recurring and ongoing white savior trope. Throughout the nine-minute film short, the Avatars continue to express their respective opinions on such topics as blood quantum, interracial (coded as intergalactic) relations, and Na'vi expressions of masculinity, all through diverse recognizably Native sensibilities.

Another 1491s mockumentary is "A Day in the Life of an Emcee" (2010). Instead of satirizing a non-Native Hollywood blockbuster about blue Natives, the 1491s turn the camera on Indian Country to satirize and razz powwow emcees. The first episode introduces the loud but somewhat lovable emcee Howard LittleHeadFiddlerOldHorn (Goldtooth) at home with his family. Viewers see, for example, Howard primp in the mirror and prepare his voice, with a range of humorous pitches and inflections, for an upcoming powwow. In episode 2, he and fellow emcee Willard BeylDearlyCoffey Jr. (Wilson) train a young Native how to be an emcee in a series of outlandish and unnecessary exercises, such as boxing to the tune of "Ten Little Indians," the children's song of genocide, but with the readjusted lyrics and flipped vantage point of "One little, two little, three little white people."[21]

In "Singing Lessons," Goldtooth plays another obnoxious character, this time an uninformed uncle "teaching" his nephew (Anishinaabe comedian Tito Ybarra) how to sing the American Indian Movement song. Whereas the nephew already knows how to sing it in a recognizably Native high-pitched register, the uncle keeps saying it is wrong and proceeds to vocally and emotionally butcher the song. When the uncle, representative of Natives who feign traditions and miseducate, says to sing it "like you're crying for the people!" the nephew finally concedes before walking off to leave the clueless uncle alone with his misguided version.[22]

In "Slapping Medicine Man," the 1491s literally slap back at Natives and their self-pity and self-abuse on problems surrounding diet, obesity, alcohol, and other concerns in Indian Country. It begins, for example, with an exchange between Ybarra and the medicine man (Noah Ellis):

> YBARRA: I've been to a lot of white doctors. No one can really tell me what's going on with me. Basically, I ain't got no singing voice, and I'm really tired all the time.
> MEDICINE MAN: Well, do you party a lot?
> YBARRA: Hell yeah!
> MEDICINE MAN: [*Slaps Ybarra*] Knock it off!

Each delivered slap to Ybarra and other members of the 1491s during the video sounds a comical and assertive wake-up call to Natives to refuse defeat and embrace survivance.[23]

The 1491s call for Natives to take control of their lives, to respect themselves and their indigenous nations, and to remember, as Taiaiake Alfred does, that decolonization starts with the self.[24] Rather than always go for laughs, the 1491s provide, for many, shared smiles of cultural recognition such as in their "Represent" series. In these video shorts, the 1491s give visual space to numerous guests, including Native college students at Dartmouth and Fort Lewis, to perform on camera a tribal tradition at their modern-day campus setting. When, for instance, her laptop stops working in a study hall, Mattie Harper (Bois Forte Ojibwe) retrieves sweetgrass from her backpack, lights it up, and suddenly the laptop works again.[25] When Eddie Morales (Comanche) takes over-the-counter pills of some sort in his kitchen, he hears within him a gourd dance song by the Kiowa Tiapiah Society. He holds onto the pill bottle for a rattle, grabs a nearby oven mitt for a fan, and begins dancing. When Elizabeth Anne Reese (Nambe Pueblo) sees a couple of guys walking by on the sidewalk beneath her upstairs apartment, she throws candy at them to signify an old tradition of a Pueblo throw. Throughout, the students represent themselves *and* a personal responsibility to their indigenous nations and tribal teachings.[26]

Before, during, and since 1492, Native Peoples (and Native humor) have always already been *here*, signed on and tuned in to an indigenous and fluid state of active presence. Indigenous producers' strategies of survivance showcase an unrelenting and undeniable recognizably Native presence. In their fast-growing collection of videos, the 1491s show their survivance strategies to be highly versatile as they smile back, laugh back, give back, love back, mock back, talk back, even slap back to each other, to indigenous struggles, to their audiences, and to media makers' visions of indigeneity.[27]

Today, Native producers like the 1491s are critical leaders and practitioners in a media decolonization movement that looks to past, current, and future generations to envision indigenous and nonindigenous futures of justice, peace, love, and, of course, laughter. Contemporary DIY digital approaches illustrate, perhaps more than ever in media history, the anti-sign-off and "always connected" ethic inherently already built into media decolonization strategies. The cultural, social, and political responsibilities, roadblocks, and quests for survival, decolonization, and indigenization coalesce, then, to transmit an incredibly important signal that has been reverberating from, across, and above indigenous homelands for thousands of years:

There is no such thing as signing off. Oko ke tsahporu nai hanipu.

Notes

PREFACE

1. Kompare, *Rerun Nation.*

2. "Crime-Free Mayberry," *The Andy Griffith Show*, CBS, Nov. 20, 1961.

3. Magoc, "Machine in the Wasteland," 27.

4. Alexie, "No Reservations."

5. Byrd, *Transit of Empire*, 11.

6. "The Snow Job," *Three's Company*, ABC, Oct. 2, 1979; "Fonzie Loves Pinky (1)," *Happy Days*, ABC, Sept. 21, 1976; "Workin' Man Blues," *Home Improvement*, ABC, Dec. 10, 1996.

7. Deloria, *Playing Indian*, 184.

8. "Junior Pathfinders Ride Again," *Dennis the Menace*, CBS, Apr. 8, 1962; "The Indian Show," *I Love Lucy*, CBS, Apr. 3, 1953; "The Brady Braves," *The Brady Bunch*, ABC, Oct. 1, 1971; "Michael's Tribe," *My Wife and Kids*, ABC, Dec. 18, 2002; "Dances with Couch," *Yes Dear*, CBS, Apr. 8, 2002.

9. "The Indians Are Coming," *The Beverly Hillbillies*, CBS, Feb. 1, 1967; "The Rains Came," *Green Acres*, CBS, May 18, 1966; "Lucy and the Indian Chief," *Here's Lucy*, CBS, Oct. 6, 1969; "The Return of Bald Eagle," *F Troop*, ABC, Oct. 12, 1965.

10. The episode's title appears to substitute Andy Taylor's name for Christopher Columbus's. Cornel Pewewardy (Comanche/Kiowa) recounts his own "learning" experience about Columbus, to which countless other Native Peoples can relate: "In public school I was taught that Christopher Columbus discovered America. Later, I found out that the man was totally lost on his voyage and named the Indigenous Peoples he 'discovered' Indios because he was looking for the country of India. Throughout my entire public school education, I was led to believe by my teachers that this was a true story." Pewewardy, "Renaming Ourselves," 11.

11. "Andy Discovers America," *The Andy Griffith Show*, CBS, Mar. 4, 1963; "Aunt Bee's Medicine Man," *The Andy Griffith Show*, CBS, Mar. 11, 1963; "The Beauty Contest," *The Andy Griffith Show*, CBS, Jan. 23, 1961; "The Pageant," *The Andy Griffith Show*, CBS, Nov. 30, 1964. Meek defines Hollywood Injun English as "a composite of grammatical 'abnormalities' that marks the way Indians speak and differentiates their speech from Standard American English." Meek, "And the Injun Goes 'How!,'" 95.

12. Books like Raymond Stedman's *Shadows of the Indian* and Sierra Adare's *"Indian" Stereotypes in TV Science Fiction* catalog representations of Indians within a racialized regime and raise important general points about stereotypes of Indians. Bending near the media imperialism polemic, however, such work on stereotypes often excludes closer cultural analysis of representational nuances.

13. Bhabha, "The Other Question," 71.

14. P. Deloria, *Indians in Unexpected Places*, 8, 9, 13.

15. In theorizing the politics of perception in response to, for example, social constructions of Natives as suddenly wealthy owners of casinos, Corntassel notably cites *The Simpsons* episode "Missionary: Impossible." Corntassel and Witmer, *Forced Federalism* 5, 31; "Missionary: Impossible," *The Simpsons*, Fox, Feb. 20, 2000.

16. Qtd. in Maggie Barrett, "Book Edited by WFU Professor Takes Serious Look at the Sitcom," Wake Forest News Service, Nov. 3, 2005, http://www.wfu.edu/wfunews/2005/110305s.html (accessed Oct. 10, 2012).

17. Morreale, *Critiquing the Sitcom*, xi; Dalton and Linder, *Sitcom Reader*, 12.

18. See Mellencamp, "SitCom, Feminism, and Freud"; Coleman, *African American Viewers*; H. Gray, *Watching Race*; V. Johnson, *Heartland TV*; Spigel, *Welcome to the Dreamhouse*; and Aniko Bodroghkozy, *Groove Tube*.

19. See Byrd, "'In the City of Blinding Lights'"; Raheja, *Reservation Reelism*; and Cox, "Muting White Noise."

INTRODUCTION

1. Taylor, "No More Test Patterns," reprinted in Taylor, *News*, 200.

2. Harris, "Television Test Patterns." In 1949, M. S. Kay said the Indian Head Test Pattern was the "most common" design. Kay, "Television Test Pattern."

3. Qtd. in Barfield, *Word from Our Viewers*, 21–22.

4. Ibid., 17, 19.

5. I once asked Chuck Pharis, who purportedly has the master artwork of the pattern and sells restored reprints (a set of which hangs in my office), about the identity of Brooks and the decision to use the Indian, but he said no one knows. He has contacted the PBS series *History Detectives* with similar questions. "They spent six months," according to Pharis, "trying to figure out who 'Brooks' was, and why the Indian Head was used, but just couldn't crack the case. They did locate the original technical data for the Indian Head test pattern and sent me a copy, but that's as far as they could go." Pharis qtd. in James E. O'Neal, "A Pattern for Testing," *TV Technology*, Sept. 16, 2010, http://www.tvtechnology.com/feature-box/0124/a-pattern-for-testing/206972 (accessed Aug. 5, 2013).

6. Berkhofer, *White Man's Indian*.

7. The first cinematic Tonto was portrayed by Victor Daniels, or Chief Thundercloud.

8. In 1908, President Theodore Roosevelt called for new coin designs in American currency. His friend William Sturgis Bigelow contacted Boston sculptor Bela Lyon Pratt, who designed the $2.50 Indian Head coin, minted 1908–1915 and 1925–1929, and the $5.00 Indian Head coin, minted 1908–1916 and in 1929. On a related currency note, another "Indian" coin has been interpellated in the *invention* of television. C. Francis Jenkins, one of the credited inventors of television, turned to the figure on the Indian Head one-cent coin (1859–1909) to illustrate how images are transmitted and reproduced on television screens. "When we were little tykes," he explained in a 1932 interview, "mother entertained us by putting a penny under a piece of paper, and, by drawing straight lines across the paper, she made a picture of the Indian appear. Well, that's the very way we do it [in television]." Qtd. in Orrin E. Dunlap, *Outlook for Television*, 53. On the Buffalo nickel, see numismatic author Q. David Bowers's *Guide Book*.

9. In this study, I generally write "indigenous," "Native Peoples," or "Natives" to refer to the original inhabitants of North America; "American Indian" to refer to the indigenous in the United States; and "First Nations," "Inuit," or "Métis" to refer to the indigenous in Canada. I also use nation-specific designations with the preferred spelling, if known, of the person(s) to whom I am referring.

10. Green, "Tribe Called Wannabee"; P. Deloria, *Playing Indian*; Huhndorf, *Going Native*; Francis, *Imaginary Indian*; V. Deloria, foreword to *Pretend Indians*, xvi.

11. The Indie Award was awarded by the Canadian Film and Television Production Association, now called the Canadian Media Production Association. "Moose TV Is Funniest at Indie Awards," *Playback*, Mar. 3, 2008, http://playbackonline.ca/2008/03/03/indie-20080303/ (accessed July 24, 2013).

12. "Birth of a Station," *Moose TV*, Showcase, Aug. 23, 2007.

13. "Ernie Makes a Drum" depicts an elder named Ernie literally making a drum on camera, a show likely inspired by the film *Dab Iyiyuu: Charlie Makes a Drum* (2004), in which "elder Charlie Etapp crafts a traditional Cree hunting drum." Ernest Webb produced *Dab Iyiyuu*, and Neil Diamond (Cree) and Philip Lewis directed it. Native Networks, Smithsonian National Museum of the American Indian, http://www.nativenetworks.si.edu/eng/orange/charlie_makes_a_drum.htm (accessed July 24, 2013).

14. Unless I refer to individuals by name, I often will broadly use the term "producer" to indicate the writers, directors, and other members of production crews of sitcom episodes. As Paul Lieberstein said of his job duties when he was an executive producer of the Fox animated sitcom *King of the Hill*, "Basically, I'm still a writer. First you're a staff writer, then a story editor, then an executive story editor, then a co-producer, producer, supervising producer, co-executive producer. All these people do exactly the same thing. There are three parts to the job: breaking new stories, writing and handling all the production work." In a nod to a collective sense of production that makes it difficult to hold only certain individuals accountable for the broadcasted content, Lieberstein added later, "Most of the writing work is group writing and editing." Wendy Paris, "Job Q&A," Monster.com, Mar. 5, 1999 (accessed Oct. 10, 2012).

15. Pratt, *Imperial Eyes*, 4.

16. Bhabha, "The Other Question," 71.

17. Alexie, "No Reservations." "Indigenous sitcom kid" narratives have not received nearly as much scholarly attention as indigenous narratives on watching cinematic westerns or other television genres. On Native perspectives in response to anti-indigenous cinema, especially western films, see, for example, Michael Yellow Bird, "Cowboys and Indians." At one point, Yellow Bird (Sahnish/Arikara and Hidatsa) reflects that "as young boys we watched the loser Indians in many westerns and, like many of our other young colonized Indian brothers who grew up on other reservations . . . , we cheered for the cowboys whenever they kicked our people's butts" (40). Citing a childhood experience of watching the heroic savior John Wayne fight murderous, kidnapping Apaches in *Rio Grande* (1950), Tom Colonnese (Santee Sioux) talks of being upset at the film's portrayals of Natives. "What was making me feel so bad," Colonnese reflects, "wasn't that I was ashamed of the bad Apaches. What was making me feel so bad was the way the movie made Indian people seem." Colonnese, "Indian Summer," 17. See also Shively, "Cowboys and Indians." On Native responses to television, see Bird, "Not My Fantasy"; and Adare, *"Indian" Stereotypes*.

18. Sherman Alexie, "Sherman Alexie, 'Sitcom American,'" *Morning Edition*, NPR, Aug. 18, 2003.

19. Alexie, *Lone Ranger and Tonto*, 184, 187.

20. Chaat Smith, "Land of a Thousand Dances," in *Everything You Know about Indians Is Wrong*, 37.

21. Cox, "Muting White Noise," 155.

22. Ibid.

23. Lyons qtd. in Alfred, *Wasáse*, 239.

24. Harjo, "Postcolonial Tale," 18.

25. Belvin qtd. in Friar and Friar, *Only Good Indian*, 260.

26. President Ronald Reagan vetoed the Fairness Doctrine in 1987. See Tim Giago, "An Indigenous Perspective on the Fairness Doctrine," *Huffington Post*, Feb. 15, 2009, http://www.huffingtonpost.com/tim-giago/an-indigenous-perspective_b_167068.html (accessed Nov. 2, 2012).

27. Jack Gould, *New York Times*, Sept. 7, 1967, qtd. in Friar and Friar, *Only Good Indian*, 274–75. For further information on *Custer* and Native protest, see V. Deloria, *Custer Died for Your Sins*, 24; and Pearson, "White Network/Red Power."

28. Redwing guest-starred as the Indian character Brave Dog in "Blazing Arrows," *Custer*, ABC, Nov. 29, 1967.

29. *What's My Line*, CBS, Feb. 2, 1958.

30. Winters's response comes a few moments before the end of the show, during which he ironically plays Indian with a raised hand to gesture "How?" to Redwing, smiles as if just playing around, and then shakes his hand.

31. Teyowisonte qtd. in Alfred, *Wasáse*, 270–71. In 2013, with the permission of Lucasfilm, Navajos translated and recorded *Star Wars* into the Navajo language. See "Jedis and Indians! Live from the 'Navajo Star Wars' Premiere," July 10, 2013, *Indian Country Today Media Network*, http://indiancountrytodaymedianetwork.com/2013/07/10/jedis-and-indians-live-navajo-star-wars-premiere-video-150361 (accessed July 11, 2013); and "The Force Is with the Navajo: 'Star Wars' Gets a New Translation," June 5, 2013, NPR, http://www.npr.org/blogs/codeswitch/2013/07/03/188676416/Star-Wars-In-Navajo (accessed July 11, 2013).

32. "Native American Poet Sherman Alexie," *PBS NewsHour Extra*, Oct. 23, 2009, http://www.pbs.org/newshour/extra/video/blog/2009/10/native_american_poet_sherman_a.html.

33. Alexie, "Sherman Alexie, 'Sitcom American.'"

34. Alexie, "Flight Patterns."

35. *Smoke Signals*, dir. Chris Eyre, Miramax, 1998.

36. Lyons, *X-Marks*, x–xiii.

37. Alexie qtd. in Bernardin, "Alexie-Vision," 52.

38. Hearne, *Native Recognition*, 265–66.

39. Alexie qtd. in Kempley, "No More Playing Dead."

40. A. Cobb, "This Is What It Means to Say *Smoke Signals*," 208.

41. *Oxford English Dictionary*, 7th ed. (Oxford: Oxford University Press, 2012).

42. The "text," as Jonathan Gray explains, is the "entire storyworld as we know it" (e.g., the entire series of the sitcom *King of the Hill*). Paratexts are "textual entities" that "create

texts, they manage them, and they fill them with many of the meanings that we associate with them" (e.g., television commercials and online discussion boards about *King of the Hill*). J. Gray, *Show Sold Separately*, 7, 16, 6.

43. J. Gray, *Watching with* The Simpsons, 4.

44. George and Sanders, "Reconstructing Tonto," 431.

45. Kilpatrick, *Celluloid Indians*, 1.

46. Barnouw, *History of Broadcasting*, vol. 3, *Image Empire, from 1953*.

47. Wolfe, "Settler Colonialism," 388.

48. Bhabha, "The Other Question," 66. On playing Indian, see P. Deloria, *Playing Indian*; Green, "Tribe Called Wannabee"; Huhndorf, *Going Native*; and Tahmahkera, "Custer's Last Sitcom."

49. "Turkey Day," *The Beverly Hillbillies*, CBS, Nov. 27, 1963; "Un-Underground Movie," *The Brady Bunch*, ABC, Oct. 16, 1970; "The First Thanksgiving," *Happy Days*, ABC, Nov. 21, 1978; "The Bird," *Everybody Loves Raymond*, CBS, Nov. 24, 2003.

50. Tahmahkera, "Custer's Last Sitcom"; Bhabha, "Of Mimicry and Man," in *Location of Culture*, 86.

51. "The Indian Show," *I Love Lucy*, CBS, Apr. 3, 1953; "Dances with Couch," *Yes, Dear*, CBS, Apr. 8, 2002; "Michael's Tribe," *My Wife and Kids*, ABC, Dec. 18, 2002; "Boston Tea Party," *The Suite Life of Zack and Cody*, Disney, June 30, 2006; Bhabha, "Of Mimicry and Man," 86.

52. Vizenor, *Manifest Manners*, 4; "The Indian," *Barney Miller*, ABC, Jan. 4, 1979; "Indian Summer," *Dharma and Greg*, ABC, Nov. 5, 1997; "Running Zack," *Saved by the Bell*, NBC, Nov. 24, 1990; "Brought to You in Dharmavision," *Dharma and Greg*, ABC, Nov. 18, 1998; "Mother and Daughter Reunion," *Dharma and Greg*, ABC, Oct. 10, 2000; "Intensive Caring," *Dharma and Greg*, ABC, Sept. 25, 2001.

53. Vizenor, *Manifest Manners*, 8.

54. Lacroix, "High Stakes Stereotypes," 3; Spilde, "Rich Indian Racism."

55. Corntassel and Witmer, *Forced Federalism*, 31; "Missionary: Impossible," *The Simpsons*, Fox, Feb. 20, 2000.

56. "Red Man's Greed," *South Park*, Comedy Central, Apr. 30, 2003.

57. Cattelino, *High Stakes*, 211.

58. "The Son Also Draws," *Family Guy*, Fox, May 9, 1999.

59. Cramer, "Common Sense," 331.

60. "Bart to the Future," *The Simpsons*, Fox, Mar. 19, 2000; Nate Birch qtd. in *The Simpsons Archive*, http://www.snpp.com/episodes/BABF13 (accessed Aug. 12, 2012).

61. On the "sound of Indian," see P. Deloria, "The Hills Are Alive . . . with the Sound of Indian," in *Indians in Unexpected Places*, 183–223.

62. For examples of "How" jokes in sitcoms, see "The Pageant," *The Andy Griffith Show*, CBS, Nov. 30, 1964; "The One with Rachel's Inadvertent Kiss," *Friends*, NBC, Mar. 18. 1999; "Red Man's Greed," *South Park*, Comedy Central, Apr. 30, 2003; "Running Zack," *Saved by the Bell*, NBC, Nov. 24, 1990; and "Michael's Tribe," *My Wife and Kids*, ABC, Dec. 18, 2002. On *The Simpsons'* use of Hill's "Hi-how-are-you?," producer Mike Scully says he and the writers "debated about whether to do it or not, but [actor] Dan [Castellaneta] did it so funny when we [read] at the table, we decided to put it in and risk offending." Another writer jokes that viewers, possible insinuating Native viewers, should "send your angry

arrows to Tom." Qtd. in "Director's Commentary: 'Bart to the Future,'" in *The Simpsons: The Eleventh Season*, DVD. "Bart to the Future," *The Simpsons*, Fox, Mar. 19, 2000. Steve Allen qtd. in the documentary *On and Off the Res' w/Charlie Hill*.

63. George and Sanders, "Reconstructing Tonto," 449.

64. "Jed Cuts the Family Tree," *The Beverly Hillbillies*, CBS, Mar. 20, 1963.

65. Mittell, *Television and American Culture*, 287; Marc, *Demographic Vistas*, 55.

66. Attallah, "Television Discourse"; Staiger, *Blockbuster TV*.

67. Hearne, *Native Recognition*, 276.

68. Howe, "The Story of America," 29, 33, 46. See also Howe, "Tribalography."

69. J. Gray, *Watching with* The Simpsons, 37.

70. Taylor co-created and was head writer of the sitcom *Mixed Blessings*. He also served as script consultant for *Moose TV*. Deer adapted her film *Mohawk Girls* into a pilot episode for a sitcom of the same title and plans to produce additional episodes.

71. *Mohawk Girls* "Press Kit," 2010, http://www.rezolutionpictures.com/wp-content/uploads/2013/03/MG_Package_Mar10_2010_MailSized.pdf (accessed July 28, 2013).

72. Warrior, *Tribal Secrets*; Vizenor, *Fugitive Poses*, 178, 15; Singer, *Wiping the War Paint*, 2; Osawa qtd. in "Native Networks," Apr. 2005, http://www.nativenetworks.si.edu/eng/rose/osawa_s.htm (accessed July 7, 2013); Lewis, *Alanis Obomsawin*, 175; Raheja, *Reservation Reelism*, 194, 200.

73. *Harold of Orange*, dir. Richard Weise, Film in the Cities, 1984.

74. Silberman, "Gerald Vizenor and *Harold of Orange*," 16–17.

75. Vizenor, *Manifest Manners*, ix.

76. Ibid., 6; Vizenor and Lee, *Postindian Conversations*, 156.

77. Vizenor, *Manifest Manners*, 12.

78. Arjun Appadurai defines mediascapes as "the distribution of the electronic capabilities to produce and disseminate information (newspapers, magazines, television stations, film production studios, etc.) . . . and . . . the images of the world created by these media." Appadurai, "Difference and Disjuncture," 298–99.

79. Vizenor and Lee, *Postindian Conversations*, 85; Vizenor, *Fugitive Poses*, 15.

80. As Vizenor would later say in an interview, Ted Velt "knows too much about the inventions, and movie simulations, but too little about native humor and tricky stories." Vizenor and Lee, *Postindian Conversations*, 72.

81. Vizenor, "Socioacupuncture," 180.

82. Another major influence was Vine Deloria Jr., when Hill saw him on *The Dick Cavett Show*. "Vine was both biting and funny, and it crystallized for me what I wanted to do." Qtd. in Minnie Two Shoes, "Conversation with Charlie Hill."

83. "Road Trip," *Moesha*, UPN, Nov. 26, 1996; Leona Hill qtd. in *On and Off the Res' w/Charlie Hill*; Charlie Hill, "Please Welcome Charlie Hill," *Joel Samuels Presents*, Tempe, Ariz., 1983. Available at http://www.youtube.com/watch?v=wh6eCALF0hY, July 7, 2009 (accessed 19 July 19, 2012).

84. *On and Off the Res' w/Charlie Hill*; "The Last Thursday in November," *Roseanne*, ABC, Nov. 21, 1995. As Barr has said of those who wrote for *Roseanne*, "I hired comics that I had worked with in clubs, rather than script writers." Barr, "And I Should Know," *New York Magazine*, May 15, 2011. Hill recalls a similar "real demeaning" proposed sketch for him called "White for a Day" on his 1977 guest appearance on *The Richard Pryor Show*.

According to Hill, Pryor refused the sketch and told Hill, "You got five minutes. You can do what you want on my show." *On and Off the Res' w/Charlie Hill.*

85. Jojola, "*Moo Mesa*," 265–66.

86. Ibid., 268, 269, 274.

87. Ibid., 273.

88. Pack, "'I Hate White People!,'" 144.

89. Lacapa qtd. in Ingles, "The Man on the Couch."

90. Eyre qtd. in Lynn Cline, "Comments from the Couch," *Santa Fe New Mexican*, Aug. 9, 2002, 80.

91. Pack, "'I Hate White People!,'" 144.

92. Attallah, "Television Discourse and Situation Comedy."

CHAPTER 1

1. Qtd. in Watson, *The Expanding Vista*, 7.

2. Rich, "Paar to Leno, J.F.K. to J.F.K."

3. Qtd. in Philp, *Indian Self-Rule*, 226. Paul Boller reports a similar incident in Wisconsin, where "Kennedy was made honorary chieftain of an Indian tribe. Donning the headdress, he exclaimed: 'Next time I go to the movies to see cowboys and Indians, I'll be us.'" Boller, *Presidential Anecdotes*, 306.

4. Thomas Clarkin says that Lyndon B. Johnson, Kennedy's running mate, visited the Blackfeet reservation in 1960 on a campaign stop. "He was decked out in a headdress, made an honorary chief, and given the name Leading Star." On June 21, 1960, in Minot, North Dakota, then vice president Richard Nixon, running against Kennedy for the presidency, also donned a headdress on the campaign trail. Clarkin, *Federal Indian Policy*, 108.

5. Kennedy, introduction, 7. As Castile notes, Kennedy signed his name to an introduction that "had been solicited through Pierre Salinger by Alvin Josephy and was drafted by someone on Udall's staff." Castile, *To Show Heart*, 14.

6. Clarkin, *Federal Indian Policy*, 78. "New Frontier" became the "New Trail" in political discourse purportedly over concerns that Native Peoples would not have fond memories of the "frontier" and its formations through physical and discursive violence that killed and forcibly removed Indians from their homelands. Yet "New Trail" risked conjuring the so-called Trail of Tears of the 1830s–1840s and James Earle Fraser's *End of the Trail* sculpture from 1915.

7. Udall, "American Indian Task Force Report," July 10, 1961, qtd. in Clarkin, *Federal Indian Policy*, 32. In all, the task force report suggested that historic treaties recognizing indigenous sovereignties are pointless if the paternalistic federal government can lead its subjects to social, economic, and cultural assimilation in a capitalistic American citizenry and quash Native calls for homelands to be returned and rights to be upheld.

8. Cowger, *National Congress*, 132.

9. Castile, *To Show Heart*, 13.

10. Ibid., 14; Clarkin, *Federal Indian Policy*, 78; Jaimes, "Hollow Icon," 34.

11. Jaimes, "Hollow Icon," 41.

12. Thom qtd. in D. Cobb, *Native Activism*, 71.

13. Spigel focuses on what she terms the "'fantastic family sitcom,' a hybrid genre that mixed family comedy with science fiction and horror," such as *The Addams Family* and *Bewitched*. Within this genre, I look briefly at *The Munsters'* episode "Big Heap Herman." Spigel, *Welcome to the Dreamhouse*, 18.

14. Ibid., 18, 116.

15. Deloria and Lytle attribute the federal government's allocation of funds due to policy on eradicating poverty, not "because the government felt responsible to fulfill treaty obligations long withheld and due [to Native nations]." They add, "Indians happened to be a group that fell well within the identifiable guidelines of the poverty program, and they therefore qualified as recipients." Deloria and Lytle, *Nations Within*, 216. On the relations between Native Peoples, Johnson, and the War on Poverty, see D. Cobb, *Native Activism*.

16. L. Johnson, "Remarks to Members."

17. Funds were distributed through the Area Redevelopment Act and overall economic development programs. Kennedy had previously signed the Area Redevelopment Act into law on May 1, 1961, to "alleviate conditions of substantial and persistent unemployment and underemployment in certain economically distressed areas." Among those noted were "Indian reservations." Qtd. in Wilkins and Stark, *American Indian Politics*, 221. On April 22, 1965, Johnson approved "H.R. 4778, a measure which authorizes increased funds for the vocational training of American Indians." Lyndon Johnson, "Statement by the President upon Signing Bill Authorizing Increased Funds for Vocational Training of American Indians," Apr. 24, 1965, http://www.presidency.ucsb.edu/ws/?pid=26913.

18. In his March 6, 1968, "Special Message to the Congress on the Problems of the American Indian: 'The Forgotten American,'" Johnson echoed Kennedy's calls for self-determination over termination and for indigenous-settler cooperation: "I propose a new goal for our Indian programs: A goal that ends the old debate about 'termination' of Indian programs and stresses self-determination; a goal that erases old attitudes of paternalism and promotes partnership self-help." http://www.presidency.ucsb.edu/ws/index.php?pid=28709.

19. Newcomb, "From Old Frontier to New Frontier," 288.

20. For an engaging account of 1950s U.S. television's public affairs and documentary coverage of real Native Peoples within political context, see Pamela Wilson's "Confronting 'The Indian Problem.'"

21. Castile says "development" and "inclusion" were Nash's most prominent themes during his tenure as commissioner of Indian Affairs. Castile, *To Show Heart*, 13.

22. Kennedy, "The New Frontier." In his August 28, 2008, Democratic acceptance speech, then senator Barack Obama spoke, in ways reminiscent of Kennedy's rhetoric, of "fulfilling America's promise," which "will require a renewed sense of responsibility from each of us to recover what John F. Kennedy called our intellectual and moral strength"; he later added, "That promise is our greatest inheritance . . . a promise that has led immigrants to cross oceans and pioneers to travel west." Numerous critics have compared the acceptance speeches, yet relatively few have noted their comparative indigenous implications. For more on relations between indigeneity, Kennedy, and Obama, see Byrd, "'In the City of Blinding Lights.'"

23. Frederick Jackson Turner, "The Significance of the Frontier in American History," in *Annual Report of the American Historical Association*; Drinnon, *Facing West*, 366; Slotkin, *Gunfighter Nation*, 2–3.

24. Kennedy, "The New Frontier." On Kennedy's use of the Frontier Myth to establish New Frontier rhetoric and policy, see Dorsey, "Myth of War and Peace"; Drinnon, *Facing West*; and Slotkin, *Gunfighter Nation*.

25. For Ojibway film critic Jesse Wente, "*Stagecoach* is the iconic western . . . that all others were modeled after." He adds, "*Stagecoach* summed up and gave the opinion of Native People for decades to the populace in the U.S." Qtd. in *Reel Injun*, dir. Neil Diamond, Domino Film & Television International, 2009.

26. Meek, "And the Injun Goes 'How!'"

27. "Pass That Peace Pipe" was nominated for an Academy Award for Best Original Song in the 1947 movie *Good News*. In the actual Indian show, Ricky's two Indians have insignificant roles. Both only stand stoically like cigar-store Indians near the club's stage entrance, lending themselves to producers' presumed wish to authenticate the show's theme and content.

28. "Droop-Along Flintstone," *The Flintstones*, ABC, Sept. 22, 1961.

29. "Droop-Along Flintstone" was reportedly banned by Canadian broadcasters due to its depictions of Indians.

30. On the quiz show scandals, see, for example, Richard Tedlow, "Intellect on Television."

31. Minow, "Television and the Public Interest."

32. Fleeson, "Call for Improved Television."

33. Minow and Cate, "Revisiting the Vast Wasteland"; Smith, *Virgin Land*; Robert Frost, "The Gift Outright," *Virginia Quarterly Review* (Spring 1942).

34. Barnouw, *Tube of Plenty*, 306. For a range of responses to *The Beverly Hillbillies*, see Staiger, *Blockbuster TV*; and Harkins, *Hillbilly*.

35. Hope qtd. in "Hope Quips Convulse Convention," *Billboard*, Apr. 13, 1963; Ryan qtd. in Harkins, *Hillbilly*, 190.

36. "Turkey Day," *The Beverly Hillbillies*, CBS, Nov. 27, 1963.

37. "The Family Tree," *The Beverly Hillbillies*, CBS, Mar. 13, 1963.

38. Ellen Brown, portrayed by *I Dream of Jeannie* star Barbara Eden, visits Mayberry and mentions the sign in "The Manicurist," *The Andy Griffith Show*, CBS, Jan. 22, 1962.

39. "The Arrest of the Fun Girls," *The Andy Griffith Show*, CBS, Apr. 5, 1965; "TV or Not TV," *The Andy Griffith Show*, CBS, Mar. 1, 1965; "The Pickle Story," *The Andy Griffith Show*, CBS, Dec. 18, 1961; "The Rivals," *The Andy Griffith Show*, CBS, Apr. 8, 1963; "The Bookie Barber," *The Andy Griffith Show*, CBS, Apr. 16, 1962.

40. Kelly qtd. in Ted Reuter, "What Andy, Opie, and Barney Fife Mean to Americans, Even in the 90s," *Christian Science Monitor* 90.39 (1998): 19.

41. Vaughn, "Why *The Andy Griffith Show* Is Important," 398.

42. See the following episodes of CBS's *The Andy Griffith Show*: "Opie's Hobo Friend," Nov. 13, 1961; "The Clubmen," Nov. 27, 1961; "Opie's Rival," Dec. 3, 1962; "Andy and Opie's Pal," Jan. 13, 1964; "Aunt Bee's Medicine Man," Mar. 11, 1963; "Bargain Day," Mar. 23, 1964.

43. Minow and Lamay, *Abandoned in the Wasteland*, 197; Kennedy, "Inaugural Address." On the parade floats, see Cowger, *National Congress*, 126.

44. John F. Kennedy, "Letter on Indian Affairs from Senator John F. Kennedy to Mr. Oliver La Farge, President, Association on American Indian Affairs," Oct. 28, 1960, *The American Presidency Project*, http://www.presidency.ucsb.edu/ws/?pid=74264 (accessed Aug. 16, 2012).

45. Castile, *To Show Heart*, 11.

46. The 1794 treaty is available at "Indian Affairs: Laws and Treaties," http://digital .library.okstate.edu/kappler/vol2/treaties/six0034.htm. Kennedy press conference, Mar. 9, 1961, qtd. in Castile, *To Show Heart*, 15.

47. Byrd, *The Transit of Empire*, 64.

48. "The Beauty Contest," *The Andy Griffith Show*, CBS, Jan. 23, 1961; Dixon, "House as Symbol," 144.

49. "The Pageant," *The Andy Griffith Show*, CBS, Nov. 30, 1964; *Cheyenne Autumn*, dir. John Ford, Warner Brothers, 1964; Wente qtd. in *Reel Injun*, dir. Neil Diamond, Domino Film & Television International, 2009.

50. L. Johnson, "The Great Society."

51. The majority of Cherokees were forced toward Indian Territory, present-day Oklahoma, in the 1830s. Those who evaded capture in North Carolina became recognized by the state in 1870 as the Eastern Band of Cherokee Indians. Today, citizenship in the Cherokee Nation in Oklahoma numbers over 288,000; the United Keetoowah Band in Oklahoma around 14,000; and the Eastern Band in North Carolina at approximately 12,500. See the Nations' official sites at http://www.cherokee.org/, http://www.ukb-nsn.gov, and http://nc-cherokee.com.

52. Actor Don Knotts, who portrayed Barney Fife, also played Indian in *Shakiest Gun in the West* (1968), in which he portrayed a bumbling anti-indigenous dentist who, near the end of the film, cross-dressed as a Comanche woman to disguise himself from white and Comanche villains.

53. Like Lucy in *I Love Lucy*, Barney is repeatedly depicted as a weak performer with high aspirations. For example, Barney thinks he has an incredible singing voice in the episodes "Barney and the Choir," Feb. 19, 1962; "Rafe Hollister Sings," Feb. 11, 1963; and "The Song Festers," Feb. 24, 1964.

54. Green, "Tribe Called Wannabe," 48.

55. "The Battle of Mayberry," *The Andy Griffith Show*, CBS, Apr. 4, 1966.

56. In "Barney's Replacement" (Oct. 9, 1961), for example, an African American woman appears in the foreground for just over thirty seconds.

57. Settler actor Norm Alden portrayed Strongbow. Among his many roles from 1957 to 2003, Alden played Captain Horton opposite Tim Conway as Rango (a Texas Ranger) and Guy Marks as Pink Cloud (a cowardly Indian sidekick) in the comedic western TV series *Rango* (1967).

58. Presumably founded in 1864 according to the 1964 centennial celebration in "The Pageant," Mayberry dates back at least a century earlier according to a cited newspaper article from 1762 about the conflict in "The Battle of Mayberry."

59. In his 1981 book *The Andy Griffith Show*, avid fan Richard Michael Kelly briefly addresses the "Battle of Mayberry" episode and reinforces anti-indigenous settler sentiment but omits the episode's inclusion of Strongbow. Kelly leaps from saying, "Everyone in town . . . believed his ancestors were the central figures in the great Battle of Mayberry

fought in the 1700s, during which the settlers bravely destroyed a savage horde of Chero-kees," to referencing Opie's travels "to the Raleigh library" (6). Kelly thus excludes mentioning the only appearance in the series of an indigenous character, who also tells a very different story involving settler-Cherokee relations.

60. Nash qtd. in Castile, *To Show Heart*, 13–14.

61. Jaimes, "Hollow Icon," 35.

62. Ibid., 34.

63. L. Johnson, "Remarks to Members."

64. Crowley, "Vanishing American."

65. Philleo Nash, American Indian Capitol Conference on Poverty, Washington, D.C., May 12, 1964.

66. "The Rains Came," *Green Acres*, CBS, May 18, 1966.

67. "The Umquaw Strip," *Petticoat Junction*, CBS, Oct. 13, 1964.

68. Incidentally, Monte Blue (born Gerard Montgomery Bluefeather) is reportedly of Cherokee and French heritage.

69. "Big Heap Herman," *The Munsters*, CBS, Jan. 20, 1966.

70. *Get Smart* may have been aware of the Oglala Lakota leader of the same name. "Washington 4, Indians 3," *Get Smart*, NBC, Oct. 23, 1965.

71. Max calls it the "second biggest arrow I've ever seen," perhaps in deference to England's Black Arrow rocket. Authorized for construction in 1964, Black Arrow launched four times from 1969 to 1971. The 1966 episode also was not too far removed from the 1958 Sputnik launch and 1962 Cuban Missile Crisis.

72. *Hekawi* derives from, Wild Eagle recounts, the tribe's earlier westward migration from "Massachusetts because Pilgrims ruined the neighborhood." During their travels, the medicine man said, "I think we lost. Where the *heck are we?*" Wild Eagle, portrayed by settler actor Frank DeKova, is credited as one of the sitcom's costars. An earlier Indian character to costar in a sitcom was Hawkeye (settler actor J. Carrol Naish) in *Guestward Ho* (1960–61). In *Rango*, the timid Indian scout Pink Cloud is a sidekick to the title character, a Texas Ranger. *Pistols 'n' Petticoats* (1966–67) includes sitcom Indians Chief Eagle Shadow, Gray Hawk, and Little Hawk. Each of these sitcoms is a comedic western series.

73. The story lines generally play on white nostalgia and tourism by appealing to market interests in historical indigeneity through Indian-made products or Indian-themed performances and historical reenactments. To some extent, the episodes could be seen as on-screen translations of Buffalo Bill's Wild West shows, Native-owned roadside stands, and Indian tourist stops in relegating Indians to playing off of the past and performing variants of the "white man's Indian." Berkhofer, *White Man's Indian*; "Scourge of the West," *F Troop*, ABC, Sept. 14, 1965.

74. *F Troop* repeatedly shows the cavalry and, by extension, settler livelihood as superior to the Hekawis and other Others. For instance, in "From Karate with Love" (Jan. 5, 1967), Miko, a young Japanese woman, flees Japan and her father's arranged marriage for her and seeks refuge at Fort Courage. A samurai has followed to take her back, but by the episode's conclusion, the samurai and Miko have fallen in love. They drop traditional attire for western wear—cowboy clothing and a pioneer dress—and shun Japan to remain together in the United States, which is held up as a beacon against the implied patriarchal tyranny in Japan. In the episode "Yellow Bird" (Oct. 20, 1966), the title character is a grown

settler born as Cynthia who was captured years earlier by Geronimo, whom Wild Eagle says is his cousin and is, for the troop *and* Hekawis, the epitome of savagery in *F Troop*. A settler account of Cynthia Ann Parker, my great-great-great-great-grandmother, may have inspired "Yellow Bird." At a young age in 1836, Parker was captured and raised by Comanches, later married Peta Nocona, bore three children, and was "rescued" by Texas Rangers at the Battle of Pease River in 1860. She repeatedly tried but failed to escape the settlers to return to her Comanche people. "Rescued" by the troop, Yellow Bird is depicted savagely, too, before reverting back to Cynthia upon seeing her white father, who arrives to take her back to Texas. In "The Return of Bald Eagle" (Oct. 12, 1965), settler comedian Don Rickles portrays Bald Eagle, Wild Eagle's son. Jealous of the attention his cousin Geronimo receives, Bald Eagle is bent on attacking settlers and "pony soldiers." The chief explains that the Hekawis are "in souvenir business, wholesale and retail," and "no attack during big end of the month sale," but Bald Eagle refuses to relent. "Kill! Kill! Ki-ii-ll!" he screams. Echoing earlier sitcoms, physical and discursive Indian-settler violence remains but primarily in references to Geronimo and other Apaches and the occasionally appearing Shug Indians, not the main tribe of Hekawis.

75. "The Indians Are Coming," *The Beverly Hillbillies*, CBS, Feb. 1, 1967. Two subsequent consecutive episodes of *The Beverly Hillbillies* also revert back to representations of the early 1960s. In "The Clampetts in Washington" (Sept. 22, 1970) and "Jed Buys the Capitol" (Sept. 29, 1970), sitcom Indians are represented not by two fictionalized and near-culture-less Crowfeet Indians but by a settler character playing Indian as Princess Sitting Hawk, last of the Columbia Indians, who speaks HIE in heavy reddish-brown makeup and attempts to swindle the Clampetts.

76. On the demise of the TV western and representations of frontier violence in the 1970s, see MacDonald, *Who Shot the Sheriff?*

77. "Lucy and the Indian Chief," *Here's Lucy*, CBS, Oct. 6, 1969. Ball is identified in the closing credits as the "executive in charge of production."

78. Lucie Arnaz, "Introduction to 'Lucy and the Indian Chief,'" *Here's Lucy: Season Two*, DVD, 2009.

79. Regarding the "rural purge," actor Pat Buttram (who portrayed Mr. Haney in *Green Acres*) reportedly said, "CBS cancelled everything with a tree." Qtd in Harkins, *Hillbilly*, 203. Although *Here's Lucy* did not feature rural characters or settings, network executives associated it with attracting a largely rural audience.

80. *Mayberry R.F.D.* was a spin-off of the former *Andy Griffith Show* with many of the same characters. As Andy Griffith left *The Andy Griffith Show*, *F Troop* star Ken Berry became the lead in *Mayberry R.F.D.*

CHAPTER 2

1. Nixon, "Special Message to the Congress on Indian Affairs"; Patterson qtd. in Jerry Reynolds, "Rating the Presidents: Richard M. Nixon," *Indian Country Today*, Mar. 2, 2004; Garment qtd. in Castile, *To Show Heart*, 75. Chaat Smith and Warrior echo this sentiment by Nixon and add that Nixon and Garment were friends and former law firm partners in New York. *Like a Hurricane*, 68–69. Nixon's involvement in Indian affairs may be attributed to Nixon's former Whittier College football coach Wallace "Chief" Newman, a citizen

of the La Jolla Band of Mission Indians, who, after Nixon's father, had the most male influence on Nixon. As Duane Champagne concludes about Newman and Nixon's friendship, "Coach Newman may not have been the source of change for Nixon's Indian policy, but he provided leadership, inspiration, teachings, and mentorship in ways that were traditional within Indian communities. He led by example and deed, and thereby sought to inspire others to do the same. Creating change through leadership and mentorship, Wallace Newman is the unsung hero of modern American Indian policy." Champagne, *Notes from the Center of Turtle Island*, 138.

2. My attention to Nixon's message thus far is not to say that he was the main catalyst for self-determination policy. As Daniel Cobb and others have outlined in painstaking detail, Native Peoples had been fighting for self-determination long before Nixon assumed the presidency. Furthermore, Philip S. Deloria's sentiment speaks loudly: "I doubt that Richard Nixon had the faintest idea of what his 1970 message contained." "Era of Indian Self-Determination," 202.

3. Wilkins and Stark, *American Indian Politics*, 116; Indian Self-Determination and Education Assistance Act of 1975 (Public Law 93-638); Johnson, "Special Message to the Congress on the Problems of the American Indian."

4. As Vine Deloria once wrote, "One of the finest things about being an Indian is that people are always interested in you and your 'plight.' Others groups have difficulties, predicaments, quandaries, problems, or troubles. Traditionally we Indians have had a 'plight.'" *Custer Died for Your Sins*, 1.

5. On "agency," see Mittell, *Television and American Culture*, 214. On "happy multiculturalism," see Fusco, "Other History," 145.

6. Melamed, *Represent and Destroy*, xx, 34.

7. Byrd, *The Transit of Empire*, xiii.

8. Bhabha, "Of Mimicry and Man," in *Location of Culture*, 122.

9. Berti, who played sitcom Indian chief Henry in "Running Zack," *Saved by the Bell*, NBC, Nov. 24, 1990, has been described as Italian American and Chiricahua Apache.

10. Chaat Smith, "Meaning of Life," in *Everything You Know about Indians Is Wrong*, 127. In May 1975, Native Peoples in California protested a real estate company's "commercial portraying American Indians with 'rubber-tipped arrows,'" prompting a San Diego TV station to remove the stereotypical ad. "Jesse Hits 'Massacre'; Blasts TV Commercial," *Los Angeles Sentinel*, July 1, 1976, A2. For J. Fred MacDonald, the short duration of *Custer*, with its "savage Indians slaughtering white men" and "stress on military glory" amid protests "over the military role of the United States in the Vietnam War," partly speaks to the fast-approaching demise of the TV western and frontier adventure series (not to mention plethora of Indian representations) that were "virtually gone from network television" by 1975. MacDonald, *Who Shot the Sheriff?*, 118, 120. Another protest MacDonald cites is from 1971, when "the Boston Indian Council protested syndicated reruns of *Daniel Boone* [1964–70] as being little more than white racist indoctrination." "Through local courts of law," he added, "a special Indian Committee was allowed to preview the *Daniel Boone* films and eventually delete 37 of the 165 episodes" due to their violent portrayals of Indians (114).

11. Brown, *Bury My Heart*, xvi.

12. V. Deloria, *God Is Red*, 28.

13. Ibid., 33.

14. Qtd. in Pearson, "White Network/Red Power," 333.

15. Nagel, *American Indian Ethnic Renewal*, 13.

16. P. Deloria, "Era of Indian Self-Determination," 203. In addition to the arrests of Billy Frank Jr. (Nisqually), Hank Adams (Assiniboine-Sioux), and many other Natives, celebrities Dick Gregory and Marlon Brando also made U.S. national headlines upon their arrests at fish-ins.

17. Chaat Smith, *Everything You Know about Indians Is Wrong*, 131. On March 9, 1964, five Lakotas occupied Alcatraz for approximately an hour. For a detailed account, see Rader, *Engaged Resistance*, 8.

18. Chaat Smith and Warrior, *Like a Hurricane*, 71. As Trudell would reflect later, Alcatraz "rekindled the spirit of the people." Qtd. in *Reel Injun*, dir. Neil Diamond, Domino Film & Television International, 2009.

19. The specific date is stated by AIM cofounder Dennis Banks (Anishinaabe), qtd. in Wilkins and Stark, *American Indian Politics*, 189. Legal scholars Jeff Corntassel (Tsalagi) and Richard C. Witmer cite the 1968 Indian Civil Rights Act as the first major law of the era in *Forced Federalism*.

20. Baylor, "Media Framing of Movement Protest," 243.

21. Chaat Smith and Warrior, *Like a Hurricane*, 158.

22. Sayers qtd. in Wilkins and Stark, *American Indian Politics*, 234. Corntassel and Witmer contend Native Peoples were politically represented during this time as "domestic dependent nations, quasi-sovereigns, militant protestors, spirit guides, environmental stewards," all of which sitcoms simultaneously tuned in. *Forced Federalism*, 10. As Chaat Smith and Warrior note, "The cast of characters in the Indian world of the early 1970s was much more complicated than the media-projected young, city-based militants versus passive reservation residents." Natives also "ran their own businesses, were corporate executives, worked at newspapers, or were accountants." In addition, "American Indian educators, health professionals, journalists, artists, lawyers, . . . actors, scholars and others formed [non-militant] organizations." *Like a Hurricane*, 100–101.

23. Wilkins and Stark, *American Indian Politics*, 233.

24. Brando, "That Unfinished Oscar Speech." In 1975 Brando reflected, "I would hope that in some way an Indian speaking to some 80 million Americans for the first time in history would have sonic effect. Maybe not a direct effect but sort of a slow motion one. I'd given [Ms. Littlefeather] my statement and under the circumstances I think she did very well. Somehow, out of callousness, stupidity, thoughtlessness—that's enough adjectives—Hollywood and American picture producers have done as much—second only to the government—to harm the lives, facts, traditions, humanity and knowledge of American Indians as any group." Qtd. in Warga, "Marlon Brando."

25. Video of the PSA is available at http://www.adcouncil.org/Our-Work/The-Classics/Pollution-Keep-America-Beautiful-Iron-Eyes-Cody. On the complex politics of Cody's identity, see Raheja, "Tears and Trash," in *Reservation Reelism*, 102–44.

26. Nagel, "American Indian Ethnic Renewal," 961.

27. V. Deloria, "Popularity of Being Indian," 232.

28. "The Brady Braves," *The Brady Bunch*, ABC, Oct. 1, 1971. In *F Troop*, the white soldiers were already "honorary Hekawi," says Chief Wild Eagle, by the sitcom's start.

29. "The Adagio," *I Love Lucy*, CBS, Dec. 6, 1951; "Junior Pathfinders Ride Again," *Dennis the Menace*, CBS, Apr. 8, 1962; "The Clampetts in Washington," *The Beverly Hillbillies*, CBS, Sept. 22, 1970; "Lucy and the Indian Chief," *Here's Lucy*, CBS, Oct. 6, 1969; "The Beauty Contest," *The Andy Griffith Show*, CBS, Jan. 23, 1961; "The Pageant," *The Andy Griffith Show*, CBS, Nov. 30, 1964.

30. "A Clubhouse Is Not a Home," *The Brady Bunch*, ABC, Oct. 31, 1969; "The Slumber Caper," *The Brady Bunch*, ABC, Oct. 9, 1970.

31. "Un-Underground Movie," *The Brady Bunch*, ABC, Oct. 16, 1970.

32. "Ghost Town, U.S.A.," *The Brady Bunch*, ABC, Sept. 17, 1971; "Grand Canyon or Bust," *The Brady Bunch*, ABC, Sept. 24, 1971; "The Brady Braves," *The Brady Bunch*, ABC, Oct. 1, 1971.

33. Neumann, *On the Rim*, 168.

34. The original version of the song, titled "The Pale Faced Indian," was recorded in 1959 by Marvin Rainwater. The Raiders' complete title is "Indian Reservation (The Lament of the Cherokee Reservation Indian)." It was the #1 song on July 24, 1971. In the October 4, 1971, edition of *Sports Illustrated*, a photo of University of Washington Huskies quarterback Sonny Sixkiller (Cherokee), the "Washington Wonder," graced the cover.

35. The Bradys would search for adventure again during the first three episodes of season 4 in Hawaii. As during their trip to the Grand Canyon, they befriend an indigenous grandfather and his grandson.

36. See Loewen, *Lies across America*, 100–101.

37. Prendergast, "Tracking the Kaibab Deer," 418, 425.

38. Meek, "And the Injun Goes 'How!'"

39. Qtd. in Echohawk, "Kennedy Report," 16.

40. "Kennedy Report" qtd. in Deloria and Lytle, *Nations Within*, 218.

41. Producers of *The Lone Ranger* had Silverheels play Tonto in heavy broken English (e.g., "Me help Lone Ranger"). Offscreen, Silverheels advocated for Native actors in Hollywood and was the first Native to receive, in 1979, a star on the Hollywood Walk of Fame.

42. The "tribe" is never mentioned by name. Eagle Cloud momentarily speaks Diné when he first appears, but it may be that he just happens to know phrases from multiple nations in the region.

43. P. Deloria, *Playing Indian*, 184.

44. On Native public television in the 1970s, see Singer, *Wiping the War Paint*, 35–41.

45. "Running Bear and Moskowitz," *The New Dick Van Dyke Show*, CBS, Feb. 26, 1972; "Archie Learns His Lesson," *All in the Family*, CBS, Mar. 10, 1973; "Three on a Porch," *Happy Days*, ABC, Nov. 18, 1975; "Westward Ho!: Part 1," *Happy Days*, ABC, Sept. 12, 1978; "The First Thanksgiving," *Happy Days*, ABC, Nov. 21, 1978; "'Native American' Premieres on TV," *Los Angeles Sentinel*, May 29, 1975, B5; "The Indian," *Barney Miller*, ABC, Jan. 4, 1979; Singer, *Wiping the War Paint*, 35–38.

46. Holte, "Unmelting Images," 106.

47. Qtd. in Bogle, *Primetime Blues*, 219.

48. "The Indian," *Barney Miller*, ABC, Jan. 4, 1979. Interestingly, White Eagle debuted on television in an episode of the short-lived *Delvecchio*, a crime drama on CBS starring Judd Hirsch right before he costarred in the popular sitcom *Taxi*. White Eagle played an Indian elder and relative of an Indian fugitive character portrayed by Erik Estrada just

months before he costarred in *CHiPs*. Maureen McCormick, the actress who portrayed Marcia Brady, played Estrada's wife in the episode "One Little Indian" (Jan. 30, 1977).

49. Ten Fingers's line is very similar to a charge often attributed to Crazy Horse at the Battle of Little Big Horn: "It's a good day to die."

50. Hill qtd. in *On and Off the Res' w/Charlie Hill*; "Indians," *Lou Grant*, CBS, Jan. 14, 1980.

51. "Bones," *Barney Miller*, ABC, Apr. 30, 1982.

52. Gail credits inspiration for the title *For All My Relations* to "the usual translation for the Lakota spiritual expression 'Mitakuye Oyasin.'" Gail, "Max Gail: Running Laps," *Ability Magazine*, www.abilitymagazine.com/dana_laps.html (accessed Aug. 15, 2012).

53. Singer, *Wiping the War Paint*, 96.

54. The skit appears to have been inspired by Hill's real-life encounter with a producer who wanted Hill to pose in Hollywood Indian costume with a surfboard for a cigarette commercial and say, "Me smokum." See *On and Off the Res' w/Charlie Hill*.

55. The brief quotes in this paragraph are from my phone interview with Gail on August 22, 2012.

56. In parts 1 (May 6, 1982), 2 (May 13, 1982), and 3 (May 20, 1982) of the series finale "Landmark" the detectives prepare to move on to separate new jobs after they learn that the station will be designated a historical landmark. Gail amusingly suggests the producers failed to envision a story line in which the history of the precinct's site could be addressed further back in time as indigenous homelands. Gail interview.

57. "Bones" would be the last of five *Barney Miller* episodes Gail directed—four in 1978–79, then "Bones" in 1982.

58. According to Gail, Charlie Hill was briefly considered for the role of Long. Gail interview.

59. Mark Banks qtd. in Rosenthal, *Reimagining Indian Country*, 135.

60. Mark Banks, unpublished interview by Nicholas Rosenthal, May 5, 2004, Chatsworth, CA. For more on Winters, see "Comedian Jonathan Winters, Cherokee, Walks On."

61. Fine-Dare, *Grave Injustice*, 76.

62. The fight to receive back other belts continues today. See, for example, Sarah Moses, "Onondaga Historical Association Returns Wampum Belt to Onondaga Nation Leaders," *Syracuse Post-Standard*, June 14, 2012, http://www.syracuse.com/news/index.ssf/2012/06/onondaga_historical_associatio_3.html (accessed Aug. 12, 2012).

63. Fine-Dare, *Grave Injustice*, 92. See, too, Hauptman, *Formulating American Indian Policy*, 86–87.

64. Fine-Dare, *Grave Injustice*, 77. A series of late nineteenth-century events directly implicates the American Museum of Natural History. In 1897, six Inuits arrived from Greenland to New York with settler explorer Robert Peary to be studied by the museum. Four Inuits soon died of tuberculosis and one returned to Greenland, leaving the sixth, a young child named Minik, to be adopted by one of the curators. Minik's father was among those who died, and the museum "staged a fake funeral" to keep Minik "from discovering that the museum had stolen the remains." The father's skeleton was then put on display. Trope and Echo-Hawk, "Native American Graves Protection," 127. See also Harper, *Give Me My Father's Body*.

65. Fine-Dare, *Grave Injustice*, 105, 104, 103–4.

66. The reference to Manhattan is in response to the popular narrative that colonists purchased the island for twenty-four dollars from the Lenapes. For an astute pedagogical lesson on a *Far Side* cartoon that reframes the Manhattan narrative, see Williams, *Like a Loaded Weapon*, xiii–xvii.

67. Three Mile Island is a nuclear power plant near Harrisburg, Pennsylvania. In 1979, it leaked radioactive gases during what many have called the worst nuclear accident in U.S. history.

68. Gail interview.

69. "Burial Ground," *Diff'rent Strokes*, NBC, Jan. 7, 1982.

70. "The Music Man," *Diff'rent Strokes*, NBC, May 6, 1982. "Ebony and Ivory" had been released five weeks earlier by Paul McCartney and Stevie Wonder. It would soon be #1 for seven weeks on Billboard charts.

71. The televised version of *Beulah* aired on ABC from 1950 to 1952. The radio program of the same title ran on CBS from 1945 to 1954.

72. Bogle, *Primetime Blues*, 225.

73. Coleman, *African American Viewers*, 99. In Indian affairs, "the great white father" has typically been ascribed to U.S. presidents.

74. The line is similar to one by Ned Romero's Indian character in *The Munsters* episode "Big Heap Herman" (CBS, Jan. 20, 1966), in which he said, "White man speak with forked tongue."

75. Bogle, *Primetime Blues*, 225.

76. The actions postulated by Willis sound eerily familiar to plans by General Services Administration leader Robert Kunzig in 1964 during the first and very brief Native occupation of Alcatraz Island. Kunzig ordered the Natives "to vacate the island" within approximately twenty-four hours, Chaat Smith and Warrior report. "After that, U.S. marshals would remove them, at gunpoint if necessary. Marshals began preparing for a full, frontal assault." Tom Hannon, administrator of GSA West Coast, opposed Kunzig's approach in favor of less violent means. Chaat Smith and Warrior, *Like a Hurricane*, 67–68.

77. Other than the 1982 episodes of *Barney Miller* and *Diff'rent Strokes*, the 1980s were relatively quiet for sitcom Indians. *Cheers* on NBC featured a cigar shop Indian named Tecumseh and a photograph of Geronimo. Illustrative of what Michelle Raheja calls the "ghosting effect," or modern spectral semblances of historical Indian figures, the wooden Tecumseh stood by the door to greet patrons of the famous Boston bar (though I swear I never heard him join in the catchphrase chorus of "Norm!"), and the famous shot of Geronimo kneeling on one knee with rifle in hand was shown in the very last shot of the series finale, a tribute to the late actor Nicholas Colasanto, who portrayed "Coach" in the first three seasons and whose dressing room included the same picture. "One for the Road," *Cheers*, NBC, May 20, 1993. In the episode "I'll Be Seeing You, Part 1" (May 3, 1984), guest star Christopher Lloyd's eccentric artist character wears what he calls "ceremonial Apache" attire. A Menominee friend informed me of a 1985 *Punky Brewster* episode in which ancient Indians suddenly appear (in a ghost story narrated by young Punky) as cave dwellers who need a white savior (enter Punky's fantasy Indian alter-ego "Princess Moon") to defeat an evil spirit and help keep their *Last of the Dogmen*–like secret existence intact. "If we don't help these people," Punky pleads to her friends, "they'll lose

everything!" I have no confirmation on Princess Punky's tribal affiliation, but all royalty signifiers proverbially point to Cherokee. "The Perils of Punky, Part I" and "The Perils of Punky Part II," *Punky Brewster*, NBC, Oct. 20, 1985. "Princess Moon" was likely a play off the name Soleil Moon Frye, the actress who portrayed Punky. The 1995 film *Last of the Dogmen* starred Tom Berenger and Barbara Hershey who "discover" a group of Cheyennes living a secret static existence in teepees and buckskin in a Montana forest.

78. "I, Done (Part II)," *The Fresh Prince of Bel-Air*, NBC, May 20, 1996.

79. Mihesuah, *Repatriation Reader*, 3–4.

80. See, for example, Crawford, "(Re)Constructing Bodies."

81. Wilkins and Stark, *American Indian Politics*, 234.

82. White, "Indians' New Harvest."

83. *Dances with Wolves*, dir. Kevin Costner, Orion Pictures, 1990.

84. Mihesuah, "American Indian History," 151.

85. The episode's title derives from what Chief Henry calls Zack. As Chief Henry explains, "You run, you're Zack, it works!"

86. See Josephy, *Nez Perce Indians*, 628–29.

87. Similarly, George Ten Fingers, a Native character in the *Barney Miller* episode "The Indian" (ABC, Jan. 4, 1979), dies after helping Wojo, a white detective, to understand more about human life and his surroundings. In the *Dharma and Greg* episodes "Brought to You in Dharmavision" (ABC, Nov. 18, 1998), "Mother and Daughter Reunion" (Oct. 10, 2000), and "Intensive Caring" (Sept. 25, 2001), deceased Native character George Littlefox appears as white character Dharma's spiritual guide.

CHAPTER 3

1. Jonathan Joss, "Jonathan Joss Visits OLLU, Part 2," Nov. 16, 2010, http://www.youtube .com/watch?v=WVU2i1mIVEw&NR=1 (accessed June 28, 2012).

2. I will generally refer to the character as Redcorn. Whereas other characters in *King of the Hill* are typically called by first name only, he almost always is called "John Redcorn" or "Redcorn."

3. Bhabha, "Sly Civility," in *Location of Culture*, 93–101.

4. Steiner, *New Indians*, 27; Clyde Warrior qtd. in Chaat Smith and Warrior, *Like a Hurricane*; Clyde Warrior, "Which One Are You?," qtd. in Steiner, *New Indians*, 307; Cook-Lynn, *New Indians*, 210; Cook-Lynn, *Anti-Indianism*, 4.

5. Bruyneel, *Third Space of Sovereignty*, 129.

6. Of programs airing on NBC, CBS, ABC, and Fox from 2005 to 2006, a Native actor reportedly occupied one recurring role, presumably Joss as Redcorn. In the organization American Indians in Film & TV's 2006 report, chairman Mark S. Reed states, "American Indians remain invisible in primetime TV. There was a combined average employment of 8,000 guest starring roles, 400 recurring roles and 1,000 regular roles cast by the four networks. It is appalling that only one recurring and two guest starring roles were filled by an American Indian." Available online at http://groups.yahoo.com/group/NatNews/ message/44921 (accessed June 5, 2013).

7. On Clinton's and Obama's relations with Indian Country, see Wilkins and Stark, *American Indian Politics*.

8. The first Indian character to costar in a sitcom was likely Hawkeye (portrayed by settler actor J. Carrol Naish) in *Guestward Ho*. As Tim Brooks and Earle Marsh note, "Fed up with the hustle and bustle of New York City, the Hootens [a settler family] decided to [move to] *Guestward Ho*, a dude ranch in New Mexico." They soon meet Hawkeye, Indian proprietor of the area's only store and one of the series' costars. Sounding similar in intellect, entrepreneurialism, and outlook to Redcorn, "Hawkeye read the *Wall Street Journal*, sold Indian trinkets that had been made in Japan, and was bound and determined to find a way to return the country to its rightful owners, *his* people. He was not really militant, just industrious and conniving." Brooks and Marsh, *Complete Directory*, 567–68.

9. In sitcoms, a character's tribe is generally not identified (e.g., nationless Indians in "The Son Also Draws," *Family Guy*, Fox, May 9, 1999) or nonexistent (e.g., Crowfeet in *The Beverly Hillbillies*). Occasionally a known Native nation is stated and geographically accurate (e.g., Danny Lightfoot as Hopi in Arizona in *Hey, Dude*). Redcorn's self-identification as Anasazi in the episode "Spin the Choice" is presumably an ode to Mike Judge's father, archaeologist Jim Judge. During his career, Jim Judge has studied and cowritten numerous publications on Anasazis, including the 1991 book *The Anasazi*. For a series that prides itself on evoking accurate likenesses of popular establishments in Texas (e.g., Mega Lo Mart as "Wal-Mart" and a "W"-logoed restaurant resembling "Whataburger"), *King of the Hill* opts for an indigenous tribe that is almost always associated today with the past. Anasazis, a Diné/Navajo term for "enemies," are often identified today more appropriately as "ancestral Pueblo peoples" or "ancient Pueblos," predominantly in New Mexico. Furthermore, contemporary Natives from the nineteen Pueblos, such as Isleta or Nambe, do not identify as "Anasazi." As the federal Bureau of Land Management, within the U.S. Department of the Interior, explains, "There never was an 'Anasazi tribe,' nor did anyone ever call themselves by that name. *Anasazi* is originally a Navajo word that archaeologists applied to people who farmed the Four Corners before 1300 AD." See "Who Were the Anasazi?," U.S. Department of the Interior, http://www.blm.gov/co/st/en/fo/ahc/who_were_the_anasazi.html#who (accessed June 5, 2012).

10. Jonathan Joss, "Jonathan Joss Visits OLLU, Part 2," Nov. 16, 2010, http://www.youtube.com/watch?v=WVU2i1mIVEw&NR=1.

11. "Making of *King of the Hill*," The Wittliff Collections, http://www.thewittliffcollections.txstate.edu/exhibitions-events/exhibitions/past/kingofhill.html (accessed July 10, 2012); J. Gray, *Show Sold Separately*, 7.

12. J. Gray, *Show Sold Separately*, 16, 6.

13. Various sources have identified Joss as Apache and/or Comanche. His official site states, "Jonathan's Family Is Descended From The White Mountain Apache," near the bottom of the page "Jonathan's Links!," which includes a link to the White Mountain Apaches' official website. See http://www.jonathanjoss.com/Links.html (accessed Aug. 5, 2012).

14. A TV series' bible is the foundational written account of the show's premise and characters. In addition to Dale's supposed cluelessness, Joseph never indicates awareness that Redcorn is his biological father. Initially Peggy is clueless, too, about the affair until season 3 in the episode "Peggy's Headache" (Oct. 6, 1998).

15. Schulman, "Red Corn Band," 27.

16. Randolph Lewis defines "representational sovereignty" as "the right, as well as the ability, for a group of people to depict themselves with their own ambitions at heart." Lewis, *Alanis Obomsawin*, 175.

17. Hilton-Morrow and McMahan, "*The Flintstones* to *Futurama*," 80–81; Groening qtd. in ibid., 79.

18. *Beavis and Butthead*, under Judge's direction, returned to MTV with new episodes in 2011.

19. Although Judge once lived in Arlen-soundalike Garland, Texas, he says Arlen is based primarily on nearby Richardson. Kathryn Shuttuck interview with Judge, "It Was Good to Be King, but What Now?" *New York Times*, Apr. 22, 2009, http://www.nytimes.com/2009/04/26/arts/television/26shat.html?_r=0. (accessed July 9, 2013).

20. On masculinity in *King of the Hill*, see Thompson, "'I Am Not Down with That'"; and Palmer-Mehta, "Wisdom of Folly."

21. *King of the Hill* often seemed anxious in its efforts to not allow Hank to be perceived as a racist. A proposed and rejected story pitch, for example, involved Hank's genealogical discovery that he descends from a slave owner (*King of the Hill* Archives).

22. The program was formerly called Fox Diversity Outreach.

23. For a critique of Indians in *The X-Files*, see Hersey, "Native Americans."

24. "Fox Opens the Door to American Indian Youth," *Indian Country Today Media Network*, Sept. 13, 2002, http://indiancountrytodaymedianetwork.com/ictarchives/2002/09/13/fox-opens-the-door-to-american-indian-youth-88048 (accessed Aug. 5, 2012).

25. Joseph is voiced by non-Native actors Brittany Murphy (1997–2000) and Breckin Meyer (2000–2009).

26. Joss says he heard Redcorn was based on "someone that Mike [Judge] knew." Phone interview with the author, July 12, 2012. It has been reported, too, that Hank and his beer-drinking friends are modeled after some of Judge's former neighbors in Dallas.

27. In my interview with Joss, he recalled a mid-1990s conversation with his friend Aaron, who expressed excitement about an upcoming show called *King of the Hill* that would bring about a change, possibly for Native actors and characters and public perception of both. Aaron, however, was killed in a car accident in 1996, a week before his fortieth birthday. *King of the Hill* producers dedicated "The Order of the Straight Arrow" to the memory of Aaron. Incidentally, Joss is also featured in the "Native Visions" calendar.

28. Thanks to one of the anonymous readers for mentioning Wind in His Hair.

29. "Order of the Arrow" is the Boy Scouts of America's National Honor Society. The addition of "Straight" by *King of the Hill* may have been prompted by the Boy Scouts' antigay policies. As the organization stated in 2004, "Boy Scouts of America believes that homosexual conduct is inconsistent with the obligations in the Scout Oath and Scout Law to be morally straight and clean in thought, word, and deed." This statement is available at http://www.bsa-discrimination.org/html/bsa_gay_policy.html. Growing up in Albuquerque, Mike Judge was a Boy Scout.

30. The flute and rustling hair were apparently an inside recurring joke attributed to Greg Daniels. Cheryl Holliday, dir. Klay Hall, "Director's Commentary: 'The Order of the Straight Arrow,'" *King of the Hill: Season One*, Twentieth Century Fox, 2003, DVD.

31. "Storynotes," May 29, 1996, *King of the Hill* Archives.

32. "First draft," June 12, 1996, *King of the Hill* Archives.

33. Preparing for Thanksgiving travels to Arizona in one episode, Redcorn suggests he has family or close friends there. "Happy Hank's Giving," *King of the Hill*, Fox, Nov. 21, 1999.

34. Playing Indian in certain youth organizations has a long history. See, for example, Wall, "Totem Poles." Neil Diamond's 2009 documentary film *Reel Injun* includes contemporary scenes of savage Indian play at a summer camp.

35. "Good Hill Hunting," *King of the Hill*, Fox, Dec. 1, 1998.

36. "Second draft," June 20, 1996, *King of the Hill* Archives.

37. "Luanne's Saga," *King of the Hill*, Fox, Feb. 16, 1997.

38. See, for example, John Redcorn's Facebook wall at http://www.facebook.com/pages/John-Redcorn/40083099075 (accessed July 2, 2012).

39. "Peggy's Headache," *King of the Hill*, Fox, Oct. 6, 1998; P. Deloria, *Indians in Unexpected Places*, 9–10.

40. "The Arrowhead," *King of the Hill*, Fox, Oct. 19, 1997.

41. In an earlier and still disparaging version of this line that subsumes women as men's property, Redcorn says, "Hank, think about what you're doing. How would you feel if I took what was precious to your people, and defiled it?" "Greg's Draft," co-creator Greg Daniels, Feb. 24, 1997, *King of the Hill* Archives.

42. A deleted scene in "The Arrowhead" shows the archaeologist asking a group of kids, "Now, who can tell me what Indian tribes are native to Arlen?" Singling out Joseph due to his appearance, the archaeologist says, "I bet you can." Joseph replies, "Um, I don't know." Jonathan Aibel and Glenn Berger, dir. Klay Hall, "Deleted and Extended Scenes: 'The Arrowhead,'" *King of the Hill: Season Two*, Twentieth Century Fox, 2003, DVD.

43. "The Indian Giver," first draft, Jan. 17, 1997, p. 7, *King of the Hill* Archives.

44. Ibid., p. 8.

45. Beat sheet, "The Indian Giver," Feb. 3, 1997, *King of the Hill* Archives.

46. "Indian Artifact Story pitch," Nov. 25, 1996, p. 4, *King of the Hill* Archives.

47. Ibid. Such moves by Aibel and Berger are not surprising when perusing their list of script resources at the end of the story pitch. The episode includes a number of settler-authored government and popular magazine sources, such as the Advisory Council on Historic Preservation's document "The National Historic Preservation Program," a *Texas Monthly* story about the Caddoan Mounds State Historic Site, and a *Natural History* article titled "A Texas Powwow: The Alabama and Coushatta Indians Make No Apologies for Their Eclectic Traditions." Additional references are made to sources about "historical Indian tribes in Texas." Upon consideration of the early script idea to declare Hank's yard "a sacred Indian burial ground," a glaring research omission is a story from four months earlier. On July 28, 1996, skeletal remains were found in Kennewick, Washington. Labeled the Kennewick Man, the remains have been argued over between white archaeologists and Indigenous Peoples in the Pacific Northwest. The bones are currently housed in the Burke Museum at the University of Washington. See Crawford, "(Re)Constructing Bodies."

48. "Indian Artifact Story Pitch."

49. Aibel and Berger wrote for *MADtv* from 1995 to 1997. In *Alvin and the Chipmunks: The Squeakquel*, the writers even resurrect their dated *King of the Hill* approach of creating a clash between indigeneity and modernity. One brief and odd scene flashes to Alaska Natives seated in an igloo watching the chipmunks on a flat-screen television, as if, in 2009, such technology consumption is to be unexpected and igloos are the housing norm.

50. Absent from the on-screen and archival tribal smorgasbord is reference to "Anasazi," Redcorn's neo-tribal affiliation starting in season 5.

51. *King of the Hill* episodes "The Wedding of Bobby Hill," Feb. 9, 1999; "Sleight of Hank," Feb. 16, 1999; "Hank's Cowboy Movie," Apr. 6, 1999; "Dog Dale Afternoon," Apr. 13, 1999; "Happy Hank's Giving," Nov. 21, 1999; "To Kill a Ladybird," Dec. 12, 1999.

52. "Nancy Boys," *King of the Hill*, Fox, Apr. 30, 2000.

53. Jonathan Joss, "Jonathan Joss vists [*sic*] OLLU, part 3," Nov. 16, 2010, http://www.youtube.com/watch?v=RltzqhVLuxg. As Gover said before a gathered assembly of indigenous political leaders, "Let us begin by expressing our profound sorrow for what this agency has done in the past," and later lamented, "On behalf of the Bureau of Indian Affairs, I extend this formal apology to Indian people for the historical conduct of this agency." Gover's speech is available at http://www.youtube.com/watch?v=zu52ig696L4.

54. The decision was overseen by then energy secretary and future governor of New Mexico Bill Richardson. For more on the decision, see Michael Janofsky, "U.S. Is Returning 84,000 Acres to Indians," *New York Times*, Jan. 14, 2000, http://www.nytimes.com/2000/01/14/us/us-is-returning-84000-acres-to-indians.html. "Spin the Choice," *King of the Hill*, Fox, Nov. 19, 2000.

55. "Returning Japanese, Part I," *King of the Hill*, Fox, May 12, 2002.

56. For more on the Ray story, see Dougherty, "For Some Seeking Rebirth, Sweat Lodge Was End."

57. In season 8's "Rich Hank, Poor Hank" (Jan. 4, 2004), Redcorn, in a less troubling vein, is opportunistic again. When he is fooled by a false rumor that Hank has suddenly become very wealthy, Redcorn pulls his hair back, dresses in a suit and bolo tie, and proposes, with blueprints in hand, an investment opportunity to Hank: the "New Age Golden Years Assisted Living Facility" for aging baby boomers. When Hank does not invest the requested $1,000,000, Redcorn replies, "Someone is going to make a lot of money off of this idea. It could have been us."

58. When asked in 2010 if his roles have caused him trouble with Native Peoples or his family, Joss replied, "Not in trouble with family, just producers. I stand up for what I believe in. Sometimes Hollywood has a misunderstanding about the Native American ideas and rituals that we do and why we do them." He then proceeded to draw a comparison. In theater, "you don't use a real Bible on stage. Very simple. So, we as Native Americans prefer not to do traditional things on film." In the same interview, regarding his roles in film and television, he said, "I've never had anyone say that I treated anyone in a negative way, I've been proud to say my entire career." "Jonathan Joss vists [*sic*] OLLU, part 3," Nov. 16, 2010, http://www.youtube.com/watch?v=RltzqhVLuxg&feature=endscreen&NR=1.

59. "Vision Quest," *King of the Hill*, Fox, Feb. 9, 2003.

60. In my interview with Joss, he said that *King of the Hill* producer Joe Bouchet once said to him something to the effect of, "You really care about this character."

61. Schulman, "Red Corn Band," 27.

62. Joss interview.

63. Joss borrowed the name Big Mountain Fudgecake from Black Angus Steakhouse, one of Hank Hill's favorite restaurants, whose menu includes the Big Mountain Chocolate Fudgecake dessert. When *King of the Hill* later used the name for Redcorn's on-screen band, Joss dropped it offscreen and chose the Red Corn Band.

64. Jonathan Joss, "Jonathan Joss Visits OLLU, Part 2," Nov. 16, 2010, http://www.youtube.com/watch?v=WVU2i1mIVEw&NR=1.

65. "Golder Driblets" refers to the CD's cover picture of Joss's friend's urine-stained toilet. Joss interview.

66. Jonathan Joss, "Jonathan Joss Visits OLLU, Part 2," Nov. 16, 2010, http://www.youtube.com/watch?v=WVU2i1mIVEw&NR=1; Joss interview.

67. As Joss told interviewer Sandra Schulman, "Mike Judge and producer Joe Bouchet liked what they heard and wrote it into the script." Schulman, "Red Corn Band," 27. My thanks to Joss for providing me with a copy of the unreleased "Golden Driblets."

68. "The Witches of East Arlen," *King of the Hill*, Fox, May 18, 2003.

69. Jonathan Joss, "Jonathan Joss Visits OLLU, Part 2," Nov. 16, 2010, http://www.youtube.com/watch?v=WVU2i1mIVEw&NR=1.

70. Schulman, "Red Corn Band: Red Corn Sessions," 26; Red Corn Band, *The Red Corn Sessions*, with Jonathan Joss, Tim Sampson, and George Multine III, prod. Adrian Brown, 2004, CD.

71. Raheja, *Reservation Reelism*, 150.

72. "Redcorn Gambles with His Future," *King of the Hill*, Fox, Apr. 10, 2005.

73. Joss was thirty-nine at the time of the episode's premiere.

74. See Cramer, "Common Sense," 331; Corntassel and Witmer, *Forced Federalism*, 31; Cattelino, *High Stakes*, 7, 210–11; and Lacroix, "High Stakes Stereotypes." On "rich Indian racism," see Spilde, "Rich Indian Racism."

75. Joss, e-mail to the author, July 23, 2012.

76. Immediately after the Tiguas' casino closed, lobbyist Jack Abramoff assured the Tiguas he would restore justice for the tribe and lead efforts to reopen the casino. However, he also secretly lobbied against them. Along with his main partner-in-crime Michael Scanlon, Abramoff soon made headlines for a major lobbying scandal that included bilking $4.2 million from the Tiguas. Abramoff was incarcerated from 2006 to 2010 for fraudulent charges in Florida, not for defrauding the Tiguas and other indigenous clients. In "Redcorn Gambles with His Future," a crooked Abramoff-like character named Henry Mankiller, who quickly self-identifies as "1/64th Creek on my mother's side," represents the Tribal Gaming Corporation that finances Redcorn's casino. When the casino is shut down, he tells Redcorn that a $23,000 payment is due immediately or else Redcorn's land will be turned into a toxic dumping site. In an episode that features settler characters advising and helping Redcorn, the only two characters blamed by Redcorn for his business failure are indigenous: Redcorn himself and Mankiller. When Mankiller attempts to fault the proverbial "white man" for the casino shutdown, Redcorn replies, "The 'white man'? How could *you* not know there was no gaming in Texas?"

77. On the tribal recognition history of the Tiguas, see M. E. Miller, "From Playing Indian to Playing Slots."

78. "As Texas Goes, What for Indian Country?," *Indian Country Today Media Network*, Aug. 23, 2002, http://indiancountrytodaymedianetwork.com/ictarchives/2002/08/23/as-texas-goes-what-for-indian-country-88002 (accessed Aug. 4, 2013).

79. Battise qtd. in Senate Hearing 107-571, "Implementation of the Texas Restoration Act," June 18, 2002, http://www.gpo.gov/fdsys/pkg/CHRG-107shrg80743/html/CHRG-107shrg80743.htm (accessed Aug. 4, 2013).

80. "Hair Today, Gone Tomorrow," *King of the Hill*, Fox, May 13, 2007.

81. "Manger Baby Einstein," *King of the Hill*, Fox, May 10, 2009. In season 12, Redcorn learns he has a daughter with an ex-girlfriend. He and the mother start seeing each other again behind the back of her new boyfriend, Bill Dauterive. Then she and her two children suddenly move in with Redcorn at the end of the episode. When the script and subsequent broadcast have Redcorn driving off with his new family to their home, Joss wondered to himself, "Is that your way of getting rid of me?" But Redcorn continued his entrepreneurial run in season 13 when he briefly ran a fireworks stand. Reminiscent of Kicking Wing's (Adam Beach) stand in the 2001 film *Joe Dirt* starring David Spade, Redcorn is approached by Hank, who wants to buy major explosives. Like the Kicking Wing character, Redcorn initially pushes the sparklers, which he says "will blow your mind, Hank. When you write in the air, the words will stay there for almost [pause] a second." Then in line with previous shady survivalist practices and at the urging of Hank, Redcorn sells him the fireworks that "are illegal in Mexico." "The Untitled Blake McCormick Project," *King of the Hill*, Fox, Feb. 17, 2008; "Born Again on the Fourth of July," *King of the Hill*, Fox, Apr. 19, 2009.

82. Qtd. in Sanford Allen, "Made in SA: Jonathan Joss Has the Specs on the Big Screen *Jonah Hex*," Aug. 7, 2009, http://missionsunknown.com/2009/08/made-in-sa-jonathan-joss-has-the-specs-on-the-big-screen-jonah-hex/.

83. Ibid.

84. Schulman, "Red Corn Band," 27.

85. Near the end of a video filmed at the 2008 Austin Rock Band Championships, Joss can be heard talking in Redcorn's voice; see http://www.youtube.com/watch?v=GouSpEBchqY. Ryan Hailey, "Faux Rockers Battle, Electronically Please the Legends of Rock," *Daily Texan*, Nov. 13, 2008; Brad Parrett, "Rock Band 2 and John Redcorn—Together at Last!" OriginalAlamo.com, Nov. 10, 2008.

86. Jonathan Joss, "Jonathan Joss Visits OLLU, Part 2," Nov. 16, 2010, http://www.youtube.com/watch?v=WVU2i1mIVEw&NR=1.

87. *One Voice Radio with Kenneth Hieber and Felipe Rose*, interview with Joss, July 25, 2012, http://www.youtube.com/watch?v=F3lu9i96tLI&NR=1&feature=endscreen; 1200 WOAI radio *San Antonio's First News* with Charlie Parker, interview with Joss, Oct. 5, 2011. Joss plays the recurring role of Ken Hotate, chief of the Wamapoke Indians, in NBC's sitcom *Parks and Recreation*.

88. In May 2011, Joss filmed an online commercial for the grill rub. See the commercial at http://www.youtube.com/watch?v=60jVwpQ_Vys.

89. For "Aboriginal *Brady Bunch*," see Taylor qtd. in Carol Levine, "A Very Special 'Occasion': Breaking Bread with Drew Hayden Taylor," *NativeVue: Film and Media Connection*, Jan. 2007, http://www.scene4.com/archivesqv6/jan-2007/html/carolelevine0107.html.

CHAPTER 4

1. See http://www.bcnationalaboriginalday.com/, http://www.nationalaboriginal-daythunderbay.ca/, http://nadottawa.wordpress.com/, and http://www.edmonton.ca/attractions_recreation/festivals_events/national-aboriginal-day.aspx.

2. The holiday is set to the tenor of collaboration: "Planning committees usually include both Aboriginal and non-Aboriginal people." "National Aboriginal Day History,"

Indian and Northern Affairs Canada, https://www.aadnc-aandc.gc.ca/eng/11001000133
39/1100100013341.

3. Taylor, "What . . . You Think You're Funny?!"

4. On Native authors' use of humor for cultural healing, see, for example, Taylor, *Me Funny*; Blaeser, "New 'Frontier'"; and Eva Gruber, "Humorous Restorifications" and *Humor in Contemporary Native North American Literature*. On Native humor, see, for example, V. Deloria, "Indian Humor," in *Custer Died for Your Sins*, 146–67; and Lincoln, *Indi'n Humor*.

5. Taylor, "What . . . You Think You're Funny?!" For scholarship on Taylor, see Young, "Bridging the Gap"; and Nunn, *Drew Hayden Taylor*. On Taylor's work in television, the main sources are Taylor's own commentaries about his experiences and observations.

6. Vizenor and Lee, *Postindian Conversations*, 160.

7. Taylor, *Funny, You Don't Look Like One*, 14.

8. Taylor qtd. in Carol Levine, "A Very Special 'Occasion': Breaking Bread with Drew Hayden Taylor," *NativeVue: Film and Media Connection*, Oct. 28, 2006, http://www.nativevue.org/blog/?p=189. *Mixed Blessings* also is the title of a 1978–80 British sitcom about an interracial black and white couple.

9. The season 2 finale is titled "Baby on the Way," APTN, Nov. 25, 2008.

10. Fort McMurray has a population of approximately 60,000. Nearby is the Fort McMurray First Nation. *Mixed Blessings* was "shot and produced in Edmonton," around three hours southwest of Beaver Lake. See "Actors Grateful for Mixed Blessings."

11. Scott founded the company in 1993. See its official site at http://www.prairiedog.ca/.

12. Scott qtd. in Heather Andrews Miller, "Ukrainian Meets Cree in Six-Part Television Series," *Alberta Sweetgrass*, Jan. 1, 2008, 8.

13. Scott qtd. in Diane Wild, "TV, Eh? Interview: Ron E. Scott of Blackstone," Feb. 1, 2012, http://www.tv-eh.com/2012/02/01/tv-eh-interview-ron-e-scott-of-blackstone/.

14. "Dot Not Feather," the *Mixed Blessings* season 3 premiere (Dec. 8, 2009), is set on National Aboriginal Day. In support of the tenor of aforementioned events, Josie says in the episode, "We're celebrating Native culture, and part of that is sharing it with others."

15. Scott qtd. in H. Miller, "Ukrainian Meets Cree," 8.

16. "Pow Wow," *Mixed Blessings*, APTN, Dec. 18, 2007.

17. Taylor qtd. in Moffatt and Tait, "'I Just See Myself as an Old-Fashioned Storyteller,'" 73; "A House Divided," *The Beachcombers*, CBC, Mar. 27, 1988.

18. Taylor, "Adventures in the Skin Trade," in *Furious Observations*, 84.

19. Taylor, "57 Channels," in ibid., 59. In another article, Taylor describes "Seeing Red" as "Native oriented humour where we make fun of the perceptions and stereotypes surrounding the First Nations culture. It could be dangerous because myself and the other two writers plan to pull the leg of white people and Native people to the point of dislocation." "Laughing Till Your Face Is Red," in ibid., 96.

20. Young, "Bridging the Gap," 197, 223.

21. Taylor qtd. in Moffatt and Tait, "'I Just See Myself as an Old-Fashioned Storyteller,'" 81–82.

22. For example, Taylor says in an interview, "As a Native person in a Native environment, I watch *The Simpsons*, I watch *Friends*, and I laugh." Interview with Rachel Chapa, June 6, 2005, http://hidvl.nyu.edu/video/000506894.html.

23. Taylor, "57 Channels," 61.

24. Alexie, "No Reservations."

25. Taylor, "Aboriginal TV," in *Funny, You Don't Look Like One*, 126–28.

26. Taylor, "TV's Electronic Smoke Signals."

27. "The Snow Job," *Three's Company*, ABC, Oct. 2, 1979; "Archie Learns His Lesson," *All in the Family*, CBS, Mar. 10, 1973.

28. Taylor, "Aboriginal TV," 126, and "TV's Electronic Smoke Signals," *Windspeaker* 19.2 (2001): 6–7.

29. Taylor, "The Things That a Person Learns while in L.A.," *Windspeaker* 21.3 (2003): 14, http://www.ammsa.com/node/26302.

30. Taylor, "57 Channels" and *Furious Observations*, 68–69. He mentions his fatigue with *Thunderheart* and *Billy Jack* in "57 Channels," 62. Taylor calls for dramatic and comedy TV series while also recognizing the unfunny and dramatic increases in costs for original fictional programming. "Drama," he writes, "is a hell of a lot more expensive, several times over in fact, than a news show." *Furious Observations*, 69.

31. Taylor, "North of Sixty, South of Accurate," in *Funny, You Don't Look Like One*, 89, 92.

32. Ibid., 92. Taylor also critiqued the NBC unaired pilot "Blood Brothers." NBC contacted Taylor in the early 2000s to invite him to submit Native-oriented programming ideas. As Taylor notes, "The network had recently polled its audiences and were shocked (their words—'shocked') to discover they had no programming for or about American Indians! And they wanted to do something about it. I was shocked that they were shocked." Ibid., 63.

33. Roth, *Something New in the Air*, 51.

34. Ibid., 106.

35. Ibid., 145–47.

36. CRTC qtd. in Roth, *Something New in the Air*, 22.

37. APTN, "About," http://www.aptn.ca/corporate/about.php.

38. Tagalik qtd. in Roth, *Something New in the Air*, 201.

39. H. Gray, *Watching Race*, 113.

40. Taylor, "What . . . You Think You're Funny?!"

41. Taylor, *Me Funny*, 3.

42. "Secret Love," *Mixed Blessings*, APTN, Nov. 13, 2007.

43. As Taylor explained in an interview, he enjoys compiling lists of indigenous pop culture trivia and incorporating pieces of them into his writings. "I'm just sitting around thinking of all the obscure Native pop culture stuff I could come up with in my head; you know, what was The Lone Ranger's real name? John Reid. You know, stuff like that. And what was the real name of Jay Silverheels, the actor who played Tonto? Harold Smith. I soak that stuff up." Taylor qtd. in Moffatt and Tait, "'I Just See Myself as an Old-Fashioned Storyteller,'" 83.

44. The song was reportedly recorded in 1960 but not released until the 1976 album *Elvis: A Legendary Performer*, vol. 2. *Flaming Star*, dir. Don Siegel, Twentieth Century Fox, 1960.

45. Nazareth, "Elvis as Anthology," 69, 41.

46. "Choices," *Mixed Blessings*, APTN, Nov. 27, 2007.

47. Taylor, "Epilogue: Everything I Learned about Life," in *Funny, You Don't Look Like One*, 139.

48. "Choices," *Mixed Blessings*, APTN, Nov. 27, 2007.

49. Taylor, upon watching *Dances with Wolves*, admits it was "Kevin Costner's epic homage to the romantic Indian," but "I kept looking for someone in the film to say, 'I never met an Indian I didn't like.'" Taylor, "Coloured Movies: Aboriginals on Parade," in *Funny, You Don't Look Like One*, 73–74, 73–76.

50. "Choices," *Mixed Blessings*, APTN, Nov. 27, 2007.

51. "Dances with Wolfy," *Mixed Blessings*, APTN, Feb. 2, 2010; "Dances with Couch," *Yes, Dear*, CBS, Apr. 8, 2002; "Dances with Groceries," *Ten Items or Less*, TBS, Feb. 17, 2009.

52. In the First Nations sitcom *Moose TV* ("Technical Difficulties," Showcase, July 26, 2007), Cree characters also find themselves up against German expectations. When a German couple visit the Cree community of Moose in Canada, they pay $10,000 "to find our place of great spiritual reunion" with, they add, the help of a "tribal elder" and "to look around" and "have, you know, intercourse with nature." Actor Gary Farmer's character, the scheming mayor of Moose, comically reasons that the couple is visiting because "they're into the noble savage thing. They're Europeans. They're rich."

53. Taylor, "If Only We Were So Popular Here," *Windspeaker* 26.10 (2009): 12, in *News*; Lutz qtd. in Dawes and Nunn, "Interview with Drew Hayden Taylor," 197.

54. Taylor, "Experiencing Fine German 'Injuneering,'" *Windspeaker* 30.3 (2012): 11.

55. Taylor qtd. in Nunn, *Drew Hayden Taylor*, 198. For an additional account by Taylor on visiting Germany, see "Ich Bin Ein Ojibway," in *News*, 36–38.

56. Wolfgang is portrayed by Noel Johansen, a rather versatile settler actor with ties to Canada, the United States, and England, as noted at http://www.noeljohansen.com/actor/index.html.

57. On the *Diff'rent Strokes* episode "Burial Ground," see chapter 2.

58. For an excellent account of visual sovereignty and its tactic of Native Peoples laughing at the camera, see Raheja, "Visual Sovereignty," in *Reservation Reelism*.

59. Taylor qtd. in Dawes and Nunn, "Interview with Drew Hayden Taylor," 196.

60. Vizenor, *Fugitive Poses*, 15.

61. Vizenor, *Manifest Manners*, 5.

62. Vizenor, *Fugitive Poses*, 15.

63. Doerfler, "Postindian Survivance," 191.

64. Scott qtd. in "Actors Grateful for Mixed Blessings."

65. Scott qtd. in *The Making of Mixed Blessings*, Prairie Dog Film + Television, available at http://www.mixedblessingstheseries.com/themakingofMB.html.

66. Taylor qtd. in Levine, "A Very Special 'Occasion.'"

67. Damberger qtd. in "Cast of Mixed Blessings," *Mixed Blessings: Season 3*, Prairie Dog Film + Television, DVD.

68. Doerfler, "Postindian Survivance," 190.

69. "Actors Grateful for Mixed Blessings."

70. Thrush received the 2011 Gemini (Canada's equivalent to the Emmy) for Best Performance by an Actress in a Continuing Leading Dramatic Role for her performance in Ron Scott's indigenous TV drama *Blackstone*. Regarding her thoughts on *Mixed Blessings* and her role, Thrush said, "We are so funny, and to be able to capture that on film

is so important. Everything is so serious, and I'm so tired of playing suicidal victims, drama, everything's always negative." Qtd. in *Making of Mixed Blessings* video, Prairie Dog Film + Television, available at http://www.mixedblessingstheseries.com/themak-ingofMB.html.

71. Belcourt qtd. in Shannon Montgomery, "Young Aboriginals Hope to Break Stereotypes through Films that Show Real Life," *Native Journal*, July 2008, http://www.nativejournal.ca/pages/2008%20sections/*2008.07.sections/2008.07.Culture.html.

72. "The Cigar Store Indian," *Seinfeld*, NBC, Dec. 9, 1993. When a female sitcom Indian did appear in U.S. sitcoms in the 1960s–1970s, they rarely spoke. Male sitcom Indians dominated Hekawi speaking roles in *F Troop*. In the *Munsters* episode "Big Heap Herman" (Jan. 20, 1966) the minor bit part of "Indian girl" included very few lines. In the *Happy Days* episode "Westward Ho!: Part 1" (Sept. 12, 1978), the mute female Indian Soft Doe appears in buckskin and on horseback in a modern-day setting. In *Son of the Beach* (2000–2001), an FX sitcom co-executive produced by Howard Stern, Joanna Bacalso (Filipina) portrayed the highly sexualized sitcom Indian female character "Firebush" in "Love, Native American-Style" (Apr. 4, 2000) and "Light My Firebush" (Apr. 17, 2001).

73. Scott qtd. in H. Miller, "Ukrainian Meets Cree," 8.

74. Susie and Sarah performed live on the first night of APTN's premiere. Michele LeTourneau, "Getting Tuned In: Aboriginal Network Launches," Northern News Services, Sept. 6, 1999, http://www.nnsl.com/frames/newspapers/1999-09/sep6_99tv.html; Eyre qtd. in *Reel Injun*, dir. Neil Diamond, Domino Film & Television International, 2009.

75. Lameman qtd. in *Making of Mixed Blessings* video, Prairie Dog Film + Television, available at http://www.mixedblessingstheseries.com/themakingofMB.html.

76. "Pow Wow," *Mixed Blessings*, APTN, Dec. 18, 2007.

77. "Cast Kookum," *Mixed Blessings* official site, http://www.mixedblessingstheseries.com/html/kookum.html.

78. When Charlie runs a moose stand at a powwow, Hank, trying to be in the cultural know, asks if he has any moose nose. "Just ran out," Charlie slyly replies. "Had a busload of seniors come by here this morning."

79. "Secret Love," *Mixed Blessings*, APTN, Nov. 13, 2007.

80. "Traditional Wedding," *Mixed Blessings*, APTN, Dec. 4, 2007.

81. "Rafter Six Ranch," *Fish Out of Water*, APTN, Jan. 25, 2008.

82. Twoyoungmen qtd. in Harbeck, "Morley Entertainer Good Medicine for Confused Youth," *Cochrane Eagle*, Mar. 12, 2008, http://www.harbeck.ca/cww/cww_080312.html.

83. As George Gerbner explains, "Representation in the fictional world signifies social existence; absence means symbolic annihilation." Gerbner qtd. in Coleman and Yokim, "Symbolic Annihilation of Race," 2.

84. Ginsburg, "Screen Memories"; Raheja, *Reservation Reelism*, 195.

85. On the use of sonic bridges in American television, see Mittell, *Television and American Culture*, 112.

86. See http://www.leannegoose.com/fr_home.cfm. (accessed Sept. 22, 2012).

87. Kinnie Starr, "Rock the Boat," *Anything*, prod. Howard Redekopp, 2006, CD.

88. Lucie Idlout, "Tonight," *Swagger*, 2009, CD.

89. On Strynadka, see Ostashewski, "Full-Fledged."

90. See http://leelagilday.com/ and http://www.myspace.com/mgirlmusic (accessed Sept. 22, 2012).

CONCLUSION

1. For more on Winn's work, see Mittell, "Cultural Power."

2. Pew Research Center, "Millennials."

3. On the complex relationship between the Internet and television, see Spigel and Olsson, *Television after TV*; Lotz, *Television Will Be Revolutionized*; and Bennett and Strange, *Television as Digital Media*.

4. "Bones" remained on the site for approximately a year before YouTube terminated the account in mid-2013 for copyright infringement, one of the major ongoing disputes in just how much freedom *you* are allowed with the *tube*, slang for television.

5. Among original Internet TV series are Internet sitcoms *The Guild, Break a Leg*, and *The Burg*.

6. Jenkins, "What Happened Before YouTube." On participatory culture, see Jenkins, *Convergence Culture*, 290.

7. Seabrook, "Streaming Dreams."

8. Whereas Indigenous Peoples around the world are actively using the Internet, many communities currently have limited or no access. For more on indigeneity and Internet usage and access, see Landzelius, "Introduction"; Dyson, Hendriks, and Grant, *Information Technology and Indigenous People*; and Dyson, "Indigenous Peoples on the Internet."

9. 1491s cofounder Dallas Goldtooth says "the first time the 1491s got together" was on the set.

10. "About," 1491s official site, http://1491s.com/about/.

11. "Wolf Pack Auditions" is available at http://www.youtube.com/watch?v=BmFx JYFSXyo, Dec. 1, 2009. Although it appears on Sterlin Harjo's YouTube channel, the video is the first to feature the 1491s together.

12. The "Kill Your TV" shirt is available at Red Corn's company Demockratees, http://www.demockratees.com/killyourtv.html (accessed Aug. 7, 2013).

13. Red Corn qtd. in "Ryan Red Corn Explains 'Smiling Indian.'"

14. Ibid. The comedic videos may also speak back to some of the current state of Native filmmaking. Evoking Drew Hayden Taylor's constant reminders to non-Native and Native TV producers that Native Peoples are funny and Native humor is very much alive, Red Corn refers to "Native film festivals" where the screenings are "really depressing. Almost all the films are about alcoholism, poverty, all that stuff." Red Corn qtd. in ibid.

15. Red Corn qtd. in ibid.; Red Corn qtd. in Verbosky, "'Smiling Indians.'"

16. The video is available at Sterlin Harjo's YouTube channel, uploaded Feb. 21, 2011, http://www.youtube.com/watch?v=ga98brEf1AU&feature=player_embedded. When NPR learned of the video, its popular program *All Things Considered* featured it and interviewed Red Corn. See Verbosky, "'Smiling Indians'"; Goeman, "Introduction to Indigenous Performances"; and Bannerji, *Returning the Gaze*.

17. The 1491s, "Wolf Pack Auditions," Dec. 1, 2009, http://www.youtube.com/watch?v=BmFxJYFSXyo; The 1491s, "Hunting," Sept. 1, 2011. http://www.youtube.com/watch?v=7oKtyYIIcaQ; Goodfox, "The 1491s."

18. Ibid.

19. The 1491s, "The Avatars," Sept. 17, 2012, http://www.youtube.com/watch?v=upimfe QXRNs; *Avatar*, dir. James Cameron, Twentieth Century Fox, 2009; Charity, "Review"; Randy Szuch, "Avatar/Pocahontas Mashup," 2010, http://vimeo.com/9389738. In an hour-long spoof on Native portrayals in Hollywood on the call-in show *Native America Calling*, guest Sterlin Harjo played a megalomaniac director who said his next project would be like *Avatar*, a multimillion-dollar blockbuster with all computer-generated imagery Indians and all voices provided by Harjo. "Win Johnny Depp!," *Native America Calling*, Jan. 18, 2011.

20. "Na'ai" is the grandfather's corrected pronunciation of Na'vi, possibly a commentary on the common mispronunciations of indigenous insider names by outsiders. The 1491s' "Turok Makto" is a play-off of "Toruk Makto," which refers to the few who can ride the giant leonopteryx creatures in *Avatar*.

21. Both characters carry hybrid names of well-known powwow emcees in Indian Country, including Dale Old Horn (Crow) and Wallace Coffey (Comanche), which provides for insider teasing in referencing well-known Natives in Indian Country, especially on the so-called powwow trail. The 1491s, "A Day in the Life of an Emcee," Mar. 31, 2010, http://www.youtube.com/watch?v=NgQGjVtZ_AQ; The 1491s, "A Day in the Life of an Emcee (Episode 2)," Mar. 30, 2010, http://www.youtube.com/watch?v=sx9jfK4wvXA. For Natives to signify real-life Native emcees suggests featuring Natives as role models. As Sandra Sunrising Osawa, director of *On and Off the Res' w/Charlie Hill*, says on the importance of indigenous filmmaking, "I thought American Indians should be portrayed as contemporary figures with a vibrant culture, full of humor and strength, and with our own inspiring role models. By claiming and defining our own history, I believe we can more easily build a better life in all other areas." "Sandra Sunrising Osawa," Native Networks, Apr. 2005, http://www.nativenetworks.si.edu/eng/rose/osawa_s.htm.

22. The 1491s, "Singing Lessons," May 22, 2011, http://www.youtube.com/watch?v=xJ89 HBfaLs4.

23. The 1491s, "Slapping Medicine Man," May 26, 2011, http://www.youtube.com/watch?v=MVWLHMZ-ceE.

24. Alfred, *Wasáse*, 164.

25. Harper could have dialed 1-800-BAD-MEDZ to contact, from a 1491s skit, the "Bad Medicine Removers," satirical swindlers led by Percy Thomas (Ryan Red Corn) who claim their Indian mojo can scare away the bad spirits in nonfunctioning office equipment, such as copy machines and computers. I would say sweetgrass was the wiser choice. See http://www.youtube.com/watch?v=DQiO4r25Euw, Nov. 22, 2011.

26. Mattie Harper, "Represent—Computer Medicine," Dec. 8, 2011, http://www.youtube.com/watch?v=TSNbTIrGQJk; Eddie Morales, "Represent—Gourd Dance," Mar. 22, 2012, http://www.youtube.com/watch?v=7JZVs_lLC2c; Elizabeth Anne Reese, "Represent—Pueblo throw," July 26, 2012, http://www.youtube.com/watch?v=tUwr4NubkL4.

27. In "Native Love," for example, Native men peel back one handwritten sign at a time on camera to express their abiding love for indigenous women, including—as the signs read—aunties, sisters, mothers, grandmas, wives, baby mamas, shack ups, and snags, and to say "thank you" for all the good they do. The 1491s, "Native Love," Feb. 15, 2010, http://www.youtube.com/watch?v=mNQAk58D9Vw. Several other videos by the

1491s are primarily serious social and political statements demanding justice. See, for example, their collaborations with the Indian Law Resource Center: "To the Indigenous Woman," Jan. 9, 2012, http://www.youtube.com/watch?v=P4UpodrnXX4, and "Ten Little Indians—Violence against Native Women" (PSA), Mar. 21, 2012, http://www.youtube.com/watch?v=TJHQutcSFQU. See also "Geronimo E-KIA" in response to the U.S. military using "Geronimo" as a code name for Osama bin Laden. These video examples significantly add to the vitality and versatility of the 1491s' overall collection of critical-creative work and further illustrate a multifaceted and complex indigenous sensibility. The 1491s, "Geronimo E-KIA," June 1, 2011, http://www.youtube.com/watch?v=y7vKu7X4aNA.

Bibliography

WORKS CITED

Acham, Christine. *Revolution Televised: Prime Time and the Struggle for Black Power.* Minneapolis: University of Minnesota Press, 2005.

"Actors Grateful for Mixed Blessings." *Edmonton Journal*, Nov. 5, 2007.

Adams, Tyrone, and Stephen Smith. *Electronic Tribes: The Virtual Worlds of Geeks, Gamers, Shamans, and Scammers.* Austin: University of Texas Press, 2008.

Adare, Sierra. *"Indian" Stereotypes in TV Science Fiction: First Nations' Voices Speak Out.* Austin: University of Texas Press, 2005.

Alexie, Sherman. "Flight Patterns." In *Ten Little Indians.* New York: Grove Press, 2004.

———. "I Hated Tonto (Still Do)." *Los Angeles Times*, June 28, 1998.

———. *The Lone Ranger and Tonto Fistfight in Heaven.* New York: HarperPerennial, 1994.

———. "No Reservations: Native American Writer Sherman Alexie Breaks the Barriers." Interview with Tamara Wieder. ThePhoenix.com, June 13–19, 2003. http://www.bostonphoenix.com/boston/news_features/qa/documents/02945557.htm (July 8, 2012).

Alfred, Taiaiake. *Wasáse: Indigenous Pathways of Action and Freedom.* Peterborough, Ont.: Broadview Press, 2005.

Amato, Christopher A. "Digging Sacred Ground: Burial Site Disturbances and the Loss of New York's Native American Heritage." *Columbia Journal of Environmental Law* 27.1 (2002): 1–44.

Andrews, Jennifer. "In the Belly of a Laughing God: Reading Humor and Irony in the Poetry of Joy Harjo." *American Indian Quarterly* 24.2 (Spring 2000): 200–218.

Annual Report of the American Historical Association for the Year 1893. Washington, D.C., 1894.

Appadurai, Arjun. "Difference and Disjuncture in the Global Cultural Economy." *Theory, Culture and Society* 7.2 (1990): 295–310.

Attallah, Paul. "Television Discourse and Situation Comedy." *Canadian Review of American Studies* 40.1 (2010): 1–24.

Bannerji, Himani, ed. *Returning the Gaze: Essays on Racism, Feminism, and Politics.* Toronto: Sister Vision, 1993.

Barfield, Ray. *A Word from Our Viewers: Reflections from Early Television Audiences.* Westport, Conn.: Praeger, 2007.

Barnouw, Erik. *A History of Broadcasting in the United States.* Vol. 3, *The Image Empire, from 1953.* New York: Oxford University Press, 1970.

———. *Tube of Plenty: The Evolution of American Television.* New York: Oxford University Press, 1990.

Bataille, Gretchen, and Charles Silet. *The Pretend Indians: Images of Native Americans in the Movies*. Ames: Iowa State University Press, 1980.

Baylor, Tim. "Media Framing of Movement Protest: The Case of American Indian Protest." *Social Science Journal* 33.3 (1996): 241–55.

Bennett, James, and Niki Strange, eds. *Television as Digital Media*. Durham: Duke University Press, 2011.

Berkhofer, Robert. *The White Man's Indian: Images of the American Indian from Columbus to the Present*. New York: Vintage, 1979.

Bernardin, Susan. "Alexie-Vision: Getting the Picture." *World Literature Today* 84.4 (2010): 52–55.

Bhabha, Homi. "Of Mimicry and Man: The Ambivalence of Colonial Discourse." In *The Location of Culture*, 121–31. New York: Routledge, 1994.

———. "The Other Question: Stereotype, Discrimination and the Discourse of Colonialism." In *The Location of Culture*, 94–120. New York: Routledge, 1994.

Bird, S. Elizabeth, ed. *Dressing in Feathers: The Construction of the Indian in American Popular Culture*. Boulder, Colo.: Westview Press, 1998.

———. "Not My Fantasy: The Persistence of Indian Imagery in *Dr. Quinn, Medicine Woman*." In *Dressing in Feathers: The Construction of the Indian in American Popular Culture*, ed. S. Elizabeth Bird, 245–62. Boulder, Colo.: Westview Press, 1998.

Blaeser, Kimberly. "The New 'Frontier' of Native American Literature: Dis-arming History with Tribal Humor." In *Native American Perspectives on Literature and History*, ed. Alan Velie, 37–50. Norman: University of Oklahoma Press, 1994.

Bodroghkozy, Aniko. *Groove Tube: Sixties Television and the Youth Rebellion*. Durham: Duke University Press, 2001.

Bogle, Donald. *Primetime Blues: African Americans on Network Television*. New York: Farrar, Straus and Giroux, 2002.

Boller, Paul. *Presidential Anecdotes*. New York: Oxford University Press, 1996.

Bowers, Q. David. *A Guide Book of Buffalo and Jefferson Nickels*. Florence, Ala.: Whitman, 2007.

Brando, Marlon. "That Unfinished Oscar Speech." *New York Times*, Mar. 30, 1973.

Brooks, Tim, and Earle Marsh. *The Complete Directory to Prime Time Network and Cable TV Shows, 1946–Present*. New York: Ballantine Books, 2007.

Brown, Dee. *Bury My Heart at Wounded Knee: An Indian History of the American West*. New York: Holt, Rinehart and Winston, 1970.

Bruyneel, Kevin. *The Third Space of Sovereignty: The Postcolonial Politics of US–Indigenous Relations*. Minneapolis: University of Minnesota Press, 2007.

Burgess, Jean, and Joshua Green. *YouTube*. Malden, Mass.: Polity, 2009.

Byrd, Jodi A. "'In the City of Blinding Lights': Indigeneity, Cultural Studies and the Errants of Colonial Nostalgia." *Cultural Studies Review* 15.2 (2009): 13–28.

———. *Transit of Empire: Indigenous Critiques of Colonialism*. Minneapolis: University of Minnesota Press, 2011.

Castile, George Pierre. *Taking Charge: Native American Self-Determination and Federal Indian Policy, 1975–1993*. Tucson: University of Arizona Press, 2006.

———. *To Show Heart: Native American Self-Determination and Federal Indian Policy, 1960–1975*. Tucson: University of Arizona Press, 1999.

Cattelino, Jessica R. *High Stakes: Florida Seminole Gaming and Sovereignty*. Durham: Duke University Press, 2008.

Chaat Smith, Paul. *Everything You Know about Indians Is Wrong*. Minneapolis: University of Minnesota Press, 2009.

Chaat Smith, Paul, and Robert Allen Warrior. *Like a Hurricane: The Indian Movement from Alcatraz to Wounded Knee*. New York: New Press, 1997.

Champagne, Duane. *Notes from the Center of Turtle Island*. Lanham, Md.: Alta Mira Press, 2010.

Charity, Tom. "Review: 'Avatar' Delivers on the Hype." Dec. 19, 2009. CNN Entertainment. http://www.cnn.com/2009/SHOWBIZ/Movies/12/17/avatar.review/.

Clarkin, Thomas. *Federal Indian Policy in the Kennedy and Johnson Administrations, 1961–1969*. Albuquerque: University of New Mexico Press, 2001.

Cobb, Amanda J. "This Is What It Means to Say *Smoke Signals*: Native American Cultural Sovereignty." In *Hollywood's Indian: The Portrayal of the Native American in Film*, ed. Peter C. Rollins and John E. O'Connor, 206–28. 2nd ed. Lexington: University Press of Kentucky, 2003.

Cobb, Daniel. *Native Activism in Cold War America: The Struggle for Sovereignty*. Lawrence: University Press of Kansas, 2008.

Coleman, Robin Means. *African American Viewers and the Black Situation Comedy: Situating Racial Humor*. New York: Garland, 2000.

Coleman, Robin Means, and Emily Chivers Yochim. "The Symbolic Annihilation of Race: A Review of the 'Blackness' Literature." *African American Research Perspectives* 12 (2008): 1–10.

Colonnese, Tom. "Indian Summer." *Wicazo sa Review* 16.2 (2001): 13–17.

"Comedian Jonathan Winters, Cherokee, Walks On." *Indian Country Today Media Network*, Apr. 13, 2013. http://indiancountrytodaymedianetwork.com/2013/04/13/comedian-jonathan-winters-cherokee-walks-148793 (accessed July 7, 2013).

Consalvo, Mia, and Charles Ess, eds. *The Handbook of Internet Studies*. Malden, Mass.: Wiley-Blackwell, 2011.

Cook-Lynn, Elizabeth. *Anti-Indianism in Modern America: A Voice from Tatekeya's Earth*. Urbana: University of Illinois Press, 2001.

———. *New Indians, Old Wars*. Urbana: University of Illinois Press, 2007.

Corntassel, Jeff. "Toward Sustainable Self-Determination: Rethinking the Contemporary Indigenous-Rights Discourse." *Alternatives: Global, Local, Political* 33.1 (2008): 105–32.

Corntassel, Jeff, and Richard C. Witmer. *Forced Federalism: Contemporary Challenges to Indigenous Nationhood*. Norman: University of Oklahoma Press, 2008.

Cowger, Thomas. *The National Congress of American Indians: The Founding Years*. Lincoln: University of Nebraska Press, 1999.

Cox, James. "Muting White Noise: The Popular Culture Invasion in Sherman Alexie's Fiction." In *Muting White Noise: Native American and European American Novel Traditions*, 145–202. Norman: University of Oklahoma Press, 2006.

Cramer, Renee Ann. "The Common Sense of Anti-Indian Racism: Reactions to Mashantucket Pequot Success in Gaming and Acknowledgment." *Law and Social Inquiry* 31.2 (Spring 2006): 313–41.

Crawford, Suzanne J. "(Re)Constructing Bodies: Semiotic Sovereignty and the Debate over Kennewick Man." In *Repatriation Reader: Who Owns American Indian Remains?*, ed. Devon A. Mihesuah, 211–36. Lincoln: University of Nebraska Press, 2000.

Crowley, Raymond. "Vanishing American." AP, Washington, D.C., Jan. 21, 1964.

Cummings, Denise K., ed. *Visualities: Perspectives on Contemporary American Indian Film and Art*. East Lansing: Michigan State University Press, 2011.

Dalton, Mary, and Laura Linder, eds. *The Sitcom Reader: America Viewed and Skewed*. Albany: State University of New York Press, 2005.

D'Ambrosio, Antonino. *A Heartbeat and a Guitar: Johnny Cash and the Making of* Bitter Tears. New York: Nation Books, 2010.

Dawes, Birgit, and Robert Nunn. "Interview with Drew Hayden Taylor." In *Drew Hayden Taylor: Essays on His Works*, ed. Robert Nunn, 190–239. Toronto: Guernica Editions, 2008.

Deloria, Philip S. "The Era of Indian Self-Determination: An Overview." In *Indian Self-Rule: First-Hand Accounts of Indian-White Relations from Roosevelt to Reagan*, ed. Kenneth Philp, 191–207. Logan: Utah State University Press, 1986.

———. *Indians in Unexpected Places*. Lawrence: University of Kansas Press, 2003.

———. *Playing Indian*. New Haven, Conn.: Yale University Press, 1998.

Deloria, Vine, Jr. "Comfortable Fictions and the Struggle for Turf: An Essay Review of *The Invented Indian: Cultural Fictions and Government Policies*." *American Indian Quarterly* 16 (Summer 1992): 397–410.

———. *Custer Died for Your Sins: An Indian Manifesto*. Norman: University of Oklahoma Press, 1969. Reprint, 1988.

———. Foreword in *The Pretend Indians: Images of Native Americans in the Movies*, by Gretchen Bataille and Charles Silet, ix–xvi. Ames: Iowa State University Press, 1980.

———. *God Is Red: A Native View of Religion*. Golden, Colo.: Fulcrum, 2003.

———. "The Popularity of Being Indian: A New Trend in Contemporary American Society." In *Spirit and Reason: The Vine Deloria, Jr., Reader*, ed. Barbara Deloria, Kristen Foehner, and Sam Scinta, 230–40. Golden, Colo.: Fulcrum, 1999.

Deloria, Vine, Jr., and Clifford M. Lytle. *The Nations Within: The Past and Future of American Indian Sovereignty*. Austin: University of Texas Press, 1984.

Dixon, Lynda Dee. "A House as Symbol, a House as Family: Mamaw and Her Oklahoma Cherokee Family." In *Our Voices: Essays in Culture, Ethnicity, and Communication*, ed. Alberto Gonzalez, Marsha Houston, and Victoria Chen, 144–48. Los Angeles: Roxbury, 2004.

Doerfler, Jill. "Postindian Survivance: Gerald Vizenor and Kimberly Blaeser." In *Gerald Vizenor: Texts and Contexts*, ed. Deborah L. Madsen and A. Robert Lee, 186–207. Albuquerque: University of New Mexico Press, 2010.

Dorsey, Leroy G. "The Myth of War and Peace in Presidential Discourse: John Kennedy's 'New Frontier' Myth and the Peace Corps." *Southern Journal of Communication* 62.1 (1996): 42–55.

Dougherty, John. "For Some Seeking Rebirth, Sweat Lodge Was End." *New York Times*, Oct. 21, 2009.

Drinnon, Richard. *Facing West: The Metaphysics of Indian-Hating and Empire-Building*. Norman: University of Oklahoma Press, 1997.

Dunlap, Orrin E. *The Outlook for Television*. New York: Harper and Brothers, 1932.

Dyson, Laurel. "Indigenous Peoples on the Internet." In *The Handbook of Internet Studies*, ed. Mia Consalvo and Charles Ess, 251–69. Malden, Mass.: Wiley-Blackwell, 2011.

Dyson, Laurel Evelyn, Max A. N. Hendriks, and Stephen Grant. *Information Technology and Indigenous People*. Hershey, Pa.: Information Science Publishing, 2007.

Echohawk, John. "The Kennedy Report." *NIEA News* 41.2 (Winter 2009/2010): 16–17.

Fagan, Kristina. "The Spiritual Tourist in the Plays of Drew Hayden Taylor." In *Drew Hayden Taylor: Essays on His Works*, ed. Robert Nunn, 124–48. Toronto: Guernica Editions, 2008.

Fine-Dare, Kathleen. *Grave Injustice: The American Indian Repatriation Movement and NAGPRA*. Lincoln: University of Nebraska Press, 2002.

Fleeson, Doris. "A Call for Improved Television." *Washington Star*, May 11, 1961, A15.

Forbes, Jack D. *Native Americans and Nixon: Presidential Politics and Minority Self-Determination, 1969–1972*. Los Angeles: American Indian Studies Center, UCLA, 1981.

Francis, Daniel. *The Imaginary Indian: The Image of the Indian in Canadian Culture*. Vancouver: Arsenal Pulp, 1992.

Friar, Ralph E., and Natasha A. Friar. *The Only Good Indian: The Hollywood Gospel*. New York: Drama Book Specialists, 1972.

Fusco, Coco. "The Other History of Intercultural Performance." *Drama Review* 38.1 (Spring 1994): 143–67.

George, Diana, and Susan Sanders. "Reconstructing Tonto: Cultural Formations and American Indians in 1990's Television Fiction." *Cultural Studies* 9.3 (Oct. 1995): 427–52.

Ginsburg, Faye. "Rethinking the Digital Age." In *Global Indigenous Media: Cultures, Poetics, and Politics*, 287–305. Durham: Duke University Press, 2008.

———. "Screen Memories: Resignifying the Traditional in Indigenous Media." In *Media Worlds: Anthropology on New Terrain*, ed. Faye D. Ginsburg, Lila Abu-Lughod, and Brian Larkin, 39–57. Berkeley: University of California Press, 2002.

Goeman, Mishuana. "Introduction to Indigenous Performances: Upsetting the Terrains of Settler Colonialism." *American Indian Culture and Research Journal* 35.4 (2011): 1–18.

Goodfox, Julia. "The 1491s Are Crazier Than That Uncle Your Parents Won't Talk About (Review)." May 31, 2011, http://juliagoodfox.com/1491s/.

Gray, Herman. *Cultural Moves: African Americans and the Politics of Representation*. Berkeley: University of California Press, 2005.

———. *Watching Race: Television and the Struggle for "Blackness."* Minneapolis: University of Minnesota Press, 1995.

Gray, Jonathan. *Show Sold Separately: Promos, Spoilers, and Other Media Paratexts*. New York: New York University Press, 2010.

———. *Television Entertainment*. New York: Routledge, 2008.

———. *Watching with* The Simpsons: *Television, Parody, and Intertextuality*. New York: Routledge, 2006.

Green, Rayna. "The Tribe Called Wannabee: Playing Indian in America and Europe." *Folklore* 99.1 (1988): 30–55.

Gregory, S. Jay. "'White Man's Book No Good': D. W. Griffith and the American Indian." *Cinema Journal* 39.4 (2000): 3–26.

Gruber, Eva. *Humor in Contemporary Native North American Literature: Reimagining Nativeness.* New York: Camden House, 2008.

———. "Humorous Restorifications: Rewriting History with Healing Laughter." In *Aboriginal Canada Revisited*, ed. Kirstin Knopf, 220–45. Ottawa: University of Ottawa Press, 2008.

Hall, Stuart. "Encoding/Decoding." In *Culture, Media, Language: Working Papers in Cultural Studies, 1972–1979*, 128–38. London: Hutchinson, 1980.

Hamamoto, Darrell. *Nervous Laughter: TV Situation Comedy and Liberal Democratic Ideology.* New York: Praeger, 1989.

Harjo, Joy. "A Postcolonial Tale." In *The Woman Who Fell from the Sky: Poems.* New York: W. W. Norton, 1994.

Harkins, Anthony. *Hillbilly: A Cultural History of an American Icon.* New York: Oxford University Press, 2003.

Harper, Kenn. *Give Me My Father's Body: The Life of Minik, the New York Eskimo.* London: Profile Books, 2001.

Harris, Steven. "Television Test Patterns." *Christian Science Monitor* 92.55 (Feb. 2000): 23.

Hauptman, Laurence M. *Formulating American Indian Policy in New York State, 1970–1986.* Albany: State University of New York Press, 1988.

Hearne, Joanna. *Native Recognition: Indigenous Cinema and the Western.* Albany: State University of New York Press, 2013.

Hersey, Eleanor. "Native Americans in *The X-Files*: Word-Healers and Code-Talkers." *Journal of Popular Film and Television* 26.3 (Fall 1998): 108–19.

Hilton-Morrow, Wendy, and David McMahan. "*The Flintstones* to *Futurama*: Networks and Prime Time Animation." In *Prime Time Animation: Television Animation and American Culture*, ed. Carol Stabile, 74–88. New York: Routledge, 2003.Hirch, Mirjam. "Subversive Humor: Canadian Native Playwrights' Winning Weapon of Resistance." In *Me Funny*, ed. Drew Hayden Taylor, 99–122. Vancouver: Douglas and McIntyre, 2005.

Holte, James Craig. "Unmelting Images: Film, Television, and Ethnic Stereotyping." *MELUS* 11.3 (Autumn 1984): 101–8.

Howe, LeAnne. "The Story of America: A Tribalography." In *Clearing a Path: Theorizing the Past in Native American Studies*, ed. Nancy Shoemaker, 29–48. New York: Routledge, 2002.

———. "Tribalography: The Power of Native Stories." *Journal of Dramatic Theory and Criticism* 1 (1999): 117–26.

Huhndorf, Shari. *Going Native: Indians in the American Cultural Imagination.* Ithaca: Cornell University Press, 2001.

Ingles, Paul. "Man on the Couch." *Albuquerque Tribune*, Sept. 13, 2002, B12.

Jaimes, M. Annette. "The Hollow Icon: An American Indian Analysis of the Kennedy Myth and Federal Indian Policy." *Wicazo Sa Review* 6.1 (1990): 34–44.

Jenkins, Henry. *Convergence Culture: Where Old and New Media Collide.* New York: New York University Press, 2009.

———. "What Happened Before YouTube." In *YouTube*, by Jean Burgess and Joshua Green, 109–25. Malden, Mass.: Polity, 2009.

Johnson, Lyndon B. "The Great Society." University of Michigan, May 22, 1964. http://www.lbjlib.utexas.edu/johnson/archives.hom/speeches.hom/640522.asp.

———. "Remarks to Members of the National Congress of American Indians." Jan. 20, 1964. http://www.presidency.ucsb.edu/ws/index.php?pid=26000.

———. "Special Message to the Congress on the Problems of the American Indian: 'The Forgotten American.'" Mar. 6, 1968. http://www.presidency.ucsb.edu/ws/index.php?pid=28709.

Johnson, Troy. *The American Indian Occupation of Alcatraz Island: Red Power and Self-Determination*. Lincoln: University of Nebraska Press, 1996.

Johnson, Victoria E. *Heartland TV: Prime Time Television and the Struggle for U.S. Identity*. New York: New York University Press, 2008.

Jojola, Theodore S. "Absurd Reality II: Hollywood Goes to the Indians." In *Hollywood's Indian: The Portrayal of the Native American in Film*, ed. Peter C. Rollins and John E. O'Connor, 12–26. 2nd ed. Lexington: University Press of Kentucky, 2003.

———. "*Moo Mesa*: Some Thoughts on Stereotypes and Image Appropriation." In *Dressing in Feathers: The Construction of the Indian in American Popular Culture*, ed. Elizabeth S. Bird, 263–79. Boulder, Colo.: Westview Press, 1998.

Josephy, Alvin M., Jr. *The Nez Perce Indians and the Opening of the Northwest*. New Haven: Yale University Press, 1965.

Judge, James. *The Anasazi*. Albuquerque: Southwest Natural Cultural Heritage Association, 1991.

Kay, M. S. "The Television Test Pattern." *Radio and Television News* 41.1 (Jan. 1949): 38–39, 135–36.

Kelly, Richard Michael. *The Andy Griffith Show*. Winston-Salem, N.C.: John F. Blair, 1981.

Kempley, Rita. "No More Playing Dead for American Indian Filmmaker Sherman Alexie." *Washington Post*, July 3, 1998, D1.

Kennedy, John F. "Inaugural Address." Jan. 20, 1961. http://www.presidency.ucsb.edu/ws/?pid=8032.

———. Introduction to *American Heritage Book of Indians*, ed. Alvin Josephy Jr., 7. New York: American Heritage, 1961.

———. "The New Frontier." Democratic National Convention Nomination Acceptance Address, Los Angeles, July 15, 1960. http://www.jfklibrary.org/Asset-Viewer/AS08q50YzoSFUZg9uOi4iw.aspx.

Kilpatrick, Jacquelyn. *Celluloid Indians: Native Americans and Film*. Lincoln: University of Nebraska Press, 1999.

King of the Hill Archives. The Wittliff Collections. Texas State University at San Marcos, 1995–2006.

Klooster, John W. *Icons of Invention: The Makers of the Modern World from Gutenberg to Gates*. Santa Barbara, Calif.: Greenwood, 2009.

Kompare, Derek. *Rerun Nation: How Repeats Invented American Television*. New York: Routledge, 2004.

Kvasnicka, Robert, ed. *The Commissioners of Indian Affairs, 1824–1977*. Lincoln: University of Nebraska Press, 1979.

Lacroix, Celeste C. "High Stakes Stereotypes: The Emergence of the 'Casino Indian' Trope in Television Depictions of Contemporary Native Americans." *Howard Journal of Communications* 22.1 (2011): 1–23.

Landzelius, Kyra. "Introduction: Native on the Net." In *Native on the Net: Indigenous and Diasporic Peoples in the Virtual Age*, ed. Kyra Landzelius, 1–42. London: Routledge, 2006.

Lewis, Randolph. *Alanis Obomsawin: The Vision of a Native Filmmaker*. Lincoln: University of Nebraska Press, 2006.

Lincoln, Kenneth. *Indi'n Humor: Bicultural Play in Native America*. New York: Oxford University Press, 1993.

Loewen, James. *Lies across America: What Our Historic Sites Get Wrong*. New York: New Press, 1999.

Lotz, Amanda. *The Television Will Be Revolutionized*. New York: New York University Press, 2007.

Lyons, Scott Richard. *X-Marks: Native Signatures of Assent*. Minneapolis: University of Minnesota Press, 2010.

MacDonald, J. Fred. *Who Shot the Sheriff? The Rise and Fall of the Television Western*. New York: Praeger, 1987.

Magoc, Chris J. "The Machine in the Wasteland: Progress, Pollution, and the Pastoral in Rural-Based Television, 1954–1971." *Journal of Popular Film and Television* 19.1 (1991): 25–34.

Marc, David. *Comic Visions: Television Comedy and American Culture*. 2nd ed. Malden, Mass.: Blackwell, 1997.

——. *Demographic Vistas: Television in American Culture*. Philadelphia: University of Pennsylvania Press, 1996.

McLuhan, Marshall. *Understanding Media: Extensions of Man*. Cambridge, Mass.: MIT Press, 1994.

Meek, Barbara. "And the Injun Goes 'How!': Representations of American Indian English in White Public Space." *Language in Society* 35.1 (2006): 93–128.

Melamed, Jodi. *Represent and Destroy: Rationalizing Violence in the New Racial Capitalism*. Minneapolis: University of Minnesota Press, 2011.

Mellencamp, Patricia. "SitCom, Feminism, and Freud: Discourses of Gracie and Lucy." In *Feminist Television Criticism: A Reader*, ed. Charlotte Brunsdon, Julie D'Acci, and Lynn Spigel, 60–73. New York: Oxford University Press, 1997.

Meyer, Carter, and Dianne Royer. *Selling the Indian: Commercializing and Appropriating American Indian Cultures*. Tucson: University of Arizona Press, 2001.

Mihesuah, Devon A. "Should American Indian History Remain a Field of Study?" In *Indigenizing the Academy: Transforming Scholarship and Empowering Communities*, ed. Devon A. Mihesuah, 143–59. Lincoln: University of Nebraska Press, 2004.

——, ed. *Repatriation Reader: Who Owns American Indian Remains?* Lincoln: University of Nebraska Press, 2000.

Miller, Mark Edwin. "From Playing Indian to Playing Slots: Gaming, Tribal Recognition, and the Tiguas of El Paso, Texas." In *Forgotten Tribes: Unrecognized Indians and the Federal Acknowledgment Process*, 209–55. Norman: University of Oklahoma Press, 2006.

Miller, Mary Jane. *Outside Looking In: Viewing First Nations Peoples in Canadian Dramatic Television Series*. Montreal: McGill-Queen's University Press, 2008.

Minow, Newton. "Television and the Public Interest." Speech before the National Association of Broadcasters, Washington, D.C., May 9, 1961.

Minow, Newton, and Fred Cate. "Revisiting the Vast Wasteland." *Federal Communications Law Journal* 55.3 (Apr. 2003): 414.

Minow, Newton, and Craig Lamay. *Abandoned in the Wasteland: Children, Television, and the First Amendment*. New York: Hill and Wang, 1995.

Mittell, Jason. "The Cultural Power of an Anti-television Metaphor." *Television and New Media* 1.2 (2000): 215–38.

———. *Television and American Culture*. New York: Oxford University Press, 2009.

Moffatt, John, and Sandy Tait. "'I Just See Myself as an Old-Fashioned Storyteller': A Conversation with Drew Hayden Taylor." *Canadian Literature* 183 (Winter 2004): 72–86.

Morreale, Joanne, ed. *Critiquing the Sitcom: A Reader*. Syracuse: Syracuse University Press, 2003.

Nagel, Joane. "American Indian Ethnic Renewal: Politics and the Resurgence of Identity." *American Sociological Review* 60.6 (1995): 947–65.

———. *American Indian Ethnic Renewal: Red Power and the Resurgence of Identity and Culture*. New York: Oxford University Press, 1997.

Nazareth, Peter. "Elvis as Anthology." In *In Search of Elvis: Music, Race, Art, Religion*, ed. Vernon Chadwick, 37–72. Boulder, Colo.: Westview, 1997.

Neumann, Mark. *On the Rim: Looking for the Grand Canyon*. Minneapolis: University of Minnesota Press, 2001.

Newcomb, Horace. "From Old Frontier to New Frontier." In *The Revolution Wasn't Televised: Sixties Television and Social Conflict*, ed. Lynn Spigel and Michael Curtin, 287–304. New York: Routledge, 1997.

Nixon, Richard. "Special Message to the Congress on Indian Affairs." July 8, 1970. http://www.presidency.ucsb.edu/ws/?pid=2573.

Nunn, Robert, ed. *Drew Hayden Taylor: Essays on His Works*. Toronto: Guernica Editions, 2008.

O'Connor, John. *The Hollywood Indian: Stereotypes of Native Americans in Films*. Trenton: New Jersey State Museum, 1980.

On and Off the Res' w/Charlie Hill. Dir. Sandra Sunrising Osawa. Upstream Productions. 2000.

Ostashewski, Marcia. "A Full-Fledged and Finely Functioning Fiddle: Humour and 'The Uke-Cree Fiddler.'" *Canadian Folk Music* 43.1 (2009): 1–5.

Pack, Sam. "'I Hate White People!'—Subverting the Televisual Gaze." *Visual Anthropology* 21.2 (2008): 136–50.

Palmer-Mehta, Valeria. "The Wisdom of Folly: Disrupting Masculinity in *King of the Hill*." *Text and Performance Quarterly* 26.2 (2006): 181–98.

Pearson, Roberta. "Custer's Still the Hero: Textual Stability and Transformation." *Journal of Film and Video* 47.1–3 (Spring–Fall 1995): 82–97.

———. "White Network/Red Power: ABC's *Custer* Series." In *The Revolution Wasn't Televised: Sixties Television and Social Conflict*, ed. Lynn Spigel and Michael Curtin, 327–48. New York: Routledge, 2001.

Pewewardy, Cornel. "Renaming Ourselves on Our Own Terms: Race, Tribal Nations, and Representation in Education." *Indigenous Nations Studies Journal* 1.1 (Spring 2000): 11–28.

Pew Research Center. "Millennials: A Portrait of Generation Next." 2010, PewSocialTrends.org, http://www.pewsocialtrends.org/files/2010/10/millennials-confident-connected-open-to-change.pdf.

Philp, Kenneth. *Indian Self-Rule: First-Hand Accounts of Indian-White Relations from Roosevelt to Reagan*. Logan: Utah State University Press, 1986.

Porter, Robert Odawi. "The Decolonization of Indigenous Governance." In *For Indigenous Eyes Only: A Decolonization Handbook*, ed. Waziyatawin Angela Wilson and Michael Yellow Bird, 87–108. Santa Fe: School of American Research, 2005.

Pratt, Mary Louise. *Imperial Eyes: Studies in Travel Writing and Transculturation*. New York: Routledge, 1992.

Prendergast, Neil. "Tracking the Kaibab Deer into Western History." *Western Historical Quarterly* 39.4 (Winter 2008): 413–38.

Prins, Harold E. L. "Visual Media and the Primitivist Perplex: Colonial Fantasies, Indigenous Imagination, and Advocacy in North America." In *Media Worlds: Anthropology on New Terrain*, ed. Faye D. Ginsburg, Lila Abu-Lughod, and Brian Larkin, 58–74. Berkeley: University of California Press, 2002.

Rader, Dean. *Engaged Resistance: American Indian Art, Literature, and Film from Alcatraz to the NMAI*. Austin: University of Texas Press, 2011.

Raheja, Michelle. *Reservation Reelism: Redfacing, Visual Sovereignty, and Representations of Native Americans in Film*. Lincoln: University of Nebraska Press, 2011.

Rath, Richard Cullen. *How Early America Sounded*. Ithaca: Cornell University Press, 2005.

Rich, Frank. "Paar to Leno, J.F.K. to J.F.K." *New York Times*, Feb. 8, 2004.

Riggs, Christopher. "American Indians, Economic Development, and Self-Determination in the 1960s." *Pacific Historical Review* 69 (2000): 431–63.

Rollins, Peter C., and John E. O'Connor, eds. *Hollywood's Indian: The Portrayal of the Native American in Film*. 2nd ed. Lexington: University Press of Kentucky, 2003.

Roome, Dorothy. "Humor as 'Cultural Reconciliation' in South African Situation Comedy: *Suburban Bliss* and Multicultural Female Viewers." *Journal of Film and Video* 51.3/4 (Fall/Winter 1999/2000): 61–87.

Rosenthal, Nicholas. *Reimagining Indian Country: Native American Migration and Identity in Twentieth-Century Los Angeles*. Chapel Hill: University of North Carolina Press, 2012.

Roth, Lorna. *Something New in the Air: The Story of First Peoples Television Broadcasting in Canada*. Montreal: McGill-Queen's University Press, 2005.

"Ryan Red Corn Explains 'Smiling Indians.'" *Indian Country Today Media Network*, Mar. 7, 2011, http://indiancountrytodaymedianetwork.com/2011/03/07/ryan-red-corn-explains-smiling-indians-21497.

Schulman, Sandra. "The Red Corn Band: From Small Screen to Concert Stage." *News from Indian Country*, Mar. 21, 2005, 27.

———. "The Red Corn Band: Red Corn Sessions." *News from Indian Country*, July 26, 2004, 26.

Seabrook, John. "Streaming Dreams: YouTube Turns Pro." *New Yorker*, Jan. 16, 2012.

Shively, JoEllen. "Cowboys and Indians: Perceptions of Western Films among American Indians and Anglos." *American Sociological Review* 57.6 (Dec. 1992): 725–34.

Silberman, Robert. "Gerald Vizenor and *Harold of Orange*: From Word Cinemas to Real Cinema." *American Indian Quarterly* 9.1 (Winter 1985): 5–21.

Singer, Beverly R. *Wiping the War Paint Off the Lens: Native American Film and Video*. Minneapolis: University of Minnesota Press, 2001.

Slotkin, Richard. *Gunfighter Nation: The Myth of the Frontier in Twentieth-Century America*. Norman: University of Oklahoma Press, 1998.

Smith, Henry Nash. *Virgin Land: The American West as Symbol and Myth*. Cambridge, Mass.: Harvard University Press, 2007.

Spigel, Lynn. *Welcome to the Dreamhouse: Popular Media and Postwar Suburbs*. Durham: Duke University Press, 2001.

Spigel, Lynn, and Michael Curtin, eds. *The Revolution Wasn't Televised: Sixties Television and Social Conflict*. New York: Routledge, 2001.

Spigel, Lynn, and Jan Olsson, eds. *Television after TV: Essays on a Medium in Transition*. Durham: Duke University Press, 2011.

Spilde, Katherine A. "Rich Indian Racism—Direct Attack on Tribal Sovereignty." *Hocak Worak*, Oct. 1999, 1–2.

Staiger, Janet. *Blockbuster TV: Must-See Sitcoms in the Network Era*. New York: New York University Press, 2000.

Stedman, Raymond. *Shadows of the Indian: Stereotypes in American Culture*. Norman: University of Oklahoma Press, 1982.

Steiner, Stan. *The New Indians*. New York: Harper and Row, 1968.

Tahmahkera, Dustin. "Custer's Last Sitcom: Decolonized Viewing of the Sitcom's 'Indian.'" *American Indian Quarterly* 32.3 (2008): 324–51.

Taylor, Drew Hayden. *Funny, You Don't Look Like One: Observations from a Blue-Eyed Ojibway*. Rev. ed. Penticton, B.C.: Theytus Books, 1998.

———. *Furious Observations of a Blue-Eyed Ojibway: Funny, You Don't Look Like One Two Three*. Penticton, B.C.: Theytus Books, 2002.

———. *Further Adventures of a Blue-Eyed Ojibway: Funny, You Don't Look Like One Two*. Penticton, B.C.: Theytus Books, 1999.

———. *News: Postcards from the Four Directions*. Vancouver: Talonbooks, 2010.

———. "Seeing Red: The Stoic Whiteman and Non-Native Humour." In *Walking a Tightrope: Aboriginal People and Their Representations*, ed. Ute Lischke and David T. McNab, 21–28. Waterloo, Ont.: Wilfrid Laurier University Press, 2005.

———. "Storytelling to Stage: The Growth of Native Theatre in Canada." *Drama Review* 41.3 (Autumn 1997): 140–52.

———. "What . . . You Think You're Funny?!" Canadian Broadcasting Corporation, June 21, 2012, http://www.cbc.ca/books/canadawrites/2012/06/drew-hayden-taylor-what-you-think-youre-funny.html.

———, ed. *Me Funny*. Vancouver: Douglas and McIntyre, 2005.

Tedlow, Richard S. "Intellect on Television: The Quiz Show Scandals of the 1950s." *American Quarterly* 28.4 (1976): 483–95.

Thompson, Ethan. "'I Am Not Down with That': *King of the Hill* and Sitcom Satire." *Journal of Film and Video* 61.2 (Summer 2009): 38–51.

Trope, Jack F., and Walter R. Echo-Hawk. "The Native American Graves Protection and Repatriation Act: Background and Legislative History." *Repatriation Reader: Who Owns American Indian Remains?*, ed. Devon A. Mihesuah, 123–68. Lincoln: University of Nebraska Press, 2000.

Two Shoes, Minnie. "A Conversation with Charlie Hill." *News from Indian Country*, Feb. 7, 2005.

Vaughn, Don Rodney. "Why *The Andy Griffith Show* Is Important to Popular Cultural Studies." *Journal of Popular Culture* 38.2 (Nov. 2004): 397–423.

Verbosky, Abby. "'Smiling Indians' Depicts a Lighter Side of Native Americans." NPR, Mar. 9, 2011, http://www.npr.org/blogs/pictureshow/2011/03/09/134394893/smiling-indians-depicts-a-lighter-side-of-native-americans.

Vizenor, Gerald. *Fugitive Poses: Native American Indian Scenes of Absence and Presence.* Lincoln: University of Nebraska Press, 2000.

——. *Manifest Manners: Narratives on Postindian Survivance.* Lincoln: University of Nebraska Press, 1999.

——. "Socioacupuncture: Mythic Reversals and the Striptease in Four Scenes." *The American Indian and the Problem of History* (1987): 180–91.

Vizenor, Gerald, and A. Robert Lee. *Postindian Conversations.* Lincoln: University of Nebraska Press, 2003.

Wall, Sharon. "Totem Poles, Teepees, and Token Traditions: 'Playing Indian' at Ontario Summer Camps, 1920–1955." *Canadian Historical Review* 86.3 (2005): 513–44.

Warga, Wayne. "Marlon Brando: Still Looking, Still Asking." *Los Angeles Times*, Aug. 10, 1975.

Warrior, Robert Allen. *Tribal Secrets: Recovering American Indian Intellectual Traditions.* Minneapolis: University of Minnesota Press, 1995.

Watson, Mary Ann. *The Expanding Vista: American Television in the Kennedy Years.* Durham: Duke University Press, 1994.

White, Robert H. "Indians' New Harvest." *New York Times*, Nov. 22, 1990, http://www.nytimes.com/1990/11/22/opinion/indians-newharvest.html?pagewanted=all&src=pm.

Wilkins, David, and Heidi Kiiwetinepinesiik Stark. *American Indian Politics and the American Political System.* 3rd ed. Lanham, Md.: Rowman and Littlefield, 2002.

Williams, Robert A. *Like a Loaded Weapon: The Rehnquist Court, Indian Rights, and the Legal History of Racism in America.* Minneapolis: University of Minnesota Press, 2005.

Wilson, Pamela. "Confronting 'The Indian Problem': Media Discourses of Race, Ethnicity, Nation, and Empire in 1950s America." In *Living Color: Race and Televisions in the United States*, ed. Sasha Torres, 35–61. Durham: Duke University Press, 1998.

Wilson, Pamela, and Michelle Stewart, eds. *Global Indigenous Media: Cultures, Poetics, and Politics.* Durham: Duke University Press, 2008.

Wilson, Waziyatawin Angela, and Michael Yellow Bird, eds. *For Indigenous Eyes Only: A Decolonization Handbook.* Santa Fe: School of American Research, 2005.

Wolfe, Patrick. "Settler Colonialism and the Elimination of the Native." *Journal of Genocide Research* 8.4 (2006): 387–409.

Yellow Bird, Michael. "Cowboys and Indians: Toys of Genocide, Icons of American Colonialism." *Wicazo sa Review* 19.2 (Fall 2004): 33–48.

Young, Dale. "Bridging the Gap: Drew Hayden Taylor, Native Canadian Playwright in His Times." Ph.D.dissertation. Bowling Green State University, 2005.

SITCOM EPISODES CITED

"Archie Learns His Lesson," *All in the Family*, CBS, Mar. 10, 1973.

"Andy and Opie's Pal," *The Andy Griffith Show*, CBS, Jan. 13, 1964.

"Andy Discovers America," *The Andy Griffith Show*, CBS, Mar. 4, 1963." The Arrest of the Fun Girls," *The Andy Griffith Show*, CBS, Apr. 5, 1965.

"Aunt Bee's Medicine Man," *The Andy Griffith Show*, CBS, Mar. 11, 1963.

"Bargain Day," *The Andy Griffith Show*, CBS, Mar. 23, 1964.

"Barney and the Choir," *The Andy Griffith Show*, CBS, Feb. 19, 1962.

"Barney's Replacement," *The Andy Griffith Show*, CBS, Oct. 9, 1961.

"The Battle of Mayberry," *The Andy Griffith Show*, CBS, Apr. 4, 1966.

"The Beauty Contest," *The Andy Griffith Show*, CBS, Jan. 23, 1961.

"The Bookie Barber," *The Andy Griffith Show*, CBS, Apr. 16, 1962.

"The Clubmen," *The Andy Griffith Show*, CBS, Nov. 27, 1961.

"Crime-Free Mayberry," *The Andy Griffith Show*, CBS, Nov. 20, 1961.

"The Manicurist," *The Andy Griffith Show*, CBS, Jan. 22, 1962.

"Opie's Hobo Friend," *The Andy Griffith Show*, CBS, Nov. 13, 1961.

"Opie's Rival," *The Andy Griffith Show*, CBS, Dec. 3, 1962.

"The Pageant," *The Andy Griffith Show*, CBS, Nov. 30, 1964.

"The Pickle Story," *The Andy Griffith Show*, CBS, Dec. 18, 1961.

"Rafe Hollister Sings," *The Andy Griffith Show*, CBS, Feb. 11, 1963.

"The Rivals," *The Andy Griffith Show*, CBS, Apr. 8, 1963.

"The Song Festers," *The Andy Griffith Show*, CBS, Feb. 24, 1964.

"Bones," *Barney Miller*, ABC, Apr. 30, 1982.

"The Indian," *Barney Miller*, ABC, Jan. 4, 1979.

"The Clampetts in New York," *The Beverly Hillbillies*, CBS, Nov. 5, 1969.

"The Clampetts in Washington," *The Beverly Hillbillies*, CBS, Sept. 22, 1970.

"The Family Tree," *The Beverly Hillbillies*, CBS, Mar. 13, 1963.

"The Grunion Invasion," *The Beverly Hillbillies*, CBS, Jan. 5, 1971.

"Honesty Is the Best Policy," *The Beverly Hillbillies*, CBS, Mar. 18, 1970.

"The Indians Are Coming," *The Beverly Hillbillies*, CBS, Feb. 1, 1967.

"Jed Buys the Capitol," *The Beverly Hillbillies*, CBS, Sept. 29, 1970.

"Jed Cuts the Family Tree," *The Beverly Hillbillies*, CBS, Mar. 20, 1963.

"Turkey Day," *The Beverly Hillbillies*, CBS, Nov. 27, 1963.

"Big Little Man," *The Brady Bunch*, ABC, Jan. 7, 1972.

"The Brady Braves," *The Brady Bunch*, ABC, Oct. 1, 1971.

"A Clubhouse Is Not a Home," *The Brady Bunch*, ABC, Oct. 31, 1969.

"Ghost Town, U.S.A.," *The Brady Bunch*, ABC, Sept. 17, 1971.

"Grand Canyon or Bust," *The Brady Bunch*, ABC, Sept. 24, 1971.

"The Slumber Caper," *The Brady Bunch*, ABC, Oct. 9, 1970.

"Un-Underground Movie," *The Brady Bunch*, ABC, Oct. 16, 1970.

"I'll Be Seeing You, Part 1," *Cheers*, NBC, May 3, 1984.

"One for the Road," *Cheers*, NBC, May 20, 1993.

"Junior Pathfinders Ride Again," *Dennis the Menace*, CBS, Apr. 8, 1962.

"Brought to You in Dharmavision," *Dharma and Greg*, ABC, Nov. 18, 1998.

"Indian Summer," *Dharma and Greg*, ABC, Nov. 5, 1997.

"Intensive Caring," *Dharma and Greg*, ABC, Sept. 25, 2001.

"Mother and Daughter Reunion," *Dharma and Greg*, ABC, Oct. 10, 2000.

"Burial Ground," *Diff'rent Strokes*, NBC, Jan. 7, 1982.

"The Music Man," *Diff'rent Strokes*, NBC, May 6, 1982.

"The Bird," *Everybody Loves Raymond*, CBS, Nov. 24, 2003.

"Dancing with Debra," *Everybody Loves Raymond*, CBS, May 10, 1999.

"The Son Also Draws," *Family Guy*, Fox, May 9, 1999.

"Rafter Six Ranch," *Fish Out of Water*, APTN, Jan. 25, 2008.

"Droop-Along Flintstone," *The Flintstones*, ABC, Sept. 22, 1961.

"I, Done (Part II)," *The Fresh Prince of Bel-Air*, NBC, May 20, 1996.

"The One with Rachel's Inadvertent Kiss," *Friends*, NBC, Mar. 18, 1999.

"From Karate with Love," *F Troop*, ABC, Jan. 5, 1967.

"The Return of Bald Eagle," *F Troop*, ABC, Oct. 12, 1965.

"Scourge of the West," *F Troop*, ABC, Sept. 14, 1965.

"Yellow Bird," *F Troop*, ABC, Oct. 20, 1966.

"Where the Buggalo Roam," *Futurama*, Fox, Mar. 3, 2002.

"Washington 4, Indians 3," *Get Smart*, NBC, Oct. 23, 1965.

"The Rains Came," *Green Acres*, CBS, May 18, 1966.

"The First Thanksgiving," *Happy Days*, ABC, Nov. 21, 1978.

"Fonzie Loves Pinky (1)," *Happy Days*, ABC, Sept. 21, 1976.

"Fonzie's New Friend," *Happy Days*, ABC, Nov. 25, 1975.

"The Other Richie Cunningham," *Happy Days*, ABC, Oct. 7, 1975.

"Three on a Porch," *Happy Days*, ABC, Nov. 18, 1975.

"Westward Ho!: Part 1," *Happy Days*, ABC, Sept. 12, 1978.

"Lucy and the Indian Chief," *Here's Lucy*, CBS, Oct. 6, 1969.

"Workin' Man Blues," *Home Improvement*, ABC, Dec. 10, 1996.

"The Adagio," *I Love Lucy*, CBS, Dec. 6, 1951.

"The Indian Show," *I Love Lucy*, CBS, Apr. 3, 1953.

"The Arrowhead," *King of the Hill*, Fox, Oct. 19, 1997.

"Born Again on the Fourth of July," *King of the Hill*, Fox, Apr. 19, 2009.

"Dog Dale Afternoon," *King of the Hill*, Fox, Apr. 13, 1999.

"Good Hill Hunting," *King of the Hill*, Fox, Dec. 1, 1998.

"Hair Today, Gone Tomorrow," *King of the Hill*, Fox, May 13, 2007.

"Hank's Cowboy Movie," *King of the Hill*, Fox, Apr. 6, 1999.

"Happy Hank's Giving," *King of the Hill*, Fox, Nov. 21, 1999.

"Luanne's Saga," *King of the Hill*, Fox, Feb. 16, 1997.

"Manger Baby Einstein," *King of the Hill*, Fox, May 10, 2009.

"Nancy Boys," *King of the Hill*, Fox, Apr. 30, 2000.

"The Order of the Straight Arrow," *King of the Hill*, Fox, Feb. 2, 1997.

"Peggy's Headache," *King of the Hill*, Fox, Oct. 6, 1998.

"Redcorn Gambles with His Future," *King of the Hill*, Fox, Apr. 10, 2005.

"Returning Japanese, Part I," *King of the Hill*, Fox, May 12, 2002.

"Rich Hank, Poor Hank," *King of the Hill*, Fox, Jan. 4, 2004.

"Sleight of Hank," *King of the Hill*, Fox, Feb. 16, 1999.

"Spin the Choice," *King of the Hill*, Fox, Nov. 19, 2000.

"To Kill a Ladybird," *King of the Hill*, Fox, Dec. 12, 1999.

"The Untitled Blake McCormick Project," *King of the Hill*, Fox, Feb. 17, 2008.

"Vision Quest," *King of the Hill*, Fox, Feb. 9, 2003.

"The Wedding of Bobby Hill," *King of the Hill*, Fox, Feb. 9, 1999.

"The Witches of East Arlen," *King of the Hill*, Fox, May 18, 2003.

"Indians," *Lou Grant*, CBS, Jan. 14, 1980.

"Casino," *Malcolm in the Middle*, Fox, Nov. 19, 2000.

"Cliques," *Malcolm in the Middle*, Fox, May 5, 2002.

"Baby on the Way," *Mixed Blessings*, APTN, Nov. 25, 2008.

"Choices," *Mixed Blessings*, APTN, Nov. 27, 2007.

"Dances with Wolfy," *Mixed Blessings*, APTN, Feb. 2, 2010.

"Dot Not Feather," *Mixed Blessings*, APTN, Dec. 8, 2009.

"Pow Wow," *Mixed Blessings*, APTN, Dec. 18, 2007.

"Secret Love," *Mixed Blessings*, APTN, Nov. 13, 2007.

"Traditional Wedding," *Mixed Blessings*, APTN, Dec. 4, 2007.

"Road Trip," *Moesha*, UPN, Nov. 26, 1996.

"Birth of a Station," *Moose TV*, Showcase, Aug. 23, 2007.

"Technical Difficulties," *Moose TV*, Showcase, July 26, 2007.

"Big Heap Herman," *The Munsters*, CBS, Jan. 20, 1966.

"Michael's Tribe," *My Wife and Kids*, ABC, Dec. 18, 2002.

"Running Bear and Moskowitz," *The New Dick Van Dyke Show*, CBS, Feb. 26, 1972.

"The Umquaw Strip," *Petticoat Junction*, CBS, Oct. 13, 1964.

"The Perils of Punky, Part I," *Punky Brewster*, NBC, Oct. 20, 1985.

"The Perils of Punky, Part II," *Punky Brewster*, NBC, Oct. 20, 1985.

"The Last Thursday in November," *Roseanne*, ABC, Nov. 21, 1995.

"Running Zack," *Saved by the Bell*, NBC, Nov. 24, 1990.

"The Cigar Store Indian," *Seinfeld*, NBC, Dec. 9, 1993.

"Bart to the Future," *The Simpsons*, Fox, Mar. 19, 2000.

"Missionary: Impossible," *The Simpsons*, Fox, Feb. 20, 2000.

"Light My Firebush," *Son of the Beach*, FX, Apr. 17, 2001.

"Love, Native American–Style," *Son of the Beach*, FX, Apr. 4, 2000.

"Red Man's Greed," *South Park*, Comedy Central, Apr. 30, 2003.

"Boston Tea Party," *The Suite Life of Zack and Cody*, Disney, June 30, 2006.

"Dances with Groceries," *Ten Items or Less*, TBS, Feb. 17, 2009.

"The Snow Job," *Three's Company*, ABC, Oct. 2, 1979.

"Dances with Couch," *Yes, Dear*, CBS, Apr. 8, 2002.

Acknowledgments
CLOSING CREDITS

This production of *Tribal Television* has been made possible by a strong and supportive crew to whom I offer words of thanks.

To my wife, Maria; to my daughter, Maya; and to my sons, Jonah, Ira, and Ezra, I say ᏌᏓᎪᎩ, a heartfelt thanks, for all the days and nights you allowed me to complete this. With you, your love, your laughter, your support, it is (finally) done. To Mom and Dave, to John and Kim, and to all my Lacefield, Tahmahkera, and Ifcic relatives, thank you for all the love and support.

My thanks go to the inspiring faculty in the English Department at Midwestern State University, especially the late Dr. Jeff Campbell, my first mentor, who turned a wandering undergrad on to knowledge with a dazzling pedagogy back in the day and whose guidance led me to become who I am today; to Dr. Tom Hoffman for the sit-com-raderie and encouragement to study and create pop culture; and to Dr. Robert Johnson for the stories and for teaching the influential seminar "Style and Voice." My thanks go to former faculty at Bowling Green State University Dr. Don McQuarie and the late Dr. John Warren for their friendship and advice. Udakok to my dear Cherokee friend and mentor Dr. Lynda Dixon for all the support and guidance over the years. Thanks go to Grandma Fawn Crawfoot for the laughter and stories in BG and to the Native American Unity Council for providing community and inviting me back to share my research. Special thanks go to my friends and colleagues in the American Indian Studies program at the University of Illinois, Urbana-Champaign, especially Robert Warrior, LeAnne Howe, Matthew Sakiestewa Gilbert, Jodi Byrd, John McKinn, Fred Hoxie, and Robert Dale Parker, for welcoming me into their incredible indigenous community as a Chancellor's Postdoctoral Fellow. My thanks go to the Department of Communication Studies, including Davi Thornton, Robert Bednar, David Olson, and Valerie Renegar, and Provost Jim Hunt at Southwestern University for their support of my research, including during my much-appreciated Faculty Sabbatical. Additional gratitude is extended to the late Corlee Bosch, Susan Lamb, Ben Nava (and the entire Nava tribe!), Laura Forbes Glass, Kenneth Mello, Laura Hobgood-Oster, Elaine Craddock, Alison Kafer, Melissa Johnson, Brenda Sendejo, Helene Meyers, and Eric Selbin. My thanks go to students in the American Indians in Media and Indigeneity courses and to other students over the years who have conversed with me about representations of the indigenous in television.

My thanks go to numerous friends and colleagues who have generously reviewed drafts and visited with me over the years about this project, especially Michael Lupro, Matthew Mace Barbee, Dale Young, Philip Deloria, Julia Johnson, Lynda Dixon, Rachel Ida Buff, Joseph Bauerkemper, Matthew Sakiestewa Gilbert, David Olson, David Delgado Shorter, Randolph Lewis, Danika Medak-Saltzman, and David Anthony Clark. Jodi Byrd's reading of the entire manuscript (twice!) and her extensive feedback have, to say the least, helped immensely in shaping the final product. Additional thanks for their support and insights go to Erik Wade, Debbie Reese, Joshua Nelson, Joanna Hearne, Jason Schmitt, Katie Feyh, Tiara Na'puti, Vince Diaz, Maricela DeMirjyn, Cary Campbell, Colin Helb, Marti Chaatsmith, Paul Chaat Smith, Julianna Brannum, Sy Hoahwah, Loriene Roy, Winona LaDuke, Circe Sturm, Travis Baker, Lisa Alexander, Christina Gerken, Stephen Swanson, Gloria Enriquez Pizana, and so many others whose names should go here.

My thanks go to Jonathan Joss and Max Gail for their generosity, time, and insights during our interviews; to the original Indi'n "sit-com kid" Sherman Alexie for welcoming a Comanche he had just met in Austin to send a draft of this manuscript to him; to Nicholas Rosenthal, who shared the transcript of his interview (with Mark Banks) in support of chapter 2; to archivist Katie Salzmann of the Wittliff Collections at Texas State University for guiding me through the library's *King of the Hill* Archives; and to Ron E. Scott and Ashley Barlow at Prairie Dog Film + Television for supporting my research on *Mixed Blessings*. Udah to the Comanche Language and Cultural Preservation Committee, especially Ron Red Elk and Barbara Goodin, for their assistance with translations. My thanks go as well to those who have invited me to share my research in presentation and song, including Gwen Westerman at the Native American Literature Symposium, Shannon Speed and Jim Cox with the Native American & Indigenous Studies program at the University of Texas–Austin, and Dan Littlefield and Robert Sanderson at the Sequoyah National Research Center. My thanks go to the Native American and Indigenous Studies Association, the American Studies Association, and the SW/TX Popular Culture Association for providing critical and creative spaces for rich discussion of indigeneity and media.

Many thanks go to the University of North Carolina Press for support and patience, especially from Mark Simpson-Vos, Caitlin Butterfield, Paula Wald, and Julie Bush. To think the relationship began with a handshake from Mark years ago in Oklahoma, and now here we are.

In closing, this book is dedicated to the memory of my grandmother Pearl Lacefield, my uncle Steve Lacefield, and my first mentor, Dr. Jeff Campbell, all of whom passed on within eight months of each other between June 2006 and February 2007. Their love and support mean more than words can express.

Index

violence, 58; "The Manicurist" episode, 185 (n. 38); "Barney's Replacement" episode, 186 (n. 56)

Anishinaabe prophecy, 139–40

Appadurai, Arjun, 182 (n. 78)

Applebaum-Hébert *Report on Federal Cultural Policy*, 147–48

Arcand, Nathaniel, 4, 5, 159

Area Redevelopment Act, 184 (n. 17)

Arnaz, Desi, Jr., 67

Arnaz, Lucie, 67, 68

Arness, James, 37

Arnold, Danny, 91

Art Institute of Chicago, 93

Ashbaugh, Emma, 159

Asian American characters, xiii, 87

Assimilation: and sitcoms, xiii, 40–41, 42, 59, 65, 72, 83, 91, 155; and Indian policies, 33; and Kennedy's discourse with Native Peoples, 39, 183 (n. 7); and multiculturalism, 74; and settler colonialism, 147

Assimilative pluralism, 74

Association on American Indian Affairs, 52

Attallah, Paul, 23, 32

Avatar (film; 2009), 172, 173, 206 (n. 20)

Bacalso, Joanna, 204 (n. 72)

Bain, Conrad, 100–101

Bainbridge, Catherine, 4, 159

Ball, Lucille, 67, 188 (n. 77)

Banks, Dennis, 92, 190 (n. 19)

Banks, Mark, 75, 92, 95

Bannerji, Himani, 171

Barney Miller: representations of the recognizably Indian in, 7; Indian representations in, 17, 87, 88, 144, 193 (n. 77); "The Indian" episode, 19, 88–90, 104, 192 (n. 49), 194 (n. 87); and vanishing Indian trope, 19, 89, 194 (n. 87); and settler self-determination, 33, 104; and indigenous-settler relations, 72, 88, 89; Native actors in, 75, 92–95; multiethnic cast of, 87–88; "Bones" episode, 89, 91–95, 101, 104, 168, 192 (n. 57), 205 (n. 4); and representational self-determination, 89–90; and Indianness, 93–94; and settler colonialism, 94; and Manhattan narrative, 94, 193 (n. 66); "Landmark," 192 (n. 56)

Barnouw, Erik, 17, 48

Barr, Roseanne, 30, 182 (n. 84)

Basaraba, Gary, 141

Battise, Kevin, 133

Baylor, Tim, 78

Beach, Adam, 4–5, 6

The Beachcombers, "A House Divided" episode, 143

Beadle's Dime Novels, 3

Bearisto, Ric, 141

Beavis and Butthead, 112

Bedard, Irene, 159

Belcourt, Allen, 159

Belvin, Harry, 11, 15, 16

Benaderet, Bea, 63

Berenger, Tom, 194 (n. 77)

Berger, Glenn, 120, 121, 122–23, 197 (n. 47)

Bering Strait theory, 121

Berkhofer, Robert, 3

Berry, Ken, 188 (n. 80)

Berti, Dehl, 19, 75, 103, 189 (n. 9)

Beulah, 96, 193 (n. 71)

The Beverly Hillbillies: Indian representations in, xiv, 18, 49–50, 108; "Turkey Day" episode, 18, 49, 67; "Jed Cuts the Family Tree" episode, 23–24; and settler-indigenous relations, 32, 49, 66, 67, 188 (n. 75); and recognizably Indian representations, 40, 188 (n. 75); and representation of violence directed at Indians, 48–49; "The Family Tree" episode, 49; "The Indians Are Coming" episode, 66–67, 188 (n. 75); cancellation of, 68; settlers playing Indian in, 80; Jed's hound in, 113; "The Clampetts in Washington" episode, 188 (n. 75); "Jed Buys the Capitol" episode, 188 (n. 75); tribes of Indian characters, 195 (n. 9)

Bewitched, 184 (n. 13)

Bhabha, Homi, xv, 7, 16, 17, 18, 75, 107, 119

Bigelow, William Sturgis, 178 (n. 8)

The Big Show, 88

Billy Jack films, 9–10, 79, 146

Black Robe (film; 1992), 102

Blackstone, 158, 161, 203 (n. 70)

Blansky's Beauties, 87

Blue, Monte, 63, 187 (n. 68)

Bogle, Donald, 87, 96–97, 98

Boller, Paul, 37–38, 183 (n. 3)

Bonanza, 12, 44

Bond, Ward, 37

Boone, Richard, 37

The Bootlegger Blues, 143

Boston Indian Council, 189 (n. 10)

Bouchet, Joe, 198 (n. 60), 199 (n. 67)

Boy Scouts of America, 115, 196 (n. 29)

The Brady Bunch: settlers playing Indian in, xiii, 18, 69, 80, 81, 83, 85; Native audiences of, 9; "Un-Underground Movie" episode, 18, 80–81; and settler self-determination, 33, 86; and indigenous-settler relations, 72–73, 80, 82–85, 132; Native actors in, 75, 83–84; "A Clubhouse Is Not a Home" episode, 80; "Slumber Caper" episode, 80; "The Brady Braves" episode, 80, 81–86, 91, 102, 103, 104, 191 (n. 42); "Ghost Town, U.S.A." episode, 81; "Grand Canyon or Bust" episode, 81; and setters' representational authority on Indians, 81–82, 86, 94; and engagement of recognizably Indian representations, 97; Indian representations in, 108, 166; in Hawaii, 191 (n. 35)

Brando, Marlon, 79, 190 (nn. 16, 24)

Broadcasting Act, 148

Brooks, Tim, 195 (n. 8)

Brown, Adrian, 128

Brown, Dee, 77

Bruyneel, Kevin, 108, 109

Buffalo Bill Wild West shows, 3, 187 (n. 73)

Buffalo nickel, 3

Bureau of Indian Affairs (BIA): and New Trail discourse, 39, 51, 61; and Great Society programs, 40, 62; and sitcoms, 65, 88–89, 123; and American Indian Movement, 78; and indigenous self-determination, 84; Gover's apology on behalf of, 124, 198 (n. 53)

Burnette, Robert, 38

Bush, George H. W., 101

Bush, George W., 133

Button, Charles, 129

Buttram, Pat, 188 (n. 79)

Byrd, Jodi, xiii, xvi, 74

Caddoan Mounds State Historic Site, 197 (n. 47)

Cameron, James, 13, 172, 173

Canada Writes, 139

Canadian Broadcasting Corporation (CBC), 139, 146

Canadian Cemeteries Act of 1976, 93

Canadian Film and Television Production Association, 179 (n. 11)

Canadianness, 4

Canadian Radio-television and Telecommunications Commission (CRTC), 147, 148

Canadian Union of Ontario Indians, 93

Cardinal, Tantoo, 159

The Carol Burnett Show, 92

Castile, George Pierre, 39, 183 (n. 5), 184 (n. 21)

Catawbas, 52

Cattelino, Jessica, 20

Cayuga Nation, 52

Chaat Smith, Paul, 10, 77, 188 (n. 1), 190 (n. 22), 193 (n. 76)

Champagne, Duane, 189 (n. 1)

Chapelle's Show, 20

Charity, Tom, 172

Charmed, 138

Cheers: "I'll Be Seeing You, Part 1" episode, 193 (n. 77); "One for the Road" episode, 193 (n. 77)

Cherokees, 54, 55, 57, 58, 59–60, 117, 151, 186 (n. 51)

Cheyenne Autumn (film; 1964), 54

174; "Bad Medicine Removers" video, 206 (n. 25); "Native Love" video, 206 (n. 27); "Geronimo E-KIA" video, 207 (n. 27); "Ten Little Indians–Violence against Native Women" PSA, 207 (n. 27); "To the Indigenous Woman" video, 207 (n. 27)

Fox, 112, 113

Francis, Daniel, 3–4

Frank, Billy, Jr., 190 (n. 16)

Frank's Place, 148

Fraser, James Earle, 3, 183 (n. 6)

Frederick, Sokaymoh, 161

Freedom of Information Act (FOIA), 123–24

The Fresh Prince of Bel-Air, 100–101

Friends, Indian representation in, 22, 144, 201 (n. 22)

Frost, Robert, 48

Frye, Soleil Moon, 194 (n. 77)

F Troop: Indian representations in, xiv, 17, 30, 31, 66, 204 (n. 72); and settler colonialism, 27, 187–88 (n. 74); and indigenous-settler relations, 33, 42, 62, 65, 66, 190 (n. 28); "Karate with Love" episode, 187 (n. 74); "Yellow Bird" episode, 187–88 (n. 74); "The Return of Bald Eagle" episode, 188 (n. 74)

Futurama, 114

Gail, Max, 87–92, 95, 192 (nn. 52, 56, 57)

Gammill, Tom, 22

Garment, Leonard, 70, 188 (n. 1)

George, Diana, 16, 22

Gerbner, George, 204 (n. 83)

Germans and perceptions of Native Peoples, 154, 203 (n. 52)

Geronimo (film; 1993), 114

Gervais, Ricky, 168

Get Smart: and indigenous-settler relations, 64–65, 66; "Washington 4, Indians 3" episode, 64–65, 187 (nn. 70, 71); and Romero, 96

Gilday, Leela, 165

Gilligan's Island, 145, 147

Gimme a Break!, 96

Ginsburg, Faye, 163, 169

Glass, Ron, 87

Goeman, Mishauna, 171

Goldtooth, Dallas, 170, 171, 172, 173

Goodfox, Julia, 171–72

Good News (film; 1947), 185 (n. 27)

Goose, Leanne, 164

Gould, Jack, 11

Gover, Kevin, 124, 198 (n. 53)

Grand Canyon National Game Preserve, 82

The Grapes of Wrath (film; 1940), 170

Gray, Herman, xvi, 148

Gray, Jonathan, 25, 110, 180–81 (n. 42)

Great Society programs: and Johnson, 32, 33, 40, 42, 55, 62, 184 (n. 17); and sitcoms, 32, 33, 41, 61–66, 167; and guidelines of poverty programs, 184 (n. 15)

Green, Rayna, 3–4, 56

Green Acres: and Indian representations, xiv, 63, 66; and indigenous-settler relations, 42, 63; "The Rains Came" episode, 63, 122; cancellation of, 68

Gregory, Dick, 190 (n. 16)

Griffith, Andy, 188 (n. 80)

Groening, Matt, 112

Guerrero, Kimberly Norris, 159

Guestward Ho, 187 (n. 72), 195 (n. 8)

Gunsmoke, 37, 44

Halbritter, Ray, 114

Hall, Klay, 115

Happy Days: and settler characters standing in for the indigenous, xiii, 18; "The First Thanksgiving" episode, 18, 87; "Westward Ho!" episode, 87, 204 (n. 72); Indian representations in, 88–89

Harjo, Joy, 11, 15

Harjo, Sterlin, 170, 171, 206 (n. 19)

Harold of Orange (film; 1984), 27, 28–29, 182 (n. 80)

Harper, Mattie, 174, 206 (n. 25)

Harris, Richard "Horse," 79

Have Gun Will Travel, 37

Hawk, Bunky Echo, 172

Hearne, Joanna, 14, 24–25

Henning, Paul, 63

Here's Lucy: and Indian representations, xiv, 66, 67–68; "Lucy and the Indian Chief" episode, 67–68; cancellation of, 68, 188 (n. 79); settlers playing Indian in, 80

Hershey, Barbara, 194 (n. 77)

Hey, Dude, 195 (n. 9)

Hieber, Kenneth, 137

Hill, Charlie: on indigenous erasure, 22; as Native actor, 27, 29–30, 75, 90, 92, 182–83 (n. 84), 192 (nn. 54, 58); on Bureau of Indian Affairs, 88–89; on Vine Deloria, 182 (n. 82)

Hill, Leona, 29

Hilton-Morrow, Wendy, 111–12

Hin-mah-too-yah-lat-kekt/Chief Joseph, 103

Hirsch, Judd, 191 (n. 48)

History Detectives, 178 (n. 5)

Hoffman, Dustin, 79

Holliday, Cheryl, 116–17

Holte, James Craig, 87, 88

Home Improvement, xiii

Hope, Bob, 48

Hopkins-Duke, A. A., 11

Horse, Michael, 31, 113

House, Dakota, 113

House Concurrent Resolution 108, 52

Howe, LeAnne, 25

Huhndorf, Shari, 3–4

Hulu, 168

Idlout, Lucie, 165

I Love Lucy: settlers playing Indian in, xiii, 16–17, 44, 80, 186 (n. 53); Indian representations in, 7, 17, 18, 41, 44–45, 52, 68, 108, 167, 185 (n. 27); "The Adagio" episode, 16–17, 44; "The Indian Show," 18, 44–46, 67, 185 (n. 27)

In a World Created by a Drunken God (made-for-television movie), 143

Indian Act (Canada), 147

Indian Child Welfare Act of 1978, 71

Indian Civil Rights Act (1968), 78, 190 (n. 19)

Indian Country Today, 86

Indian Education Act of 1972, 71

Indian Gaming Regulatory Act (1988), 132, 133

Indian Head half-eagle gold coins, 3, 178 (n. 8)

Indian Head nickel, 3

Indian Head one-cent coin, 178 (n. 8)

Indian Head quarter-eagle gold coins, 3, 178 (n. 8)

Indian Head test pattern (IHTP): as international iconic image, 1, 2; viewers adjusting television sets with, 1, 2; viewers watching of, 2; unidentified Brooks as artist of, 2, 178 (n. 5); as "white man's Indian," 3; as settler colonial image, 4; in *Moose TV,* 4, 6; and color television, 57; history of, 167

Indian in the Cupboard (film; 1995), 153

Indianness: American cultural ambivalence with, xiii; and sitcoms, xiii, 80, 83, 85, 93–94, 101–2; and multiculturalism, 74; and indigenous-settler relations, 77, 83, 85, 108; and ecology, 79, 117; settler-centered occupation of, 104; and new Indian, 106–9, 110, 111, 115, 118, 125–26, 129, 138, 166, 167; and cultural identity, 108; and postcolonial resistance, 108, 109

Indian representations: repetitious nature of Indian characters, xii; settlers playing Indian, xiii, 4, 16–17, 76, 197 (n. 34); as visible representations, xiii–xiv; complexity of, xiv, xvi, 22–23; and Hollywood Injun English, xiv, 177 (n. 11); and stereotypes of Indians, xiv–xv, 17, 20, 177 (n. 12); and Indian Head test pattern, 1–3; and settler colonial images, 3–4; and fixed Indian versus flexible Native, 6, 8, 17, 158; adjustments and readjustments of, 6–7, 15,

17, 25, 32, 35, 41, 73, 149–57; multiplicity
of, 15; expectations of, 109. *See also*
Recognizably Indian representations;
Recognizably Native representations;
and specific sitcoms
"Indian Reservation" (song), 81, 191 (n. 34)
Indian Restoration Act (1987), 133
Indian Self-Determination and Education
Assistance Act of 1975, 71–72
Indians of All Tribes, 78, 81
Indian Territory, 54, 186 (n. 51)
Indian Time, 90
Indie Award for *Moose TV,* 4, 179 (n. 11)
Indigeneity: politics of perception of, xv, 7,
16, 20, 24, 26, 27–28, 77–78, 178 (n. 15);
in sitcoms, xvi; adjustment and read-
justment of representations of, 6–7, 15,
17, 25, 32, 35, 41, 73, 149–57; televisual,
7, 20; theoretical framework of, 13; and
New Frontier discourse, 47; public
discourse on, 77; historical, market
interests in, 77, 187 (n. 73); limited
perceptions of, 118–19; performative,
settler expectations of, 119; clashes with
modernity, 122, 197 (n. 49); and Native
humor, 142; non-Native appropriation
of, 156–57; and Internet, 169, 170–71,
205 (n. 8)
Indigenous authenticity, 4, 19, 82, 97, 117,
171–72
Indigenous critical intertextuality, 25–26
Indigenous-nonindigenous intercultural
relations: public perceptions of, xv;
and Natives' narratives recontextual-
izing the Indian, 4; and contact zones
of televisual production spaces, 7; representational conflicts and resolutions
in, 7; in sitcoms, 7, 8–15; multiplicity of,
15; and New Frontier discourse, 39–40
Indigenous self-determination: and Kennedy's discourse with Native Peoples,
38, 39, 83; and sitcoms, 40, 41, 72, 75,
100, 104, 166; and Nixon's discourse
with Native Peoples, 70–71, 189 (n. 2);
and Native Peoples' activism, 71–72,

74, 189 (n. 2); federal policy on, 71–72,
78, 84, 101, 104, 167, 190 (n. 19); and paternalism, 74; and Johnson's discourse
with Native Peoples, 184 (n. 18)
Indigenous-settler relations: public perception of, xv; in sitcoms, xvi, 33–34,
40–42, 44–45, 53, 58–61, 74–75, 76, 107;
televisual representations of, 6–7, 20,
21, 22–24, 37; and televisual tribalography, 25; and New Frontier discourse,
39, 40, 51, 53; and New Trail discourse,
51; and cooperative conflict resolutions, 51, 53, 54, 56, 58–61, 62, 63, 71,
76; and colonial mimicry, 75; and violence, 80, 81; and Johnson's discourse
with Native Peoples, 184 (n. 18). *See
also specific sitcoms*
Indigenous social movements, 76, 90, 190
(n. 22). *See also specific groups*
In Living Color, 112, 143
Institute of Indian Arts, Santa Fe, 77
Intercultural healing and Native humor,
140
Internet: influence of, 167–68, 175; and
indigeneity, 169, 170–71, 205 (n. 8). *See
also* YouTube
Intertextual convergences, 42
Intertribal Friendship Houses, 90
Into the West (HBO miniseries), 162
Inuit Broadcasting Corporation, 147
Inuits, 147, 192 (n. 64)
Inuit Tapirisat of Canada, 147
It's Garry Shandling's Show, 112

Jackson, Janet, 96
Jaimes, M. Annette, 39
Jenkins, C. Francis, 178 (n. 8)
Jenkins, Henry, 168
The Jetsons, 112
Joe Dirt (film; 2001), 200 (n. 81)
Johansen, Noel, 203 (n. 56)
Johnny Quest, 112
Johnson, Lyndon B.: and Great So-
ciety programs, 32, 33, 40, 42, 55,
62, 184 (n. 17); and indigenous

self-determination, 41; discourse with Native Peoples, 41, 72, 184 (n. 18); and federal Indian policy, 52; and Civil Rights Act, 54; inaugural State of the Union address, 61–62; and public opinion of Indian people, 70; "Forgotten American" message to Congress, 72; visit to Blackfeet reservation, 183 (n. 4)

Johnson, Victoria, xvi

Jojola, Ted, 30–31

The Jonathan Winters Show, 92

Joseph, Victor, 14

Josephy, Alvin, 183 (n. 5)

Joss, Jonathan: offscreen representations of Redcorn, 34, 106, 107, 110–11, 127–30, 136–37, 138; on influence of Redcorn character, 106, 110; on Redcorn character's contributions, 109, 110–11, 127; as uncredited producer, 110; offscreen Red Corn Band of, 110, 128–30, 136–37, 198 (n. 63); heritage of, 110, 195 (n. 13); effect of Redcorn character on, 111, 127–36, 137, 138, 198 (n. 60), 199 (n. 74); and representational sovereignty, 111, 138, 195 (n. 16), 198 (n. 58); voice-over debut of, 119; and Redcorn character's business ventures, 123–27, 128, 132–36, 200 (n. 81); on white person's apologies to Native Peoples, 124; John Redcorn Big Mountain Fudgecake band, 128, 130, 131, 137, 198 (n. 63); on cancellation of *King of the Hill,* 136; and *Parks and Recreation,* 137, 138, 200 (n. 87); performing in Redcorn voice for Austin Rock Band Championships, 137, 200 (n. 85); Redcorn as recurring role in sitcom, 194 (n. 6); on Aaron, 196 (n. 27); on basis of characters of *King of the Hill,* 196 (n. 26)

Judas Priest, 124

Judge, Jim, 195 (n. 9)

Judge, Mike: and *Beavis and Butthead,* 32, 112, 196 (n. 18); and *King of the Hill* Archives, 109; as producer of *King of the Hill,* 110; and Joss's representations of

Redcorn, 111, 199 (n. 67); and Redcorn character's Anasazi identification, 195 (n. 9); Boy Scout background of, 196 (n. 29); and character of *King of the Hill,* 196 (n. 26); on setting of *King of the Hill,* 196 (n. 19)

Justice League, 138

Kaibab Indian Reservation, 82

Keaton, Buster, 44

"Keep American Beautiful" public service announcement (1971), 79, 117

Kelly, Richard Michael, 50, 186–87 (n. 59)

Kennedy, John F.: and New Frontier discourse, 32, 39, 41, 42–43, 51, 183 (n. 6), 184 (n. 22); as honorary chieftain, 32, 183 (n. 3); discourse with Native Peoples, 37–39, 51–53, 71, 183 (n. 7); and indigenous self-determination, 38, 39, 83; and introduction to *The American Heritage Book of Indians,* 38, 183 (n. 5); and New Trail discourse, 38–39, 40, 43, 51–52, 61, 183 (n. 6); and Minow's appointment, 46–47; acceptance speech of 1960, 48, 55; inaugural address of, 51; and racial equality, 54; and public opinion of Indian people, 70; and Area Redevelopment Act, 184 (n. 17)

Kennewick Man, 197 (n. 47)

Kids in the Hall, 172

Kilgallen, Dorothy, 12

Kilmer, Val, 102

Kilpatrick, Jacquelyn, 17

King, Martin Luther, Jr., 57

King of the Hill: recognizably Indian representations in, 7, 34, 105, 107, 109, 110, 115, 118, 122, 127, 128, 166; Redcorn character's New Age healing practices, 105, 111, 118–19, 124, 125–26, 136; and new Indian identity, 106–7, 108, 110, 111, 115, 118, 125–26, 129, 138, 166, 167; and indigenous-settler relations, 106–7, 109, 115–17, 119, 120, 121, 123–26, 127, 128, 132, 133–35, 199 (n. 76); archives of, 109–10, 120; Redcorn character's

Mac, Bernie, 113, 121
MacDonald, J. Fred, 189 (n. 10)
MacDonald, Peter, 101
MacFarlane, Seth, 21
MADtv, 122, 197 (n. 49)
Magoc, Chris, xii
Malcolm in the Middle, 113–14, 159
A Man Called Horse (film; 1970), 79
Manifest Destiny doctrine, 42, 43, 47
The Many Lives of Dobie Gillis, 96
Marc, David, 23, 48
Marks, Guy, 186 (n. 57)
Married with Children, 112, 145
Marsh, Earle, 195 (n. 8)
The Mary Tyler Moore Show, 92
Maude, 68
May, Karl, 154
Mayberry R.F.D., 68, 188 (n. 80)
McCartney, Paul, 96, 193 (n. 70)
McCormick, Maureen, 192 (n. 48)
McHale's Navy, 96
McMahan, David, 111–12
Means, Bill, 91
Means, Russell, 79, 91
Mediascapes, 28, 182 (n. 78)
Meek, Barbra, xiv, 177 (n. 11)
Melamed, Jodi, 74
Mellencamp, Patricia, xvi
Menominees, 52
Merasty, Billy, 4
Meyer, Brecklin, 196 (n. 25)
M'Girl, 165
Mihesuah, Devon, 102
Miles, Elaine, 159
Miller, Derek, 165
Minow, Newton, 46–48, 51, 53
Mister Ed, 12, 75
Mittell, Jason, 23, 73
Mixed Blessings: Taylor as head writer of, 26, 34, 141, 143, 144, 147, 149–50, 153, 160, 182 (n. 70); and decolonization of audience views of rigid indigeneity, 26, 35, 166; and sitcom sovereignty, 34, 147, 149, 159, 163, 167; and tribalography, 141, 157, 164; setting of, 141, 201 (n. 10); and

interculturality, 141–42, 143, 148, 149, 150–56, 158, 162–63, 165, 166, 204 (n. 78); and indigenous-settler relations, 142, 149, 151, 152, 153, 162, 166; and Native humor, 142–43, 144, 148, 149, 156–57, 161; on APTN, 148; and Native music, 149, 157, 163–65; and recognizably Native representations, 149–50, 151–52, 156–66, 167, 204 (n. 78); and politics of indigenous identity, 150, 155–56; and Elvis Presley, 150–52; "Dances with Wolfy" episode, 154–57, 164; and survivance, 157, 158–59, 163, 166; casting of, 159–63, 165; and guest stars, 161; "Traditional Wedding" episode, 162, 163; "Dot Not Feather" episode, 201 (n. 14)
Moesha, "Road Trip" episode, 29–30
Mohawk Girls (documentary), 26, 182 (n. 70)
Momaday, Scott, 77
Monias, Richard, 161
Moose TV: Indian Head test pattern in, 4, 6; visuality and perception of the indigenous in, 4–6, 7; premise of, 5–6; cast of, 159; Taylor as script consultant for, 159, 182 (n. 70); on YouTube, 169; and German expectations, 203 (n. 52)
Morales, Eddie, 174
Morgan, Arthur E., 52
Morreale, Joanne, xv–xvi
Morris, Zack, 103, 104–5
Moses, Robert, 52
MTV, 112, 196 (n. 18)
Multiculturalism: and recognizably Indian representations, 73–74, 75, 76, 81–86, 97, 103; production of, 74
Multine, George III, 129, 130
The Munsters: and indigenous-settler relations, 42; "Big Heap Herman" episode, 64, 184 (n. 13), 193 (n. 74), 204 (n. 72); Native actors in, 75, 96, 193 (n. 74)
Murphy, Brittany, 196 (n. 25)
Museum of the American Indian, 93
Mutual of Omaha, 3
My Favorite Martian, 64

Oneida Nation, 114
Oneida people, 52
One Voice Radio, 137
Online indigenous comedy. *See* YouTube
Onondaga people, 52, 93
Ortman, Laura, 171
Osawa, Sandra Sunrising, 26, 29, 86, 206
    (n. 21)
Ostwelve, 164–65

Paar, Jack, 37, 42
Pack, Sam, 32
Paleface (film; 1922), 44
"The Pale Faced Indian" (song), 191 (n. 34)
Paratexts: meanings shaped by, 15, 25,
    180–81 (n. 42); of DVD commentaries,
    20, 21, 22, 68, 181–82 (n. 62); in *King of*
    the Hill Archives, 109–10, 120
Parker, Cynthia Ann, 188 (n. 74)
Parker, Trey, 20
Parks and Recreation, 137, 138, 200 (n. 87)
Paternalism, 71, 72, 74, 99, 100, 132, 183
    (n. 7), 184 (n. 18)
Patterson, Brad, 70
Peary, Robert, 192 (n. 64)
Pelly, Wilma, 159, 160–61, 163
Pensoneau, Migizi, 170, 171
Peter Pan (made-for-television movie), 47
Petticoat Junction: and indigenous-settler
    relations, 42, 63–64, 66; "The Umquaw
    Strip" episode, 63–64, 91; cancellation
    of, 68
Petty, Tom, 130
Pewewardy, Cornel, 177 (n. 10)
Pew Research Center, 167–68
Pharis, Chuck, 178 (n. 5)
Pickering Treaty (1794), 52
Pistols 'n' Petticoats, 187 (n. 72)
Pocahontas (film; 1995), 32
Podemski, Jennifer, 4, 159
Podemski, Tamara, 159
Positive pluralism, 74
Postcolonial resistance, 108, 109
Powell-Arcand, Griffin, 159
Powwow Highway (film; 1989), 102

Prairie Dog Film + Television, 141
Pratt, Bela Lyon, 178 (n. 8)
Pratt, Mary Louise, 6–7
Presley, Elvis, 12, 150–51
Pryor, Richard, 183 (n. 84)
Pulp Fiction (film; 1994), 128
Punky Brewster, "The Perils of Punky"
    episodes, 193–94 (n. 77)

Race and racism: rich Indian racism,
    20, 132; racial hierarchies in sitcoms,
    42; and racial equality, 54; and racial
    politics, 57; and multiculturalism, 74;
    and racial attitudes, 98; and racialized
    discourse, 113, 132, 153; and multiracial
    identity, 140; and race relations, 145
Radio Corporation of America (RCA), 1, 3
Radio Free Alcatraz, 78
Raheja, Michelle, xvi, 26–27, 129, 193 (n. 77)
Raiders, 81, 191 (n. 34)
Rainwater, Marvin, 191 (n. 34)
Rango, 186 (n. 57), 187 (n. 72)
Ray, James Arthur, 126
Reagan, Ronald, 180 (n. 26)
Recognizably Indian representations: in
    redface, xiii, 18, 19, 45, 54, 56, 57, 67, 72,
    79, 80, 93, 98, 103; and non-Native per-
    formers, 4, 12, 13–14, 18, 19, 55–56, 58–59,
    68, 76, 79, 113, 153, 186 (n. 57), 187 (n. 72);
    in sitcoms, 7, 8, 16, 17–24, 36, 40, 62, 76;
    and ideology of television producers,
    15–16, 17, 20–21, 22, 41; and vanish-
    ing Indian trope, 19, 23, 89, 102; and
    representational self-determination,
    19, 33, 72–74, 75, 76, 89–90; and casino
    Indians, 19–22, 66, 114, 132; in paratexts
    of DVD commentaries, 20, 68; and In-
    dian speech, 22, 30, 40, 45, 55, 56, 63, 72,
    81, 82, 103, 155, 181–82 (n. 62), 191 (n. 41);
    heterogeneous representations, 22–24,
    73; relationship to recognizably Native
    representations, 24–25, 26, 34–35, 73, 76,
    104, 109, 138, 144, 149–50, 152, 157, 163,
    166; and Kennedy's discussions with
    Native Peoples, 38; and Hollywood

Index **239**

Seinfeld: Indian representations in, 17, 144; "The Cigar Store Indian" episode, 159

Seinfeld, Jerry, 159

Senecas, 52

Sesame Street, 86

Settler characters: diversity of, xii; standing in for indigenous, xiii, 18, 72, 76; discursive violence toward non-Native characters posing as Indians, 41, 48, 51, 58, 188 (n. 74); and TV westerns, 44

Settler colonialism: and dominance over the indigenous, xii–xiii, 3, 9, 17, 18, 27, 43, 48, 53–54; and ideology of recognizably Indian representations, 16, 17, 22, 119; postindians' resistance to, 28; and cross-cultural cooperation, 41, 51, 53, 54, 56, 58–61, 62; and Kennedy, 42–43; and New Frontier discourse, 47–48; and assimilation, 147

Settler self-determination and sitcoms, 33–34, 73, 74, 76, 77–79, 86, 99–100, 104–5, 121, 130

Shakiest Gun in the West (film; 1968), 12, 57, 186 (n. 52)

Shebala, Marley, 114

Sierra, Gregory, 87

Silberman, Robert, 27

Silverheels, Jay, 9–10, 75, 83, 191 (n. 41), 202 (n. 43)

Simpson, Rose, 173

The Simpsons: Indian representations in, 17, 144, 201 (n. 22); casino Indians in, 19, 20, 21, 22, 132, 178 (n. 15); "Missionary: Impossible" episode, 20, 178 (n. 15); "Bart to the Future" episode, 21, 22, 181–82 (n. 62); parodic critiques of American television culture, 25; as animated sitcom, 112; recognizably Indian representations in, 114; and politics of perception of Natives as wealthy owners of casinos, 178 (n. 15)

Singer, Beverly, 26

Sitcoms: as influence on worldview, xii, 9, 10, 13, 16; Indianness in, xiii, 80, 83, 85, 93–94, 101–2; public perceptions

shaped by, xv; complexity of narratives, xv–xvi; recognizably Indian representations in, 7, 8, 16, 17–24, 36, 40, 62, 76; recognizably Native representations in, 8, 26–32, 36; and New Frontier discourse, 32–33, 39, 40, 41, 42–51, 61, 66, 167, 184 (n. 13); and settler self-determination, 33–34, 73, 74, 76, 77–79, 86, 99–100, 104–5, 121, 130; televisual violence in, 44–46, 48–49, 51, 58, 65, 66, 188 (n. 74), 189 (n. 10); and rural purge, 68, 188 (n. 79); ambiguity of indigenous self-determination in, 72; animated, reemergence of in 1990s, 111–12; characters' unidentified tribes, 195 (n. 9). *See also specific sitcoms*

Sitcom sovereignty: enactment of, 26, 73; and Native television producers, 26–27; and recognizably Native representations, 26–27, 34–35, 159; of *Mixed Blessings,* 34, 147, 149, 159, 163, 167; and Taylor's critiques, 146–47; development of, 147–49

Sixkiller, Sonny, 191 (n. 34)

Six Nations, 52

Six Nations Council of Chiefs, 93

Skye, Harriet, 86

Slotkin, Richard, 43

Smith, Henry Nash, 48

Smithsonian Institution, 93

Smoke Signals (1998), 6, 13, 14, 160

Socioacupuncture, 28–29

Son of the Beach, "Love, Native-American Style" episode, 204 (n. 72)

Soo, Jack, 87

The Sopranos, 20

Southern Paiutes, 82

South Park: Indian representations in, 17; casino Indians in, 19, 20, 22, 24, 132; "Red Man's Greed," 20, 22, 24

Spade, David, 200 (n. 81)

Speaking Rock Casino, El Paso, 132, 133, 199 (n. 76)

Speaking Rock Entertainment Center, El Paso, 134

Made in the USA
Monee, IL
05 August 2021